C

By EXAMPLE

que

Greg Perry

C By Example

©1992 by Que

Library of Congress Catalog Card Number: 92-70890

ISBN: 0-88022-813-X

96 95 94 93 92   8 7 6 5 4 3 2

Interpretation of the printing code: the rightmost double-digit number is the year of the book's printing; the rightmost single-digit number, the number of the book's printing. For example, a printing code of 92-1 shows that the first printing of the book occurred in 1992.

Publisher
Richard K. Swadley

Publishing Manager
Joseph B. Wikert

Managing Editor
Neweleen A. Trebnik

Acquisitions Editor
Gregory Croy

Development Editor
Stacy Hiquet

Production Editor
Jodi Jensen

Editors
Susan Pink
Andy Saff
Gayle Johnson
Rich Limacher
Christine Pfeiffer
Erik Dafforn
Lori Cates
Fran Hatton

Editorial Coordinator
Becky Freeman

Technical Editor
Robert Zigon

Editorial Assistants
Rosemarie Graham
San Dee Phillips

Cover Designer
Jean Bisesi

Production Director
Jeff Valler

Production Manager
Corinne Walls

Book Designer
Michele Laseau

Production Analyst
Mary Beth Wakefield

Page Layout Coordinator
Matthew Morrill

Proofreading/Indexing Coordinator
Joelynn Gifford

Graphics Image Specialists
Dennis Sheehan
Jerry Ellis

Production
Keith Davenport, Book Shepherd
Phil Worthington, Assistant Shepherd
Paula Carroll
Brook Farling
Laurie Lee
Linda Quigley
Kelli Widdifield
Allan Wimmer

Indexer
Johnna VanHoose

Composed in Palatino and MCPdigital typefaces by Prentice Hall Computer Publishing.
Screen reproductions in this book were created by means of the program Collage Plus from Inner Media, Inc., Hollis, NH.

Dedication

My thanks to Diane Moore is long past due. Her daily support of my work at Tulsa Junior College gives me reason to strive for excellence in teaching.

About the Author

Greg Perry has been a programmer and trainer for the past 14 years. He received his first degree in computer science, then he received a Masters degree in corporate finance. He currently is a professor of computer science at Tulsa Junior College, as well as a computer consultant and lecturer. Mr. Perry is the author of 10 other computer books, including *QBASIC By Example*. In addition, he has published articles in several publications, including *PC World, Data Training*, and *Inside First Publisher*. He has attended computer conferences and trade shows in several countries and is fluent in nine computer languages.

Acknowledgments

I appreciate Stacy Hiquet and Joseph Wikert at Prentice Hall/Que for trusting me completely with the direction and style of this book.

The rest of my editors—Jodi Jensen, Susan Pink, Andy Saff, Gayle Johnson, Rich Limacher, Christine Pfeiffer, Erik Dafforn, Lori Cates, Fran Hatton, and Robert Zigon—kept me on track so that readers can have an accurate and readable text.

Gary Farrar is one of the primary reasons for this book's accuracy and readability. Gary is an excellent example of the pupil who surpassed the teacher. I am grateful for your help, Gary.

The Tulsa Junior College administration continues to support my writing. More importantly, Diane Moore, head of the Business Services Division, puts up with my antics and motivates me to look forward to each day.

When Dr. Richard C. Burgess and his wonderful wife, Ellen, recently stepped back into my life, they filled a void. Rick, you are the reason I am who I am today. Ellen, you have always been *simpatica, molta!*

As always, my beautiful bride Jayne, my parents Glen and Bettye Perry, and of course, Luke, the bischon, are my closest daily companions. It is for them that I work.

Trademark Acknowledgments

Que Corporation has made every attempt to supply trademark information about company names, products, and services mentioned in the book. Trademarks indicated below were derived from various sources. Que Corporation cannot attest to the accuracy of this information.

ANSI is a registered trademark of American National Standards Institute.

DEC is a registered trademark of Digital Equipment Corporation.

IBM is a registered trademark of International Business Machines Corporation.

Microsoft QuickC and MS-DOS are registered trademarks of Microsoft Corporation.

Turbo C is a registered trademark of Borland International, Inc.

UNIX is a trademark of AT&T.

X Window System is a trademark of The Massachusetts Institute of Technology.

Overview

Introduction 1

Part I Introduction to C 9

1 Welcome to C 11
2 What Is a Program? 33
3 Your First C Program 47
4 Variables and Constants 63
5 Character Arrays and Strings 91
6 Preprocessor Directives 105
7 Simple Input and Output 123

Part II C Operators 155

8 Math Operators and Precedence 157
9 Relational Operators 181
10 Logical Operators 203
11 Additional C Operators 217
12 Bitwise Operators 233

Part III C Constructs 247

13 The while Loop 249
14 The for Loop 275
15 Other Loop Options 297
16 The switch and goto Statements 311

Part IV Variable Scope and
Modular Programming 331

17 Writing C Functions 333
18 Variable Scope 353
19 Passing Values 379
20 Function Return Values and Prototypes 397

Part V Character Input, Output,
and Library Functions 415

21 Device and Character I/O 417
22 Character, String, and Numeric Functions 439

Part VI Arrays and Pointers.....................461

23	Introducing Arrays	463
24	Array Processing	483
25	Multidimensional Arrays	509
26	Pointers	531
27	Pointers and Arrays	545

Part VII Structures and File I/O 569

28	Structures	571
29	Arrays of Structures	593
30	Sequential Files	613
31	Random Access Files	635
A	Memory Addressing, Binary, and Hexadecimal Review	653
B	Answers to Review Questions	673
C	ASCII Table	691
D	C Precedence Table	697
E	Keyword and Function Reference	701
F	The Mailing List Application	705
	Glossary	715
	Index	727

Contents

Introduction 1

Who Should Use This Book 1
The Book's Philosophy 2
Overview 3
  Part I: Introduction to C 3
  Part II: C Operators 3
  Part III: C Constructs 3
  Part IV: Variable Scope and Modular Programming 4
  Part V: Character Input, Output, and Library Functions ... 4
  Part VI: Arrays and Pointers 4
  Part VII: Structures and File I/O 5
  Conventions 5
  Index to the Icons 5
  Margin Graphics 6
  Pseudocode 8
Companion Disk Offer 8

Part I Introduction to C

1 Welcome to C 11

What C Can Do for You 11
The Background of C 13
C Compared to Other Languages 14
C and Microcomputers 16
An Overview of Your Computer 17
  Hardware 17
  Software 27
Review Questions 31
Summary 31

2 What Is a Program? 33

Computer Programs 34
Program Design 36
Using a Program Editor 38
Using a C Compiler 40

Running a Sample Program 41
Handling Errors 44
Review Questions 46
Summary 46

3 Your First C Program 47

Looking at a C Program 48
    The Format of a C Program 49
    Readability Is the Key 50
    Uppercase Versus Lowercase 51
    Braces and main() 51
    Comments in C 52
Explaining the Sample Program 56
Review Questions 62
Summary 62

4 Variables and Constants 63

Variables 64
    Naming Variables 64
    Variable Types 65
    Declaring Variables 67
    Looking at Data Types 69
    Assigning Values to Variables 73
Constants 76
    Integer Constants 76
    String Constants 78
    Character Constants 83
Review Questions 87
Review Exercises 88
Summary 89

5 Character Arrays and Strings 91

Character Arrays 92
Character Arrays Versus Strings 95
Review Questions 102
Review Exercises 102
Summary 103

6   Preprocessor Directives 105

Understanding Preprocessor Directives 106

The #include Directive 106

The #define Directive 112

Review Questions 120

Review Exercises 121

Summary 122

7   Simple Input and Output 123

The printf() Function 124

Printing Strings 124

Conversion Characters 127

String Conversion Character %s 128

Character Conversion Character %c 129

Integer and Floating-Point Conversion
Characters %d and %f 130

Hex and Octal Conversion
Characters %x and %o 134

Exponential Conversion Characters %e and %g 135

Conversion Character Modifiers 137

Keeping Count of Output 142

The scanf() Function 144

Review Questions 151

Review Exercises 152

Summary 153

Part II C Operators

8   Math Operators and Precedence 157

C's Primary Math Operators 158

The Unary Operators 159

Division and Modulus 161

The Order of Precedence 162

Using Parentheses 164

The Assignment Statements 168

Multiple Assignments 168

Compound Assignments 171

Mixing Data Types in Calculations 174

Type Casting 174

Review Questions 177

Review Exercises 178

Summary 178

9   Relational Operators 181

Defining Relational Operators 182

The if Statement 185

The else Statement 195

Review Questions 199

Review Exercises 200

Summary 201

10   Logical Operators 203

Defining Logical Operators 203

Logical Operators and Their Use 205

C's Logical Efficiency 207

Logical Operators and Their Precedence 211

Review Questions 213

Review Exercises 214

Summary 215

11   Additional C Operators 217

The Conditional Operator 218

The Increment and Decrement Operators 221

The sizeof Operator 226

The Comma Operator 228

Review Questions 230

Review Exercises 231

Summary 232

12   Bitwise Operators 233

Bitwise Logical Operators 234

Bitwise Compound Operators 240

Bitwise Shift Operators 242

Review Questions 244

Review Exercises 245

Summary 245

Part III C Constructs

13   The while Loop **249**

The while Statement 250

The Concept of Loops 251

The do-while Loop 256

The if Loop Versus the while Loop 259

The exit() Function and break Statement 260

Counters and Totals 264

Review Questions 272

Review Exercises 273

Summary 274

14   The for Loop **275**

The for Statement 275

The Concept of for Loops 276

Nested for Loops 288

Review Questions 293

Review Exercises 294

Summary 295

15   Other Loop Options **297**

Timing Loops 298

The break and for Statements 300

The continue Statement 305

Review Questions 309

Review Exercises 310

Summary 310

16   The switch and goto Statements **311**

The switch Statement 312

The goto Statement 321

Review Questions 327

Review Exercises 328

Summary 328

Part IV Variable Scope and Modular Programming

17 Writing C Functions 333

Function Basics 334
Breaking Down Problems 335
More Function Basics 337
Calling and Returning Functions 339
Review Questions 350
Summary 351

18 Variable Scope 353

Global Versus Local Variables 354
    Defining Variable Scope 355
    Use Global Variables Sparingly 363
    The Need for Passing Variables 363
Automatic Versus Static Variables 369
Three Issues of Parameter Passing 374
Review Questions 375
Review Exercises 375
Summary 377

19 Passing Values 379

Passing by Value (by Copy) 379
Passing by Address (by Reference) 384
    Variable Addresses 385
    Sample Program 386
    Passing Nonarrays by Address 390
Review Questions 394
Review Exercises 395
Summary 396

20 Function Return Values and Prototypes ...397

Function Return Values 398
Function Prototypes 405
    Prototype for Safety 408
    Prototype All Functions 408
Review Questions 412
Review Exercises 413
Summary 413

Part V Character Input, Output, and Library Functions

21 Device and Character I/O 417

Character Stream I/O 418
Standard Devices 419
    Redirecting Devices from MS-DOS and UNIX 421
    Printing Formatted Output 423
Character I/O Functions 424
    The getc() and putc() Functions........................... 424
    The getchar() and putchar() Functions 428
    The getch() and putch() Functions 434
Review Questions 436
Review Exercises 437
Summary 438

22 Character, String, and Numeric Functions 439

Character Functions 440
    Character Testing Functions............................... 440
    Alphabetic and Digital Testing 440
    Special Character Testing Functions 442
    Character Conversion Functions 443
String Functions 445
    Useful String Functions 445
    String I/O Functions 446
    Converting Strings to Numbers 449
Numeric Functions 451
    Useful Mathematical Functions 451
    Trigonometric Functions................................... 454
    Logarithmic Functions 454
    Random-Number Processing 455
Review Questions 457
Review Exercises 458
Summary 459

Part VI Arrays and Pointers

23 Introducing Arrays **463**

Array Basics 464

Initializing Arrays 469

    Initializing Elements at Declaration Time 469

    Initializing Elements in the Program 476

Review Questions 481

Review Exercises 481

Summary 482

24 Array Processing **483**

Searching Arrays 484

Searching for Values 485

Sorting Arrays 491

Advanced Referencing of Arrays 498

Review Questions 506

Review Exercises 506

Summary 507

25 Multidimensional Arrays **509**

Multidimensional Array Basics 510

Reserving Multidimensional Arrays 512

Mapping Arrays to Memory 515

Defining Multidimensional Arrays 517

Tables and for Loops 520

Review Questions 527

Review Exercises 528

Summary 529

26 Pointers **531**

Introduction to Pointer Variables 532

    Declaring Pointers 533

    Assigning Values to Pointers 535

    Pointers and Parameters 536

Arrays of Pointers 541

Review Questions 543

Summary 544

27 Pointers and Arrays 545

Array Names as Pointers 546
Pointer Advantages 548
Using Character Pointers 551
Pointer Arithmetic 556
Arrays of Strings 562
Review Questions 566
Review Exercises 567
Summary 568

Part VII Structures and File I/O

28 Structures 571

Introduction to Structures 572
Defining Structures 575
Initializing Structure Data 579
Nested Structures 588
Review Questions 590
Review Exercises 591
Summary 592

29 Arrays of Structures 593

Declaring Arrays of Structures 594
Arrays as Members 603
Review Questions 610
Review Exercises 611
Summary 612

30 Sequential Files 613

Why Use a Disk? 614
Types of Disk File Access 615
Sequential File Concepts 616
Opening and Closing Files 617
Writing to a File 623
Writing to a Printer 626
Adding to a File 627
Reading from a File 628
Review Questions 632
Review Exercises 633
Summary 634

31 Random Access Files 635

Random File Records 636
Opening Random Access Files 637
The `fseek()` Function 639
Other Helpful I/O Functions 646
Review Questions 649
Review Exercises 650
Summary 651

**A Memory Addressing, Binary,
and Hexadecimal Review 653**

Computer Memory 654
   Memory and Disk Measurements 654
   Memory Addresses 655
Bits and Bytes 656
The Order of Bits 659
Binary Numbers 660
Binary Arithmetic 664
Binary Negative Numbers 666
Hexadecimal Numbers 668
Why Learn Hexadecimal? 670
How Binary and Addressing Relates to C 671

B Answers to Review Questions 673

Chapter 1 Answers 673
Chapter 2 Answers 674
Chapter 3 Answers 674
Chapter 4 Answers 675
Chapter 5 Answers 675
Chapter 6 Answers 676
Chapter 7 Answers 677
Chapter 8 Answers 677
Chapter 9 Answers 678
Chapter 10 Answers 679
Chapter 11 Answers 679
Chapter 12 Answers 680
Chapter 13 Answers 680
Chapter 14 Answers 681
Chapter 15 Answers 682

Chapter 16 Answers 682
Chapter 17 Answers 683
Chapter 18 Answers 683
Chapter 19 Answers 683
Chapter 20 Answers 684
Chapter 21 Answers 684
Chapter 22 Answers 685
Chapter 23 Answers 685
Chapter 24 Answers 686
Chapter 25 Answers 686
Chapter 26 Answers 687
Chapter 27 Answers 687
Chapter 28 Answers 688
Chapter 29 Answers 688
Chapter 30 Answers 688
Chapter 31 Answers 689

C ASCII Table 691

D C Precedence Table 697

E Keyword and Function Reference 701

    `<stdio.h>` 702
    `<ctype.h>` 702
    `<string.h>` 703
    `<math.h>` 703
    `<stdlib.h>` 703

F The Mailing List Application 705

Glossary 715

Index 727

Introduction

Every day, more and more people learn and use the C programming language. I have taught C to hundreds of students, and I grow more fond of the language with each course I teach. The C programming language is now the mainstream computer course in colleges. Knowledge of C is an essential prerequisite for employment in the computer industry. I hope this book helps fill a need that the vast number of C books currently in print do not fill: the need for a book with a straightforward, friendly, and comfortable feel that provides a stepping-stone style to C for beginners.

C By Example is one of several books in Que's new *By Example* series. The philosophy of these books is simple: The best way to teach computer programming concepts is with multiple examples. Command descriptions, format syntax, and language references are not enough to teach a newcomer a programming language. Only by looking at numerous examples in which new commands are immediately used, and by running sample programs, can programming students get more than just a "feel" for the language.

Who Should Use This Book

This book teaches at three levels: beginning, intermediate, and advanced. Text and numerous examples are aimed at readers on each level. If you are new to C, and even if you are new to computers, this book attempts to put you at ease and gradually build your C programming skills. If you are an expert at C, this book tries to provide a few extras for you along the way.

The Book's Philosophy

This book focuses on programming *correctly* in C by teaching structured programming techniques and proper program design. Emphasis is always placed on a program's readability rather than "tricks of the trade" code examples. In this changing world, programs should be clear, properly structured, and well-documented, and this book does not waver from the importance of this philosophy.

This book teaches you C using a holistic approach. In addition to learning the mechanics of the language, you learn some tips and warnings, how to use C for different types of applications, and a little of the history and interesting asides about the computing industry.

Many other books build single applications, adding to them a little at a time with each chapter. The chapters of this book are stand-alone chapters, showing you complete programs that fully demonstrate the commands discussed in the chapter. There is a program for every level of reader, from beginning to advanced.

This book contains more than 200 sample program listings. These programs show ways that you can use C for personal finance, school and business record-keeping, math and science, and general-purpose applications that almost everybody with a computer can use. This wide variety of programs shows you that C is a very powerful language that is easy to learn and use.

Appendix F is a complete application—much longer than any of the other programs in the book—that brings together your entire working knowledge of C. The application is a computerized mailing list manager. Throughout the chapters that come before the program, you learn how each command in the program works. You might want to modify the program to suit your own needs. (The comments in the program suggest changes you can make.)

Overview

This book is divided into seven parts. Part I introduces you to the C environment, as well as to introductory programming concepts. Starting with Part II, the book presents the C programming language commands and built-in functions. After mastering the language, you then can use the book as a reference. When you need help with a specific C programming problem, turn to the area that describes that part of the language to see numerous examples of code.

To give you an idea of the book's layout, here is a description of each part of the book.

Part I: Introduction to C

Part I explains what C is by presenting a brief history of the C programming language and then outlining C's advantages over other languages. This part describes your computer's hardware, how you develop your C programs, and the steps you follow to enter and run programs. You write your first C programs in Chapter 3.

Part II: C Operators

Part II teaches the entire set of C operators. The rich assortment of operators (C has more operators than any other programming language except APL) makes up for the fact that the C programming language is very small. The operators and their order of precedence are more important in C than they are in most programming languages.

Part III: C Constructs

C data processing is powerful due to the looping, comparison, and selection constructs that C offers. Part III shows you how to write programs that flow correctly and have control computations that produce accurate and readable code.

Part IV: Variable Scope and Modular Programming

To support true structured programming techniques, C must allow for local and global variables, as well as offer several ways to pass and return variables between functions. Part IV illustrates the strength of C as a structured language that attempts—if the programmer is willing to "listen to the language"—to protect local variables by making them visible only to the parts of the program that need them.

Part V: Character Input, Output, and Library Functions

C has no commands that perform input or output. To make up for this apparent oversight, C compiler writers supply several useful input and output functions. By separating input and output functions from the language, C achieves better portability between computers; if your program runs on one computer, it should work on any other.

Part V describes these input and output functions. It also describes several of the other built-in math, character, and string functions available with C. These functions keep you from having to write your own routines to perform common tasks.

Part VI: Arrays and Pointers

C offers single- and multidimensional arrays. These arrays hold multiple occurrences of repeating data but do not require much effort on your part to process.

Unlike many other programming languages, C also uses pointer variables frequently. Pointer variables and arrays, the subject of Part VI, work together to give you flexible data storage, which enables you to sort and search data easily.

Part VII: Structures and File I/O

Variables, arrays, and pointers are not enough to hold the types of data that your programs will require. Structures allow for more powerful groupings of many different kinds of data into manageable units.

Your computer would be too limiting if you could not store data to the disk and retrieve that data back into your programs. Disk files are required by most "real world" applications. Part VII describes how C processes sequential- and random-access files and teaches the fundamental principles needed to effectively save data to the disk.

Conventions

The following typographic conventions are used in this book:

♦ Command and function names are in `lowercase monospace`. In addition to code lines, variable names and any text you would see on-screen are also in `monospace`.

♦ Placeholders in code are in *`italic monospace`*.

♦ User input following a prompt is in **`bold monospace`**.

♦ Filenames are in uppercase regular text.

♦ New terms, which can be found in the glossary at the back of this book, are in *italic*.

Index to the Icons

 Beginning information

 Intermediate information

Advanced information

 Tip

 Caution

 Note

 Pseudocode

Code continuation—indicates that the code line was too long to fit within the margins of this book. Simply leave one space and continue typing the second line.

Margin Graphics

To further help your understanding of C, this book includes numerous *margin graphics*. These margin graphics are similar to *flowcharts* you might have seen before. Both use standard symbols to represent program logic. You might have heard the adage "A picture is worth a thousand words." You may find it easier to look at the margin graphics to get a feel for the overall logic before dissecting programs line-by-line.

Throughout this book, these margin graphics are used in two places. Some graphics appear when a new command is introduced, to show you how the command works. Others are placed where new commands are shown in sample programs for the first time.

No attempt is made to give you complete, detailed graphics of every statement in each program. The margin graphics are kept simple to give you an overview of the statements you are reading about at the time.

The symbols used in margin graphics throughout this book, along with descriptions of those symbols, are shown in the following.

Terminal symbol
(`{` , `}` , `Return...`)

Assignment statement (`total = total + newvalue; ctr = ctr + 1;...`)

Input/output
(`scanf` , `printf...`)

Calling a function

Small circle; loop begin

Large dot; beginning and end of `IF-THEN`, `IF-THEN-ELSE`, and `SWITCH`

Input/output of arrays; assumes implied `FOR` loop(s) needed to deal with array I/O

Comment bracket; used for added info, such as name of a function

You will find the graphics presented here easy to interpret. Their goal is to be self-explanatory, even if you have not fully learned the commands they represent. The margin graphics, the program listings, the program comments, and the program descriptions in this book give you many vehicles for learning the C programming language.

Pseudocode

Pseudocode appears in italics and precedes many of the program listings in this book. Pseudocode is a description, written in English, of what tasks you want your program to perform. Writing pseudocode before you write your program can help you conceptualize your program's purpose.

Companion Disk Offer

If you'd like to save yourself hours of tedious typing, use the order form at the back of this book to order the companion disk for *C By Example*. This disk contains the source code for all complete programs and sample code in the book, as well as the complete mailing list application that appears in Appendix F. Additionally, the answers to many of the review exercises are also included on this disk.

Part I

Introduction to C

Welcome to C

C is one of the most popular programming languages in use today. The C programming language is a high-level, efficient language that has been standardized and made available to work on almost every computer in the world. Whether you are a beginning, an intermediate, or an expert programmer, C has the programming tools you need to make your computer do just what *you* want it to do. This chapter introduces you to C, briefly describes its history, shows you the advantages of using C over other computer languages, and concludes by introducing you to hardware and software concepts.

What C Can Do for You

ANSI C was defined by the American National Standards Institute to achieve conformity between versions of C.

Have you ever wanted your computer to perform exactly as you wished? Maybe you have looked for a program that keeps track of your household budget—exactly as you prefer—but haven't found one. Perhaps you want to track the records of a small (or large) business with your computer, but you have found nothing that prints reports exactly as you'd like them. Possibly you have thought of a new use for a computer that no one else has thought of, and you would like to implement your idea. C gives you the power to develop all these uses for your computer.

If your computer could understand English, you would not need to learn a programming language. But because it does not, you must learn to write instructions in a language your computer recognizes. C is a small but powerful programming language. Several companies have written different versions of C, but almost all C languages available today conform to the ANSI standard. *ANSI C-compatible* means that the C language in question conforms to the standard defined by the American National Standards Institute (ANSI). This group of computer professionals has attempted to develop a uniform C language. If you program using the ANSI C standard, your program should successfully run on any other computer in the world that also uses ANSI C. Whether something is ANSI C-compatible is important to people who want to write and sell programs that work on many different types of computers.

This book shows you how to program in ANSI C. Whether you use a PC, a minicomputer, a mainframe, or a supercomputer, the C language that you learn here should work on them all.

When some people attempt to learn C, even if they are programmers in other computer languages, they find that C can be cryptic and difficult to understand. This does not have to be the case. When you are taught to write clear and concise C code, in an order that builds on fundamental programming concepts, C is no more difficult to learn or use than any other programming language. Actually, after you get started, C's modularity makes it even easier to use.

Even if you've never programmed a computer before, you may soon understand that programming in C is rewarding. Becoming an expert programmer in C—or in any other computer language—takes time and dedication. Nevertheless, you can start writing simple programs with very little effort. After you learn the fundamentals of C programming, you can build on what you learn and hone your skills as you write more powerful programs. You might also see new uses for your computer and develop programs that others can use.

The importance of C cannot be overly stressed. Over the years, several programming languages have been developed that were designed to be "the only programming language you would ever need." PL/I was heralded as such back in the early 1960s. It turned out to be so large and took so many system resources that it simply became another language programmers used, along with COBOL, FORTRAN, and many others. In the mid-1970s, Pascal was developed for smaller computers. Microcomputers had just been invented, and the Pascal language was small enough to fit in their limited memory space while still offering advantages over many other languages. Pascal became very popular and still is used frequently. It never became *the* answer for all programming tasks, however, and failed at being "the only programming language you would ever need."

When C became known to the mass computer markets in the late 1970s, it also was promoted as "the only programming language you would ever need." What has surprised so many skeptics (including this author) is that C has almost fulfilled this promise! An incredible number of programming shops have converted to C. The appeal of C's efficiency, combined with its portability between computers, makes it the language of choice. Most of today's familiar spreadsheets, databases, and word processors have been written in C.

C's use seems to be growing. The computer professional help-wanted ads seem to seek more and more C programmers every day. By learning this popular language, you will stay up with the programming crowds and keep your skills current. You have taken the first step: with this book, you learn the C language particulars as well as many programming tips to use and pitfalls to avoid. This book attempts to make you not just a C programmer, but a better programmer in general by applying the structured, long-term programming habits that professionals require in today's business and industry.

The Background of C

The UNIX operating system was written almost entirely in C.

Before you jump into C, you might find it helpful to know a little about the evolution of the C programming language. Bell Labs first developed this language in the early 1970s, primarily so Bell programmers could write their UNIX operating system for a new DEC (Digital Equipment Corporation) computer. Until that time, operating systems were written in assembly language, which is tedious, time-consuming, and difficult to maintain. The Bell Labs people knew they needed a higher-level programming language to implement their project quicker and to make its code easier to maintain.

Because other high-level languages at the time (COBOL, FORTRAN, PL/I, and Algol) were too slow for an operating system's code, the Bell Labs programmers decided to write their own language. They based their new language on Algol and BCPL. Algol is still used in the European markets, but is not used much in America. BCPL strongly influenced C, although it did not offer the various data types that the makers of C required. After a few versions, these Bell programmers developed a language that met their goals very well. C is efficient (it is sometimes called a high low-level language due to its speed of execution) and flexible, and contains the proper constructs that enable it to be maintained over time.

C Compared to Other Languages

If you have programmed before, you should understand a little about how C differs from other programming languages on the market. Besides being a very efficient language, C is known also as a *weakly-typed* language; that is, the data types you assign to variables do not necessarily require that same type of data. (Function prototyping under the new ANSI standards, however, helps to alleviate this problem.) For example, if you declare an integer variable, then decide to put a character value into it, C lets you do this. The data may not be in the format you expect, but C does its best. This is much different from stronger-typed languages such as COBOL and Pascal. Although you can get into trouble a little easier, C enables you to view the same data in different ways.

C's philosophy is this: Trust the programmers—they *must* know what they're doing!

This places much more responsibility on the programmer. C is an extremely flexible language. It must be flexible to be used to write operating systems. At any one time, an operating system does not know what is coming down the line. If, for example, an operating system expects an integer but instead receives a character, its language must be flexible enough to handle this different data without aborting.

The added responsibility of the weakly-typed, flexible C language adds to the programmer's burden of being careful while programming. The trade-off is worth it, however. The designers of C did not want to hamper C programmers by adding lots of strict rules to the language.

C is a small, block-structured programming language. It has fewer than 40 keywords. To make up for its small vocabulary, C has one of the largest assortment of *operators* (second only to APL). The large number of operators in C could tempt programmers to write cryptic programs that do a lot with a small amount of code. As you learn throughout this book, however, making the program more readable is more important than squeezing out bytes. This book teaches you how to use the C operators to their fullest extent, while maintaining readable programs.

C's large number of operators (more than the number of keywords) requires a more judicious use of an *operator precedence* table. The C operator precedence table is provided on the inside covers of this book as well as in Appendix D. Unlike most other languages that have only four or five levels of precedence, C has fifteen. As you learn C, you must master each of these fifteen levels. This is not as difficult as it sounds, but its importance cannot be overstated.

C also has no input or output statements. You might want to read that sentence again! C has *no* commands that perform input or output. This is one of the most important reasons why C is available on so many different computers. The *I/O* (input/output) statements of most languages tie those languages to specific hardware. BASIC, for instance, has almost twenty I/O commands—some of which write to the screen, to the printer, to a modem, and so forth. If you write a BASIC program for a microcomputer, chances are good that it cannot run on a mainframe without considerable modification.

C's input and output is performed through the abundant use of *function calls*. With every C compiler comes a library of standard I/O functions that your program calls to perform input and output. These standard routines are *hardware independent*, because they work on any device and on any computer that conforms to the ANSI C standard (as most do).

To master C completely, you must be more aware of your computer's hardware than most other languages would require you to be. You certainly do not have to be a hardware expert, but understanding the internal data representation makes C much more usable and meaningful. It also helps if you can become familiar with binary and hexadecimal numbers. You might want to read Appendix A for a tutorial on these topics before you start to learn the C language. If you do not want to explore these topics, you can still become a very good C programmer. Knowing what goes on "under the hood," however, can make C more meaningful to you.

C and Microcomputers

C was a relatively unknown language until it was placed on the microcomputer. With the invention and growth of the microcomputer, C blossomed into a worldwide computer language. Most readers of this book are probably working on a microcomputer-based C system. If you are new to computers, it might help you to know how microcomputers were developed.

In the 1970s, NASA created the *microchip*, a tiny wafer of silicon that occupies a space smaller than a postage stamp. Computer components could be placed on these microchips, so computers required much less space than before. NASA produced these smaller computers in response to their need to send rocket ships to the moon with on-board computers. The computers on Earth could not provide split-second accuracy for rockets because radio waves took several seconds to travel between the Earth and the moon. Through development, these microchips became small enough so that the computers could travel with a rocket and safely compute the rocket's trajectory.

The space program was not the only beneficiary of computer miniaturization. Because microchips became the heart of the *micro*computer, computers could now fit on desktops. These microcomputers cost much less than their larger counterparts, so many people started buying them. Thus, the home and small-business computer market was born.

Today, microcomputers are typically called PCs (for personal computers), from the widespread use of the original IBM PC. The early PCs did not have the memory capacity of the large computers used by government and big business. Nevertheless, PC owners still needed a way to program these machines. The first programming language chosen for PCs was BASIC. Over the years, many other languages were ported from larger computers down to the PC. However, no language was as successful as C in becoming the worldwide standard programming language.

Before diving into C, you might take a few moments to familiarize yourself with some of the hardware and software components of your own PC. The next section, "An Overview of Your Computer," introduces you to computer components that C interacts with, such as the operating system, memory, disks, and input/output devices. If you are already familiar with your computer's hardware and software, you might want to skip to Chapter 2, "What Is a Program?," and begin using C right away.

An Overview of Your Computer

Your computer system consists of two parts: *hardware* and *software*. The hardware consists of all the physical parts of the machine. Hardware has been defined as "anything you can kick." Although this definition is coarse, it illustrates that your computer's hardware consists of whatever components you can touch. The software is everything else. Software is made up of programs and data that interact with your hardware. The C language is an example of software. You can use C to create even more software programs and data.

Hardware

Figure 1.1 shows a typical PC system. Before using C, you should have a general understanding of what hardware is and how your hardware components work together.

The System Unit and Memory

The *system unit* is the large, boxlike component of the computer. This unit houses the PC's microprocessor. You may hear the microprocessor called the *CPU*, or *central processing unit*. The CPU acts like a traffic cop, directing the flow of information throughout your computer system. The CPU is analogous to the human brain. When you use a computer, you are actually interacting with its CPU. All the other hardware exists so that the CPU can send information to you (through the monitor or the printer), and you can give instructions to the CPU (through the keyboard or the mouse).

Figure 1.1. A typical PC system.

The system unit also houses the computer's internal *memory*. Although the memory has several names, it is commonly referred to as RAM (random-access memory). RAM is where the CPU looks for software and data. When you run a C program, for example, you are instructing your computer's CPU to look in RAM for that program and carry out its instructions. C takes up space in RAM when it is loaded.

RAM is used for many things, and is one of the most important components of your computer's hardware. Without RAM, your computer would have no place for its instructions and data. The amount of RAM can also affect the computer's speed. In general, the more RAM your computer has, the more work it can do and the faster it can process data.

A *byte* is a single
character of memory.

The amount of RAM is measured by the number of characters it can hold. PCs generally hold approximately 640,000 characters of RAM. A character in computer terminology is called a *byte*, and a byte can be a letter, a number, or a special character such as an exclamation point or a question mark. If your computer has 640,000 bytes of RAM, it can hold a total of 640,000 characters.

All the zeros following RAM measurements can get cumbersome. You often see the shortcut notation *K* (which comes from the metric system's *kilo*, meaning *1000*) in place of the last three zeros. In computer terms, K means exactly 1024 bytes; but this number is usually rounded down to 1000 to make it easier to remember. Therefore, 640K means approximately 640,000 bytes of RAM. See the sidebar titled "The Power of Two."

The limit of RAM is similar to the limits of audiocassette tapes. If a cassette is manufactured to hold 60 minutes of music, it cannot hold 75 minutes of music. Likewise, the total number of characters that make up your program (the C data) and your computer's system programs cannot exceed the RAM's limit (unless you save some of the characters to disk).

You want as much RAM as possible to hold the C program, your programs, and the system programs. Generally, 640K is ample room for anything you might want to do in C. Computer RAM is relatively inexpensive, so if your computer has less than 640K bytes of memory, you should consider purchasing additional memory to increase the total RAM to 640K. You can put more than 640K in most PCs. There are two types of additional RAM: *extended* memory and *expanded* memory. You can access this extra RAM with some C systems, but most C programmers have no need to worry about RAM beyond 640K.

The Power of Two

Although K means approximately 1000 bytes of memory, K equates to 1024. Computers function using *on* and *off* states of electricity. These are called *binary* states. At the computer's lowest level, it does nothing more than turn electricity on and off with many millions of switches called *transistors*. Because these switches have two possibilities, the total number of states of these switches—and thus the total number of states of electricity—equals a number that is a power of 2.

The closest power of 2 to 1000 is 1024 (2 to the 10th power). The inventors of computers designed memory so that it is always added in kilobytes, or multiples of 1024 bytes at a time. Therefore, if you add 128K of RAM to a computer, you are actually adding a total of 131,072 bytes of RAM (128 times 1024 equals 131,072).

Because K actually means *more* than 1000, you always get a little more memory than you bargained for! Even though your computer might be rated at 640K, it really holds more than 640,000 bytes (655,536 to be exact). See Appendix A for a more detailed discussion of memory.

The computer stores C programs to RAM as you write them. If you have used a word processor before, you have used RAM. As you type words in your word-processed documents, your words appear on the video screen and also go to RAM for storage.

Despite its importance, RAM is only one type of memory in your computer. RAM is *volatile*; that is, when you turn the computer off, all RAM is erased. Therefore, you must store the contents of RAM to a nonvolatile, more permanent memory device (such as a disk) before you turn off your computer. Otherwise, you lose your work.

Disk Storage

A *disk* is another type of computer memory, sometimes called *external memory*. Disk storage is nonvolatile. When you turn off your computer, the disk's contents do not go away. This is very important. After typing a long C program into RAM, you do not want to retype the same program every time you turn your computer back on. Therefore, after creating a C program, you save the program to disk, where it remains until you're ready to retrieve it again.

Disk storage differs from RAM in ways other than volatility. Disk storage cannot be processed by the CPU. If you have a program or data on disk that you want to use, you must transfer it from the disk into RAM. That is the only way the CPU can work with the program or data. Luckily, most disks hold many times more data than the RAM's 640K. Therefore, if you fill up RAM, you can store its contents on disk, and continue working. As RAM continues to fill up, you or your C program can keep storing the contents of RAM to the disk.

This might sound complicated, but you only have to understand that data must be brought into RAM before your computer can process it and saved to disk before you shut your computer off. Most of the time, a C program runs in RAM and brings in data from the disk as it needs it. Later in the book, you learn that working with disk files is not difficult.

There are two types of disks: *hard disks* and *floppy disks*. Hard disks (sometimes called *fixed disks*) hold much more data and are many times faster to work with than floppy disks. Most of your C programs and data should be stored on your hard disk. Floppy disks are good for backing up hard disks, and for transferring data and programs from one computer to another. These removable floppy disks are often called *diskettes*. Figure 1.2 shows two common sizes, the 5 1/4-inch and the 3 1/2-inch diskettes. These diskettes can hold from 360K to 1.4 million bytes of data.

Figure 1.2. 5 1/4-inch diskette and 3 1/2-inch diskette.

Before using a new box of diskettes, you need to format them (unless you buy disks that are already formatted). Formatting prepares the diskettes for use on your computer by writing a pattern of paths, called *tracks*, where your data and programs will be stored. Refer to your operating system's instruction manual for the correct formatting procedure.

Disk drives house the disks in your computer. Usually, the disk drives are stored in your system unit. The hard disk stays sealed inside the hard disk drive, and you never remove it (expect for repairs). In general, the floppy disk drives also are contained in the system unit, but with these drives you must insert and remove your diskettes manually.

Disk drives have names. The computer's first floppy disk drive is called drive A. The second floppy disk drive, if you have one, is called drive B. The first hard disk (many computers have only one) is called drive C. If you have more than one hard disk, or if your hard disk is logically divided into more than one, the others are named drive D, drive E, and so on.

Disk size is measured in bytes, just as RAM is. Disks can hold many millions of bytes of data. A 40-million-byte hard disk is common. In computer terminology, a million bytes is called a *megabyte* and is abbreviated as *M*. Therefore, if you have a 20-megabyte hard disk, it can hold approximately 20 million characters of data before it runs out of space.

The Monitor

The television-like screen is called the *monitor*. Sometimes the monitor is called the *CRT* (which stands for the primary component of the monitor, the cathode-ray tube). The monitor is one place where the output of the computer can be sent. When you want to look at a list of names and addresses, you could write a C program to list the information on the monitor.

The advantage of screen output over printing is that screen output is faster and does not waste paper. Screen output, however, is not permanent. When text is *scrolled* off-screen (displaced by additional text coming on-screen), it is gone and you may not always be able to see it again.

All monitors have a *cursor*, which is a character such as a blinking underline or a rectangle. The cursor moves when you type letters on-screen, and always indicates the location of the *next* character to be typed.

Monitors that can display pictures are called *graphics monitors*. Although many PC monitors are capable of displaying graphics and text, some can display only text.

If your monitor cannot display colors, it is called a *monochrome* monitor.

Your monitor plugs into a *display adapter* located in your system unit. The display adapter determines the amount of resolution and number of possible on-screen colors. *Resolution* refers to the number of row and column intersections. The higher the resolution, the more rows and columns are present on your screen and the sharper your text and graphics appear. Some common display adapters are MCGA, CGA, EGA, and VGA.

The Printer

The printer provides a more permanent way of recording your computer's results. It is the "typewriter" of the computer. Your printer can print C program output to paper. Generally, you can print anything that appears on your screen. You can use your printer to print checks and envelopes too, because most types of paper have been made to work with computer printers.

The two most common PC printers are the *dot-matrix* printer and the *laser* printer. A dot-matrix printer is inexpensive, fast, and uses a series of small dots to represent printed text and graphics. A laser printer is faster and more expensive than a dot-matrix. Its output is much sharper because a laser beam burns toner ink into the paper. For many people, a dot-matrix printer provides all the speed and quality they need for most applications. C can send output to either type of printer.

The Keyboard

Figure 1.3 shows a typical PC keyboard. Most of the keys are the same as those on a standard typewriter. The letter and number keys in the center of the keyboard produce their indicated characters on the screen. If you want to type an uppercase letter, be sure to press one of the Shift keys before typing the letter. Pressing the Caps Lock key puts the keyboard into an all-uppercase mode, but you still must press the Shift key to type one of the special characters above a number. For instance, to type the percent sign (%), you would press Shift-5, even with the Caps Lock on.

Figure 1.3. The various PC keyboards.

Like the Shift keys, the Alt and Ctrl keys can be used in conjunction with other keys. Some C programs require that you press Alt or Ctrl before pressing another key. For instance, if your C program prompts you to press Alt-F, you should press the Alt key, then press F while still holding down Alt, then release both keys. Do not hold them both down for long, however, or the computer keeps repeating your keystrokes as if you typed them more than once.

The key marked Esc is called the *escape* key. In many C programs, you can press Esc to "escape" out of, or exit from, something you started and then want to stop. For example, if you prompt your C compiler for help and then you no longer need the help message, you can press Esc to remove the help message from the screen.

The group of numbers and arrows on the far right of the keyboard is called the *numeric keypad*. People familiar with a 10-key adding machine usually prefer to enter numbers from the keypad rather than from the top row of the alphabetic key section. The numbers on the keypad work only when you press the Num Lock key. If you press Num Lock a second time, you disable these number keys and make the arrow keys work again. To prevent confusion, many keyboards have separate arrow keys and a keypad used solely for numbers.

The arrows help you move the cursor from one area of the screen to another. To move the cursor toward the top of the screen, you need to press the up-arrow key continuously. To move the cursor to the right, you press the right-arrow key, and so on. Do not confuse the Backspace key with the left-arrow key. Pressing Backspace moves the cursor backward one character at a time—erasing everything as it moves. The left-arrow key simply moves the cursor backward, without erasing.

The keys marked Insert and Delete (Ins and Del on some keyboards) are useful for editing. Your C program editor probably takes advantage of these two keys. Insert and Delete work in C programs the same way they work in a word processor's text. If you do not have separate keys labeled Insert and Delete, you probably need to press Num Lock and use the keypad key 0 (for Insert) and period (for Delete).

PgUp and PgDn are the keys to press when you want to scroll the screen (that is, move your on-screen text either up or down). Your screen acts like a camera that pans up and down your

C programs. You can move down through your text by pressing PgDn, and up through your text by pressing PgUp. (Like Insert and Delete, you may have to use the keypad for these operations.)

The keys labeled F1 through F12 (some keyboards go only to F10) are called *function keys*. The function keys are located either across the top of the alphabetic section or to the left of it. These keys perform advanced functions. When you press one of them, you usually want to issue a complex command, such as searching for a specific word in a program. The function keys in your C program, however, do not necessarily produce the same results as they might in another program, such as a word processor. Functions keys are *application-specific*.

> **CAUTION:** Computer keyboards have a key for number 1. Do not substitute the lowercase *l* to represent the number 1, as you might on a typewriter. To C, a 1 is very different from the letter *l*. You should be careful also to use 0 when you mean zero, and *O* when you want the uppercase letter *O*.

The Mouse

The mouse is a relatively new input device. The mouse moves the cursor to any location on the screen. If you have never used a mouse before, you should take a little time to become skillful in moving the cursor with it. Your C editor (described in the next chapter, "What is a Program?") might use the mouse for selecting commands from its menus.

Mouse devices have two or three buttons. Most of the time, pressing the third button produces the same results as simultaneously pressing both keys on a two-button mouse.

The Modem

A *modem* can be used to communicate between two distant computers.

A PC *modem* enables your PC to communicate with other computers over telephone lines. Some modems, called *external modems*, sit in a box outside your computer. *Internal modems* reside inside the system unit. It does not matter which one you have because they operate identically.

Some people have modems so that they can share data between their computer and that of a long-distance friend or off-site co-worker. You can write programs in C that communicate with your modem.

A Modem by Any Other Name...

The term *digital computer* comes from the fact that your computer operates on binary (on and off) digital impulses of electricity. These digital states of electricity are perfect for your computer's equipment, but they cannot be sent over normal telephone lines. Telephone signals are called *analog* signals, which are much different from the binary digital signals in your PC.

Therefore, before your computer can transmit data over a telephone line, the information must be *modulated* (converted) into analog signals. The receiving computer then must have a way to *demodulate*—convert those signals back to digital.

The modem is the means by which computer signals are modulated and demodulated from digital to analog and vice versa. Thus, the device that *mod*ulates and *dem*odulates these signals is called a *modem*.

Software

No matter how fast, large, and powerful your computer's hardware is, its software determines what work gets done and how the computer does it. Software is to a computer what music is to a stereo system. You store software on the computer's disk and load it into your computer's memory when you are ready to process the software, just as you store music on a tape and play it when you want to hear music.

Programs and Data

No doubt you have heard the phrase, *data processing*. This is what computers really do: they take data and manipulate it into meaningful output. The meaningful output is called *information*. Figure 1.4 shows the *input-process-output* model, which is the foundation of everything that happens in your computer.

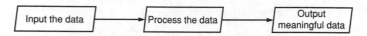

Figure 1.4. Data processing at its most elementary level.

In Chapter 2, "What Is a Program?," you learn the mechanics of programs. For now, you should know that the programs you write in C process the data that you input into the programs. Both data and programs make up the software. The hardware acts as a vehicle to gather the input and produce the output. Without software, computers would be worthless, just as an expensive stereo would be useless without some way of playing music so that you can hear it.

The input comes from input devices, such as keyboards, modems, and disk drives. The CPU processes the input and sends the results to the output devices, such as the printer and the monitor. A C payroll program might get its input (the hours worked) from the keyboard. It then would instruct the CPU to calculate the payroll amounts for each employee in the disk files. After processing the payroll, the program could then print checks on the printer.

MS-DOS

MS-DOS (Microsoft Disk Operating System) is a system that lets your C programs interact with hardware. MS-DOS (commonly called DOS for short) is always loaded into RAM when you power-up your computer. DOS controls more than just the disks; DOS is there so that your programs can communicate with all the computer's hardware, including the monitor, keyboard, and printer.

Figure 1.5 illustrates the concept of DOS as the "go-between" with your computer's hardware and software. Because DOS understands how to control every device hooked to your computer, it stays in RAM and waits for a hardware request. For instance, printing the words "C is fun!" on your printer takes many computer instructions. However, you do not have to worry about all of those instructions. When your C program wants to print something, it tells DOS to print it. DOS always knows how to send information to your printer, so it takes your C program requests and does the work of routing that data to the printer.

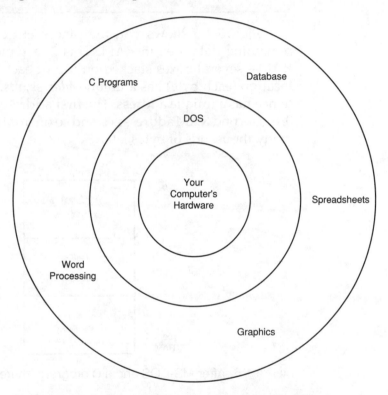

Figure 1.5. DOS interfaces between hardware and software.

Many people program computers for years and never take the time to learn why DOS is there. You do not have to be an expert in DOS, or even know more than a few simple DOS commands, to be proficient with your PC. Nevertheless, DOS does some things that C cannot do, such as formatting diskettes and copying files to your disks. As you learn more about the computer, you may see the need to better understand DOS. For a good introduction to using DOS, refer to the book *MS-DOS 5 QuickStart* (Que Corporation).

> **NOTE:** As mentioned, DOS always resides in RAM and is loaded when you start the computer. This is done automatically so that you can use your computer and program in C without worrying about how to get DOS into RAM. It is important to remember that DOS always takes up some of your total RAM.

Figure 1.6 shows you the placement of DOS, C, and your remaining data area in RAM. This is a typical way to represent RAM—several boxes stacked on top of each other. Each memory location (each byte) has a unique *address*, just as everybody's residence has a unique address. The first address in memory begins at 0, the second RAM address is 1, and so on until the last RAM location many thousands of bytes later.

Figure 1.6. After MS-DOS and a C program, there is less RAM for data.

Your operating system (whether you use MS-DOS, PC DOS, DR DOS, or UNIX) takes part of the first few thousand bytes of memory. The amount of RAM that DOS takes varies with each computer's configuration. When working in C, the C system sits on top of DOS, leaving you with the remainder of RAM for your program and data. This explains why you may have a total of 512K of RAM and still not have enough memory to run some programs—DOS is sitting there taking some of it for itself.

Review Questions

Answers to review questions are in Appendix B.

1. What is the name of one of the programming languages that C was developed from?

2. In what decade was C developed?

3. True or false: C is too large to fit on many microcomputers.

4. Which usually holds more data: RAM or the hard disk?

5. What device is needed for your PC to communicate over telephone lines?

6. Which of the following device types best describes the mouse?

   a. Storage

   b. Input

   c. Output

   d. Processing

7. What key would you press to turn off the numbers on the numeric keypad?

8. What operating system is written almost entirely in C?

9. Why is RAM considered volatile?

10. True or false: The greater the resolution, the better the appearance of graphics on-screen.

11. How many bytes is 512K?

12. What does *modem* stand for?

Summary

C is an efficient, powerful, and popular programming language. Whether you are new to C or an experienced programmer, C is all you need to produce computer programs that make the computer work the way you want it to.

This chapter presented the background of C by walking you through the history of the C programming language. C offers some of the most advanced programming language commands that exist today.

The rest of this book is devoted to teaching you C. Chapter 2, "What Is a Program?," explains program concepts so that you can begin to write C programs.

What Is a Program?

This chapter introduces you to fundamental programming concepts. The task of programming computers has been described as rewarding, challenging, easy, difficult, fast, or slow. Actually, it is a combination of all these descriptions. Writing complex programs to solve advanced problems can be frustrating and time-consuming, but you can have fun along the way, especially with the rich assortment of features that C has to offer.

This chapter describes the concept of programming, from a program's inception to its execution on your computer. The most difficult part of programming is breaking up the problem into logical steps that the computer can carry out. Before you finish this chapter, you will have typed and executed your first C program.

This chapter introduces you to

♦ The concept of programming

♦ The program's output

♦ Program design

♦ Using an editor

♦ Using a compiler

◆ Entering and running a C program

◆ Handling errors

After you complete this chapter, you should be ready throughout the rest of this book to learn the C programming language elements in greater detail.

Computer Programs

Before you can make C work for you, you must write a C program. You have seen the word *program* used several times in this book. A program is a set of instructions that enables a computer to perform certain tasks.

Keep in mind that computers are only machines. They're not smart; in fact, they're quite the opposite! They don't do anything until they are given very detailed instructions. A word processor, for example, is a program somebody wrote—in a language such as C— that tells your computer exactly how to behave when you type words into it.

You are familiar with the concept of programming if you have ever followed a recipe, which is a "program," or a set of instructions, telling you how to prepare a certain dish. A good recipe lists these instructions in their proper order and with enough description so that you can carry out the directions successfully, without any need to make assumptions.

If you want your computer to help with your budget, or keep track of names and addresses, or compute your gas mileage, it needs a program telling it how to do those things. You can supply that program in two ways: buy a program somebody else wrote or write the program yourself.

Writing the program yourself has a big advantage for many applications: The program does exactly what *you* want it to do. If you buy one that is already written, you have to adapt your needs to those of whomever wrote the program. This is where C comes in. With the C programming language (and a little study) you can make your computer carry out your own tasks precisely.

To give C programming instructions to your computer, you need an *editor* and a *C compiler*. An editor is similar to a word processor; it is a program that lets you type a C program into memory, make changes (such as moving, copying, inserting, and deleting text), and save the program more permanently in a disk file. After you use the editor to type the program, you must compile it before you can run it.

The C programming language is called a *compiled* language. You cannot write a C program and run it on your computer unless you have a C compiler. This compiler takes your C language instructions and translates them into a form that your computer can read. A C compiler is the tool your computer needs to understand the C language instructions in your programs. Many compilers come with their own built-in editor. If yours does, you probably feel that your C programming is more integrated. A later section in this book discusses editors and compilers in more detail.

To some beginning programmers, the process of compiling a program before running it may seem like an added and meaningless step. If you know the BASIC programming language, you may not have heard of a compiler or understand the need for one. That's because BASIC (also APL and some versions of other computer languages) is not a compiled language, but an *interpreted* language. Instead of translating the entire program into machine-readable form (as a compiler does in one step), an interpreter translates each program instruction—and then executes it—before translating the next one. The difference between the two is subtle, but the bottom line is not: Compilers produce *much* more efficient and faster-running programs than interpreters do. This seemingly extra step of compiling is worth the effort (and with today's compilers, there is not much extra effort needed).

Because computers are machines that do not think, the instructions you write in C must be very detailed. You cannot assume your computer understands what to do if some instruction is not in your program, or if you write an instruction that does not conform to C language requirements.

After you write and compile a C program, you must *run* (or *execute)* it. Otherwise, your computer would not know that you want it to follow the instructions in the program. Just as a cook must follow a recipe's instructions before the dish is made, so too your computer must execute a program's instructions before it can accomplish what you want it to do. When you run a program, you are telling the computer to carry out your instructions.

> **The Program and Its Output**
>
> While you are programming, remember the difference between a program and its output. Your program contains only the C instructions that you write. But the computer follows your instructions only *after* you run the program.
>
> Throughout this book, you often see a *program listing* (that is, the C instructions in the program) followed by the results that occur when you run the program. The results are the output of the program, and they go to an output device such as the screen, the printer, or a disk file.

Program Design

Design your programs before you type them.

You must plan your programs before typing them into your C editor. When builders construct houses, for example, they don't immediately grab their lumber and tools and start building! They first find out what the owner of the house wants, then they draw up the plans, order the materials, gather the workers, and, finally, start building the house.

The hardest part of writing a program is breaking it into logical steps that the computer can follow. Learning the C language is a requirement, but it is not the only thing to consider. There is a method of writing programs, a formal procedure you should learn, that makes your programming job easier. To write a program you should:

1. Define the problem to be solved with the computer.
2. Design the program's output (what the user should see).
3. Break the problem into logical steps to achieve this output.
4. Write the program (using the editor).

5. Compile the program.

6. Test the program to make sure it performs as you expect.

As you can see from this procedure, the typing of your program occurs toward the end of your programming. This is important, because you first need to plan how to tell the computer how to perform each task.

Your computer can perform instructions only step-by-step. You must assume that your computer has no previous knowledge of the problem, so it is up to you to provide that knowledge, which, after all, is what a good recipe does. It would be a foolish recipe for baking a cake if all it said was: "Bake the cake." Why? Because this *assumes* much too much on the part of the baker. But even if a recipe is written out in step-by-step fashion, proper care must be taken (through planning) to be sure the steps are in sequence. Wouldn't it be foolish also to instruct a baker to put the ingredients into the oven before stirring them?

Throughout the book, the preceding programming procedure is adhered to, as each program is presented. Before you see the actual program, you see it thought out in advance. The goals of the program are presented first, then these goals are broken down into logical steps, and finally the program is written.

Designing the program in advance makes the entire program structure more accurate, and keeps you from having to make many changes later. A builder, for example, knows that a room is much harder to add after the house is built. So, if you do not properly plan every step, it is going to take you longer to create the final, working program. It is always more difficult to make major changes after your program is written.

Planning and developing according to these six steps becomes much more important as you write longer and more complicated programs. Throughout this book, you learn helpful tips for program design. But now it's time to launch into C, so that you can experience typing in your own program and seeing it run.

Using a Program Editor

The instructions in your C program are called the *source code*. You type source code into your computer's memory by using your program editor. After you type your C source code (your program), you should save it to a disk file before compiling and running the program. Most C compilers expect C source programs to be stored in files with filenames ending in .C. For example, the following are valid filenames for most C compilers:

MYPROG.C

SALESACT.C

EMPLYEE.C

ACCREC.C

Many C compilers include a built-in editor. Two of the most popular C compilers (both conform to the ANSI C standard and include their own extended language elements) are Borland's Turbo C and Microsoft's QuickC. These two programs run in fully-integrated environments that relieve the programmer from having to worry about finding a separate program editor or learning many compiler-specific commands.

Figure 2.1 shows a Turbo C screen. Across the top of the screen (as with QuickC) is a menu that offers pull-down editing, compiling, and running options. The middle of the screen contains the body of the program editor, and this is the area where the program goes. From this screen, you type, edit, compile, and run your C source programs. Without an *integrated environment*, you would have to start an editor, type your program, save the program to disk, exit the editor, run the compiler, and only *then* run the compiled program from the operating system. With Turbo C and QuickC, you simply type the program into the editor, and then—in one step—you select the proper menu option that compiles and runs the program.

If you do not own an integrated environment such as Turbo C or QuickC, you need to find a program editor. Word processors can act as editors, but you must learn how to save and load files in a true ASCII text format. It is often easier to use an editor than it is to make a word processor work like one.

```
≡  File  Edit  Search  Run  Compile  Debug  Project  Options    Window  Help
[■]━━━━━━━━━━━━━━━ \CBOOK\C10AGE.C ━━━━━━━━━━━━━━━2=[↑]┐
/* Filename: C10AGE.C
   Program that helps ensure age values are reasonable */
#include <stdio.h>
main()
{
    int age;

    printf("What is your age");
    if ((age > 10) && (age < 100))
      { printf(" \x07 \x07 \n");    /* Beep twice */
        printf("*** The age must be between 10 and 100 ***\n"); }
    else
      { printf("You entered a valid age."); }
    return;
━━ 1:1 ━━━□
━━━━━━━━━━━━━━━━━ Message ━━━━━━━━━━━━━━━1



F1 Help  F2 Save  F3 Open  Alt-F9 Compile  F9 Make  F10 Menu
```

Figure 2.1. Turbo C's integrated environment.

On PCs, DOS Version 5 comes with a nice, full-screen editor, called EDIT. It offers menu-driven commands and full cursor-control capabilities. EDIT is a simple program to use and is a good beginner's program editor. Refer to your DOS manual or a good book on DOS, such as *MS-DOS 5 QuickStart* (Que Corporation), for more information on this program editor.

Another editor, called EDLIN, is available for earlier versions of DOS. EDLIN is a line editor that does not allow full-screen cursor control, and it requires you to learn some cryptic commands. But, the advantage to learning EDLIN is that it is always included with any PC that uses a release of DOS prior to Version 5.

If you use a computer other than a PC, such as a UNIX-based minicomputer or a mainframe, you need to learn which editors are available. Most UNIX systems include the vi editor. If you program on a UNIX operating system, it would be worth your time to learn vi. It is to UNIX what EDLIN is to PC operating systems, and it is available on almost every UNIX computer in the world.

Mainframe users have other editors available, such as the ISPF editor. You may have to check with your systems department to find an editor accessible from your account.

NOTE: Because this book teaches the ANSI C standard programming language, no attempt is made to tie in editor or compiler commands—there are too many on the market to cover them all in one book. As long as you write ANSI C-specific programs, the tools you use to edit, compile, and run those programs are secondary; your goal of good programming is the result of whatever applications you produce.

Using a C Compiler

After you type and edit your C program's source code, you must compile the program. The process you use to compile your program depends on the version of C and the computer you are using. Turbo C and QuickC users need only press Alt-R to compile and run their programs. When you compile programs on most PCs, your compiler eventually produces an *executable* file whose name begins with the same name as the source code, but ends with an .EXE file extension. For example, if your source program is named GRADEAVG.C the PC would produce a compiled file called GRADEAVG.EXE, which you could execute at the DOS prompt by typing the name GRADEAVG.

NOTE: Each program in this book contains a comment that specifies a recommended filename for the source program. You do not have to follow the file-naming conventions used in this book; the filenames are only suggestions. If you use a mainframe, you need to follow the dataset-naming conventions set up by your system administrator. Each program name on the sample disk (see the order form at the back of the book), however, matches the filename of the corresponding program listing in the book.

UNIX users generally have to use the cc compiler. This produces an executable file whose name (by default) is A.OUT. You can then run the A.OUT file from the UNIX prompt. Mainframe users generally have company-standard procedures for compiling C source programs and storing their results in a test account.

Unlike many other programming languages, your C program must be routed through a *preprocessor* before it is compiled. C source code can contain *preprocessor directives* that control the way your programs compile. The preprocessor step is performed automatically by your C compiler, so it requires no additional effort or commands to learn on your part.

You may have to refer to your compiler's reference manuals or to your company's system personnel to learn how to compile programs for your programming environment. Again, learning the programming environment is not as critical as learning the C language. The compiler is just a way to transform your program from a source code file to an executable file.

Your program must go through one additional stage after compiling and before running. It is called the *linking*, or the *link editing*, stage. When your program is linked, needed run-time information (which is not always available to the compiler) is supplied to your program. You can also combine several compiled programs into one executable program by linking them. Most of the time, however, your compiler initiates the link editing stage (this is especially true with integrated compilers such as Turbo C and QuickC) and you do not have to worry about the process.

Figure 2.2 shows the steps that your C compiler and link editor perform to produce an executable program.

Running a Sample Program

Before delving into the specifics of the C language, you should take a few moments to become familiar with your editor and C compiler. Starting with the next chapter, "Your First C Program," you should put all your concentration into the C programming language and not worry about using a specific editor or compiling environment.

Figure 2.2. Compiling C source code into an executable program.

Following this paragraph is a block of pseudocode, which describes in English what you want your program to do. Following the pseucocode is a short program. Start your editor of choice and type the program into your computer. Be as accurate as possible— a single typing mistake could cause the C compiler to generate a series of errors. You do not have to understand the program's content at this point; the goal is simply to give you practice in using your editor and compiler.

Identify the program and include the necessary header file. This program will print a name five times, then make a beep sound. Define a constant called BELL that is the character code for a beep. We need a counter that counts from 1 to 5, so make ctr an integer equal to 0. We need a variable to hold the user's answer, so make fname a character array that holds 20 elements.

Ask the user for his or her first name. Get the user's answer and assign it to fname. *If the counter is less than 5, print the user's answer, add 1 to the counter, and repeat. Make a beep sound.*

```
/* Filename: C2FIRST.C
   Requests a name, prints the name 5 times, and rings a bell */

#include <stdio.h>
#define BELL '\a'

main()
{
   int ctr=0;          /* Integer variable to count through loop */
   char fname[20];     /* Define character array to hold name    */

   printf("What is your first name? ");      /* Prompt the user */
   scanf(" %s", fname);          /* Get the name from the keyboard */
   while (ctr < 5)                       /* Loop to print the name */
   {                                     /* exactly 5 times        */
     printf("%s\n", fname);
     ctr++;
   }
   printf("%c", BELL);               /* Ring the terminal's bell */
   return;
}
```

Be as accurate as possible. In most programming languages—and especially in C—the characters you type in a program must be accurate. In this sample C program, for instance, you see parentheses (), brackets [], and braces {}, but you cannot use them interchangeably.

The *comments* (words between the two symbols /* and */) to the right of some lines do not need to end in the same alignments that you see in the listing. However, you should familiarize yourself with your editor and learn to space characters accurately so you can type this program exactly as shown.

Compile the program and execute it. Granted, the first time you do this you may have to check your reference manuals or contact someone who already knows your C compiler. But do not worry about damaging your computer: Nothing you do from the keyboard can harm the physical computer. The worst thing you can do at this point is erase portions of your compiler software or change the compiler's options—all of which can be easily corrected by reloading the compiler from its original source. (But it is only remotely likely that you would do anything like this, even if you are a beginner.)

Handling Errors

Because you are typing instructions for a machine, you must be very accurate. If you misspell a word, leave out a quotation mark, or make another mistake, your C compiler informs you with an error message. In Turbo C and QuickC, the error probably appears in a separate window, as shown in Figure 2.3. The most common error is a *syntax error* and usually implies a misspelled word.

```
≡  File  Edit  Search  Run  Compile  Debug  Project  Options    Window  Help
                         ─── \CBOOK\C10AGE.C ───────────────────2─
/* Filename: C10AGE.C
   Program that helps ensure age values are reasonable */
#isnclude <stdio.h>
main()
{
   int age;

   printf("What is your age");
   if ((age > 10) && (age < 100))
     { printf(" \x07 \x07 \n");     /* Beep twice */
       printf("*** The age must be between 10 and 100 ***\n"); }
   else
      { printf("You entered a valid age."); }
   return}
─*─── 3:2 ─────────────────────────────────────────────────────
─[■]────────────────────── Message ──────────────────────1=[↑]─
Compiling E:\CBOOK\C10AGE.C:
Error E:\CBOOK\C10AGE.C 3: Unknown preprocessor directive: 'isnclude'



◄■─────────────────────────────────────────────────────────────►
F1 Help  Space View source  ◄┘ Edit source  F10 Menu
```

Figure 2.3. The compiler reporting a program error.

When you get an error message (or more than one), you must return to the program editor and correct the error. If you don't understand the error, you may have to check your reference manual or scour your program's source code until you find the offending problem.

Getting the Bugs Out

One of the first computers, owned by the military, refused to print some important data one day. After its programmers tried for many hours to find the problem in the program, a programmer by the name of Grace Hopper decided to check out the printer.

She found a small moth lodged between two important wires. When she removed the moth, the printer started working perfectly (although the moth did not have the same luck).

The late Grace Hopper retired as an admiral from the Navy. Although she is responsible for developing many important computer concepts (she was the author of the original COBOL language), she may be best known for discovering the first computer bug.

Ever since Admiral Hopper discovered that moth, errors in computer programs have been known as *computer bugs*. When you test your programs, you may have to *debug* them—remove the errors by correcting typing mistakes or changing the logic so your program does exactly what you want it to do.

After you have typed your program correctly using the editor (and you get no compile errors), the program should run properly by asking for your first name, then printing it five times on the screen. After it prints your name for the fifth name, you hear the computer's bell ring.

This example helps to illustrate the difference between a program and its output. You must type the program (or load one from disk), then run the program to see its output.

Review Questions

Answers to review questions are in Appendix B.

1. What is a program?

2. What are the two ways to obtain a program that does what you want?

3. True or false: Computers can think.

4. What is the difference between a program and its output?

5. What do you use for typing C programs into the computer?

6. What filename extension do all C programs have?

7. Why is typing in the program one of the *last* steps in the programming process?

8. What does the term *debug* mean?

9. Why is it important to write ANSI C-compatible programs?

10. True or false: You must link a program before compiling it.

Summary

After reading this chapter, you should understand the steps necessary to write a C program. You know that planning makes writing the program much easier, and that your program's instructions produce the output only after you run the program.

You also learned how to use your program editor and compiler. Some program editors are as powerful as word processors. Now that you know how to run C programs, it is time to start learning the C programming language itself.

Your First C Program

This chapter introduces you to some important C language commands and other elements. But before looking at the language more specifically, many people like to "walk through" a few simple programs to get the overall feel of what a C program is like. This is done here. The rest of the book covers these commands and elements more formally.

This chapter introduces the following topics:

♦ An overview of C programs and their structure

♦ Variables and constants

♦ Simple math operators

♦ Screen output format

This chapter gives you a few general tools to become familiar with the C programming language. The rest of the book concentrates on more specific areas of the language itself.

Looking at a C Program

Figure 3.1 shows the outline of a typical small C program. No C commands are shown in the figure. Although there is much more to a program than this outline implies, this is the general format of the beginning examples in this book.

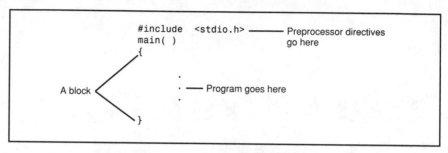

Figure 3.1. A skeleton outline of a simple C program.

To get acquainted with C programs as fast as possible, you should begin to look at a C program in its entirety. Here is a listing of a very simple C program. It doesn't do much, but it enables you to see the general format of C programming. The next few sections discuss elements from this and other programs. You may not understand everything in this program, even after finishing the chapter, but it is a good place to start.

```
/* Filename: C3FIRST.C
   Initial C program that demonstrates the C comments
   and shows a few variables and their declarations */

main()
{
   int i, j;    /* These 3 lines declare 4 variables */
   char c;
   float x;

   i = 4;       /* i and j are both assigned integer constants */
   j = i + 7;
```

```
    c = 'A';      /* All character constants are
                     enclosed in single quotes */
    x = 9.087;    /* x requires a floating-point value since it
                     was declared as a floating-point variable */
    x = x * 4.5;  /* Change what was in x with a formula */

  /* Sends the values of the variables to the screen */
    printf("%d %d %c %f", i, j, c, x);

    return;    /* ALWAYS end programs and functions with return */
}
```

For now, familiarize yourself with this overall program. See if you can understand any part or all of it. If you are new to programming, you should know that the computer looks at each line of the program, starting with the first line and working its way down, until it has carried out all the instructions in the program. (Of course, you first need to compile and link the program, as described in Chapter 2.)

The output of this program is minimal: It simply displays four values on the screen after performing some assignments and calculations of arbitrary values. Just concentrate on the general format at this point.

The Format of a C Program

C is a free-form language.

Unlike some other programming languages, such as COBOL, C is a *free-form* language. That is, programming statements can start in any column of any line. You can insert blank lines in a program if you want. This sample program is called C3FIRST.C (you can find the name of each program in this book in the first line of each program listing). It contains several blank lines to help separate parts of the program. In a simple program such as this, the separation is not as critical as it might be in a longer, more complex program.

Generally, spaces in C programs are free-form as well. Your goal should not be to make your programs as compact as possible. Your goal should be to make your programs as readable as possible.

For example, the C3FIRST.C program shown in the previous section could be rewritten as follows:

```
/* Filename: C3FIRST.C Initial C program that demonstrates the
C comments and shows a few variables and their declarations */
main() {int i, j;
/* These 3 lines declare 4 variables */
char c;float x;i=4;/* i and j are both assigned integer constants
*/
j=i+7;c='A';/* All character constants are enclosed in single
quotes */x=9.087;/* x requires a floating-point value since it
was declared as a floating-point variable */x=x*4.5;/* Change
what was in x with a formula */printf("%d %d %c %f",i,j,c,x);
/* Sends the values of the variables to the screen */return;
/* ALWAYS end programs and functions with return*/}
```

To your C compiler, the two programs are exactly the same, and they produce exactly the same result. However, to people who have to read the program, the first style is *much* more readable. Granted, this is an extreme example.

Readability Is the Key

As long as programs do their job and produce correct output, who cares how well they are written? Even in today's world of fast computers and abundant memory and disk space, *you* should still care. Even if nobody else ever looks at your C program, you might need to make a change at a later date. The more readable you make your program, the faster you can find what needs changing, and then make your changes.

If you work as a programmer for a company, you can almost certainly expect to modify someone else's source code, and others will modify yours. In programming departments, it is said that long-term employees write readable programs. Given this new global economy and all the changes that will face business in the years ahead, companies are seeking programmers who write for the future. Consequently, programmers whose programs are straightforward, readable, abundant with *white space* (separating lines and spaces), and devoid of hard-to-read "tricks" that make for messy programs may have the best employment opportunities.

Use lots of white space so you can have separate lines and spaces throughout your programs. Notice that the first few lines of C3FIRST.C start in the first column, but the body of the program is indented a few spaces. This helps programmers "zero in" on the important code. When you write programs that contain several sections (called *blocks*), your use of white space helps the reader's eye drop down to, and recognize, the next indented block.

Uppercase Versus Lowercase

Use lowercase abundantly in C!

Your uppercase and lowercase letters are much more significant in C than in most other programming languages. You can see that most of C3FIRST.C is in lowercase. The entire C language is in lowercase. For example, you must type the keywords int, char, and return into programs using lowercase characters. If you use uppercase letters, your C compiler would produce many errors and refuse to compile the program until you correct the errors. Appendix E shows a list of every command in the C programming language. You can see that none of the commands have uppercase letters.

Many C programmers reserve uppercase characters for some words and messages sent to the screen, printer, or disk file; they use lowercase letters for almost everything else. There is, however, one exception to this rule that you will read about in Chapter 6, "Preprocessor Directives," which covers the #define preprocessor directive.

Braces and main()

All C programs require the following lines:

```
main()
{
```

A C block is enclosed between two braces.

The statements that follow main() are the first statements executed. The section of a C program that begins with main(), followed by an opening brace ({), is called the *main function*. A C program is actually a collection of functions (small sections of code). The function called main() is always required and always the first function executed.

In the sample program in this chapter, almost the entire program is main() because the matching closing brace that follows main()'s opening brace is at the end of the program. Everything between two matching braces is called a *block*. You will read more about blocks later. For now, just note that this sample program contains only one function, main(), and the entire function is a single block because there is only one pair of braces.

All *executable* C statements must be followed by a semicolon (;) so C knows where the statements end. Because the computer ignores all comments, do *not* put semicolons after your comments. Notice that the lines containing main() and the braces do not end with semicolons either. These lines simply define the beginning and end of the function and do not execute.

As you become better acquainted with C, you will learn when to include the semicolon and when to leave it off. Many beginning C programmers learn quickly when semicolons are required; your compiler certainly lets you know if you forget to include a semicolon where one is needed.

Figure 3.2 repeats the sample program shown in Figure 3.1. It contains additional markings to help acquaint you with these new terms as well as other items described in the remainder of this chapter.

All executable C statements must end with a semicolon (;).

Comments in C

In Chapter 2, you learned the difference between a program and its output. Most users of a program do not see the program itself; they see the output from the execution of the program's instructions. Programmers, on the other hand, look at the program listings and add new routines, change old ones, and update for advancements in computer equipment.

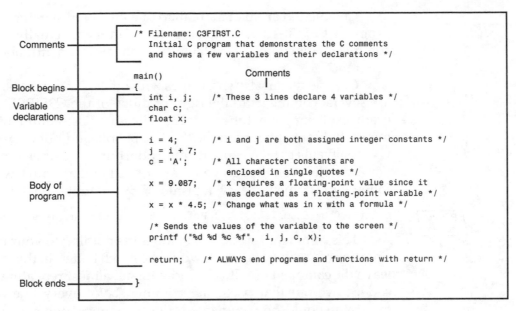

Figure 3.2. The parts of the sample program.

Document
your C
program

Comments tell
people what the
program is doing.

As explained earlier, the readability of a program is important so that you and other programmers can look through it easily. Nevertheless, no matter how clearly you write C programs, you can always enhance their readability by adding comments throughout.

Comments are messages that you insert into your C programs, explaining what is going on at that point in the program. For example, if you write a payroll program, you might put a comment before the check-printing routine that describes what is about to happen. You never put C language statements inside a comment, because a comment is a message for people—not computers. Your C compiler ignores all comments in every program.

NOTE: C comments always begin with a /* symbol and end with a */ symbol.

Comments can span more than one line. Notice in the sample program, C3FIRST.C, that the first three lines are actually a single comment. This comment explains the filename and a little about the program.

Comments can also share lines with other C commands. There are several comments to the right of much of the C3FIRST.C program, explaining what the individual lines do. Use abundant comments, but remember who they're for: people and not computers. Use comments to help explain your code, but do not *over*comment. For example, even though you may not be familiar with C yet, the following statement is easy: It prints "C By Example" on the screen.

```
printf("C By Example");   /* Print C By Example on the screen */
```

This comment is redundant and adds nothing to your understanding of the line of code. It would be much better, in this case, to leave the comment out. If you find yourself almost repeating the C code, leave out that particular comment. Not every line of a C program should be commented. Only comment whenever code lines need explaining—in English —to the people looking at your program.

It does not matter if you use uppercase, lowercase, or a mixture of both in your comments because C ignores them. Most C programmers capitalize the first letter of sentences in comments, just as you would in everyday writing. Because only people read comments, use whatever case seems appropriate for the letters in your message.

CAUTION: C comments cannot be *nested*. That is, you cannot put a comment within another comment. If you do, the C compiler gets confused when it sees the first comment end in the middle of a second one.

The section of a C program that follows is illegal because one comment resides within another:

```
sales = 3456.54 * bonus;
/* This is an example of a C program
   /* It does NOT
      comment correctly! */
   The first comment did not end before the second began. */
```

This sometimes confuses programmers who are just learning C, but who know another programming language. In C, you cannot *comment out* large sections of code just by inserting /* at the beginning of the section and */ at the end if *any* lines within that section already have comments. In some languages, programmers can comment out several lines in a program so that those lines do not execute. This enables the programmer to test remaining lines independently from those commented out. If you try this in C—and create nested comments —your compiler becomes confused.

Comment As You Go

Insert your comments *as you write your programs*. You are most familiar with your program logic at the time you are typing the program into the editor. Some people put off adding comments until after the program is written. More often than not, however, those comments never get put in, or else they are written halfheartedly.

If you comment as you write your code, you can glance back at your comments while working on later sections of the program—instead of having to decipher the previous code itself. This is a great help whenever you want to see something earlier in the program.

Examples

1. Suppose you want to write a C program that produces a fancy boxed title containing your name with flashing dots around it (like a marquee). The C code to do this might be difficult to understand and may not, by itself, be understandable to others who look at your program later. So, before such code, you might want to insert the following comment:

```
/* The following few lines draw a fancy box around
a name, then display flashing dots around the
name like a Hollywood movie marquee. */
```

This would not tell C to do anything because a comment is not a command, but it would make the next few lines of code more understandable to you and others. The comment explains in English, for people reading the program, exactly what the program is getting ready to do.

2. You should also put the disk filename of the program in one of the first comments. For example, in the C3FIRST.C program shown earlier, the first line is really the beginning of a comment:

```
/* Filename: C3FIRST.C
```

The comment continues to the following two lines, but this part of it tells you which disk file the program is stored in. Throughout this book, programs have comments that include a possible filename under which the program can be stored. The program names provided begin with C*x*, where *x* is the chapter number in which they appear (for example, C6VARPR.C and C10LNIN.C). This helps you to find these programs when they are referred to in another section of the book.

> **TIP:** It may be a good idea to put your name at the top of a program in a comment. If people need to modify your program at a later date, they first might want to consult with you, the original programmer, before they change it.

Explaining the Sample Program

Now that you have an overview of a C program, its structure, and its comments, the rest of this chapter walks you through the entire sample program. Do not expect to become a C expert just by completing this section—that is what the rest of the book is for! For now, just sit back and follow this walk-through of the program code.

As described earlier, this sample program contains several comments. The first three lines of the program are comments:

```
/* Filename: C3FIRST.C
   Initial C program that demonstrates the C comments
   and shows a few variables and their declarations */
```

This comment tells you the filename and explains the purpose of the program. This is not the only comment in the program; others appear throughout the rest of the code.

The next two lines (following the blank separating line) are shown here:

```
main()
{
```

This begins the main() function. Basically, the main() function's opening and closing braces enclose the body of this program and the instructions that execute. C programs often contain more than one function, but they *always* contain a function called main(). The main() function does not need to be the first one, but it usually is. The opening brace begins the first and only block of this program.

When this program is compiled and run, the computer looks for main() and starts executing whatever instruction follows main()'s opening brace. Here are the three lines that follow:

```
int i, j;     /* These 3 lines declare 4 variables */
char c;
float x;
```

These three lines *declare variables*. A variable declaration describes all variables used in that block of code.

A C program processes data into meaningful results. All C programs include the following:

♦ Commands

♦ Data

Data is made up of *variables* and *constants*. As the name implies, a *variable* is data that can change (become variable) while the program runs. A *constant* remains the same. In life, a variable might be your salary. It increases over time (if you are lucky). A constant would be your first name or social security number, because each remains with you throughout life and does not usually change.

Chapter 4, "Variables and Constants," fully explains these concepts. However, to give you an overview of the sample program's elements, the following discussion explains variables and constants in this program.

C enables you to use several kinds of *constants*. For now, you simply need to understand that a C constant is any number, character, word, or phrase. The following are all valid C constants:

```
5.6

-45

'Q'

"Mary"

18.67643

0.0
```

As you can see, some constants are numeric and some are character-based. The single and double quotation marks around two of the constants, however, are not part of the constants themselves. A single character constant requires single quotation marks around it; a string of characters, such as "Mary", requires double quotation marks.

Look for the constants in the sample program. You can find these:

```
4

7

'A'

9.087

4.5
```

A variable is like a box inside your computer that holds something. That "something" might be a number or a character. You can have as many variables as your program needs to hold data that changes in the program. After you put a value into a variable, it stays in that variable until you change it or put something else into it.

Variables have names so you can tell them apart. You use the assignment operator, the equal sign (=), to assign values to variables. The following statement

```
sales=25000;
```

puts the constant value 25000 into the variable named sales. In the sample program, you can find the following variables:

```
i

j

c

x
```

The three lines of code that follow the opening brace of the sample program declare these variables. This variable declaration lets the rest of the program know that two integer variables named i and j as well as a character variable called c and a floating-point variable called x appear throughout the program. The terms *integer* and *floating-point* basically refer to two different types of numbers: Integers are whole numbers, and floating-point numbers contain decimal points.

You can see the variables being assigned values in the next few statements of the sample program.

```
i = 4;       /* i and j are both assigned integer constants */
j = i + 7;
c = 'A';     /* All character constants are
                enclosed in single quotes */
x = 9.087;   /* x requires a floating-point value since it
                was declared as a floating-point variable */
x = x * 4.5; /* Change what was in x with a formula */
```

The first line puts 4 in the integer variable i. The second line adds 7 to the variable i's value to get 11, which then gets assigned to (or put into) the variable called j. The plus sign (+) in C works just like it does on calculators. The other primary math operators are shown in Table 3.1.

Table 3.1. The Primary Math Operators.

Operator	Meaning	Example
+	Addition	4 + 5
-	Subtraction	7 - 2
*	Multiplication	12 * 6
/	Division	48 / 12

The character constant A is assigned to the c variable. The number 9.087 is assigned to the variable called x, then x is immediately overwritten with a new value: itself (9.087) multiplied by 4.5. This helps illustrate why computer designers use an asterisk (*) for multiplication and not a lowercase x as people generally do to show multiplication; the computer would confuse the variable x with the multiplication symbol x if both were allowed.

TIP: If mathematical operators are on the right side of the equal sign, the math is completely carried out before the assignment is performed.

The next line (after the comment) includes the following special—and, at first, confusing—statement:

```
printf("%d %d %c %f", i, j, c, x);
```

When the program runs and gets to this line, it prints the contents of the four variables to the screen. It does *not* print %d %d %c %f, even though it might look as if it does. The "%d %d %c %f" is called a *format string*, which describes the format of what is to follow. The %d means that a decimal integer prints in that location. The %c and %f mean that a character and a floating-point value, respectively, print in those locations. This should make more sense to you later.

For now, you can ignore format strings inside printf lines until Chapter 7 explains them more fully. The important part of this line is that the four values for i, j, c, and x print on the screen.

The output from this line is:

```
4 11 A 40.891499
```

Because this is the only printf in the program, this is the only output the sample program produces. You might think that the program is rather long for such a small output. After you learn more about C, you should be able to write more useful programs.

The printf is not a C command. You might recall from Chapter 2 that C has no built-in input/output commands. The printf is a built-in *function,* not an actual command. You have seen one function already, main(), which is one *you* write the code for. The C programming designers have already written the code for the printf function. At this point, you can think of printf as being a command that outputs values to the screen, but it is really a built-in function.

To differentiate printf from regular C commands, parentheses are used after the name, as in printf(). All function names have parentheses following them in a C program. Sometimes these parentheses have something between them, and sometimes they are blank.

The last two lines in the program are shown here:

```
    return;    /* ALWAYS end programs and functions with return */
}
```

Put a return
statement at the end
of each function.

The return command simply tells C that this function is finished. C returns control to whatever was controlling the program before it started running. In this case, because there was only one function, control is returned to DOS or to the C editing environment.

Actually, the return statement is optional. C would know when it reached the end of the program without this statement. But it is a good programming practice to put a return statement at the end of every function, including main(). Because some functions require a return statement (if you are returning values), it is better to get in the habit of using them, rather than run the risk of leaving one out when you really need it.

The closing brace after the return does two things in this program. It signals the end of a block (begun earlier with the opening brace), which is the end of the main() function, and it signals the end of the program.

Review Questions

Answers to review questions are in Appendix B.

1. What must go before and after each comment in a C program?

2. What is a variable?

3. What is a constant?

4. True or false: You can put a comment within another comment.

5. What are four C math operators?

6. What operator puts a value into a variable? (Hint: It is called the assignment operator.)

7. True or false: A variable can consist of only two types: integers and characters.

8. What is the built-in function that writes output to the screen?

9. Is the following a variable name or a string constant?

   ```
   city
   ```

10. What, if anything, is wrong with the following C statement?

    ```
    RETURN;
    ```

Summary

This chapter focused on writing helpful and appropriate comments for your programs. You also learned a little about variables and constants, which hold the program's data. Without them, the term *data processing* would no longer be meaningful.

Now that you have a feel for what a C program looks like, it is time to begin looking at specifics of the commands. Starting with the next chapter, you begin to write your own programs. The next chapter picks up where this one left off; it takes a detailed look at constants and variables, and better describes their uses and how you choose their names.

Variables and Constants

To understand data processing with C, you must understand how C creates, stores, and manipulates data. This chapter teaches you how C handles data by introducing the following topics:

♦ The concepts of variables and constants

♦ The types of C variables and constants

♦ Special constants

♦ Naming and using variables

♦ Declaring variables

♦ Assigning values to variables

Now that you have seen an overview of the C programming language, you can start writing C programs. In this chapter, you begin to write your own programs from scratch.

Garbage in, garbage out!

You learned in the last chapter that C programs consist of commands and data. Data is the heart of all C programs; if you do not correctly declare or use variables and constants, your data is inaccurate and your results are going to be inaccurate as well. A computer adage says the if you put garbage in, you are going to get garbage out. This is very true. People usually blame computers for mistakes, but the computers are not always at fault. Rather, their data is often not entered properly into their programs.

This chapter spends a lot of time focusing on numeric variables and numeric constants. If you are not a "numbers" person, do not fret. Working with numbers is the computer's job. You need to understand only how to tell the computer what you want it to do.

Variables

Variables have characteristics. When you decide your program needs another variable, you simply declare a new variable and C makes sure you get it. You declare all C variables at the top of whatever block of code needs them. To declare a variable, you must understand the possible characteristics, which are

◆ Each variable has a name

◆ Each variable has a type

◆ Each variable holds a value that you put there, by assigning it to that variable

The following sections explain each of these characteristics.

Naming Variables

Because you can have many variables in a single program, you must assign names to them so you can keep track of them. Variable names are unique, just as house addresses are unique. If two variables have the same name, C would not know which you mean when you request one of them.

Variable names can be as short as a single letter or as long as 31 characters. Their names must begin with a letter of the alphabet but, after the first letter, they can contain letters, numbers, and under-score (_) characters.

TIP: Spaces are not allowed in a variable name, so the under-score character helps separate parts of the name.

The following variable names are all valid:

```
salary   aug91_sales   i   index_age   amount
```

It is traditional to use lowercase letters for C variable names. You do not need to follow this tradition, but you should know that upper-case letters in variable names are different from lowercase letters. For example, each of the following four variables are viewed differently by your C compiler.

```
sales   Sales   SALES   sALES
```

Be very careful with the Shift key when you type a variable name. Do not inadvertently change the case of a variable name throughout a program. If you do, C thinks they are distinct and separate variables.

Do not give variables the same name as a command or built-in function.

Variables cannot have the same name as a C command or function. Appendix E shows a list of all C command and function names that you must watch out for whenever you are naming variables.

The following are *invalid* variable names:

```
81_sales   Aug91+Sales   MY AGE   printf
```

TIP: Although you can call a variable any name that fits the naming rules (as long as it is not being used by another variable in the program), you should always use meaningful variable names. Give your variables names that help describe the values they are holding.

For example, keeping track of total payroll in a variable called `total_payroll` is much more descriptive than using the variable name `XYZ34`. Even though both names are valid, `total_payroll` is easier to remember and you have a good idea of what the variable holds by looking at its name.

Variable Types

Variables can hold different *types* of data. Table 4.1 lists the different types of C variables. For instance, if a variable holds an integer, C assumes no decimal point or fractional part (the part to the right of the decimal point) exists for the variable's value. A very large number of types are possible in C. For now, the most important types that you should concentrate on are char, int, and float. You can append the prefix long to make some of them hold larger values than they would hold otherwise. Using the unsigned prefix enables them to hold positive numbers only.

Table 4.1. Some C variable types.

Declaration Name	Type
char	Character
unsigned char	Unsigned character
signed char	Signed character (same as char)
int	Integer
unsigned int	Unsigned integer
signed int	Signed integer (same as int)
short int	Short integer
unsigned short int	Unsigned short integer
signed short int	Signed short integer (same as short_int)
long	Long integer
long int	Long integer (same as long)
signed long int	Signed long integer (same as long_int)
unsigned long int	Unsigned long integer
float	Floating-point
double	Double floating-point
long double	Long double floating-point

The next section more fully describes each of these types. For now, you need to concentrate on the importance of declaring them before using them.

Declaring Variables

There are two places that you can declare a variable:

♦ After the opening brace of a block of code (usually at the top of a function)

♦ Before a function name (such as before `main()` in the program)

The first of these is the most common, and is used throughout much this book. (If you declare a variable before a function name, it is called a *global* variable. Later chapters address the pros and cons of global variables.) To declare a variable, you must state its type, followed by its name. In the previous chapter, you saw a program that declared four variables in the following way.

Declare the variables i and j as integers.
Declare the variable c as a character.
Declare the variable x as a floating-point variable.

```
main()
{
    int i, j;    /* These 3 lines declare 4 variables */
    char c;
    float x;
    /* Rest of program follows */
```

This declares two integer variables named i and j. You have no idea what is inside those variables, however. You generally cannot assume that a variable holds zero—or any other number—until you assign it a value. The first line basically tells C the following:

"I am going to use two integer variables somewhere in this program. Be expecting them. I want them named i and j. When I put a value into i or j, I ensure that the value is an integer."

Without such a declaration, you could not assign i or j a value later. All variables must be declared before you use them. This does not necessarily hold true in other programming languages, such as

Declare all variables in a C program before you use them.

BASIC, but it does for C. You could declare each of these two variables on lines by themselves, as in the following code:

```
main()
{
    int i;
    int j;
    /* Rest of program follows */
```

You do not gain any readability by doing this, however. Most C programmers prefer to declare variables of the same type on the same line.

The second line in this example declares a character variable called c. Only single characters should be placed there. Next, a floating-point variable called x is declared.

Examples

1. Suppose you had to keep track of a person's first, middle, and last initials. Because an initial is obviously a character, it would be prudent to declare three character variables to hold the three initials. In C, you could do that with the following statement:

```
main()
{
    char first, middle, last;
    /* Rest of program follows */
```

This statement could go after the opening brace of main(). It lets the rest of the program know that you require these three character variables.

2. You could declare these three variables also on three separate lines, although it does not necessarily improve readability to do so. This could be accomplished with the following:

```
main()
{
    char first;
    char middle;
```

```
char last;
/* Rest of program follows */
```

3. Suppose you want to keep track of a person's age and weight. If you want to store these values as whole numbers, they would probably go in integer variables. The following statement would declare those variables:

```
main()
{
    int age, weight;
    /* Rest of program follows */
```

Looking at Data Types

You might wonder why it is important to have so many variable types. After all, a number is just a number. But C has more data types than almost all other programming languages. The variable's type is critical, but choosing the type among the many offerings is not as difficult as it may first appear.

The character variable is easy to understand. A character variable can hold only a single character. You cannot put more than a single character into a character variable.

> **NOTE:** Unlike many other programming languages, C does not have a string variable. Also, you cannot hold more than a single character in a C character variable. To store a string of characters, you must use an *aggregate* variable type that combines other fundamental types, such as an array. Chapter 5, "Character Arrays and Strings," explains this more fully.

Integers hold whole numbers. Although mathematicians may cringe at this definition, an integer is really just any number that does not contain a decimal point. All of the following expressions are integers:

```
45      -932    0     12     5421
```

Floating-point numbers contain decimal points. They are known as *real* numbers to mathematicians. Any time you need to store a salary, a temperature, or any other number that may have a fractional part (a decimal portion), you must store it in a floating-point variable. All of the following expressions are floating-point numbers, and any floating-point variable can hold them:

```
45.12    -2344.5432   0.00    .04594
```

Sometimes you need to keep track of very large numbers, and sometimes you need to keep track of smaller numbers. Table 4.2 shows a list of ranges that each C variable type might hold.

> **CAUTION:** All true ANSI C programmers know that they cannot count on using the exact values in Table 4.2 on every computer that uses C. These ranges are typical on a PC, but may be much different on another computer. Use this table only as a guide.

Table 4.2. Typical ranges that C variables might hold.

Type	Range*
char	−128 to 127
unsigned_char	0 to 255
signed_char	−128 to 127
int	−32768 to 32767
unsigned_int	0 to 65535
signed_int	−32768 to 32767
short_int	−32768 to 32767
unsigned_short_int	0 to 65535
signed_short_int	−32768 to 32767
long_int	−2147483648 to 2147483647

Type	Range*
signed_long_int	–2147483648 to 2147483647
float	–3.4E+38 to 3.4E+38
double	–1.7E+308 to 1.7E+308
long_double	–1.7E+308 to 1.7E+308

* *Use this table only as a guide; different compilers and different computers may allow different ranges.*

NOTE: The floating-point ranges in Table 4.2 are shown in scientific notation. To determine the actual range, take the number before the E (meaning *Exponent*) and multiply it by 10 raised to the power after the plus sign. For instance, a floating-point number (type float) can contain a number as small as -3.4×10^{38}.

Notice that long integers and long doubles tend to hold larger numbers (and therefore, have a higher precision) than regular integers and regular double floating-point variables. This is due to the larger number of memory locations used by many of the C compilers for these data types. Again, this is usually—but not always—the case.

Do Not Over-Type a Variable

If the long variable types hold larger numbers than the regular ones, you might initially want to use long variables for all your data. This would not be required in most cases, and would probably slow your program's execution.

As Appendix A describes, the more memory locations used by data, the larger that data can be. However, every time your computer has to access more storage for a single variable (as is usually the case for long variables), it takes the CPU much longer to access it, calculate with it, and store it.

Use the long variables only if you suspect your data overflows the typical data type ranges. Although the ranges differ between computers, you should have an idea of whether your numbers may exceed the computer's storage ranges. If you are working with extremely large (or extremely small and fractional) numbers, you should consider using the long variables.

Generally, all numeric variables should be signed (the default) unless you know for certain that your data contains only positive numbers. (Some values, such as age and distances, are always positive.) By making a variable an unsigned variable, you gain a little extra storage range (as explained in Appendix A), but that extra range of values must always be positive.

Obviously, you must be aware of what kinds of data your variables hold. You certainly do not always know exactly what all variables are holding, but you can have a general idea. For example, in storing a person's age, you should realize that a long integer variable would be a waste of space, because nobody can live to an age that can't be stored by a regular integer.

At first, it may seem strange for Table 4.2 to state that character variables can hold numeric values. In C, integers and character variables frequently can be used interchangeably. As explained in Appendix A, the ASCII table characters each have a unique number that corresponds to their location in the table. If you store a number in a character variable, C treats the data as if it were the ASCII character that matched that number in the table. Conversely, you can store character data in an integer variable. C finds that character's ASCII number, and stores that number instead of the character. Examples that help illustrate this follow a little later in the chapter.

Designating Long, Unsigned, and Floating-Point Constants

When you type a number, C interprets its type as the smallest type that can hold that number. For example, if you print 63, C knows that this number fits into a signed integer memory location. It does not treat the number as a long integer, because 63 is not large enough to warrant a long integer constant size.

However, you can append a suffix character to numeric constants to override the default type. If you put an L at the end of an integer, C interprets that integer as a long integer. The number 63 is an integer constant, but the number 63L is a long integer constant.

Assign the U suffix to designate an unsigned integer constant. The number 63 is, by default, a signed integer constant. If you type 63U, C treats it as an unsigned integer. The suffix UL indicates an unsigned long constant.

C interprets all floating-point constants (numbers that contain decimal points) as double floating-point constants. This ensures the maximum accuracy in such numbers. If you use the constant 6.82, C treats it as a double floating-point data type, even though it would fit in a regular float. You can append the floating-point suffix (F) or the long double floating-point suffix (L) to constants that contain decimal points to represent a floating-point constant or a long double floating-point constant, respectively, instead of the default double constant value.

You may rarely use these suffixes, but if you need to assign a constant value to an extended or unsigned variable, you may gain a little more accuracy if you add U, L, UL, or F (their lowercase equivalents work too) to the end of the constant.

Assigning Values to Variables

Assign value of expression to variable

Now that you know about the C variable types, you are ready to learn the specifics of putting values into those variables. You do this with the *assignment* statement. The equal sign (=) is used for assigning values to variables. The format of the assignment statement is

```
variable=expression;
```

The *variable* is any variable that you declared earlier. The *expression* is any variable, constant, expression, or combination that produces a resulting data type that is the same as the *variable*'s data type.

> **TIP:** Think of the equal sign as a left-pointing arrow. Loosely, the equal sign means you want to take the number, variable, or expression on the right side of the equal sign and put it into the variable on the left side of the equal sign.

Examples

1. If you want to keep track of your current age, salary, and dependents, you could store these values in three C variables. You first declare the variables by deciding on correct types and good names for them. You then assign values to them. Later in the program, these values may change (for example, if the program calculates a new pay increase for you).

   Good variable names would be age, salary, and dependents. To declare these three variables, the first part of the main() function might look like this:

```
/* Declare and store three values */
main()
{
    int age;
    float salary;
    int dependents;
```

Notice that you do not need to declare all integer variables together. After these variables are declared, the next three statements could assign them values, such as:

```
    age=32;
    salary=25000.00;
    dependents=2;
/* Rest of program follows */
```

This example is not very long and doesn't do much, but it illustrates using and assigning values to variables.

2. Do not put commas in values that you assign to variables. Numeric constants should *never* contain commas. The following statement is *invalid*:

```
salary=25,000.00;
```

3. You can assign variables or mathematical expressions to other variables. Suppose you stored your tax rate in a variable called `tax_rate` earlier in a program, then decided to use your tax rate for your spouse's rate as well. At the proper point in the program, you could code the following:

```
spouse_tax_rate = tax_rate;
```

(Putting spaces around the equal sign is all right with the C compiler, but you do not have to.) At this point in the program, the value in `tax_rate` would be copied to a new variable named `spouse_tax_rate`. The value in `tax_rate` would still be there after this line finishes. This assumes that the variables were declared earlier in the program.

If your spouse's tax rate is going to be 40 percent of yours, you can assign an expression to the spouse's variable, as in

```
spouse_tax_rate = tax_rate * .40;
```

Any of the four mathematical symbols you learned in the last chapter, as well as the additional ones you learn about later in the book, can be part of the expression you assign to a variable.

4. If you want to assign character data to a character variable, you must enclose the character in single quotation marks. All C character constants must be enclosed in single quotation marks.

The following section of a program declares three variables, then assigns three initials to them. The initials are character constants because they are enclosed in single quotation marks.

```
main()
{
   char first, middle, last;
   first = 'G';
   middle = 'M';
   last = 'P';
   /* Rest of program follows */
```

Because these are variables, you can put other values into them later if the program warrants it.

CAUTION: Do not mix types. In most cases, C lets you do this, but the results are unpredictable. For instance, in the middle variable presented in the last example, you could have stored a floating-point constant:

```
middle = 345.43244;    /* Do not do this! */
```

If you did so, middle would hold a strange value that would seem to be meaningless. Make sure that values you assign to variables match the variable's type. The only major exception to this occurs when you assign an integer to a character variable, or a character to an integer variable, as you learn shortly.

Constants

As with variables, there are several types of C constants. Remember that a constant does not change. Integer constants are whole numbers that do not contain decimal points. Floating-point constants are numbers that contain a fractional portion (a decimal point with an optional value to the right of the decimal point).

Integer Constants

You already know that an integer is any whole number without a decimal point. C lets you assign integer constants to variables, use integer constants for calculations, and print integer constants in the printf() function.

A regular integer constant cannot begin with a leading 0. To C, the number 012 is *not* the number twelve. If you precede an integer constant with a 0, C thinks it is an *octal* constant. An octal constant is a base-8 number. The octal numbering system is not used much in today's computer systems. The newer versions of C retain octal capabilities for compatibility with previous versions.

An octal integer constant contains a leading 0, and a hexadecimal constant contains a leading 0x.

A special integer in C that *is* still greatly used today is the base-16, or *hexadecimal*, constant. Appendix A describes the hexadecimal numbering system. If you want to represent a hexadecimal integer constant, add the 0x prefix to it. All of the following numbers are hexadecimal numbers:

0x10   0x2C4   0xFFFF   0X9

Notice that it does not matter if you use a lowercase or uppercase letter *x* after the leading zero, or an uppercase or lowercase hexadecimal digit (for hex numbers *A* through *F*). If you write business application programs in C, you may think you never have the need for using hexadecimal, and you might be correct. For a complete understanding of C and your computer in general, however, you should become a little familiar with the fundamentals of hexadecimal numbers.

Table 4.3 shows a few integer constants represented in their regular decimal, hexadecimal, and octal notations. Each row contains the same number in all three bases.

Table 4.3. Integer constants represented in three different bases.

Decimal (Base 10)	Hexadecimal (Base 16)	Octal (Base 8)
16	0x10	020
65536	0xFFFF	0100000
25	0x19	031

NOTE: Floating-point constants may begin with a leading zero, for example, 0.7. They will be properly interpreted by C. Only integers are hexadecimal or octal constants if preceded by a zero.

Your Computer's Word Size Is Important

If you write a lot of system programs that use hexadecimal numbers, you probably want to store those numbers in *unsigned* variables. This keeps C from improperly interpreting positive numbers as negative numbers.

For example, if your computer stores integers in 2-byte words (as most PCs do), the hexadecimal constant 0xFFFF represents either –1 or 65536, depending on how the sign bit is interpreted. If you declared an unsigned integer, such as

```
unsigned_int i_num = 0xFFFF;
```

C knows you want it to use the sign bit as data and not as the sign. If you declared the same value as a signed integer, however, as in

```
int i_num = 0xFFFF;   /* The word "signed" is optional */
```

C thinks this is a negative number (–1) because the sign bit is turned on. (If you were to convert 0xFFFF to binary, you would get sixteen 1s.) Appendix A describes these concepts in more detail.

String Constants

A string constant is always enclosed in double quotation marks.

One type of C constant, called the string constant, does not have a matching variable. A string constant is *always* enclosed in double quotation marks. Here are examples of string constants:

```
"C Programming"    "123"    " "    "4323 E. Oak Road"    "x"
```

Any string of characters between double quotation marks—even a single character between double quotation marks—is considered to be a string constant. A single space, a word, or a group of words between double quotation marks are all C string constants. If the string constant contains only numeric digits, it is *not* a number; it is a string of numeric digits that you cannot use to perform mathematics. You can perform math only on numbers, not on string constants that contain numbers or even on a character constant that might contain a number (enclosed in single quotation marks).

> **NOTE:** A string constant is *any* character, digit, or group of characters enclosed in double quotation marks. A character constant is any character enclosed in single quotation marks.

The double quotation marks are never considered part of the string constant. The double quotation marks surround the string and simply inform your C compiler that it is a string constant and not another type of constant.

It is easy to print string constants. Simply put the string constants in a `printf()` function. No other `printf()` characters you have seen, such as `"%d"` or `"%c"`, are needed. Here is an example of what you need to type to print a string constant to the screen.

Print C By Example to the screen.

```
printf("C By Example");
```

Examples

1. The following program displays a simple message on-screen. No variables are needed because no data is stored or calculated.

```
/* Filename: C4ST1.C
   Display a string on-screen */

main()
{
    printf("C programming is fun!");
    return;
}
```

Remember to make the last line in your C program (before the closing brace) a return statement.

2. You probably want to label the output from your programs. Do not print the value of a variable unless you print also a string constant that describes that variable. The following program computes sales tax for a sale and prints the tax. Notice a message is printed first that tells the program user what the next number means.

```
/* Filename: C4ST2.C
   Compute sales tax and display it with an appropriate
   message */

main()
{
    float sale, tax;
    float tax_rate = .08;    /* Sales tax percentage */

    /* Determine the amount of the sale */
    sale = 22.54;

    /* Compute the sales tax */
    tax = sale * tax_rate;

    /* Print the results */
    printf("The sales tax is");
    printf("%f", tax);

    return;
}
```

String-Constant Endings

An additional aspect of string constants sometimes confuses beginning C programmers. All string constants end with a zero. You do not see the zero, but C makes sure it stores the zero at the end of the string in memory. Figure 4.1 shows what the string "C Program" looks like in memory.

Figure 4.1. In memory, a string constant always ends with 0.

You do not need to worry about putting the zero at the end of a string constant; C does it for you every time it stores a string. If your program contained the string "C Program", for example, the compiler would recognize it as a string constant (from the double quotation marks) and store the zero at the end.

The zero is important to C. It is called the *string delimiter*. Without it, C would not know where the string constant ended in memory. (Remember that the double quotation marks are not stored as part of the string, so C cannot use them to determine where the string ends.)

All string constants end in a null zero (also called binary zero or ASCII zero).

The string-delimiting zero is *not* the same as the character zero. If you look at the ASCII table in Appendix C, you can see that the first entry, ASCII number 0, is the *null* character. (If you are unfamiliar with the ASCII table, you should read Appendix A for a review.) This differentiates the string-delimiting zero from the character '0', whose ASCII value is 48.

As explained in Appendix A, all memory locations in your computer actually hold bit patterns for characters. If the letter *A* is stored in memory, an *A* is not really there; the binary bit pattern for the ASCII *A* (01000001) is stored there. Because the binary bit pattern for the null zero is 00000000, the string-delimiting zero is also called a *binary zero*.

To illustrate this further, Figure 4.2 shows the bit patterns for the following string constant when stored in memory:

`"I am 30."`

Figure 4.2. The bit pattern showing that a null zero and a character zero are different.

Figure 4.2 shows how a string is stored in your computer's memory at the binary level. It is important for you to recognize that the character *0*, inside the number *30*, is not the same zero (at the bit level) as the string-terminating null zero. If it were, C would think this string ended after the *3*, which would be incorrect.

This is a fairly advanced concept, but you truly need to understand it before continuing. If you are new to computers, reviewing the material in Appendix A will help you understand this concept.

String Lengths

The length of a string constant does not include the null binary zero.

Many times, your program needs to know the length of a string. This becomes critical when you learn how to accept string input from the keyboard. The length of a string is the number of characters up to, but not including, the delimiting null zero. Do *not* include the null character in that count, even though you know C adds it to the end of the string.

Examples

1. The following are all string constants:

   ```
   "0"      "C"       "A much longer string constant"
   ```

2. The following table shows some string constants and their corresponding string lengths.

String	Length
"C"	1
"0"	1
"Hello"	5
" "	0
"30 oranges"	10

Character Constants

All C character constants should be enclosed within single quotation marks. The single quotation marks are not part of the character, but they serve to delimit the character. The following are valid C character constants:

```
'w'  'W'  'C'  '7'  '*'  '='  '.'  'K'
```

C does not append a null zero to the end of character constants. You should know that the following are very different to C.

```
'R'    and     "R"
```

'R' is a single character constant. It is one character long, because *all* character constants (and variables) are one character long. "R" is a string constant because it is delimited by double quotation marks. Its length is also one, but it includes a null zero in memory so C knows where the string ends. Because of this difference, you cannot mix character constants and character strings. Figure 4.3 shows how these two constants are stored in memory.

'R' in RAM

"R" in RAM

Figure 4.3. The difference in memory between 'R' as a character constant and "R" as a string constant.

All of the alphabetic, numeric, and special characters on your keyboard can be character constants. Some characters, however, cannot be represented with your keyboard. They include some of the higher ASCII characters (such as the Spanish Ñ). Because you do not have keys for every character in the ASCII table, C lets you represent these characters by typing their ASCII hexadecimal number inside single quotation marks.

For example, the hexadecimal ASCII number for the Spanish Ñ is A5. To store Ñ in a variable, add the prefix \x to A5 and enclose it in single quotation marks, so C will know to use the special character. You could do that with the following code:

```
char sn='\xA5';    /* Puts the Spanish N into the variable
                      called sn */
```

This is the way to store (or print) any character from the ASCII table, even if that character does not have a key on your keyboard.

The single quotation marks still tell C that a *single* character is inside the quotation marks. Even though '\xA5' contains four characters inside the quotation marks, those four characters represent a single character, not a character string. If you were to include those four characters inside a string *constant*, C would treat \xA5 as a single character within the string. The following string constant

```
"An accented a is \xA0"
```

is a C string that is 18 characters long, not 21 characters. C interprets the \xA0 character as the *á*, just as it should.

CAUTION: If you are familiar with entering ASCII characters by typing their ASCII numbers with the Alt-keypad combination, do *not* do this in your C programs. They might work on your computer (not all C compilers support this), but your program might not be portable to another computer's C compiler.

Any character preceded by a backslash, \, (such as these have been) is called an *escape sequence*, or *escape character*. Table 4.4 shows some additional escape sequences that come in handy when you want to print special characters.

TIP: Include \n in a printf() if you want to skip to the next line.

Table 4.4. Special C escape sequence characters.

Escape Sequence	Meaning
\a	Alarm (the terminal's bell)
\b	Backspace
\f	Form feed (for the printer)
\n	Newline (carriage return and line feed)
\r	Carriage return
\t	Tab
\v	Vertical tab
\\	Backslash (\)
\?	Question mark
\'	Single quotation mark
\"	Double quotation mark
\ooo	Octal number

continues

Table 4.4. continued

Escape Sequence	Meaning
\xhh	Hexadecimal number
\0	Null zero (or binary zero)

Math with C Characters

Because C links characters so closely with their ASCII numbers, you can perform arithmetic on character data. The following section of code

```
char c;
c = 'T' + 5;      /* Add 5 to the ASCII character */
```

actually stores a *Y* in c. The ASCII value of the letter *T* is 84. Adding 5 to 84 produces 89. Because the variable c is not an integer variable, but is a character variable, C knows to put in c the ASCII character for 89, not the number itself. Conversely, you can store character constants in integer variables. If you do, C stores the matching ASCII number for that character. The following section of code

```
int i='P';
```

does not put a letter *P* in i because i is not a character variable. C assigns the number 80 in the variable because 80 is the ASCII number for the letter *P*.

Examples

1. To print two names on two different lines, include the \n between them.

Print the name Harry *to the screen; drop the cursor down to a new line and print* Jerry.

```
printf("Harry\nJerry");
```

When the program gets to this line, it prints

```
Harry
Jerry
```

2. The following short program rings the bell on your computer by assigning the \a escape sequence to a variable and then printing that variable.

```
/* Filename: C4BELL.C
   Rings the bell */
main()
{
   char bell='\a';
   printf("%c", bell);   /* "%c" means print a character
                             value */
   return;
}
```

Review Questions

Answers to review questions are in Appendix B.

1. Which of the following variable names are valid?

   my_name   89_sales   sales_89   a-salary

2. Which of the following constants are characters, strings, integers, and floating-point constants?

   0   -12.0   "2.0"   "X"   'X'   65.4   -708   '0'

3. How many variables do the following statements declare, and what are their types?

```
int i, j, k;
char c, d, e;
float x=65.43;
```

4. What do all string constants end with?

5. True or false: An unsigned variable can hold a larger value than a signed variable.

6. How many characters of storage does the following constant take?

   `'\x41'`

7. How is the following string stored at the bit level?

   `"Order 10 of them."`

8. How is the following string (called a *null string*) stored at the bit level? (Hint: The length is zero, but there is still a terminating character.)

   `" "`

Review Exercises

1. Write the C code to store in three variables your weight (you can fib), height in feet, and shoe size. Declare the variables, then assign them values in the body of your program.

2. Rewrite your program from #1, adding proper `printf()` statements to print the values to the screen. Use appropriate messages (by printing string constants) to describe the numbers that are printed.

3. Write a program that stores a value into, and prints, each type of variable you have learned in this chapter.

4. Write a program that stores a value into every type of variable C allows. You must first declare each variable at the top of your program. Put numbers in them and print them to see how C stores and prints them.

Summary

A firm grasp of C's fundamentals is critical to your better understanding of the more detailed material that follows. This was one of the last general-topic chapters in the book. You learned about variable types, constant types, how to name variables, and how to assign variable values. These issues are critical to your understanding of the rest of C.

This chapter taught you how to store almost every type of constant into variables. There is no string variable, so you cannot store string constants in string variables (as you can in other programming languages). However, you can "fool" C into *thinking* it has a string variable by using a character array to hold strings. You learn this important concept in the next chapter.

Character Arrays and Strings

Even though C has no string variables, you can make C think it has them by using character arrays. The concept of arrays may be new to you, but this chapter explains how easy they are to declare and use. After you declare these arrays, they can hold character strings— just as if they were real string variables. This chapter introduces

♦ Character arrays

♦ How character arrays and strings are alike and different

♦ Examples of using character arrays and strings

After you master this chapter, you are on your way toward being able to manipulate almost every type of variable C offers. Manipulating characters and words is one thing that separates your computer from a powerful calculator; this capability gives computers true data processing capabilities.

Character Arrays

A string constant can be stored in an array of characters.

Almost every type of data in C has a variable, but there is no variable for holding character strings. The authors of C realized that you need some way to store strings in variables, but instead of storing them in a string variable (as in some languages such as BASIC or Pascal) you must store them in an *array* of characters.

If you have never programmed before, an array might be new to you. An array is a list (sometimes called a *table*) of variables, and most programming languages allow the use of such lists. Suppose you had to keep track of the sales records of 100 salespeople. You could make up 100 variable names and assign to each one a different salesperson's sales record.

All those different variable names, however, are difficult to track. If you were to put them in an array of floating-point variables, you would need to keep track of only a single name (the array name) and could reference each of the 100 values by a numeric subscript.

Part 6, "Arrays and Pointers," covers array processing in more detail. However, to work with character string data in your early programs, you need to become familiar with the concept of an array of characters (called a *character array*).

Because a string is simply a list of one or more characters, a character array is the perfect place to hold strings of information. Suppose you want to keep track of a person's full name, age, and salary in variables. The age and salary are easy because there are variable types that can hold such data. You would write the following code to declare those two variables:

```
int age;
float salary;
```

You have no string variable to hold the name, but you can create an appropriate array of characters (which is really one or more character variables next to each other in memory) with the following declaration:

```
char name[15];
```

This reserves a character array. An array declaration always includes brackets, [], that declare the storage C needs to reserve for the array. This array is 15 characters long. The array name is name.

You can also assign to the character array a value at the time you declare it. The following declaration statement not only declares the character array, but also assigns the name "Michael Jones" at the same time:

Declare the character array called name *as 15 characters long, and assign* Michael Jones *to that array.*

```
char name[15]="Michael Jones";
```

Figure 5.1 shows what this array looks like in memory. Each of the 15 boxes of the array is called an *element*. Notice the null zero (the string-terminating character) at the end of the string. Notice also that the last character of the array contains no data. You filled only the first fourteen elements of the array with the data and the data's null zero. The fifteenth element actually has a value in it—but we are not concerned with whatever follows the string's null zero.

Figure 5.1. A character array after being declared and assigned a string value.

You can access individual elements within an array, or you can access the array as a whole. This is the primary advantage of an array over the use of many differently named variables. You can assign values to the individual array elements by putting the elements' location, called a *subscript*, in brackets, as follows:

```
name[3]='k';
```

This overwrites the h in the name Michael with a k. The string now looks like the one in Figure 5.2.

Figure 5.2. The array contents (see Figure 5.1) after changing one of the elements.

All array subscripts begin at 0.

All array subscripts start at zero. Therefore, to overwrite the first element, you must use 0 as the subscript. Assigning name[3] (as is done in Figure 5.2) changes the value of the fourth element in the array.

You can print the entire string—or, more accurately, the entire array—with a single printf() function, as follows:

```
printf(name);
```

or

```
printf("%s", name);
```

Notice that when you print an array, you do not put the brackets after the array name. Also, as long as a character array holds a string—and it does as long as you put in a string, or ensure that a null zero is at the end of its character data—you can print it with or without the "%s" (string) format code.

But you must be sure to reserve enough characters in the array to hold the entire string. The following

```
char name[5]="Michael Jones";
```

would be incorrect because it reserves only 5 characters for the array, while the name and its null zero require 14 characters. However, C would *not* give you an error message if you tried to do this; instead, it would overwrite whatever follows the `name` array in memory. This could cause unpredictable results and would never be correct.

Always reserve enough array elements to hold the string, plus its null-terminating character. It is easy to forget the null character, but don't do it. If your string contains 13 characters, it must have also a 14th for the null zero—or it will never be treated like a string. To help eliminate this error, C gives you a shortcut. The following two character array statements are the same:

```
char horse[9]="Stallion";
```

and

```
char horse[]="Stallion";
```

If you assign a value to a character array at the same time you declare the array, C counts the string's length, adds one for the null zero, and reserves that much array space for you automatically.

Never declare a character array (or any other type of array) with empty brackets, if you do not also assign values to that array at the same time. The following statement

```
char people[];
```

does *not* reserve any space for the array called `people`. Because you did not assign the array a value when you declared it, C assumes this array contains zero elements. Therefore, you have no room to put values into this array later. Most compilers generate an error if you attempt this.

Character Arrays Versus Strings

In the previous section, you saw how to put a string into a character array. Strings can exist in C only as string *constants*, or stored in character arrays. At this point, you need to understand only that strings must be stored in character arrays. As you read through this book and become more familiar with arrays and strings, however, you should become more comfortable with their use.

> **NOTE:** Strings must be stored in character arrays, but not all character arrays contain strings.

Look at the two arrays shown in Figure 5.3. The first one, called cara1, is a character array, but it does not contain a string. Instead of a string, it contains a list of several characters. The second array, called cara2, contains a string because it has a null zero at the end.

Figure 5.3. Two character arrays: the one above contains characters, and the one below contains a character string.

These arrays could be initialized with the following declaration statements.

Declare the array cara1 with ten individual characters.
Declare the array cara2 with the character string "Excellent".

```
char cara1[10]={'a', 'b', 'c', 'd', 'e', 'f', 'g', 'h', 'i', 'j'};
char cara2[10]="Excellent";
```

If you want to put only individual characters into an array, you must enclose the list of characters in braces, as shown. You could also initialize cara1 later in the program, using assignment statements, as the following code section does.

Initialize each element of array

```
char cara1[10];
cara1[0]='a';
cara1[1]='b';
cara1[2]='c';
cara1[3]='d';
cara1[4]='e';
cara1[5]='f';
cara1[6]='g';
cara1[7]='h';
cara1[8]='i';
cara1[9]='j';       /* Last element possible with subscript of 9 */
```

Because the cara1 character array does not contain a null zero, it does *not* contain a string of characters. It does contain characters that can be stored in the array—and used individually—but they cannot be treated in a program as if they were a string.

> **CAUTION:** You cannot assign string values to character arrays in a regular assignment statement, except when you first declare them, as shown.

Because a character array is not a string variable (it can be used only to hold a string), it cannot go on the left side of an equal (=) sign. The program that follows is *invalid*:

```
main()
{
    char petname[20];      /*  Reserve space for the pet's name */
    petname = "Alfalfa";   /* INVALID! */
    printf(petname);
    return;
}
```

Because the pet's name was not assigned *at the time the character array was declared*, it cannot be assigned a value later. But the following is allowed, because you can assign values individually to a character array:

```
main()
{
    char petname[20];    /* Reserve space for the pet's name */
    petname[0]='A';   /* Assign values one element at a time */
    petname[1]='l';
    petname[2]='f';
    petname[3]='a';
    petname[4]='l';
    petname[5]='f';
    petname[6]='a';
    petname[7]='\0';   /* Needed to ensure this is a string! */
    printf(petname);   /* NOW the pet's name prints properly */
    return;
}
```

The petname character array now holds a string because the last character is a null zero. How long is the string in petname? It is seven characters long because the length of a string never includes the null zero.

You cannot assign more than 20 characters to this array because its reserved space is only 20 characters. However, you can store any string of 19 (leaving one for the null zero) or fewer characters to the array. If you put the "Alfalfa" string into the array as shown, and then assign a null zero to petname[3] as in

```
petname[3]='\0';
```

the string in `petname` is now just three characters long. You have, in effect, shortened the string. There are still 20 characters reserved for `petname`, but the data inside it is the string `"Alf"` ending with a null zero.

There are many other ways to assign a value to a string. You can use the `strcpy()` function, for example. This is a built-in function—like `printf()`—that lets you copy a string constant into a string. To copy the `"Alfalfa"` pet name into the `petname` array, you could type:

```
strcpy(petname, "Alfalfa");   /* Copies Alfalfa into the array */
```

The `strcpy()` ("string copy") function assumes that the first value in the parentheses is a character array name, and that the second value is a valid string constant or another character array that holds a string. You must be sure that the first character array in the parentheses is long enough (in number of reserved elements) to hold whatever string you copy into it.

Other methods of initializing arrays are explored throughout the rest of this book.

The `strcpy()` function puts string constants into string arrays.

Examples

1. Suppose you want to keep track of your aunt's name in a program so you can print it. If your aunt's name is Ruth Ann Cooper, you need to reserve at least 16 elements—15 to hold the name and one to hold the null character. The following statement properly reserves a character array to hold the name:

```
char aunt_name[16];
```

2. If you want to put your aunt's name in the array at the same time you reserve the array storage, you could do it like this:

```
char aunt_name[16]="Ruth Ann Cooper";
```

You could also leave out the array size and let C count the number needed:

```
char aunt_name[]="Ruth Ann Cooper";
```

3. Suppose you want to keep track of the names of three friends. The longest name is 20 characters (including the null zero). You simply need to reserve enough character-array space to hold each friend's name. The following would do it:

```
char friend1[20];
char friend2[20];
char friend3[20];
```

These array declarations should go towards the top of the block, along with any integer, floating-point, or character variables you need to declare.

4. The next example asks the user for a first and last name. It then prints the user's initials on-screen by printing the first character of each name in the array. The program must print each array's 0 subscript because the first subscript of any array begins at 0, not 1.

```
/* Filename: C5INIT.C
   Print the user's initials */
#include <stdio.h>
main()
{
    char first[20];   /* Holds the first name */
    char last[20];    /* Holds the last name */

    printf("What is your first name? ");
    scanf(" %s", first);
    printf("What is your last name? ");
    scanf(" %s", last);

    /* Print the initials */
    printf("Your initials are %c.%c.", first[0], last[0]);
    return;
}
```

5. The following program takes your three friends' character arrays and assigns them string values, by using the three methods shown in this chapter:

```
/* Filename: C5STR.C
   Store and initialize 3 character arrays for 3 friends */

main()
{
   /* Declare all arrays, and initialize the first one */
   char friend1[20]="Jackie Paul Johnson";
   char friend2[20];
   char friend3[20];

/* Use a function to initialize the second array */
   strcpy(friend2, "Julie L. Roberts");

   friend3[0]='A';  /* Initialize the last, an element at a
                        time */
   friend3[1]='d';
   friend3[2]='a';
   friend3[3]='m';
   friend3[4]=' ';
   friend3[5]='G';
   friend3[6]='.';
   friend3[7]=' ';
   friend3[8]='S';
   friend3[9]='m';
   friend3[10]='i';
   friend3[11]='t';
   friend3[12]='h';
   friend3[13]='\0';

   /* Print all three names */
   printf("%s\n", friend1);
   printf("%s\n", friend2);
   printf("%s\n", friend3);
   return;
}
```

The last method of initializing a character array with a string—one element at a time—is not used as often as the other methods.

Review Questions

Answers to review questions are in Appendix B.

1. How would you declare a character array called `my_name` that holds the following string constant?

   `"This is C"`

2. How long is the string in #1?

3. How many bytes of storage does the string in #1 take?

4. What do all string constants end with?

5. How many variables do the following statements declare, and what are their types?

   ```
   char name[25];
   char address[25];
   ```

6. True or false: The following statement assigns a string constant to a character array.

   `myname[]="Kim Langston";`

7. True or false: The following declaration puts a string into the character array called `city`.

   `char city[]={'M', 'i', 'a', 'm', 'i', '\0'};`

8. True or false: The following declaration puts a string into the character array called `city`.

   `char city[]={'M', 'i', 'a', 'm', 'i'};`

Review Exercises

1. Write the C code to store your weight, height in feet, shoe size, and name in four variables. Declare the variables, then assign them values in the body of your program.

2. Rewrite the program in #1, adding proper `printf()` statements to print the values to the screen. Use appropriate messages (by printing string constants) to describe the values that are printed.

3. Write a program to store and print the names of your two favorite television programs. Store these programs in two character arrays. Initialize one of the strings (assign it the first program's name) at the time you declare the array. Initialize the second value in the body of the program with the `strcpy()` function.

4. Write a program that puts ten different initials into ten elements of a single character array. Do not store a null zero. Print the list backward, one initial on each line.

Summary

This has been a short, but powerful, chapter. You learned about character arrays that hold strings. Even though C has no string variables, character arrays can hold string constants. After you put a string into a character array, you can print or manipulate it as if it were a string.

Starting with the next chapter, you begin to hone the C skills you are building. Chapter 6 introduces preprocessor directives, which are not part of the C language but help you work with your source code as a whole before your program is compiled.

Preprocessor Directives

As you may recall from Chapter 2, the C compiler routes your programs through a *preprocessor* before it compiles them. The preprocessor might be called a "pre-compiler" because it preprocesses and prepares your source code for compiling before your compiler receives it.

Because this *preprocess* is so important to C, you should familiarize yourself with it before learning more specialized commands in the language itself. Regular C commands do not affect the preprocessor. You must supply special non-C commands, called *preprocessor directives*, to control the preprocessor. These directives enable you, for example, to effect changes to your source code before it reaches the compiler. To teach you about the C preprocessor, this chapter describes

♦ What preprocessor directives are

♦ The #include preprocessor directive

♦ The #define preprocessor directive

♦ Examples of both

Almost every proper C program contains preprocessor directives. This chapter teaches you the two most common: `#include` and `#define`.

Understanding Preprocessor Directives

Preprocessor directives are commands that you supply to the preprocessor. All preprocessor directives begin with a pound sign (#). Never put a semicolon at the end of preprocessor directives, because they are preprocessor commands and not C commands. Preprocessor directives typically begin in column 1 of your source program. They could begin in any column, of course, but you should stay with tradition and start them in the first column wherever they appear. Figure 6.1 illustrates a program that contains three preprocessor directives.

Preprocessor directives cause your C preprocessor to change your source code, but these changes last only as long as the compilation takes. When you look at your source code again, the preprocessor is finished with your file and its changes are no longer in the file. Your preprocessor does not in any way compile your program or look at your actual C commands. Some beginning C students tend to get confused by this, but you shouldn't as long as you realize your program *has yet to be compiled* when your preprocessor directives execute.

It has been said that a preprocessor does nothing more than text-editing to your program. This analogy holds true throughout this chapter.

Preprocessor directives temporarily change your source code.

The #include Directive

The `#include` preprocessor directive *merges* a disk file into your source program. Remember that a preprocessor directive does nothing more than a word processing command might do to your

program; word processors are also capable of file merging. The
format of the #include preprocessor directive follows:

```
#include <filename>
```

or

```
#include "filename"
```

Merge file
into source
code

```
/* Filename: C6PRE.C
   C program that demonstrates preprocessor directives */

#include <stdio.h>
#define AGE 28
#define MESSAGE "Hello, world."

main()
{
   int i = 10, age;   /* i is assigned a value at declaration */
                      /* age is still UNDEFINED */

   age = 5;           /* Puts 5 in the variable age */

   i = i * AGE;       /* AGE is not the same as the variable age
*/

   printf("%d %d %d", i, age, AGE);  /* Prints 280 5 28 */
   printf(MESSAGE);   /* "Hello world" gets printed on screen */

   return;
}
```

Preprocessor
directives

Figure 6.1. Program containing three preprocessor directives.

In the #include directive, the *filename* must be an ASCII text file
(just as your source file must be) that resides on your disk. To better
illustrate this, it may help to leave C for just a moment. The following
example shows the contents of two files on disk. One is called
OUTSIDE and the other is called INSIDE.

The OUTSIDE file contains the following:

```
Now is the time for all good men
#include <INSIDE>
to come to the aid of their country.
```

The INSIDE file consists of the following:

```
A quick brown fox jumped
over the lazy dog.
```

Assume you can run the OUTSIDE file through the C preprocessor, which would find the #include directive and replace it with the entire file called INSIDE. In other words, the C preprocessor directive would merge the INSIDE file into the OUTSIDE file—at the #include location—and OUTSIDE would expand to include the merged text. After the preprocessing ends, OUTSIDE would look like this:

```
Now is the time for all good men
A quick brown fox jumped
over the lazy dog.
to come to the aid of their country.
```

The INSIDE file remains on disk in its original form. Only the file containing the #include directive is changed. But note that this change is only *temporary*; that is, OUTSIDE is expanded by the included file only for as long as it takes to compile the program.

A few examples that are more usable with C might help, because the OUTSIDE and INSIDE files are not C programs. You might want to #include a file containing common code that you frequently use. Suppose you print your name and address often in your C programs. You *could* type the following few lines of code in every program that prints your name and address:

```
printf("Kelly Jane Peterson\n");
printf("Apartment #217\n");
printf("4323 East Skelly Drive\n");
printf("New York, New York\n");
printf("           10012\n");
```

Instead of having to retype the same five lines everywhere you want your name and address to print, you could just type them *once* and save them in a file called MYADD.C. From then on, you would only need to type the single line:

```
#include <myadd.c>
```

This not only saves typing, but it also maintains consistency and accuracy. (Sometimes this kind of repeated text is known as *boilerplate*.)

You usually can use angled brackets, <>, or double quotation marks, "", around the included filename with the same results. The angled brackets tell the preprocessor to look for the *include* file in a default include directory, set up by your compiler. The double quotes tell the preprocessor first to look for the include file in the directory where the source code is stored and, if missing, then to look for it in the system's include directory.

Most of the time, you do see angled brackets around the included filename. If you want to include sections of code in other programs, be sure to store that code in the system's include directory (if you use angled brackets).

Even though #include works well for inserted source code, there are other ways to include common source code that are more efficient. You learn about these methods, called *external functions*, in Chapter 17, "Writing C Functions."

> The #include directive is most often used for system header files.

This source code #include example serves well to explain what the #include preprocessor directive does. Despite this fact, #include seldom is used to include source code text, but is more often used to include special system files called *header* files. These system files inform C how to interpret the many built-in functions that you use. Your C compiler comes with its own header files. When you (or your system administrator) installed your C compiler, these header files were automatically stored on your disk in the system's include directory. Their filenames always end in *.h* to differentiate them from regular C source code.

The most common header file is named stdio.h. This gives your C compiler needed information about the built-in printf() function, as well as other very useful and common built-in routines that perform input and output. The name "stdio.h" stands for *standard input/output header*.

At this point, you don't really need to understand the stdio.h file. You should, however, place this file before `main()` in every program you write. It is rare that a C program does *not* need stdio.h included, but if it isn't needed, including it does no harm. Your programs can work without stdio.h (you've already seen it happen in this book); nevertheless, your programs are more accurate and hidden errors come to the surface much faster if you include this file.

Throughout this book, whenever a new built-in function is described, the function's matching header file is also given. Because almost every C program you write includes a `printf()` to print to the screen, almost every program contains the following line.

Include the built-in C header file stdio.h.

```
#include <stdio.h>
```

In the last chapter, you saw the `strcpy()` function. Its header file is called string.h. Therefore, if you write a program that contains `strcpy()`, you should also include its matching header file at the same time you include `<stdio.h>`. These go on separate lines, such as:

```
#include <stdio.h>
#include <string.h>
```

The order of your include files does not matter as long as you include them before the functions that need them. Most C programmers include all of their needed header files before `main()`.

These header files are nothing more than text files. If you like, search your disk with your C editor and find one, such as stdio.h, and look at it. The file may seem very complex at this point, but there is nothing "hidden" about it. If you do look at a header file, however, do *not* change it in any way. If you do, you may have to reload your compiler from scratch to restore the file.

Examples

1. The following program is very short. It includes the name-and-address printing routine described earlier. After printing the name and address, it ends.

```
/* Filename: C6INC1.C
    Illustrates the #include preprocessor directive */
main()
{
#include "myadd.c"
return;
}
```

The double quotes are used because the file named
MYADD.C is stored in the same directory as the source file.
Remember that if you type this program into your computer
(after typing and saving the MYADD.C file) and then compile your program, the MYADD.C file is included only as
long as it takes to compile the program. Your compiler does
not see this file. Your compiler sees—and "thinks" you
typed—the following:

```
/* Filename: C6INCL1.C
    Illustrates the #include preprocessor directive */
main()
{
printf("Kelly Jane Peterson\n");
printf("Apartment #217\n");
printf("4323 East Skelly Drive\n");
printf("New York, New York\n");
printf("              10012\n");
    return;
}
```

This explains what is meant by a preprocessor: the changes
are made to your source code *before* it's compiled. Your
original source code is restored as soon as the compile is
finished. When you look at your program again, it is back in
its original form, as originally typed, with the #include
statement.

2. Because this program uses printf(), it should also include
   the standard input/output header file as follows:

```
/* Filename: C6INCL2.C
   Illustrates the #include preprocessor directive */

#include <stdio.h>

main()
{
#include "myadd.c"
   return;
}
```

3. The following program copies a message into a character array and prints it to the screen. Because the printf() and strcpy() built-in functions are used, both of their header files should also be included.

```
/* Filename: C6INCL3.C
   Uses two header files */

#include <stdio.h>
#include <string.h>

main()
{
   char message[20];
   strcpy(message, "This is fun!");
   printf(message);
   return;
}
```

The #define Directive

The #define preprocessor directive is also commonly used in many C programs. This directive might seem strange at first, but it really does nothing more than a search-and-replace command does on a word processor. The format of #define follows:

```
#define ARGUMENT1 argument2
```

where ARGUMENT1 is a single word containing no spaces. Use the same naming rules for the #define statement's first argument as for variables (see Chapter 4). For the first argument, it is traditional to use uppercase letters—one of the only uses of uppercase in the entire C language. At least one space separates ARGUMENT1 from argument2. The argument2 can be any character, word, or phrase; it also can contain spaces or anything else you can type on the keyboard. Because #define is a preprocessor directive and not a C executable command, do *not* put a semicolon at the end of its expression.

> The #define directive replaces every occurrence of a first argument with a second argument.

The #define preprocessor directive replaces the occurrence of ARGUMENT1 everywhere in your program with the contents of argument2. In most cases, the #define directive should go before main() (along with any #include directives). Look at the following #define directive.

Define the AGELIMIT constant to 21.

```
#define AGELIMIT 21
```

If your program includes one or more occurrences of the term AGELIMIT, the preprocessor replaces every one of them with the number 21. The compiler then reacts as if you actually had typed 21 instead of AGELIMIT, because the preprocessor changes all occurrences of AGELIMIT to 21 before your compiler sees the source code. But, again, the change is only temporary. After your program is compiled, you see it as you originally typed it, with #define and AGELIMIT still intact.

AGELIMIT is *not* a variable, because variables are declared and assigned values only at the time when your program is compiled and run. The preprocessor changes your source file *before* the time it is compiled.

You may wonder why you would ever need to go to this much trouble. If you want 21 everywhere AGELIMIT occurs, you could type 21 to begin with! But the advantage of using #define over constants is that if the age limit ever *changes* (perhaps down to 18), you need to change only *one* line in the program—and not every single occurrence of the constant 21.

> The #define directive creates defined constants.

Because #define enables you easily to define and change constants, the replaced arguments of the #define directive are sometimes called *defined constants*. You can define any type of constant, including string constants. The following program contains a defined string constant that replaces a string in two places.

```
/* Filename: C6DEF1.C
   Defines a string constant and uses it twice */

#include <stdio.h>
#define MYNAME "Phil Ward"

main()
{
   char name[]=MYNAME;
   printf("My name is %s\n", name);   /* Prints the array */
   printf("My name is %s\n", MYNAME); /* Prints the defined constant
*/
   return;
}
```

The first argument of #define is in uppercase to distinguish it
from variable names in the program. Variables are usually entered
in lowercase. Although your preprocessor and compiler would not
get confused, people who look at your program can more quickly
scan through and tell which items are defined constants and which
are not. They know when they see an uppercase word (if you follow
the recommended standard for this first #define argument) to look at
the top of the program for its actual defined value.

The fact that defined constants are not variables is made even
clearer in the following program. This program prints five values.
Try to guess what those five values are before you look at the answer
following the program.

```
/* Filename: C6DEF2.C
   Illustrates that #define constants are not variables */

#include <stdio.h>

#define X1 b+c
#define X2 X1 + X1
#define X3 X2 * c + X1 - d
#define X4 2 * X1 + 3 * X2 + 4 * X3

main()
{
```

```
    int b = 2;      /* Declares and initializes four variables */
    int c = 3;
    int d = 4;
    int e = X4;

    printf("%d  %d  %d  %d  %d", e, X1, X2, X3, X4);
    return;
}
```

The output from this program is

```
44   5   10   17   44
```

If you had treated X1, X2, X3, and X4 as variables, you would not get the correct answers. X1 through X4 are not variables; they are defined constants. Before your program is compiled, the preprocessor looks at the first line and knows to change every occurrence of X1 to b+c. This occurs before the next #define is processed. Therefore, after the first #define, the source code looks like this:

```
/* Filename: C6DEF2.C
   Illustrates that #define constants are not variables */

#include <stdio.h>

#define X2 b+c + b+c
#define X3 X2 * c + b+c - d
#define X4 2 * b+c + 3 * X2 + 4 * X3

main()
{
    int b=2;      /* Declares and initializes four variables */
    int c=3;
    int d=4;
    int e=X4;

    printf("%d  %d  %d  %d  %d", e, b+c, X2, X3, X4);
    return;
}
```

After the first #define finishes, the second one takes over and changes every occurrence of X2 to b+c + b+c. Your source code at that point becomes the following:

```
/* Filename: C6DEF2.C
   Illustrates that #define constants are not variables */

#include <stdio.h>

#define X3 b+c + b+c * c + b+c - d
#define X4 2 * b+c + 3 * b+c + b+c + 4 * X3

main()
{
   int b=2;      /* Declares and initializes four variables */
   int c=3;
   int d=4;
   int e=X4;

   printf("%d  %d  %d  %d  %d", e, b+c, b+c + b+c, X3, X4);
   return;
}
```

After the second #define finishes, the third one takes over and changes every occurrence of X3 to b+c + b+c * c + b+c - d. Your source code then becomes

```
/* Filename: C6DEF2.C
   Illustrates that #define constants are not variables */

#include <stdio.h>

#define X4 2 * b+c + 3 * b+c + b+c + 4 * b+c + b+c * c + b+c - d

main()
{
   int b=2;      /* Declares and initializes four variables */
   int c=3;
   int d=4;
   int e=X4;

   printf("%d  %d  %d  %d  %d", e, b+c, b+c + b+c, b+c + b+c * c +
          b+c - d, X4);
   return;
}
```

The source code is growing rapidly! After the third `#define` finishes, the fourth and last one takes over and changes every occurrence of X4 to 2 * b+c + 3 * b+c + b+c + 4 * b+c + b+c * c + b+c - d. Your source code at this last point becomes

```
/* Filename: C6DEF2.C
   Illustrates that #define constants are not variables */

#include <stdio.h>

main()
{
    int b=2;      /* Declares and initializes four variables */
    int c=3;
    int d=4;
    int e=2 * b+c + 3 * b+c + b+c + 4 * b+c + b+c * c + b+c - d;

    printf("%d  %d  %d  %d  %d", e, b+c, b+c + b+c, b+c +
           b+c * c + b+c - d, 2 * b+c + 3 * b+c + b+c +
           4 * b+c + b+c * c + b+c - d);
    return;
}
```

This is what your compiler actually sees. You did not type this complete listing; you typed the original listing that was shown first. The preprocessor expanded your source code into this longer form, just as if you *had* typed it this way.

This may be an extreme example, but it serves to illustrate how `#define` works on your source code and doesn't define any variables. The `#define` really behaves like a word processor's search-and-replace command. Because of this, you can even rewrite the C language itself!

If you are used to BASIC, you might be more comfortable typing **PRINT** instead of C's **printf()** when you want to print on-screen. If so, the following `#define` statement:

```
#define PRINT printf
```

allows you to print in C with these statements:

```
PRINT("This is a new printing technique\n");
PRINT("I could have used printf() instead."\n);
```

This works because by the time your compiler sees the program, it sees only the following:

```
printf("This is a new printing technique\n");
printf("I could have used printf() instead."\n);
```

Also, you cannot replace a defined constant if it resides in another string constant. For example, you could not use the following #define statement:

```
#define AGE
```

to replace information in this printf()

```
printf("AGE");
```

because AGE is a string constant, and it prints literally just as it appears inside the double quotes. The preprocessor can replace only defined constants that do not appear within quotation marks.

Do Not Overdo #define

Many early C programmers enjoyed redefining parts of the language to suit whatever they were used to in another language. The printf() to PRINT example is one example of this. You can redefine virtually any C statement or function to "look" any way you like.

But there is a danger to this, and you should be very wary of using #define for this purpose. Redefining the language becomes *very* confusing to others who may need to modify your program later. Also, as you become more familiar with C, you should naturally start using the true C language more and more. When you are comfortable with C, older programs that you redefined will be confusing even to *you*!

So if you are going to program in C, use the language conventions that C provides. Shy away from trying to redefine commands in the language. Think of the #define directive as a great way to define numeric and string constants. If those constants ever change, you need only change one line in your program. "Just say NO" to any temptation to redefine commands and built-in functions.

Examples

1. Suppose you want to keep track of your company's target sales amount of $55,000.00. That target amount has not changed for the last two years. Because it probably will not change soon (sales are flat), you decide to start using a defined constant to represent this target amount. Then, if target sales do change, you just have to change the amount on the #define line. It would look like:

```
#define TARGETSALES 55000.00
```

which defines a floating-point constant. You can then assign TARGETSALES to floating-point variables and print it, just as if you had typed 55000.00 throughout your program, as these lines show:

```
amt = TARGETSALES;
printf("%f",TARGETSALES);
```

2. If you find yourself defining the same constants in many programs, you might consider putting them in their own file on disk and then #include them. This saves typing your defined constants at the top of every program. If you store these constants in a file, called MYDEFS.C, in your program's directory, you could include it with the following #include statement:

```
#include "mydefs.c"
```

(To use angled brackets, you would have to store the file in your system's include directory.)

3. Defined constants are good for array sizes. For example, suppose you declare an array for a customer's name. When you write the program, you know you don't have a customer whose name is longer than 22 characters (including the null). Therefore, you can do this:

```
#define CNMLENGTH 22
```

When you define the array, you can use this:

```
char cust_name[CNMLENGTH]
```

Other statements that need to know the array size can also use CNMLENGTH.

4. Many C programmers define a list of error messages. Once they define the messages with an easy-to-remember name, they can print those constants if an error occurs—while still maintaining consistency throughout their programs. Often, you might see something like the following towards the top of C programs.

Define string constants

```
#define DISKERR "Your disk drive seems not to be working"
#define PRNTERR "Your printer is not responding"
#define AGEERR  "You cannot enter an age that small"
#define NAMEERR "You must enter a full name"
```

Review Questions

Answers to review questions are in Appendix B.

1. True or false: You can define variables with the preprocessor directives.

2. Which preprocessor directive merges another file into your program?

3. Which preprocessor directive defines constants throughout your program?

4. True or false: You can define character, string, integer, and floating-point constants with the #define directive.

5. Which happens first: your program is compiled or preprocessed?

6. When would you use the angled brackets in an `#include`, and when would you use double quotes?

7. Which are easier to change: defined constants or constants that you type throughout a program? Why?

8. Which header file should be included in almost every C program you write?

9. True or false: The `#define` in the following:

    ```
    #define MESSAGE "Please press Enter to continue..."
    ```

    would change this statement:

    ```
    printf("MESSAGE");
    ```

10. What is the output from the following program?

    ```
    /* Filename: C6EXER,C */

    #include <stdio.h>
    #define AMT1 a+a+a
    #define AMT2 AMT1 - AMT1

    main()
    {
        int a=1;
        printf("Amount is %d", AMT2);
        return;
    }
    ```

Review Exercises

1. Write a program that prints your name to the screen. Use a defined constant for the name. Do not use a character array, and don't type your actual name inside the `printf()`.

2. Suppose your boss wanted you to write a program that produced an "exception report." If the company's sales are less than $100,000.00 or more than $750,000.00, your boss wants your program to print the appropriate message. You learn how to produce these types of reports later in the book, but for now just write the #define statements that define these two floating-point constants.

3. Write the printf() statements that print your name and birth date to the screen. Store these statements in their own file. Write a second program that includes the first file in order to print your name and birth date. Be sure also to include <stdio.h>, because the included file contains printf() statements.

4. Write a program that defines the ten digits, 0 through 9, as constants ZERO through NINE. Add these ten defined digits together and print the result.

Summary

This chapter taught you the #include and #define preprocessor directives. Although these are the only two preprocessor directives you know so far, they are the two used in most C programs. Despite the fact that these directives are not executed, they temporarily change your source code by merging and defining constants into your program.

The next chapter explains printf() in more detail. There are many printf() options that you might want to use as you write programs. You also learn a way to get keyboard input into your C programs.

Simple Input and Output

You have already seen the printf() function, which prints values to the screen. But printf() does much more than that. Because the screen is such a common output device, you must understand how to take advantage of printf()'s various features in order to have it print exactly the way *you* want your data to appear. Also, your programs become much more powerful if you learn how to obtain input from the keyboard. The scanf() is a function that mirrors printf(). But, instead of sending output values to the screen, scanf() accepts values that the user types at the keyboard.

printf() is your basic screen output function, and scanf() is your basic keyboard input function. The printf() and scanf() functions offer beginning C programmers output and input functions they can use with relative ease. Both of these functions are limited—especially scanf()—but they do enable your programs to send output and to receive input.

This chapter introduces you to

♦ The printf() function

♦ Control strings

◆ Conversion characters

◆ Conversion character modifiers

◆ The scanf() function

You may be surprised at how much more advanced your programs can become, after you learn these input/output functions.

The printf() Function

The printf() function sends output to the screen.

The printf() function sends data to the standard output device, which is generally the screen—unless you redirect the standard output to a different device. If you are unfamiliar with device redirection at the operating system level, you can learn more about it in Part 5 of this book. But for now, if you do nothing special, printf() sends all output to the screen.

The format of printf() is a little different from that of regular C commands. The values that go inside the parentheses vary, depending upon the data you are printing. However, as a general rule, the following printf() format holds true:

Print data
to screen

```
printf(control_string [, one or more values]);
```

Notice that printf() always requires a *control_string*. This is a string, or a character array containing a string, that determines how the rest of the values (if any are listed) print. These values can be variables, constants, expressions, or a combination of all three.

> **TIP:** Despite its name, printf() sends output to the screen and not to the printer.

Printing Strings

The easiest data to print with printf() are strings. To print a string constant, you simply put that string constant inside the printf() function. For example, to print the string The rain in Spain, you would simply type the following:

Print the phrase The rain in Spain *to the screen.*

```
printf("The rain in Spain");
```

Remember, though, that `printf()` does *not* perform an automatic carriage return. This means that the screen's cursor remains after the last character printed. Subsequent `printf()`s begin right next to that last-printed character.

To better understand this, try to predict the output from these three printf() functions:

```
printf("Line 1");
printf("Line 2");
printf("Line 3");
```

This produces

```
Line 1Line 2Line 3
```

which is probably not what is intended. Therefore, you must include the newline character, \n, whenever you want to move the cursor to the next line. The following three `printf()` functions produce a three-line output:

```
printf("Line 1\n");
printf("Line 2\n");
printf("Line 3\n");
```

The output from these `printf()` functions is

```
Line 1
Line 2
Line 3
```

The \n character sends the cursor to the next line—no matter where you insert it. The following three `printf()` functions also produce the correct three-line output:

```
printf("Line 1");
printf("\nLine 2\n");
printf("Line 3");
```

The second `printf()` prints a new line before it prints anything else. It then prints its string followed by another new line. The third string prints on that new line.

You also can print strings stored in character arrays by putting the array name inside the `printf()`. For example, if you were to store your name in an array defined as

```
char my_name[] = "Lyndon Harris";
```

you could print the name with this `printf()`:

```
printf(my_name);
```

Examples

1. The following section of code prints three string constants on three different lines:

```
printf("Nancy Carson\n");
printf("1213 Oak Street\n");
printf("Fairbanks, Alaska\n");
```

2. The `printf()` function is often used to label output. Before printing an age, amount, salary, or any other numeric data, you should always print a string constant that tells the user what the number means. The following `printf()` lets the user know that the next number to be printed is an age. Without this `printf()`, the user may not recognize that the number is an age.

```
printf("Here is the age that was found in our files:");
```

3. All four of these `printf()`s produce different output, because all four string constants are different.

```
printf("Come back tomorrow\n");
printf("Come  back  tomorrow\n");
printf("cOME BACK TOMORROW\n");
printf("C o m e  b a c k  t o m o r r o w\n");
```

4. You can print a blank line by printing two newline characters, \n, next to each other after your string, as in

```
printf("Prepare the invoices...\n\n");
```

5. The following program assigns a message in a character array, then prints that message.

```
/* Filename: C7PS.C
   Prints a string stored in a character array */
#include <stdio.h>
main()
{
    char_message[] = "Please turn on your printer";
    printf(message);
    return;
}
```

This prints the string stored in message—and keeps printing until the null zero is reached. This is why the null zero is so important; it tells C where your string in the array ends.

Conversion Characters

Inside many of the printf()s that you have seen in the last few chapters were several *conversion characters*. These special characters tell printf() exactly how the data (following the characters) are to be interpreted. Table 7.1 shows a list of several conversion characters. Because any type of data can go inside the printf()'s parentheses, these conversion characters are needed any time you print more than a string constant. If you don't want to print a string, then the string constant must contain at least one of the conversion characters.

Table 7.1. The `printf()` conversion characters.

Conversion Character	Output
%s	String of characters (until null zero is reached)
%c	Character
%d	Decimal integer
%f	Floating-point numbers
%e	Exponential notation floating-point numbers
%g	Use the shorter of %f or %e
%u	Unsigned integer
%o	Octal integer
%x	Hexadecimal integer
%%	Prints a percent sign (%)

NOTE: You can insert an l (lowercase *l*) or L before the integer and floating-point conversion characters (such as `%ld` and `%lf`) to indicate that a long integer or long double floating-point is to be printed.

The first four conversion characters are used much more often than the others. Any character that is not shown in Table 7.1 prints exactly as it appears in the control string. Each of the following sections describe these conversion characters and their uses in `printf()`.

String Conversion Character %s

If you print a string constant, the string conversion character is not required. The following two `printf()`s are identical.

Print the sentence c is fun! *and then put the cursor on the next line. Print the same thing using the string conversion character.*

```
printf("C is fun!\n");
printf("%s", "C is fun!\n");
```

The %s informs the printf() function that a string follows. Because C does not need the %s to print strings, the %s is redundant. You also can include the %s if you print strings stored in character arrays but, again, the %s is not needed. If cary were a character array containing a valid string, both of the following printf()s would work.

```
printf("%s", cary);   /* Prints the string in cary */
print(cary);          /* Works as long as cary is an array */
                      /* that holds a valid string      */
```

The reason C does not need the %s conversion character is because anything *not* a conversion character prints exactly as it appears in the control string.

Character Conversion Character %c

You must, however, use the %c conversion character any time you print single characters, whether they are character constants or character variables. You would use the following printf() to print three character constants.

Print the characters A, B, and C using the character conversion character.

```
printf("%c %c %c", 'A','B','C');
```

These three character constants print with one blank between them. Figure 7.1 shows why this is the case. Each %c informs C that a character appears in its place, and the blank that follows the first two %c conversion characters print as blanks.

In your program:

The screen output: A   B   C

Figure 7.1. Conversion characters in action.

You must also use the %c conversion character when you print character variables. This includes single elements (such as c[3]) from a character array. The following program stores the three letters into three character variables, then prints them.

```
/* Filename: C7PC.C
   Stores and prints the contents of 3 variables */
#include <stdio.h>
main()
{
   char first, second, last;
   first='A';
   second='B';
   last='C';

   printf("%c %c %c", first, second, last);
   return;
}
```

Integer and Floating-Point Conversion Characters %d and %f

When you want to print a numeric constant or variable, you must include the proper conversion character inside the printf() control string. If i, j, and k are integer variables, you *cannot* print them with the printf() that follows:

```
printf(i,j,k);
```

Because printf() is a function and not a command, this printf() function has no way of knowing what type the variables are. The results are unpredictable, and you may see garbage on your screen—if anything appears at all.

When you print numbers, you must first print a control string that includes the format of those numbers. The following printf() prints a string. In the output from this line, a string appears with an integer (%d) and a floating-point number (%f) printed inside that string.

```
printf("I am Betty, I am %d years old, and I make %f\n", 35,
    34050.25);
```

This produces the following output:

```
I am Betty, I am 35 years old, and I make 34050.25
```

Figure 7.2 shows how C interprets the control string and the variables that follow. Be sure you understand this example before moving on. It is the foundation of the printf() function.

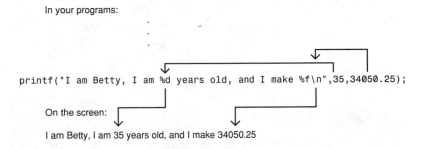

Figure 7.2. Control string in action.

You can also print integer and floating-point variables in the same manner.

NOTE: The %i also works as an integer printf() conversion character. This is easier to remember (%i for *integer*), but it is rarely used by C programmers. You should follow the standard and use %d for printing integers.

Examples

1. The following program stores a few values in three variables, then prints the results.

```
/* Filename: C7PRNT1.C
   Print values in variables */
#include <stdio.h>

main()
{
    char first='E';         /* Store some character, integer, */
    char middle='W';          /* and floating-point variables */
    char last='C';
    int age=32;
    int dependents=2;
    float salary=25000.00;
    float bonus=575.25;

    /* Print the results */
    printf("%c%c%c", first, middle, last);
    printf("%d%d", age, dependents);
    printf("%f%f", salary, bonus);
    return;
}
```

2. The previous program, however, doesn't help the user at all. The output is not labeled, and it all prints on a single line. Here is the same program with a few messages printed before the numbers, and some newline characters placed where they are needed:

```
/* Filename: C7PRNT2.C
   Print values in variables with appropriate labels */
#include <stdio.h>

main()
{
    char first='E';         /* Store some character, integer, */
    char middle='W';          /* and floating-point variables */
    char last='C';
```

```
int age=32;
int dependents=2;
float salary=25000.00;
float bonus=575.25;
/* Print the results */
printf("Here are the initials:\n");
printf("%c%c%c\n\n", first, middle, last);
printf("The age and number of dependents are:\n");
printf("%d    %d\n\n", age, dependents);
printf("The salary and bonus are:\n");
printf("%f %f", salary, bonus);
return;
}
```

The output from this program is:

```
Here are the initials:
EWC
The age and number of dependents are:
32    2
The salary and bonus are:
25000.000000 575.250000
```

The floating-point values print with too many zeros, of course, but the numbers are correct. The next section shows you how to limit the number of leading and trailing zeros that are printed.

3. If you need to print a table of numbers, you can use the \t tab character. Place the tab character between each of the numbers that print. The following program prints a list of baseball team names and the number of hits for each during the first three weeks of the season.

Print columns
of data

```
/* Filename: C7TEAM.C
   Prints a table of team names and hits for three weeks */
#include <stdio.h>

main()
{
   printf("Parrots\tRams\tKings\tTitans\tChargers\n");
   printf("%d\t%d\t%d\t%d\t%d\n", 3,5,2,1,0);
```

```
printf("%d\t%d\t%d\t%d\t%d\n", 2,5,1,0,1);
printf("%d\t%d\t%d\t%d\t%d\n", 2,6,4,3,0);

return;
}
```

This program produces the following table. You can see that, even though the names are of different widths, the numbers print correctly beneath them. The \t character forces the next name or value into the next tab position (every 8 characters for most C compilers).

Parrots	Rams	Kings	Titans	Chargers
3	5	2	1	0
2	5	1	0	1
2	6	4	3	0

Hex and Octal Conversion Characters %x and %o

The %x and %o are used to print hexadecimal and octal numbers. Even if you store a hexadecimal number in an integer variable (with the leading 0x characters, such as 0x3C1), that variable prints as a decimal value if you use the %d conversion character. To print the value in hex, you must use the %x conversion character.

TIP: You can print any integer value as a hexadecimal number if you use the %x conversion character. You do not need to store the integer as a hex number first.

Example

Suppose you were working on a systems program, and needed to add five hexadecimal values together to test the result. You could write a short C program that does just that. You could then print the answer as a hexadecimal number, by using the %x conversion character as shown in the following program.

```
/* Filename: C7HEX.C
   Add five hexadecimal numbers and print the answer */
#include <stdio.h>

main()
{

    /* Store the five numbers to add together */
    int num1=0x4c, num2=0x52, num3=0xd1, num4=0xdc, num5=0x1f;
    int hex_ans;    /* This will hold the result */

    hex_ans = num1 + num2 + num3 + num4 + num5;

    /* Print the answer */
    printf("The hexadecimal numbers add up to: %x \n",
           hex_ans);
    return;
}
```

This program produces the following single line of output:

```
The hexadecimal numbers add up to: 26a
```

Exponential Conversion Characters %e and %g

The %e exponential conversion character is used to print very large, or very small, floating-point numbers. It prints these numbers in scientific notation format. Scientific notation is a shortcut method for representing numbers of extreme values. Many people program in C for years and never use scientific notation. But if you understand it (and it *is* simple), you should feel at home with many language reference manuals, and you might not be so surprised someday if a C program prints a number on your screen in scientific notation.

It is easiest to learn scientific notation by looking at a few examples. Basically, you can represent any number in scientific notation, but it makes sense to do so only with extremely large or small numbers. All scientific notation numbers are floating-point (or double floating-point if they need the larger storage) numbers. Table 7.2 lists some scientific notational numbers and their equivalents.

Table 7.2. Examples of scientific notation.

Scientific Notation	Equivalent
3.08E+12	3,080,000,000,000
–9.7587E+02	–97,587
+5.164E–4	0.0005164
–4.6545E–9	–0.0000000046545
1.654E+302	1.654×10^{302}

Scientific notational numbers have the letter *E* in them. Positive scientific numbers begin with a plus sign (+), or they have no sign at all. Negative scientific numbers begin with a minus sign (–).

It is easy to figure out the rest. Take the portion of the number at the left and multiply it by 10 raised to the number on the right. In other words, +2.164E+3 means to take 2.164 and multiply it by 1,000 (10 raised to the 3rd power, or 10^3). Similarly, –5.432E–4 means negative 5.432 times .0001 (10 raised to the –4 power, or 10^{-4}).

You can print any floating-point value or variable using scientific notation, if you use the %e conversion character. If you are unsure whether the number needs scientific notation, use the %g conversion character. When C sees %g, it prints the number as a regular floating-point constant, if it can, and uses scientific notation only if it must, in order to output the number more accurately.

Examples

1. The speed of light travels at 186,000 miles per second. To store 186,000 in a floating-point variable using scientific notation, you would type:

```
float light_speed = 1.86E+5;
```

When you start using C to perform calculations, use the %g conversion character if you suspect the number may be large or small enough to warrant it. Any number can be printed in scientific notation, but extremely large floating-point values must be. Use the following printf() to print this variable:

```
printf("The speed of light is %g\n", light_speed);
```

2. The sun is 93,000,000 miles from the earth. (You are learning a lot of space-travel trivia while practicing programming!) The moon is only about 264,000 miles from the earth. To store these two distances in scientific notation, you would code them as follows:

```
float sun_dist = 9.3E+7;
float moon_dist = 2.68E+5;
```

3. You can combine the previous declarations into a single statement by separating them with commas.

```
float sun_dist = 9.3E+7, moon_dist = 2.68E+5;
```

Conversion Character Modifiers

You can modify the way conversion characters print.

You already have seen the need for additional program output control. All floating-point numbers print (using %f) with too many decimal places for most applications. What if you want to print only dollars and cents (two decimal places), or print an average with a single decimal place? If you want to control the way these conversion characters produce output, you have to include a modified conversion character.

You can insert a modifying number inside many of the numeric conversion characters. This number tells C how many print positions to use. For example, the following printf() prints the number 456, using three positions (the length of the data):

```
printf("%d", 456);
```

If the 456 were stored in an integer variable, it would still use three positions to print because the number of digits printed is three. However, if you insert a number before the d in the conversion character, you can exactly control how many positions print. The following printf() prints the number 456 in five positions (with two leading spaces):

```
printf("%5d", 456);
```

You typically use the width number when you want to print data in uniform columns. The following program shows you the importance of the width number. Each `printf()` output is described in the adjacent comment.

```
/* Filename: C7MOD1.C
   Illustrates various integer width printf() modifiers */
#include <stdio.h>
main()
{                             /* The output appears below */
   printf("%d%d%d \n", 456, 456, 456);     /* 456456456 */
   printf("%5d%5d%5d \n", 456, 456, 456);  /*   456  456  456 */
   printf("%7d%7d%7d \n", 456, 456, 456);  /*     456     456    456 */
   return;
}
```

When you put a width number inside a conversion character, C right-justifies the number in the width you specify. In other words, when you specify an 8-digit width, C prints a value inside those 8 digits, padding the number with leading blanks if the number does not fill the full width.

> **NOTE:** If you do not specify a width large enough to hold the number, C ignores your width request and prints the number in its entirety.

If you put a minus sign before the width specifier, C left-justifies the number inside the width. For example, the following program prints its numbers to the left of its fields, as shown especially in the final two comments.

```
/* Filename: C7MOD2.C
   Illustrates various integer width printf() modifiers */
#include <stdio.h>
main()
{                             /* The output appears below */
   printf("%d%d%d \n", 456, 456, 456);       /*456456456*/
   printf("%-5d%-5d%-5d \n", 456, 456, 456); /*456  456  456  */
   printf("%-7d%-7d%-7d \n", 456, 456, 456); /*456    456    456    */
   return;
}
```

You can control the width of strings in the same manner, by using the width modifier in the `%s` string conversion character. If you do not specify enough width to output the full string, C ignores your width. The mailing list application at the back of this book uses the same technique to print names on mailing labels.

The width specifiers become more important when you want to print floating-point numbers. The format of the floating-point width specifier is:

`%width.decimalsf`

The floating-point conversion character, `%6.2f`, tells C to print a floating-point number within six positions, including the decimal point and the fractional part. It also informs C to print two decimal places. If C has to round the fractional part, it does so. The following `printf()`:

```
printf("%6.2f", 134.568767);
```

produces this output:

```
134.57
```

Without the format modifier, C would print

```
134.568767
```

> **TIP:** When printing floating-point numbers, C always prints the entire portion to the left of the decimal (to maintain as much accuracy as possible) no matter how many positions wide you specify. Therefore, many C programmers ignore the width specifier for floating-point numbers and specify only the decimal part, as in `%.2f`.

Examples

1. Earlier, you saw how the \t tab character can be used to print columns of data. The tab character is limited to eight columns. If you want more control over the width of your data, use a modifying width in the output conversion characters. The following program is a modified version of the C7TEAM.C that uses the width specifier instead of the tab character. It ensures that each column is ten characters wide.

```c
/* Filename: C7TEAMMD.C
   Prints a table of team names and hits for three weeks
   using width modifying conversion characters */
#include <stdio.h>

main()
{
    printf("%10s%10s%10s%10s%10s\n",
    "Parrots","Rams","Kings","Titans","Chargers");
    printf("%10d%10d%10d%10d%10d\n", 3,5,2,1,0);
    printf("%10d%10d%10d%10d%10d\n", 2,5,1,0,1);
    printf("%10d%10d%10d%10d%10d\n", 2,6,4,3,0);

    return;
}
```

2. The following program is a payroll program. The output prints dollar amounts (to two decimal places).

```c
/* Filename: C7PAY1.C
   Computes and prints payroll data properly in dollars and
   cents */
#include <stdio.h>

main()
{
    char emp_name[]="Larry Payton";
    char pay_date[]="03/09/92";
    int hours_worked=40;
    float rate=7.50;            /* Pay per hour */
    float tax_rate=.40;         /* Tax percentage rate */
    float gross_pay, taxes, net_pay;
```

BEGIN

Calculate
pay
amounts

Print
results

END

```
/* Compute the pay amount */
gross_pay = hours_worked * rate;
taxes = tax_rate * gross_pay;
net_pay = gross_pay - taxes;

/* Print the results */
printf("As of %s\n", pay_date);
printf("%s worked %d hours\n", emp_name, hours_worked);
printf("and got paid %6.2f\n", gross_pay);
printf("After taxes of %5.2f\n", taxes);
printf("his take-home pay was: $%6.2f\n", net_pay);

return;
}
```

The following is the output from this program. Remember that the floating-point variables still hold their full precision (to six decimal places). The modifying width numbers affect only how the variables are output, not what is stored in them.

```
As of: 03/09/92
Larry Payton worked 40 hours
and got paid 300.000000
After taxes of 120.000000
his take-home pay was $180.000000
```

3. Most C programmers do not use the width specifier to the left of the decimal point when printing dollars and cents. Here again is the payroll program that uses the shortcut floating-point width method. Notice the last three printf() statements include the %.2f modifier. C knows to print the full number to the left of the decimal, but only two places to the right.

```
/* Filename: C7PAY2.C
   Computes and prints payroll data properly using the short-
   cut modifier */
#include <stdio.h>

main()
{
   char emp_name[]="Larry Payton";
   char pay_date[]="03/09/92";
   int hours_worked=40;
   float rate=7.50;              /* Pay per hour */
   float tax_rate=.40;           /* Tax percentage rate */
   float gross_pay, taxes, net_pay;

   /* Compute the pay amount */
   gross_pay = hours_worked * rate;
   taxes = tax_rate * gross_pay;
   net_pay = gross_pay - taxes;

   /* Print the results */
   printf("As of: %s\n", pay_date);
   printf("%s worked %d hours\n", emp_name, hours_worked);
   printf("and got paid %.2f\n", gross_pay);
   printf("After taxes of %.2f\n", taxes);
   printf("his take-home pay was $%.2f\n", net_pay);

   return;
}
```

This program's output is the same as that of the last one.

Keeping Count of Output

Make sure your printed values match the control string supplied with them. The printf() function cannot fix problems resulting from mismatched values and control strings. Don't try to print floating-point values with character string control codes. If you list five integer variables in a printf(), be sure to include five %d conversion characters in the printf() as well.

Printing ASCII Values

There is one exception to the rule of printing with matching conversion characters. If you want to print the ASCII value of a character, you can print that character (whether it is a constant or a variable) with the integer %d conversion character. Instead of printing the character, C prints the matching ASCII number for that character.

Conversely, if you print an integer with a %c conversion character, you see the character that matches that integer's value from the ASCII table.
The following printf()s illustrate this:

```
printf("%c", 65);  /* Prints letter A */
printf("%d", 'A'); /* Prints number 65 */
```

Depending on your C compiler, your output may be empty—or produce garbage on the screen—if you mismatch your parameters. The following example illustrates some of the problems that can occur. Because these printf()s are mismatched (the control strings don't always match the variables and constants being printed), you should check the comment to the right for the probable output or error that might occur.

```
/* Filename: C7PROB.C
   Program to demonstrate possible printf() problems */

main()
{
   int i, j, k;
   char a, b, c;

   i = 4;
   j = 5;
   k = 6;

   a = 'I';
   b = 'B';                        /*****************************/
   c = 'M';                        /* Output is shown below:   */
                                   /*                          */
```

```
printf("This is a message\n");        /* This is a message   */
printf("%d %d %d\n", i, j, k);        /*     4 5 6           */
printf(i, j, k);                      /* (unpredictable)     */
printf("\n%c %d  %c %d", a, i, c, j); /*   I 4  M 5          */
printf("\nB%cB%cB%c\n", a, a, a);     /* BIBIBI              */
printf(a, b, c);                      /* (unpredictable)     */
printf("\nHi.\n", a, b, c);           /* Hi.                 */
printf("%d %d\n", i, j, k);           /* 4 5                 */
printf("%c %c %c %c\n", a, b, c);     /* I B M  (garbage)    */
printf("%cc%dd\n", a, i);             /* Ic4d                */
printf("%s\n", "No conv. char. needed");
                                      /*No conv. char. needed*/
printf("No conv. char. needed");      /*No conv. char. needed*/
printf("\n%s %c", "A", 'A');          /* A A                 */
printf("\n%s %c", 'A', "A");          /*       (unpredictable)*/
printf("\nNumber in string %d, see?", i);
                                      /* Number in string 4, see? */
printf("\nWatch your types! %d %c", b, j);
                                      /* Watch your types!(garbage)*/
                                      /****************************/
return;
}
```

The bottom line is this: Avoid these types of problems by making sure every conversion character inside your `printf()` control string matches the data that follows the control string.

The scanf() Function

The scanf() function stores keyboard input into variables.

You now understand how C represents data and variables, and how to print those data. However, there is another part of this programming you haven't seen: how a user inputs data into your programs.

Until now, every program has had no input of data. All the data you've worked with have been assigned to variables within the programs. However, this is not always the best way to input data; and also, you rarely know what your data are going to be at the time you write your programs. Most data only become known when you run the programs, or another user runs them.

The scanf() function is one way to get input from the keyboard. When your programs reach the line with a scanf(), the user at the keyboard can enter values directly into variables. Then your program can process those variables and produce output. Figure 7.3 illustrates the difference between printf() and scanf().

Your Screen

printf ( ) ⟶

Your Keyboard

⟶ scanf ( )

Figure 7.3. Difference between printf() and scanf().

The scanf() Function Fills Variables with Values

There is a major difference between scanf() and the assignment statements (such as i=17;) that you have seen. Both fill variables with values. However, the assignment statement assigned specific values to variables *at programming time*. When you run a program with assignment statements, you know from the program's listing exactly what values are going into the variables, because you wrote the program to store those values there. Every time you run the program, the results are exactly the same because the same values go into (are assigned to) the same variables.

In contrast, you have no idea, when you write programs that use scanf(), what values are going into the scanf()'s variables, because their values are not known until the *program is run and the user enters those values*. This makes for much more flexible programs, which can be used by a greater variety of people. Every time the program is run, different results are output, depending upon what the user types at each scanf() in the program.

The `scanf()` function has its drawbacks (discussed later in this section), but if you understand the `printf()` function, `scanf()` shouldn't pose too much of a problem. Therefore, the next few chapters make use of `scanf()` until you learn even more powerful (and flexible) input methods.

Get data from keyboard

The `scanf()` function looks very much like `printf()`. It contains a control string and one or more variables to the right of the control string. The control string describes to C exactly what the incoming keyboard values look like, and what their types are. The format of `scanf()` is

```
scanf(control_string, one or more values);
```

The stdio.h header file contains the information C needs for `scanf()`, so include it whenever you use `scanf()`.

The `scanf()` *control_string* uses almost the same conversion characters as the `printf()` *control_string*, with two slight differences. You should never include the newline character, `\n`, in a `scanf()` control string. The `scanf()` function "knows" the input is finished when the user presses Enter. If you supply an additional newline code, `scanf()` gets confused and may not terminate properly. Also, always put a beginning space inside every `scanf()` control string. This does not affect the user's input, but `scanf()` sometimes requires it to work properly. Later examples clarify this.

The scanf() function requires that your user type correctly. This is not always possible to guarantee!

As mentioned earlier, `scanf()` poses a few problems. The `scanf()` function requires that your user type the input *exactly* the way *control_string* specifies. Because you cannot control your user's typing, this cannot always be ensured. For example, you might want the user to enter an integer value followed by a floating-point value (your `scanf()` control string might expect it too), but your user might decide to enter something else! If this happens, there is not much you can do. The resulting input will be incorrect, but your C program has no reliable method for testing user accuracy—for the user—before your program is run.

For the next few chapters, assume that the user knows to enter the proper values. However, for your own programs used by others, be on the lookout for additional methods to get better input.

> **CAUTION:** The user's keyboard input values *must* match, in number and type, the control string contained in each `scanf()`.

Another problem with `scanf()` is not as easy to explain at this point in the book. The `scanf()` function requires that you use pointer variables, not regular variables, in its parentheses. Although this sounds complicated, it doesn't have to be. You should have no problem with `scanf()`'s pointer requirements if you remember the following two simple rules.

1. Always put an ampersand (&) before variable names inside a `scanf()`.

2. Never put an ampersand (&) before an array name inside a `scanf()`.

Despite these strange `scanf()` rules, you can learn this function very quickly by looking at a few examples.

Examples

1. If you want a program that computes a 7% sales tax, you could use the `scanf()` statement to get the sales, compute the tax, then print the results as the following program shows.

```
/* Filename: C7SLTX1.C
   Get a sales amount and print the sales tax */
#include <stdio.h>
main()
{
   float total_sale;    /* User's sale amount will go here */
   float stax;

   /* Get the sales amount from user */
   scanf(" %f", &total_sale);   /* Don't forget the beginning
                                    space and & */

   /* Calculate sales tax */
   stax = total_sale * .07;

   printf("The sales tax for %.2f is %.2f", total_sale,
   stax);
   return;
}
```

If you run this program, the program waits for you to enter a value for the total sale. Remember to use the ampersand in front of the total_sale variable when you put it in the scanf() function. After you press the Enter key, the program calculates the sales tax and prints the results.

If you entered 10.00 as the sale amount, you would see the following output:

```
The sales tax for 10.00 is 0.70
```

2. The previous program is fine for introducing scanf(), but it contains a serious problem. The problem is not in the code itself, but in the program's assumption about the user; it does not tell the user what it expects him or her to enter. Because the scanf() assumes too much already, your programs that use scanf() should inform your users *exactly* what they are to type. The following revision of this program prompts the user with an appropriate message before getting the sale amount.

BEGIN

↓

Prompt for
amount

↓

Get amount
from keyboard

↓

Calculate
sales tax

↓

Print
sales
tax

↓

END

```
/* Filename: C7SLTX2.C
   Prompt for a sales amount and print the sales tax */
#include <stdio.h>
main()
{
    float total_sale;    /* User's sale amount will go here */
    float stax;

    /* Display a message for the user */
    printf("What is the total amount of the sale? ");

    /* Get the sales amount from user */
    scanf(" %f", &total_sale);    /* Don't forget the beginning
                                     space and & */

    /* Calculate sales tax */
    stax = total_sale * .07;

    printf("The sales tax for %.2f is %.2f", total_sale, stax);
    return;
}
```

Because the first `printf()` does not contain a newline character, `\n`, the user's response to the prompt appears directly to the right of the question mark.

3. Use the string `%s` conversion character to input keyboard strings into character arrays with `scanf()`. You are limited, however, to getting one word at a time, because the `scanf()` does not let you type more than one word into a single character array. The following program asks users for their first and last names. It must store these two names in two different character arrays, because `scanf()` cannot get both names at once. The program then prints the names in reverse order.

```c
/* Filename: C7PHON1.C
   Program that gets the user's name and prints it
   to the screen as it would appear in a phone book. */
#include <stdio.h>
main()
{
   char first[20], last[20];
   printf("What is your first name? ");
   scanf(" %s", first);
   printf("What is your last name? ");
   scanf(" %s", last);
   printf("\n\n");    /* Print 2 blank lines */
   printf("In a phone book, your name would look like this:\n");
   printf("%s, %s", last, first);
   return;
}
```

Figure 7.4 shows a sample run from this program. Notice that you do not include the ampersand before an array name, only before "single" nonarray variables.

```
What is your first name? Martha
What is your last name? Roberts


In a phone book, your name would like like this:
Roberts, Martha
```

Figure 7.4. The screen after a user has input her name.

4. Suppose you want to write a program, for your seven year-old daughter, that does simple addition. The following program prompts her for two numbers. The program then waits for her to type an answer. When she gives her answer, the program displays the correct result so she can see how well she did. (Later, you learn how you can immediately let her know whether her answer is correct.)

```c
/* Filename: C7MATH.C
   Program to help children with simple addition.
   Prompt child for 2 values, after printing a title message */
#include <stdio.h>
main()
{
    int num1, num2, ans;
    int her_ans;

    printf("*** Math Practice ***\n");
    printf("\n\n");     /* Print 2 blank lines */
    printf("What is the first number? ");
```

```
scanf(" %d", &num1);
printf("What is the second number? ");
scanf(" %d", &num2);

/* Compute answer and give her a chance to wait for it */
ans=num1+num2;

printf("\nWhat do you think is the answer? ");
scanf(" %d", &her_ans);    /* Nothing is done with this */

/* Print answer after a blank line */
printf("\n%d plus %d is: %d\n", num1, num2, ans);
printf("\nHope you got it right!");
return;
}
```

Review Questions

Answers to review questions are in Appendix B.

1. What is the difference between `printf()` and `scanf()`?

2. Why is a prompt message important before using `scanf()` for input?

3. How many values are entered with the following `scanf()`, and what are their types?

   ```
   scanf(" %d %d %f %s", &i, &j, &k, l);
   ```

4. True or false: The `%s` conversion character is usually not required in `printf()` control strings.

5. Which types of variables do *not* require the ampersand (&) character in `scanf()` functions?

6. Because they both put values into variables, is there any difference between assigning values to variables and using `scanf()` to give them values?

7. What is the output produced by the following `printf()`?

   ```
   printf("The backslash, \"\\\" character is special");
   ```

8. What is the output of the following `printf()`?

   ```
   printf("%8.3f", 123.456789);
   ```

9. True or false: To print a number in octal, hex, and decimal, you need to store it in three different variables.

10. Convert the following scientific-notation numbers to their floating-point equivalents.

    1.234E+6   1.234E-6   -1.234E+6   -1.234E-6

Review Exercises

1. Write a program that prompts users for name and weight. Store these values in separate variables and print them on the screen.

2. Assume you are a college professor needing to average grades for ten students. Write a program that prompts you for ten different grades, and then displays their average.

3. Modify your program in #2 to ask for each student's name as well as grade. Print the list on-screen with each student's name and grade in two columns. Make sure the columns align by using a width modifier on the grade. At the bottom, print the average of all grades. (Hint: Store the ten names and ten grades in different variables with different names.) This program is easy, but it takes thirty or so lines, plus appropriate comments and prompts. Later, you will learn ways to streamline this program.

4. Write a program that prompts users for their full names (store each—first, middle, and last—in three separate character arrays), hours worked, hourly rates, and tax rates, and then displays taxes and net pay, using the appropriate dollars-and-cents print codes.

5. Modify the child's math program shown earlier in this chapter (C7MATH.C) to include subtraction, multiplication, and division, after the child has finished practicing the addition.

6. This tests your understanding of the backslash conversion character: Write a program that uses `printf()` functions to produce the following picture on your screen.

Summary

After learning the `printf()` and `scanf()` functions in this chapter, you should be able to print almost anything on-screen. By studying the conversion characters and how they behave, you can control your output more thoroughly than ever before. Also, because you now can receive keyboard values, your programs are much more powerful. No longer do you need to know your data values at the time when you write your programs. With `scanf()`, you can ask the user to enter values into variables for you.

You now have the tools you need to begin writing programs that fit the data processing model of "Input-Process-Output." This chapter concludes the preliminaries of the C programming language. So far, this book has attempted to give you an overview of the language, and to teach you enough of C's elements so you can begin writing helpful programs as soon as possible.

The next chapter begins a new type of discussion. You learn how C's math and relational operators work on data, as well as the importance of their table of precedence.

Part II

C Operators

Math Operators and Precedence

You may be dreading this chapter if you don't like math—but relax! C does all your math for you! It is a misconception that you must be good at math in order to understand how to program computers. In fact, the opposite is true. Your computer is there to be your "slave," to follow your instructions, and to do all calculations for you. This chapter explains how C computes, by introducing you to

♦ Primary math operators

♦ Order of operator precedence

♦ Assignment statements

♦ Mixed data type calculations

♦ Type casting

Many people who dislike math actually enjoy learning how the computer handles it. After learning the math operators and a few simple ways in which C uses them, you should feel comfortable putting calculations into your programs. Computers are very fast, and they can perform math operations many times faster than you can!

C's Primary Math Operators

A C *math operator* is a symbol used for adding, subtracting, multiplying, dividing, as well as other operations. C operators are not always mathematical in nature, but many are. Table 8.1 explains these operator symbols and their primary meanings.

Table 8.1. C primary operators.

Symbol	Meaning
*	Multiplication
/	Division and Integer Division
%	Modulus or Remainder
+	Addition
-	Subtraction

Most of these operators work in the familiar way that you are used to. Multiplication, addition, and subtraction (and the division operator *usually*) produce the same results you get when you do these math functions with a calculator. Table 8.2 shows four samples that illustrate four of these simple operators.

Table 8.2. Typical operator results.

Formula	Result
4 * 2	8
64 / 4	16
80 - 15	65
12 + 9	21

Table 8.2 contains examples of *binary operations* performed with the four operators. Don't confuse this term with *binary numbers*. When an operator is used between two constants, variables, or a combination of both, it is called a *binary operator* because it operates

using two values. When you use these operators (such as assigning their results to variables), C does not "care" whether you put spaces around the operators or not.

> **CAUTION:** For multiplication, use the asterisk (*), *not* an x as you might normally do. An x cannot be used as the multiplication sign because C would confuse it with a variable called x. C would not know whether you mean to multiply or to use the value of a variable called x.

The Unary Operators

A *unary operator* operates on, or affects, a single value. For instance, you can assign a variable a positive or negative number by using a unary + or –. You can also assign a variable another positive or negative number by using a unary + or –.

Examples

1. The following section of code assigns four variables a positive or a negative number. The plus and minus signs are all unary because they are not used between two values.

   Make a equal to negative 25. Make b equal to positive 25. Make c equal to negative a. Make d equal to positive b.

   ```
   a = -25;   /* Assign 'a' a negative 25 */
   b = +25;   /* Assign 'b' a positive 25 (+ is not needed) */
   c = -a;    /* Assign 'c' the negative of 'a' (-25) */
   d = +b;    /* Assign 'd' the positive of 'b' (+ is not needed) */
   ```

2. You generally do not need to use the unary plus sign. C assumes that a number or variable is positive, even if you don't put a plus in front of it. The following four statements are equivalent to the last, except that they do not contain plus signs:

```
a = -25;    /* Assign 'a' a negative 25 */
b =  25;    /* Assign 'b' a positive 25 */
c = -a;     /* Assign 'c' the negative of 'a' (-25) */
d =  b;     /* Assign 'd' the positive of 'b' */
```

3. The unary negative comes in handy when you want to negate a single number or variable. The negative of a negative is positive. Therefore, the following short program assigns a negative number (using the unary –) to a variable, and then prints the negative of that same variable. Because it had a negative number to begin with, the printf() produces a positive result.

```
/* Filename: C8NEG.C
   The negative of a variable that contains a negative value */
#include <stdio.h>
main()
{
    signed int temp=-12;  /* 'signed' is not needed because */
                          /* that is the default */
    printf("%d", -temp);  /* Produces a 12 on the screen */

    return;
}
```

The variable declaration does not need the *signed* prefix, because all integer variables are signed by default.

4. If you want to subtract the negative of a variable, make sure you put a space before the unary minus sign. For example, the following line

```
new_temp = old_temp - -inversion_factor;
```

temporarily negates the inversion_factor and then subtracts that negated value from new_temp.

Division and Modulus

The division sign, /, and the modulus operator, %, may behave in ways unfamiliar to you. They're usually as easy to use, however, as the other operators you have just seen.

The forward slash (/) always divides. However, it produces an integer divide if integer values (constants, variables, or a combination of both) appear on both sides of the slash. If there is a remainder, C discards it.

The modulus (%) computes remainders in division.

The percent sign (%) produces a *modulus*, or a *remainder*, of an integer division. It requires that integers be on both sides of the symbol, or it does not work.

Examples

Compute weekly salary

1. Suppose you want to compute your weekly pay. The following program asks for your yearly pay, divides it by 52, and prints the results to two decimal places:

```
/* Filename: C8DIV.C
   Displays user's weekly pay */
#include <stdio.h>
main()
{
    float weekly, yearly;
    printf("What is your annual pay? ");  /* Prompt user */
    scanf("%f", &yearly);

    weekly = yearly/52;  /* Computes the weekly */
    printf("\n\nYour weekly pay is $%.2f", weekly);
    return;
}
```

Because a floating-point number is used in the division, C produces a floating-point result. Here is a sample run from such a program:

```
What is your annual pay? 38000.00
Your weekly pay is $730.77
```

2. Integer division does not round its results. If you divide two integers and the answer is not a whole number, C ignores the fractional part. The following `printf()`s help show this. The output that would result from each `printf()` appears in the comment to the right of each line.

```
printf("%d \n", 10/2);      /* 5  (no remainder) */
printf("%d \n", 300/100);   /* 3  (no remainder) */
printf("%d \n", 10/3);      /* 3  (discarded remainder) */
printf("%d \n", 300/165);   /* 1  (discarded remainder) */
```

The Order of Precedence

Knowing the meaning of the math operators is the first of two steps toward your understanding of C calculations. You must also understand the *order of precedence*. The order of precedence (sometimes called the *math hierarchy*, or *order of operators*) determines exactly how C computes formulas. The precedence of operators is exactly the same as that used in high school algebra courses. (But don't worry, this is the *easy* part of algebra!) To see how the order of precedence works, try to determine the result of the following simple calculation:

`2 + 3 * 2`

If you said 10, you would not be alone; many people would respond with 10. However, 10 is correct only if you interpret the formula from left to right. But what if you calculated the multiplication first? If you took the value of 3 * 2 and got an answer of 6, and then added the 2 to it, you would end up with an answer of 8—which is exactly the same answer that C computes!

C performs multiplication, division, and modulus *before* addition and subtraction.

C always performs multiplication, division, and modulus first, and then addition and subtraction. Table 8.3 shows the order of the operators you have seen so far. Of course, there are many more levels to C's precedence table of operators than shown in Table 8.3. Unlike most computer languages, C has 15 levels of precedence. Appendix D contains the complete precedence table, and you might notice in this appendix that multiplication, division, and modulus reside on level 3, one level higher than level 4's addition and subtraction. In the next few chapters, you learn how to use the remainder of this precedence table in your C programs.

Table 8.3. Order of precedence for primary operators.

Order	Operator
First	Multiplication, division, modulus remainder (*, /, %)
Second	Addition, subtraction (+, -)

Examples

1. It is easy to follow C's order of operators if you follow the intermediate results one at a time. The three calculations in Figure 8.1. C's order of operators with lines indicating precedence.

2. Looking back at the order of precedence table again, you might notice that multiplication, division, and modulus are on the same level. This implies that there is no hierarchy on that level. If more than one of these operators appear in a calculation, C performs the math from left to right. The same is true of addition and subtraction—the leftmost operation is done first.

   Figure 8.2 illustrates an example showing this.

   Because the division appears to the left of the multiplication, it is computed first, because division and multiplication are on the same level.

   You now should be able to follow the order of these C operators. You really don't need to worry about the math because C does all the actual work. However, you should understand this order of operators so you know how to structure your calculations. Now that you have *mastered* this order, it's already time to see how you can override it with parentheses!

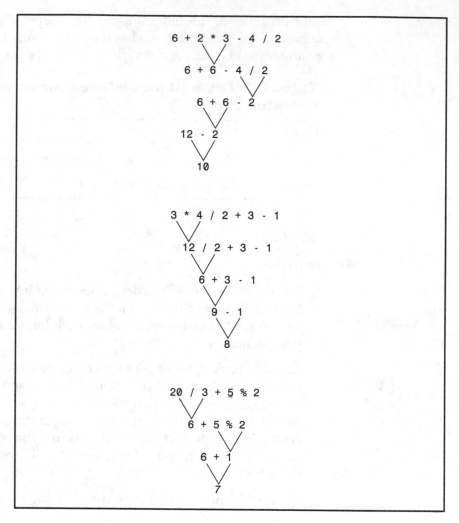

Figure 8.1. C's order of operators with lines indicating precedence.

Using Parentheses

Parentheses override
the usual order of
math.

If you want to override the order of precedence, you can put parentheses in the calculation. The parentheses actually reside on a level above the multiplication, division, and modulus in the precedence table. In other words, *any* calculation in parentheses—whether it is addition, subtraction, division, or whatever—is always calculated before the rest of the line. The other calculations are then performed in their normal operator order.

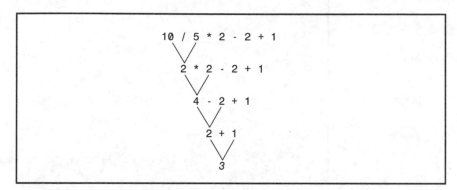

Figure 8.2. C's order of operators from left to right with lines indicating precedence.

The first formula in this chapter, *2 + 3 * 2*, produced an 8 because the multiplication was performed before addition. However, by adding parentheses around the addition, as in *(2 + 3) * 2*, the answer becomes 10.

In the precedence table shown in Appendix D, the parentheses reside on level 1 (the highest level in the table). Being higher than the other levels makes parentheses take precedence over multiplication, division, and all other operators.

Examples

1. The calculations shown in Figure 8.3 illustrate how parentheses override the regular order of operators. These are the same three formulas shown in the last section, but their results are calculated differently because the parentheses override the normal order of operators.

2. If an expression contains parentheses-within-parentheses, C evaluates the innermost parentheses first. The expressions in Figure 8.4 illustrate this.

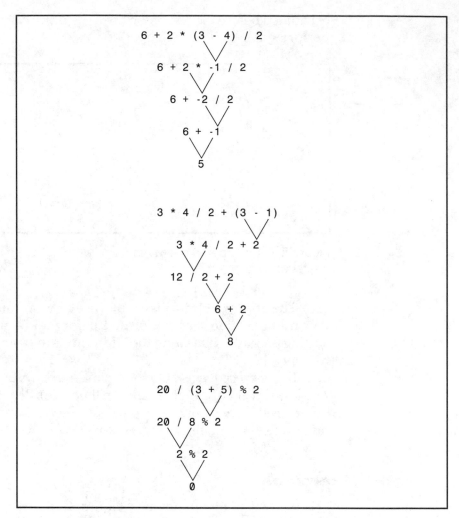

Figure 8.3. Example of parentheses as the highest precedence level with lines indicating precedence.

3. The following program produces an incorrect result, even though it looks as if it should work. See if you can spot the error!

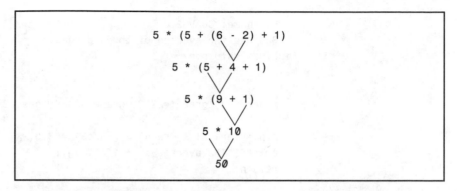

Figure 8.4. Precedence example of parentheses-within-parentheses with lines indicating precedence.

Identify the program and include the necessary header file. This program will average some grades. We need variables for the average and each of the three grades, so declare avg, grade1, grade2, *and* grade3 *as floating-point variables. Make the average equal to the three grades divided by 3. Print the average to the screen.*

```
/* Filename: C8AVG1.C
   Compute the average of three grades */
#include <stdio.h>
main()
{
    float avg, grade1=87.6, grade2=94.8, grade3=74.5;

    avg = grade1 + grade2 + grade3 / 3.0;
    printf("The average is %.1f", avg);
    return;
}
```

The problem is that division is performed first. Therefore, the third grade is first divided by 3.0, and then the other two grades are added to that result. To correct this problem, you would simply have to add one set of parentheses, as shown in the following:

```
/* Filename: C8AVG2.C
   Compute the average of three grades */
#include <stdio.h>
main()
{
   float avg, grade1=87.6, grade2=94.8, grade3=74.5;

   avg = (grade1 + grade2 + grade3) / 3.0;
   printf("The average is %.1f", avg);
   return;
}
```

TIP: Use plenty of parentheses in your C programs to make the order of operators clearer, even when you don't have to override their default order. It sometimes makes the calculations easier to understand later, when you might need to modify the program.

The Assignment Statements

In C, the assignment operator, =, behaves differently from what you might be used to in other languages. So far, you have seen it used for simple assignment of values to variables, which is consistent with its use in most other programming languages.

However, the assignment operator *also* can be used in other ways, such as multiple assignment statements and compound assignments, as the following sections illustrate.

Multiple Assignments

Initialize several variables

If two or more equals signs appear in an expression, each of them performs an assignment. This introduces a new aspect of the precedence order you should understand. Consider the following expression:

```
a=b=c=d=e=100;
```

Shorter Is Not Always Better

When you program computers for a living, it is much more important to write programs that are easy to understand than programs that are short, or that include tricky calculations.

Maintainability is the computer industry's word for changing and updating programs that were written in a simple style earlier. The business world is changing rapidly, and the programs that companies have used for years must often be updated to reflect this changing environment. Businesses do not always have the resources to write programs from scratch. They usually make do by modifying the ones they have.

Years ago when computer hardware was much more expensive, and when computer memories were much smaller, it was important to write small programs, which often relied on clever, individualized tricks and shortcuts. Unfortunately, such programs are often difficult to revise, especially if the original programmers leave and someone else (you!) must step in and modify all their original code.

Companies are realizing the importance of spending time to write programs that are easy to modify and that do not rely on tricks, or "quick and dirty" routines that are hard to follow. You can be a much more valuable programmer if you write clean programs, with lots of white space, lots of remarks, and very straightforward code. Put parentheses around formulas if it makes them clearer, and use variables for storing results in case you need the same answer later in the program. Break long calculations into several smaller ones.

Throughout the rest of this book, you can read tips on writing maintainable programs. You and your colleagues might appreciate these tips when you incorporate them into your own C programs.

This may at first seem confusing, especially if you know other computer languages. To C, the equals sign always means: assign the value on the right to the variable on the left. This right-to-left order is described in Appendix D's precedence table. The third column in the table is labeled *Associativity*, which describes the direction of the operation. The assignment operator associates from right to left, whereas some of the other C operators associate from left to right.

Because the assignment associates from right to left, the preceding expression first assigns the 100 to the variable named e. This produces a value, 100, of the expression. In C, all expressions produce values, typically the result of assignments. Therefore, this value, 100, is then assigned to the variable d. The value of that, 100, is assigned to c, then to b, and finally to a. Whatever values were in the five variables previous to this statement would be replaced by 100 after the statement finishes.

Because C does not automatically set variables to zero before you use them, you might want to zero them out before you use them with a single assignment statement. The following section of variable declarations and initializations is performed using multiple assignment statements.

```
#include <stdio.h>
main()
{
    int ctr, num_emp, num_dep;
    float sales, salary, amount;

    ctr=num_emp=num_dep=0;
    sales=salary=amount=0;
    /* Rest of program follows */
```

In C, you can include the assignment statement almost anywhere in a program, even within another calculation. For example, consider the statement

```
value = 5 + (r = 9 - c);
```

which is a perfectly legal C statement. The assignment operator resides on the first level of the precedence table, and always produces a value. Because its associativity is right to left, the r is first assigned 9 - c because the rightmost equal sign is evaluated first. The subexpression (r = 9 - c) produces a value (whatever is placed into r) that is added to 5 before storing that result in value.

Example

Because C does not initialize variables to zero before you use them, you may want to include a multiple assignment operator to zero them out before using them. The following section of code ensures that all variables are initialized before the rest of the program uses them.

```
#include <stdio.h>
main()
(
    int num_emp, dependents, age;
    float salary, hr_rate, taxrate;

    /* Initialize all variables to zero */
    num_emp=dependents=age=hours=0;
    salary=hr_rate=taxrate=0.0;

    /* Rest of program follows */
```

Compound Assignments

Many times in programming, you may want to update the value of a variable. That is, you need to take a variable's current value, add or multiply that value by an expression, and then assign it back into the original variable. The following assignment statement demonstrates this

```
salary=salary*1.2;
```

This expression multiplies the old value of salary by 1.2 (in effect, raising the value in salary by 20 percent), then assigns it back into salary. C provides several operators, called *compound operators*, that you can use any time the same variable appears on both sides of the equals sign. The compound operators are shown in Table 8.4.

Table 8.4. C's compound operators.

Operator	Example	Equivalent
+=	bonus+=500;	bonus=bonus+500;
-=	budget-=50;	budget=budget-50;
*=	salary*=1.2;	salary=salary*1.2;
/=	factor/=.50;	factor=factor/.50;
%=	daynum%=7;	daynum=daynum%7;

The compound operators are low in the precedence table. They typically are evaluated very late in equations that use them.

Examples

1. You have been storing your factory's production amount in a variable called prod_amt, and your supervisor has just informed you of a new addition that needs to be applied to that production value. You could code this update in a statement that looks like this:

```
prod_amt = prod_amt + 2.6;  /* Add 2.6 to current
                                production */
```

Instead of this formula, you should use C's compound addition operator by coding it like this:

```
prod_amt += 2.6;  /* Add 2.6 to current production */
```

2. Suppose you are a high school teacher who wants to adjust your students' grades upward. You gave a test that seemed too difficult, and the grades were not up to your expectations. If you had stored each of the student's grades in variables named grade1, grade2, grade3, and so on, you could update the grades from within a program with the following section of compound assignments:

```
grade1*=1.1;      /* Increase each student's grade by 10
                     percent */
grade2*=1.1;
grade3*=1.1;
/* Rest of grade changes follow */
```

3. The precedence of the compound operators requires important consideration when you decide how to code compound assignments. Notice from Appendix D that the compound operators are on level 14, much lower than the regular math operators. This means you must be careful how you interpret them.

For example, suppose you want to update the value of a `sales` variable with this formula:

```
4-factor+bonus
```

You could update the `sales` variable with the following statement:

```
sales += 4 - factor + bonus;
```

This adds the quantity `4-factor+bonus` to `sales`. Although this returns the same value as the following statement, the two are evaluated differently.

```
sales = sales + 4 - factor + bonus;
```

Because the `+=` operator is much lower in the precedence table than `+` or `-`, it is performed last, and from right-to-left associativity. Therefore, the following *are* equivalent, from a precedence viewpoint:

```
sales += 4 - factor + bonus;
```

and

```
sales = sales + (4 - factor + bonus);
```

Mixing Data Types in Calculations

C attempts to convert the smaller data type to the larger one in a mixed data type expression.

You can mix data types in C, such as adding together an integer and a floating-point value. C generally converts the smaller of the two types into the other. For instance, if you add a double to an integer, C first converts the integer into a double value, then performs the calculation. This produces the most accurate result possible. The automatic conversion of data types is only temporary; the converted value is back in its original data type as soon as the expression is finished.

If C converted two different data types to the smaller value's type, the higher-precision value would be truncated, or shortened too much, and accuracy would be lost. For example, in the following short program, the floating-point value of sales is added to an integer called bonus. Before C computes the answer, it converts bonus to floating-point which results in a floating-point answer.

Compute total pay

```
/* Filename: C8DATA.C
   Demonstrate mixed data type in an expression */
#include <stdio.h>
main()
{
   int bonus=50;
   float salary=1400.50;
   float total;

   total=salary+bonus;   /* bonus becomes floating-point
                             temporarily */
   printf("The total is %.2f", total);
   return;
}
```

Type Casting

Most of the time, you don't have to worry about C's automatic conversion of data types. However, problems can occur if you mix unsigned variables with variables of other data types. Because of differences in computer architecture, unsigned variables do not always convert to the larger data type. This can result in loss of accuracy, and even incorrect results.

You can override C's default conversions by specifying your own *temporary* type change. This is called *type casting*. When you type cast, you temporarily change a variable's data type from its declared data type to a new one. The format of a type cast is

```
(data type) expression
```

where `data type` can be any valid C data type, and the `expression` can be a variable, constant, or an expression that combines both. The following code type casts the integer variable `age` into a double floating-point variable, temporarily, so it can be multiplied by the double floating-point `factor`.

```
age_factor = (double)age * factor;   /* Temporarily change age */
                                     /* to double           */
```

Examples

1. Suppose you want to verify the interest calculation used by your bank on a loan. The interest rate is 15.5 percent, stored as .155 in a floating-point variable. The amount of interest you owe is computed by multiplying the interest rate by the amount of the loan balance, and then multiplying that by the number of days in the year since the loan originated. The following program finds the daily interest rate by dividing the annual interest rate by 365, the number of days in a year. C must convert the integer 365 to a floating-point constant automatically, because it is used in combination with a floating-point variable.

```
/* Filename: C8INT1.C
   Calculate interest on a loan */
#include <stdio.h>
main()
{
    int days=45;   /* Days since loan origination */
```

```
    float principle = 3500.00; /* Original loan amount */
    float interest_rate=0.155;    /* Annual interest rate */
    float daily_interest;    /* Daily interest rate */

    daily_interest=interest_rate/365;   /* Compute floating-
                                            point value */

    /* Because days is integer, it too will be converted to
       float next */
    daily_interest = principle * daily_interest * days;
    principle+=daily_interest;   /* Update the principle with
                                    interest */
    printf("The balance you owe is %.2f", principle);
    return;
}
```

The output of this program follows:

```
The balance you owe is 3566.88
```

2. Instead of letting C perform the conversion, you may want to type cast all mixed expressions to ensure they convert to your liking. Here is the same program as in the first example, except type casts are used to convert the integer constants to floating-points before they are used.

```
/* Filename: C8INT2.C
   Calculate interest on a loan using type casting */
#include <stdio.h>
main()
{
    int days=45;   /* Days since loan origination */
    float principle = 3500.00;    /* Original loan amount */
    float interest_rate=0.155;    /* Annual interest rate */
    float daily_interest;         /* Daily interest rate */

    daily_interest=interest_rate/(float)365;   /* Type cast
                                                  days to float */

    /* Since days is integer, convert it to float too */
    daily_interest = principle * daily_interest * (float)days;
```

```
principle+=daily_interest;    /* Update the principle with
                                  interest */
printf("The balance you owe is %.2f", principle);
return;
}
```

The output from this program is exactly the same as from the previous one.

Review Questions

Answers to review questions are in Appendix B.

1. What is the result for each of the following expressions?

    a. `1 + 2 * 4 / 2`

    b. `(1 + 2) * 4 / 2`

    c. `1 + 2 * (4 / 2)`

2. What is the result for each of the following expressions?

    a. `9 % 2 + 1`

    b. `(1 + (10 - (2 + 2)))`

3. Convert each of the following formulas into its C assignment equivalents.

    a. $a = \dfrac{3 + 3}{4 + 4}$

    b. $x = (a - b)*(a - c)^2$

    c. $d = \dfrac{(8 - x^2)}{(x - 9)} - \dfrac{(4 * 2 - 1)}{x^3}$

4. Write a short program that prints the area of a circle, when its radius equals 4 and π equals 3.14159. (Hint: The area of a circle is computed by `π * radius`^{2}.)

5. Write the assignment and `printf()` statements that print the remainder of 100/3.

Review Exercises

1. Write a program that prints each of the first 8 powers of 2. That is, 2^1, 2^2, 2^3,...2^8. Please include comments that include your name at the top of the program. Print string constants that describe each answer printed. The first two lines of your output should look like this:

```
2 raised to the first power is: 2
2 raised to the second power is: 4
```

2. Change C8PAY.C so it computes and prints a bonus of 15% of the gross pay. Taxes are not to be taken out of the bonus. After printing the four variables, `gross_pay`, `tax_rate`, `bonus`, and `gross_pay`, print a check on the screen that looks like a printed check. Add string constants so it prints the payee and put your name as the payer at the bottom of the check.

3. Store the weights and ages of three people in variables. Print a table, with titles, of the weights and ages. At the bottom of the table, print the average of the weights and ages.

4. Assume that a video store employee works 50 hours. She gets paid $4.50 for the first 40 hours; she gets time-and-a-half (1.5 times the regular pay rate) for the first five hours over 40; and she gets double-time pay for all hours over 45. Assuming a 28% tax rate, write a program that prints her gross pay, taxes, and net pay to the screen. Label each amount with appropriate titles (using string constants) and add appropriate comments in the program.

Summary

You now understand C's primary math operators and the importance of the precedence table. Parentheses group operations together so they can override the default precedence levels. C deviates from some other programming languages in that every operator in C has a meaning, no matter where it appears in an expression. This enables you to use the assignment operator (the equals sign) in the middle of other expressions.

When you perform math with C, you also must be aware of how C interprets data types, especially when you mix them within the same expression. Of course, you can temporarily type cast a variable or constant so that you can override its default data type.

This chapter has introduced you to a part of the book concerned with C operators. The following two chapters extend this introduction to include relational and logical operators. They enable you to compare data and then compute accordingly.

Relational
Operators

Sometimes you actually *don't* want every statement in your C program to execute every time the program runs. So far, every program in this book has started executing at the top and has continued, line by line, until the last statement stopped executing. But, depending on your application, you may not always want this to happen.

Such programs are known as *data-driven* programs. That is, the data should dictate what the program does. You would not want the computer to print all paychecks for every pay period, for example, because some employees might have taken a leave of absence, or they might be paid on commission and not have made a sale during that period. Printing paychecks with zero dollars would be ridiculous. You want the computer to print checks only for employees who have pay coming, and for nobody else!

This chapter shows you how to create data-driven programs. These programs do not execute the same way every time they are run. This is possible through the use of *relational* operators that *conditionally* control other statements. Relational operators first "look" at the constants and variables in the program, and then operate according to what they "find." This may sound like difficult programming, but it is actually quite straightforward and intuitive.

This chapter introduces you to

◆ Relational operators

◆ The `if` statement

◆ The `else` statement

Not only does this chapter introduce these comparison commands, but it prepares you for much more powerful programs that become possible once you learn the relational operators.

Defining Relational Operators

Relational operators compare data.

In addition to the math operators you learned in Chapter 8, there are also operators that you use for data comparisons. They are called *relational operators*, and their task is to compare data. They enable you to know whether two variables are equal, not equal, or which one is less or more than the other. Table 9.1 lists each relational operator and its meaning.

Table 9.1. The relational operators.

Operator	Description
==	Equal to
>	Greater than
<	Less than
>=	Greater than or equal to
<=	Less than or equal to
!=	Not equal to

The six relational operators form the foundation of comparing data in C programming. They always appear with two constants, variables, expressions (or some combination of these), with one on each side of the operator. These relational operators are so useful that you should learn them as well as you know the +, -, *, /, and % mathematical operators.

> **NOTE:** Unlike many programming languages, C uses a double equal sign (==) as a test for equality. The single equal sign (=) is reserved for assignment of values only.

Examples

1. Assume that a program initializes four variables as follows:

```
int a=5;
int b=10;
int c=15;
int d=5;
```

The following statements are then True:

a is equal to d, so a == d

b is less than c, so b < c

c is greater than a, so c > a

b is greater than or equal to a, so c >= a

d is less than or equal to b, so d <= b

b is not equal to c, so b != c

These are not C statements; they are statements of comparison (*relational logic*) between values in the variables. Relational logic is easy.

Relational logic always produces a *True* or *False* result. In C, unlike some other programming languages, you can directly use the True or False result of relational operators inside other expressions. You will soon learn how to do this; but for now, you need only understand that the following True and False evaluations are correct:

◆ A True relational result evaluates to 1.

◆ A False relational result evaluates to 0.

Each of the statements presented earlier in this example evaluate to a 1, or True, result.

2. If you assume the same values as stated for the previous example's four variables, then each of these statements about those values is False (0):

```
a == b

b > c

d < a

d > a

a != d

b >= c

c <= b
```

You should study these statements to see *why* each is False and evaluates to 0. The variables a and d, for example, are exactly equal to the same value (5), so neither is greater or less than the other.

You deal with relational logic in everyday life. Think of the following statements:

"The generic butter costs less than the name brand."

"My child is younger than Johnny."

"Our salaries are equal."

"The dogs are not the same age."

Each of these statements can be either True or False. There is no other possible answer.

Watch the Signs!

Many people say they are "not math-inclined" or "not very logical," and you may be one of them. But, as mentioned earlier in the book, you do not need to be good in math to be a good computer programmer. Neither should you be frightened by the term "relational logic," because you just saw how you may be using it every day. Nevertheless, some people get confused about symbols and their meanings.

The two *primary* relational operators, *less than* (<) and *greater than* (>), are easy to remember. You may have been taught which is which in school, and forgotten them since. Actually, their signs tell you what they mean.

The arrow points to the lesser of the two values. Notice how, in the True examples (#1), the arrow (the point of the < or >) always points to the lesser number. The larger, open part of the arrow points to the larger number.

The relation is False if the arrow is pointing the wrong way. In other words, 4 > 9 is False because the operator symbol is pointing to the 9, which is *not* the lesser number. In English this says, "4 is greater than 9," which is clearly false.

The if Statement

You incorporate relational operators in C programs with the if statement. Such an expression is called a *decision statement* because it tests a relationship—using the relational operators—and, based on the test's result, makes a decision about which statement to execute next.

The if statement is formatted as follows:

```
if (condition)
   { block of 1 or more C statements }
```

The condition includes any relational comparison, and it must be enclosed in parentheses. You saw several relational comparisons earlier, such as `a==d`, `c<d`, and so on. The `block of 1 or more C statements` is any C statement, such as an assignment or `printf()`, enclosed in braces. The block of the `if`, sometimes called the *body* of the `if` statement, is usually indented a few spaces for readability. This enables you to see, at a glance, exactly what executes if the `condition` is True.

If only one statement follows the `if`, the braces are not required (but it is always good to include them). The block executes only if the `condition` is True. If the `condition` is False, C ignores the block and simply executes the next appropriate statement in the program that follows the `if` statement.

The `if` statement makes a decision.

Basically, you can read an `if` statement in the following way: "If the condition is True, perform the block of statements inside the braces. Otherwise, the condition must be False; so *do not* execute that block, but continue executing the rest of the program as though this `if` did not exist."

The `if` is used to make a decision. The block of statements following the `if` executes if the decision (the result of the relation) is True, but the block does not execute otherwise. As with relational logic, you also use `if` logic in everyday life. Consider the statements that follow:

"If the day is warm, I will go swimming."

"If I make enough money, we will build a new house."

"If the light is green, go."

"If the light is red, stop."

Each of these statements is *conditional*. That is, if *and only if* the condition is true do you perform the activity.

> **CAUTION:** Do *not* put a semicolon after the parentheses of the relational test. Semicolons go after each statement inside the block.

Expressions as the Condition

C interprets *any* nonzero value as True, and zero always as False. This enables you to insert regular non-conditional expressions within the if logic. To see this, consider the following section of code:

```
main()
{
   int age=21;   /* Declares and assigns age as 21 */
   if (age=85)
   { printf("You have lived through a lot!"); }
   /* Rest of program goes here */
```

At first, it may seem as though the printf() does not execute, *but it does!* Because a regular assignment operator (=) is used (and not a relational operator, ==), C performs the assignment of 85 to age. This, as with all assignments you saw in Chapter 8, produces a value for the expression of 85. Because 85 is nonzero, C interprets the if condition as True and then performs the body of the if statement. Mixing up the relational equality test (==) and the regular assignment operator (=) is a common error made in C programs, and the nonzero True test makes this bug even more difficult to find.

The designers of C didn't intend for this to confuse you. They wanted you to take advantage of this feature whenever you could. Instead of putting an assignment before an if, and then testing the result of that assignment, you can combine the assignment and if into a single statement. Test your understanding of this by considering: Would C interpret the following condition as True or False?

```
if (10 == 10 == 10)...
```

Be careful! At first glance, it seems True; but C "thinks" the expression is False! Because the == operator associates from left to right, the first 10 is compared to the second. Because they are equal, the result is 1 (for True) and the 1 is then compared to the third 10—which results in a 0 (for False)!

Examples

1. The following are examples of valid C if statements.

   Make sales a variable representing the salesperson's sales. Make bonus a variable representing the salesperson's bonus. If the salesperson's sales are greater than 5000, he or she gets a bonus of 500.

```
if (sales > 5000)
    { bonus = 500; }
```

If this is part of a C program, the value inside the variable sales determines what happens next. If sales contains more than 5,000, the next statement that executes is the one inside the block which initializes bonus. If, however, sales contains 5,000 or less, the block does not execute, and the line following the if's block executes.

If the person's age is less than or equal to 21:
   Tell the user that he or she is a minor.
   Ask for the user's grade.
   Get the user's answer.

```
if (age <= 21)
    { printf("You are a minor.\n");
      printf("What is your grade?");
      scanf(" %d", &grade); }
```

If the value in age is less than or equal to 21, the lines of code within the block execute next. Otherwise, C skips the entire block and continues with the remaining program.

If the person's current balance is higher than the acceptable overdue amount, print a Past due! message.

```
if (balance > low_balance)
    {printf("Past due!\n"); }
```

If the value in balance is more than that in low_balance, execution of the program continues at the block and the message Past due! prints on-screen. You can compare two variables to each other (as in this example) or a variable to a constant (as in the previous examples) or a constant to a constant (although this is rarely done) or a constant to any expression in place of any variable or constant. The following if statement shows an expression included within the if.

If an employee's pay times the tax rate equals the minimum salary, assign 1400.60 to a variable.

```
If (pay * tax_rate == minimum)
   { low_salary = 1400.60; }
```

The precedence table of operators in Appendix D includes the relational operators. They are at levels 6 and 7, lower than the other primary math operators. When you use expressions such as the one shown in this example, you can make these expressions much more readable by enclosing them in parentheses (even though this is not required). Here is a rewrite of this if statement with ample parentheses:

```
If ((pay * tax_rate) == minimum)
   { low_salary = 1400.60; }
```

2. The following is a simple program that computes a salesperson's pay. The salesperson gets a basic flat rate of $4.10 per hour. In addition, if the sales are more than $8,500, the salesperson also receives an additional $500 as a bonus. This is a good introductory example of conditional logic that depends on a relation between two values, sales and $8500.

```
/* Filename: C9PAY1.C
   Calculates a salesperson's pay based on his or her sales */
#include <stdio.h>
main()
{
   char sal_name[20];
   int hours;
   float total_sales, bonus, pay;
```

```
        printf("\n\n");          /* Print 2 blank lines */
        printf("Payroll Calculation\n");
        printf("------------------\n");

        /* Ask the user for needed values */
        printf("What is salesperson's last name? ");
        scanf(" %s", sal_name);    /* No & because it's an array */
        printf("How many hours did the salesperson work? ");
        scanf(" %d", &hours);
        printf("What were the total sales? ");
        scanf(" %f", &total_sales);

        bonus = 0;      /* Initially, there is no bonus */

        /* Compute the base pay */
        pay = 4.10 * (float)hours;  /* Type cast the hours */

        /* Add bonus only if sales were high */
        if (total_sales > 8500.00)
           { bonus = 500.00; }

        printf("%s made $%.2f \n", sal_name, pay);
        printf("and got a bonus of $%.2f", bonus);

        return;
}
```

The following output shows the result of running this program twice, each time with different input values. Notice that the program does two different things: It computes a bonus for one employee, but doesn't for the other. The $500 bonus is a direct result of the if statement. The assignment of $500 to bonus is executed only if the value in total_sales is more than $8500.

```
Payroll Calculation
------------------
What is salesperson's last name? Harrison
How many hours did the salesperson work? 40
What were the total sales? 6050.64
Harrison made $164.00
and got a bonus of $0.00
```

```
Payroll Calculation
-------------------
What is salesperson's last name? Robertson
How many hours did the salesperson work? 40
What were the total sales? 9800
Robertson made $164.00
and got a bonus of $500.00
```

3. While programming the way users will input data, you are often wise to program *data validation* on the values they type. If they enter a bad value (for instance, a negative number when you know the input cannot be negative), you can inform them of the problem and ask them to reenter the data.

Not all data can be validated, of course, but most of it can be checked for reasonableness. For example, if you write a student record-keeping program, in order to track each student's name, address, age, and other pertinent data, you could check to see whether the age falls within a reasonable range. If the user enters **213** for the age, you know the value is incorrect. If the user enters **-4** for the age, you know this value is also incorrect. Not all erroneous input for age can be checked, however. If the user is 21, for instance, and types **22**, your program would have no way of knowing whether this is correct, because 22 falls within a reasonable age range for students.

The following program is a routine that requests an age, and checks to make sure it is more than 10. This is certainly not a foolproof test (because the user can still enter incorrect ages), but it takes care of extremely low values. If the user enters a bad age, the program asks for it again inside the if statement.

BEGIN

Get age

Is age < 10? — No

Yes

Print error

END

```c
/* Filename: C9AGE.C
   Program that helps ensure age values are reasonable */
#include <stdio.h>
main()
{
    int age;
```

```
printf("\nWhat is the student's age? ");
scanf(" %d", &age);
if (age < 10)
  { printf("%c", '\x07');    /* BEEP */
    printf("*** The age cannot be less than 10 ***\n");
    printf("Try again...\n\n");
    printf("What is the student's age? ");
    scanf(" %d", &age);
  }

printf("Thank you. You entered a valid age.");
return;
}
```

This routine could also be a section of a longer program. You learn later how to prompt repeatedly for a value until a valid input is given. This program takes advantage of the bell (ASCII 7) to warn the user that a bad age was entered.

If the entered age is less than 10, the user receives an error message. The program beeps and warns the user about the bad age before asking for it again.

The following shows the result of running this program. Notice that the program "knows," due to the if statement, whether age is more than 10.

```
What is the student's age? 3
*** The age cannot be less than 10 ***
Try again...

What is the student's age? 21
Thank you.  You entered a valid age.
```

4. Unlike many languages, C does not include a square math operator. Remember that you "square" a number by multiplying it times itself (3*3, for example). Because many computers do not allow for integers to hold more than the square of 180, the following program uses if statements to make sure the number fits as an integer answer when it is computed.

The program takes a value from the user and prints its square—unless it is more than 180. The message Square is not allowed for numbers over 180 appears on-screen if the user types an overly large number.

```c
/* Filename: C9SQR1.C
   Print the square of the input value
   if the input value is less than 180 */
#include <stdio.h>
main()
{
   int num, square;

   printf("\n\n");  /* Print 2 blank lines */
   printf("What number do you want to see the square of? ");
   scanf(" %d", &num);

   if (num <= 180)
   { square = num * num;
     printf("The square of %d is %d", num, square);
   }

   if (num > 180)
   { printf("%c", '\x07');    /* BEEP */
     printf("\n*** Square is not allowed for numbers over 180 ***");
     printf("\nRun this program again and try a smaller value.");
   }

   printf("\nThank you for requesting square roots.\n");
   return;
}
```

The following output shows a couple of sample runs with this program. Notice that both conditions work: If the user enters a number less than 180, the calculated square appears, but if the user enters a larger number, an error message appears.

```
What number do you want to see the square of? 45
The square of 45 is 2025
Thank you for requesting square roots.
```

```
What number do you want to see the square of? 212

*** Square is not allowed for numbers over 180 ***
Run this program again and try a smaller value.
Thank you for requesting square roots.
```

This program is improved when you learn the else statement later in this chapter. This code includes a redundant check of the user's input. The variable num must be checked once to print the square if the input number is less than or equal to 180, and checked again for the error message if it is greater than 180:

5. The value of 1 and 0 for True and False, respectively, can help save you an extra programming step, which you are not necessarily able to save in other languages. To understand this, examine the following section of code:

```
commission = 0;   /* Initialize commission */

if (sales > 10000)
   { commission = 500.00; }

pay = net_pay + commission;   /* Commission is 0 unless high
                                 sales */
```

This program can be streamlined and made more efficient by combining the if's relational test because you know that if returns 1 or 0:

```
pay = net_pay + (commission = (sales > 10000) * 500.00);
```

This single line does what it took the previous four lines to do. Because the rightmost assignment has precedence, it gets computed first. The variable sales is compared to 10000. If it is more than 10000, a True result of 1 is returned. That 1 is multiplied by 500.00 and stored in commission. If, however, the sales were not more than 10000, a 0 would result, and 0 multiplied by 500.00 still returns 0.

Whichever value (500.00 or 0) is assigned to commission also becomes the value of that expression. That value is then added to net_pay and stored in pay.

The else Statement

The else statement never appears in a program without an if statement. This section introduces the else statement by showing you the popular if-else combination statement. Its format is

```
if (condition)
   { A block of 1 or more C statements }
else
   { A block of 1 or more C statements }
```

The first part of the if-else is identical to the if statement. If the *condition* is True, then the block of C statements following the if executes. However, if the *condition* is False, the block of C statements following the else executes instead. Whereas the simple if statement determines what happens only when the *condition* is True, the if-else also determines what happens if the *condition* is False. No matter what the outcome is, the statement following the if-else executes next.

The following describes the nature of the if-else:

◆ If the *condition* test is True, the entire block of statements following the if is performed.

◆ If the *condition* test is False, the entire block of statements following the else is performed.

NOTE: You can also compare characters, in addition to numbers. When you compare characters, C uses the ASCII table to determine which character is "less than" (lower in the ASCII table) than the other. But you cannot compare character strings or arrays of character strings directly with relational operators.

Examples

1. The following program asks the user for a number. It then prints whether or not the number is greater than zero, by using the if-else statement.

```
/* Filename: C9IFEL1.C
   Demonstrates if-else by printing whether an
   input value is greater than zero or not */
#include <stdio.h>
main()
{
   int num;

   printf("What is your number? ");
   scanf(" %d", &num);   /* Get the user's number */

   if (num > 0)
      { printf("More than 0\n"); }
   else
      { printf("Less or equal to 0\n"); }

  /* No matter what the number was, the following executes */
   printf("\n\nThanks for your time!");
   return;
}
```

There is no need to test for *both* possibilities when you use an
else. The if tests to see whether the number is greater than
zero, and the else automatically takes care of all other possibilities.

2. The following program asks the user for his or her first
   name, and then stores it in a character array. The first character
   of the array is checked to see whether it falls in the first
   half of the alphabet. If it does, an appropriate message is
   displayed.

```
/* Filename: C9IFEL2.C
   Tests the user's first initial and prints a message */
#include <stdio.h>
main()
{
   char last[20];   /* Holds the last name */
   printf("What is your last name? ");
   scanf(" %s", last);
```

```
/* Test the initial */
if (last[0] <= 'P')
   { printf("Your name is early in the alphabet.\n");}
else
   { printf("You have to wait a while for YOUR name to be
     called!");}
return;
}
```

Notice that because a character array element is being compared to a character constant, you must enclose the character constant inside single quotes. The data type on each side of each relational operator must match.

3. The following program is a more complete payroll routine than you have seen. It uses the if to illustrate how to compute overtime pay. The logic goes something like this:

If employees work 40 hours or fewer, they get paid regular pay (their hourly rate times the number of hours worked). If employees work between 40 and 50 hours, they get one-and-a-half times their hourly rate for those hours over 40, in addition to their regular pay for the first 40. All hours over 50 are paid at double the regular rate.

```
/* Filename: C9PAY2.C
   Compute the full overtime pay possibilities */
#include <stdio.h>
main()
{
   int hours;
   float dt, ht, rp, rate, pay;

   printf("\n\nHow many hours were worked? ");
   scanf(" %d", &hours);
   printf("\nWhat is the regular hourly pay?");
   scanf(" %f", &rate);

   /* Compute pay here */
   /* Double-time possibility */
   if (hours > 50)
      { dt = 2.0 * rate * (float)(hours - 50);
```

```
            ht = 1.5 * rate * 10.0;   /* Time + 1/2 for 10 hours */
     }
     else
        { dt = 0.0; }   /* Either none or double for those hours
                                over 50 */

     /* Time and a half */
     if (hours > 40)
        { ht = 1.5 * rate * (float)(hours - 40); }

     /* Regular Pay */
     if (hours >= 40)
        { rp = 40 * rate; }
     else
        { rp = (float)hours * rate; }

     pay = dt + ht + rp;    /* Add up 3 components of payroll */

     printf("\nThe pay is %.2f", pay);
     return;
}
```

4. The block of statements following the if can contain any valid C statement—even another if statement! This sometimes comes in handy, as the following example shows.

This program could be run to give an award to employees based on their years of service to your company. In this example, you are giving a gold watch to those with more than 20 years of service, a paperweight to those with more than 10 years, and a pat on the back to everyone else!

```
/* Filename: C9SERV.C
   Prints a message depending on years of service */
#include <stdio.h>
main()
{
   int yrs;
   printf("How many years of service? ");
   scanf(" %d", &yrs);    /* Get the years they have worked */

   if (yrs > 20)
```

```
        { printf("Give a gold watch\n"); }
    else
       { if (yrs > 10)
         { printf("Give a paper weight\n"); }
         else
            { printf("Give a pat on the back\n"); }
       }
    return;
}
```

You should probably not rely on the if within an if to take care of *too many* conditions, because more than three or four conditions can add confusion. You might get into some messy logic, such as: "If this is True, and then if this is also True, then do something; but if not that, but something else is True, then..." (and so on). The switch statement that you learn about in a later chapter handles these types of multiple if selections much better than a long if within an if statement does.

Review Questions

Answers to review questions are in Appendix B.

1. Which operator tests for equality?

2. State whether each of these relational tests is True or False:

   a.   4 >= 5

   b.   4 == 4

   c.   165 >= 165

   d.   0 != 25

3. True or false: C is fun prints on-screen when the following statement is executed.

```
if (54 <= 54)
   { printf("C is fun"); }
```

4. What is the difference between an `if` and an `if-else` statement?

5. Does the following `printf()` execute?

```
if (3 != 4 != 1)
    { printf("This will print"); }
```

6. Using the ASCII table (see Appendix C), state whether these character relational tests are True or False:

a.   `'C' < 'c'`

b.   `'0' > '0'`

c.   `'?' > ')'`

Review Exercises

1. Write a weather-calculator program that asks for a list of the previous five days' temperatures, then prints `Brrrr!` every time a temperature falls below freezing.

2. Write a program that asks for a number and then prints the square and cube (the number multiplied by itself three times) of the number you input, if that number is more than `1`. Otherwise, the program does not print anything.

3. In a program, ask the user for two numbers. Print a message telling how the first one relates to the second. In other words, if the user enters `5` and `7`, your program would print "`5 is less than 7.`"

4. Write a program that prompts the user for an employee's pre-tax salary, and then prints the appropriate taxes. The taxes are 10% if the employee makes less than $10,000; 15% if the employee earns $10,000 up to, but not including, $20,000; and 20% if the employee earns $20,000 or more.

Summary

You now have the tools to write powerful data-checking programs. This chapter showed you how to compare constants, variables, and combinations of both by using the relational operators. The `if` and the `if-else` statements rely on such data comparisons in order to determine which code to execute next. You can now *conditionally execute* statements within your programs.

The next chapter takes this one step further by combining relational operators in order to create logical operators (sometimes called *compound conditions*). These logical operators further improve your program's ability to make selections based on data comparisons.

Logical Operators

C's *logical operators* enable you to combine relational operators into more powerful data-testing statements. The logical operators are sometimes called *compound relational operators*. As C's precedence table shows, relational operators take precedence over logical operators when you combine them. The precedence table plays an important role in these types of operators, as this chapter stresses.

This chapter introduces you to

♦ The logical operators

♦ How logical operators are used

♦ How logical operators take precedence

This chapter concludes your study of the conditional testing that C enables you to perform, and it illustrates many examples of if statements in programs that work on compound conditional tests.

Defining Logical Operators

There may be times when you need to test more than one set of variables. You can combine more than one relational test into a *compound relational test* by using C's logical operators, as shown in Table 10.1.

Table 10.1. Logical operators.

Operator	Meaning
&&	AND
¦¦	OR
!	NOT

Logical operators
enable compound
relational tests.

The first two logical operators, && and ¦¦, never appear by themselves. They typically go between two or more relational tests.

Table 10.2 shows you how each logical operator works. These are called *truth tables* because they show you how to achieve True results from an if statement that uses these operators. Take some time to study these tables.

Table 10.2. Truth tables.

The AND (&&) truth table
Both sides must be True

True AND True = True

True AND False= False

False AND True = False

False AND False= False

The OR (¦¦) truth table
One or the other side must be True

True OR True = True

True OR False= True

False OR True = True

False OR False= False

The NOT (!) truth table	
Causes an opposite relation	
NOT True = False	
NOT False = True	

Logical Operators and Their Use

The True and False on each side of the operators represent a relational `if` test. The following statements, for example, are valid `if` tests that use logical operators (sometimes called *compound relational operators*).

If a is less than b, and c is greater than d, print Results are invalid to the screen.

```
if ((a < b) && (c > d))
   { printf("Results are invalid."); }
```

The variable `a` must be less than `b` and, at the same time, `c` must be greater than `d` in order for the `printf()` to execute. The `if` statement still requires parentheses around its complete conditional test. Consider this portion of a program:

```
if ((sales > 5000) || (hrs_worked > 81))
   { bonus=500; }
```

The `sales` must be more than 5000, or the `hrs_worked` must be more than 81, before the assignment executes.

```
IF (!(sales < 2500))
   { bonus = 500; }
```

The || is sometimes called *inclusive OR*. Here is a program segment that includes the not (!) operator:

If `sales` is greater than or equal to 2500, `bonus` is initialized. This illustrates an important programming tip: Use `!` sparingly. Or, as some professionals so wisely put it: "Do *not* use `!` or your programs will *not* be !(unclear)." It would be much clearer to rewrite this last example by turning it into a positive relational test:

```
if (sales >= 2500)
   { bonus 500; }
```

But the ! operator is sometimes helpful, especially when you test for end-of-file conditions. Most of the time, however, you can avoid using ! by using the reverse logic shown in the following:

!(var1 == var2) is the same as (var1 != var2)

!(var1 <= var2) is the same as (var1 > var2)

!(var1 >= var2) is the same as (var1 < var2)

!(var1 != var2) is the same as (var1 == var2)

!(var1 > var2) is the same as (var1 <= var2)

!(var1 < var2) is the same as (var1 >= var2)

Notice that the overall format of the if statement is retained when you use logical operators, but the relational test is expanded to include more than one relation. You even can have three or more, as in the following statement:

```
if ((a == B) && (d == f) || (1 = m) || !(k <> 2)) ...
```

This is a little too much, however, and good programming practice dictates using *at most* two relational tests inside a single if statement. If you need to combine more than two, use more than one if statement to do so.

As with other relational operators, you also use the following logical operators in everyday conversation:

"If my pay is high and my vacation time is long, we can go to Italy this summer."

"If you take the trash out or clean your room, you can watch TV tonight."

"If you aren't good, you'll be punished."

> **Internal Truths**
>
> The True or False results of relational tests occur internally at the bit level. For example, take the `if` test
>
> ```
> if (a == 6) ...
> ```
>
> to determine the truth of the relation, `(a==6)`. The computer takes a binary 6, or 00000110, and compares it, bit by bit, to the variable a. If a contains 7, a binary 00000111, the result of this *equal* test would be False, because the right bit (called the *least-significant bit*) is different.

C's Logical Efficiency

C attempts to be more efficient than other languages. If you combine multiple relational tests with one of the logical operators, C does not always interpret the full expression. This ultimately makes your programs run faster, but there are dangers! For example, if your program is given the conditional test:

```
if ((5 > 4) || (sales < 15) && (15 != 15))...
```

then C only "looks at" the first condition, `(5 > 4)`, and realizes it does not need to look further. Because `(5 > 4)` is True and because `||` (OR) anything that follows it is still True, C does not bother with the rest of the expression. The same holds true for the following statement:

```
if ((7 < 3) && (age > 15) && (initial == 'D'))...
```

Here C looks only at the first condition, which is False. Because of the `&&` (AND) anything else that follows it is also going to be False, C does not interpret the expression to the right of `(7 < 3)`. Most of the time, this doesn't pose any problem, but you should be aware that the following expression may not fulfill your expectations:

```
if ((5 > 4) || (num = 0))...
```

The `(num = 0)` assignment never executes, because C only needs to interpret `(5 > 4)` to see whether the entire expression is True or False. Because of this danger, do *not* include assignment expressions in the same condition as a logical test. The following single `if` condition:

```
if ((sales > old_sales) ¦¦ (inventory_flag = 'Y'))...
```

should be broken into two statements, such as:

```
inventory_flag) = 'Y';
if ((sales > old_sales) ¦¦ (inventory_flag))...
```

so that the inventory_flag is always assigned the 'Y' value, no matter how the (sales > old_sales) expression tests.

Examples

1. The summer Olympics are held every four years during each year that is divisible evenly by 4. The U.S. Census is taken every ten years, in each year that is evenly divisible by 10. The following short program asks for a year, and then tells the user if it is a year of the summer Olympics, a year of the census, or both. It uses relational operators, logical operators, and the modulus operator to determine this output.

```c
/* Filename: C10YEAR.C
   Determines if it is Summer Olympics year, */
   U.S. Census year, or both              */
#include <stdio.h>
main()
{
    int year;
    /* Ask for a year */
    printf("What is a year for the test? ");
    scanf(" %d", &year);

    /* Test the year */
    if (((year % 4)==0) && ((year % 10)==0))
      { printf("Both Olympics and U.S. Census!"); }
    if ((year % 4)==0)
      { printf("Summer Olympics only"); }
    else
      { if ((year % 10)==0)
          { printf("U.S. Census only"); }
      }
    return;
}
```

2. Now that you know about compound relations, you can write an age-checking program like the one presented in Chapter 9, C9AGE.C. That example ensured the age would be above 10. This is another way you can validate input for reasonableness. The following program includes a logical operator in its if, to see whether the age is greater than 10 and less than 100. If either of these is the case, the program knows that the user did not enter a valid age.

```
/* Filename: C10AGE.C
   Program that helps ensure age values are reasonable */
#include <stdio.h>
main()
{
   int age;
   scanf(" %d", &age);
   printf("What is your age? ");
   if ((age < 10) ¦¦ (age > 100))
     { printf(" \x07 \x07 \n");    /* Beep twice */
       printf("*** The age must be between 10 and 100***\n"); }
   else
     { printf("You entered a valid age."); }
   return;
}
```

3. The following program might be used by a video store to calculate a discount, based on the number of rentals people transact as well as their customer status. Customers are classified either R for *Regular* or S for *Special*. Special customers have been members of the rental club for more than one year. They automatically receive a 50-cent discount on all rentals. The store also holds "value days" several times a year. On value days, all customers get the 50-cent discount. Special customers do not receive an additional 50 cents off during value days, because every day is a discount for them.

The program asks for each customer's status and whether or not it is a value day. It then uses the ¦¦ relation to test for the discount. Even before you started learning C, you would probably have looked at this problem with the following idea in mind.

"If a customer is Special or if it is a value day, deduct 50 cents from the rental."

That's basically the idea of the `if` decision in the following program. Even though Special customers do not get an additional discount on value days, there is one final `if` test for them that prints an extra message at the bottom of the screen's indicated billing.

```
/* Filename: C10VIDEO.C
   Program to compute video rental amounts and gives
   appropriate discounts based on the day or customer status.
*/
#include <stdio.h>
main()
{
    float tape_charge, discount, rental_amt;
    char first_name[15];
    char last_name[15];
    int num_tapes;
    char val_day, sp_stat;

    printf("\n\n *** Video Rental Computation ***\n");
    printf("      -----------\n"); /* Underline title */

    tape_charge = 2.00;     /* The before-discount tape fee per
                                tape */

    /* Get input data */
    printf("\nWhat is customer's first name? ");
    scanf(" %s", first_name);
    printf("What is customer's last name? ");
    scanf(" %s", last_name);

    printf("\nHow many tapes are being rented? ");
    scanf(" %d", &num_tapes);

    printf("Is this a Value day (Y/N)? ");
    scanf(" %c", &val_day);

    printf("Is this a Special Status customer (Y/N)? ");
    scanf(" %c", &sp_stat);
```

```
/* Calculate rental amount */
discount = 0.0;    /* Increase the discount IF they are
                      eligible */
if ((val_day == 'Y') || (sp_stat == 'Y'))
  { discount = 0.5;
    rental_amt = (num_tapes * tape_charge) - (discount *
      num_tapes); }

/* Print the bill */
printf("\n\n** Rental Club **\n\n");
printf("%s %s rented %d tapes\n", first_name, last_name,
    num_tapes);
printf("The total was %.2f\n", rental_amt);
printf("The discount was %.2f per tape\n", discount);

/* Print extra message for Special Status customers */
if (sp_stat == 'Y')
   { printf("\nThank them for being a Special Status
     customer");}
return;
}
```

Figure 10.1 shows the output from a sample run of this program. Notice that Special customers have the extra message at the bottom of the screen. This program, due to its if statements, performs differently depending on the data entered. No discount is applied for Regular customers on nonvalue days.

Logical Operators and Their Precedence

The math precedence order you read about in Chapter 8 did not include the logical operators. To be complete, you should be familiar with the entire order of precedence, as presented in Appendix D. As you can see, the math operators take precedence over the relational operators, and the relational operators take precedence over the logical operators.

```
*** Video Rental Computation ***
---------------------------------

What is customer's first name? Diane
What is customer's last name? Moore

How many tapes are being rented? 3
Is this a Value day (Y/N)? N
Is this a Special Status customer (Y/N)? Y


** Rental Club **

Diane Moore rented 3 tapes
The total was 4.50
The discount was 0.50 per tape

Thank them for being a Special Status customer
```

Figure 10.1. Logical if giving special discounts to certain customers.

You might wonder why the relational and logical operators are included in a precedence table. The following statement helps show you why:

```
if ((sales < min_sal * 2 && yrs_emp > 10 * sub) ...
```

Without the complete order of operators, it would be impossible to determine how such a statement would execute. According to the precedence order, this if statement would execute as follows:

```
if ((sales < (min_sal * 2)) && (yrs_emp > (10 * sub))) ...
```

This still may be confusing, but it is less so. The two multiplications would be performed first, followed by the relations < and >. The && is performed last because it is lowest in the precedence order of operators.

To avoid such ambiguous problems, be sure to use ample parentheses—even if the default precedence order is still your intention. It is also wise to resist combining too many expressions inside a single if relational test.

Notice that ¦¦ (OR) has lower precedence than && (AND). Therefore, the following if tests are equivalent:

```
if ((first_initial == 'A') && (last_initial == 'G') ||
    (id == 321)) ...
if (((first_initial == 'A') && (last_initial == 'G')) ||
    (id == 321)) ...
```

The second is clearer, due to the parentheses, but the precedence table makes them identical.

Review Questions

Answers to review questions are in Appendix B.

1. What are the three logical operators?

2. The following compound relational tests produce True or False comparisons. Determine which are True and which are False.

    a.   ! (True || False)

    b.   (True && False) && (False || True)

    c.   ! (True && False)

    d.   True || (False && False) || False

3. Given the statement

    ```
    int i=12, j=10, k=5;
    ```

    what are the results (True or False) of the following statements? (Hint: Remember that C interprets *any* nonzero statement as True.)

    a.   i && j

    b.   12 - i || k

    c.   j != k && i != k

4. What is the value printed in the following program? (Hint: Don't be misled by the assignment operators on each side of the ||.)

```
/* Filename: C10LOGO.C
   Logical operator test */
#include <stdio.h>
main()
{
   int f, g;

   g = 5;
   f = 8;
   if ((g = 25) || (f = 35))
      { printf("g is %d and f got changed to: %d", g, f); }
   return;
}
```

5. Using the precedence table, determine whether the following statements produce a True or False result. After this, you should *really* appreciate the abundant use of parentheses!

a.   5 == 4 + 1 || 7 * 2 != 12 - 1 && 5 == 8 / 2

b.   8 + 9 <> 6 - 1 || 10 % 2 != 5 + 0

c.   17 - 1 > 15 + 1 && 0 + 2 ! 1 == 1 || 4 != 1

d.   409 * 0 != 1 * 409 + 0 || 1 + 8 * 2 >= 17

6. Does the following `printf()` execute?

```
if (((first intial =='A') && (last initial == 'G')) ||
      (id == 321)))
```

Review Exercises

1. Write a program to determine whether the user enters an odd positive number, by using a single compound `if` statement.

2. Write a program that asks the user for two initials. Print a message telling the user if the first initial falls alphabetically before the second.

3. Write a number-guessing game. Assign a value to a variable called number at the top of the program. Give a prompt that asks for five guesses. Get the user's five guesses with a single scanf(). See whether any of the guesses matches the number and print an appropriate message if one does.

4. Write a tax-calculation routine, as follows: A family pays no tax if its income is less than $5,000. It pays a 10% tax if its income is $5,000 to $9,999 inclusive. It pays a 20% tax if the income is $10,000 to $19,999 inclusive. Otherwise, it pays a 30% tax.

Summary

This chapter extended the if statement to include the &&, ||, and ! logical operators. These operators enable you to combine several relational tests into a single test. C does not always need to look at every relational operator when you combine them in an expression.

This chapter concludes the explanation of the if statement. The next chapter explains the remaining regular C operators. As you saw in this chapter, the precedence table is still very important to the C language. Whenever you are evaluating expressions, keep the precedence table in the back of your mind (or at your fingertips) at all times!

Additional C Operators

C also has several other operators that you should learn. In fact, C has more operators than most programming languages. Unless you become familiar with them, you might think C programs are cryptic and difficult to follow. But C's heavy reliance on its operators, and operator precedence, produces the efficiency that enables your programs to run more smoothly and quickly.

This chapter teaches you the following:

♦ The ?: conditional operator

♦ The ++ increment operator

♦ The -- decrement operator

♦ The sizeof operator

♦ The (,) comma operator

Most of the operators described in this chapter are unlike those found in any other programming language. Even if you have programmed in other languages for many years, you still may be surprised by the power of these C operators.

The Conditional Operator

The conditional operator is a ternary operator.

The *conditional operator* is C's only *ternary* operator, which requires three operands (as opposed to the unary's single and the binary's double operand requirements). The conditional operator is used to replace if-else logic in some situations. The conditional operator is a two-part symbol, ?:, whose format follows:

```
conditional_expression ? expression1 : expression2;
```

The conditional_expression is any expression in C that results in a True (nonzero) or False (zero) answer. If the result of the conditional_expression is True, expression1 executes. Otherwise, if the result of the conditional_expression is False, expression2 executes. Only one of the expressions following the question mark ever executes. Put a single semicolon at the end of expression2. The internal expressions, such as expression1, should not have a semicolon.

Figure 11.1 illustrates the conditional operator a little more clearly.

```
                        If conditional    If conditional
                        expression is     expression is
                            True              False
                          execute           execute
                            this              this
                             ↓                 ↓
     Conditional expression ?  expression1  :  expression2 ;


                        If sales > 8000   If sales are not
     Example:             execute          > 8000 only
                            only            execute
                            this             this
                             ↓                ↓
     (Sales > 8000) ?  Bonus = 500  :  Bonus = ∅ ;
```

Figure 11.1. Format of the conditional operator.

If you require simple if-else logic, the conditional operator usually provides a more direct and succinct method, although you should *always* prefer readability over compact code.

To get a glimpse of the conditional operator at work, consider the section of code that follows.

```
if (a > b)
   { ans = 10; }
else
   { ans = 25; }
```

You can easily rewrite this kind of if-else code by using a single conditional operator.

If the variable a is greater than the variable b, make the variable ans equal to 10; otherwise, make ans equal to 25.

```
a > b ? (ans = 10) : (ans = 25);
```

Although parentheses are not required around the *conditional_expression* to make it work, they usually improve readability. This statement's readability could be improved by using parentheses, as follows:

```
(a > b) ? (ans = 10) : (ans = 25);
```

Because each C expression has a value—in this case, the value being assigned—this statement could be made *even more* succinct, without loss of readability, by assigning ans the answer to the left of the conditional:

```
ans = (a > b) ? (10) : (25);
```

This expression says: If a is greater than b, assign 10 to ans; otherwise, assign 25 to ans. Almost any if-else statement can be rewritten as a conditional, and vice versa. You should practice converting one to the other, in order to acquaint yourself with the conditional operator's purpose.

NOTE: Any valid if C statement can be a *conditional_expression*, including all relational and logical operators as well as any of their possible combinations.

Examples

1. Suppose you are looking over your early C programs, and you notice the following section of code.

```
if (production > target)
   { target *= 1.10; }
else
   { target *= .90; }
```

You realize that such a simple if-else statement can be rewritten, using a conditional operator, and that more efficient code would result. So you could therefore change it to the following single statement.

```
(production > target) ? (target *= 1.10) : (target *= .90);
```

2. Using a conditional operator, you can write a routine to find the minimum value between two variables. This is sometimes called a *minimum routine*. The statement to do this is

```
minimum = (var1 < var2) ? var1 : var2;
```

If var1 is less than var2, the value of var1 is assigned to minimum. If var2 is less, the value of var2 is assigned to minimum. If the variables are equal, the value of var2 is assigned to minimum, because it does not matter which is assigned.

3. A *maximum routine* can be written just as easily:

```
maximum = (var1 > var2) ? var1 : var2;
```

4. Taking the previous examples a step further, you can also test for the sign of a variable. The following conditional expression assigns –1 to the variable called sign if testvar is less than 0; 0 to sign if testvar *is* zero; and +1 to sign if testvar is 1 or more.

```
sign = (testvar < 0) ? -1 : (testvar > 0);
```

It may be easy to spot why the less-than test results in a –1, but the second part of the expression might be confusing. This works well because of C's 1 and 0 (for True and False, respectively) return values from a relational test. If testvar is 0 or greater, sign is assigned the answer of (testvar > 0). The value of (testvar > 0) is 1 if True (therefore, testvar is more than 0) or 0 if testvar is equal to 0.

The preceding statement shows C's efficient conditional operator very well. It may also help you to write this using typical if-else logic. Here is the same problem written with a typical if-else statement:

```
if (testvar < 0)
    { sign = -1; }
else
    { sign = (testvar > 0); }   /* testvar can only be
                                   0 or more here */
```

The Increment and Decrement Operators

The ++ operator adds 1 to a variable. The -- operator subtracts 1 from a variable.

C offers two unique operators that add or subtract 1 to or from variables. These are the *increment* and *decrement* operators, ++ and --. Table 11.1 shows how these operators relate to other types of expressions you have seen. Notice that the ++ and -- can go on either side of the modified variable. If the ++ or -- appears on the left, it is known as a *prefix* operator. If it appears on the right, it is a *postfix* operator.

Table 11.1. The ++ and -- operators.

Operator	Example	Description	Equivalent	Statements
++	i++;	postfix	i = i + 1;	i += 1;
++	++i;	prefix	i = i + 1;	i += 1;
--	i--;	postfix	i = i - 1;	i -= 1;
--	--i;	prefix	i = i - 1;	i -= 1;

Any time you need to add 1 to a variable, or subtract 1 from a variable, you can use these two operators. As Table 11.1 shows, if you need to increment or decrement only a single variable, these operators enable you to do so.

Increment and Decrement Efficiency

The increment and decrement operators are straightforward, efficient methods for adding 1 to a variable and subtracting 1 from a variable. You often need to do this during counting or processing loops, as shown in Part 3 of this book.

These two operators compile directly into their assembly language equivalents. Almost all computers include, at their lowest binary machine-language commands, increment and decrement instructions. If you use C's increment and decrement operators, you ensure that they compile down into these low-level equivalents.

If, however, you *code* expressions to add or subtract 1 (as you would do in other programming languages), such as the expression i = i - 1, you *do not* actually ensure that C compiles this instruction into its efficient machine-language equivalent.

Whether you use prefix or postfix does not matter—if you are incrementing or decrementing single variables on lines by themselves. However, when you combine these two operators with other operators in a single expression, you must be aware of their differences. Consider the following program section. Here, all variables are integers because the increment and decrement operators work only on integer variables.

Make a equal to 6. Increment a, then subtract 1 from it, then assign the result to b.

```
a = 6;
b = ++a - 1;
```

What are the values of a and b after these two statements finish? The value of a is easy to determine: it is incremented in the second statement, and so it is 7. However, b is either 5 or 6 depending upon *when* the variable a increments. To determine when a increments, consider the following rule:

◆ If a variable is incremented or decremented with a *prefix* operator, the increment or decrement occurs *before* the variable's value is used in the rest of the expression.

♦ If a variable is incremented or decremented with a *postfix* operator, the increment or decrement occurs *after* the variable's value is used in the rest of the expression.

In the previous code, a contains a prefix increment. Therefore, its value is first incremented to 7, then 1 is subtracted from 7, and the result (6) is assigned to b. But if a postfix increment is used, as in

```
a = 6;
b = a++ - 1;
```

a is 6, therefore, 5 is assigned to b because a does not increment to 7 until after its value is used in the expression. The precedence table in Appendix D shows that prefix operators contain much higher precedence than almost every other operator, especially low-precedence postfix increments and decrements.

TIP: If the order of prefix and postfix confuses you, break your expressions into two lines of code, putting the increment or decrement before or after the expression that uses it.

By taking advantage of this tip, you can now rewrite the previous example as follows:

```
a = 6;
b = a - 1;
a++;
```

There is now no doubt as to when a gets incremented: a increments after b is assigned to a-1.

Even parentheses cannot override the postfix rule. Consider the following statement.

```
x = p + (((amt++)));
```

There are too many unneeded parentheses here, but even the redundant parentheses are not enough to increment amt before adding its value to p. Postfix increments and decrements *always* occur after their variables are used in the surrounding expression.

> **CAUTION:** Do not attempt to increment or decrement an expression. You can apply these operators only to variables. The following expression is *invalid*:
>
> ```
> sales = ++(rate * hours);   /* Not allowed! */
> ```

Examples

1. As you should with all other C operators, keep the precedence table in mind when you evaluate expressions that increment and decrement. Figures 11.2 and 11.3 show you some examples that illustrate these operators.

```
int i=1;
int j=2;
int k=3;
ans = i++ * j - --k;
```

```
          i++ * j -  2

                2   -  2

                    0
```

ans = 0, then i increments by 1 to its final value of 2.

```
int i=1;
int j=2;
int k=3;
ans = ++i * j - k--;
```

```
           2  * j - k--

              4    - k--

                 1
```

ans = 1, then k decrements by 1 to its final value of 2.

Figure 11.2. C operators incrementing (above) and decrementing (below) by order of precedence.

2. The precedence table takes on even more meaning when you see a section of code such as that shown in Figure 11.3.

```
int i=0;
int j=-1;
int k=0;
int m=1;
ans = i++ && ++j || k || m++;
           |
    i++ &&  0  || k || m++

             0     || k || m++

                 0      || m++

                     1
```

`ans = 1`, then `i` increments by 1 to its final value of 1, and `m` increments by 1 to its final value of 2.

Figure 11.3. Another example of C operators and their precedence.

3. Considering the precedence table—and, more importantly, what you know about C's relational efficiencies—what is the value of the `ans` in the following section of code?

```
int i=1, j=20, k=-1, l=0, m=1, n=0, o=2, p=1;
ans = i || j-- && k++ || ++l && ++m || n-- & !o || p--;
```

This, at first, seems to be extremely complicated. Nevertheless, you can simply glance at it and determine the value of `ans`, as well as the ending value of the rest of the variables.

Recall that when C performs a relation `||` (or), it ignores the right side of the `||` if the left value is True (any nonzero value is True). Because True or any other value is still True, C does not "think" it needs to look at the values on the right. Therefore, C performs this expression as shown:

```
ans = i || j-- && k++ || ++l && ++m || n-- & !o || p--;
       |
       1 (TRUE)
```

> **NOTE:** Because i is True, C "knows" the entire expression is True and ignores the rest of it after the first ||. Therefore, *every other increment and decrement expression is ignored.* The result is that only ans is changed by this expression; the rest of the variables, j through p, are never incremented or decremented, even though several of them contain increment and decrement operators. If you use relational operators, be aware of this problem and break out all increment and decrement operators into statements by themselves, placing them on lines before the relational statements that use their values.

The sizeof Operator

There is another operator in C that does not look like an operator at all. It looks like a built-in function, but it is called the sizeof operator. In fact, if you think of sizeof as a function call, you may not get too confused because it works in a very similar way. The format of sizeof is follows:

Determine size of data

```
sizeof data
```

or

```
sizeof(data type)
```

The sizeof operator is unary, because it operates on a single value. This operator produces a result that represents the size, in bytes, of the *data* or *data type* specified. Because most data types and variables require different amounts of internal storage on different computers, the sizeof operator is provided to enable programs to maintain consistency on different types of computers.

> **TIP:** Most C programmers use parentheses around the sizeof argument, whether that argument is *data* or *data type*. Because you *must* use parentheses around *data type* arguments and you *can* use them around *data* arguments, it doesn't hurt you to always use them for both kinds of arguments.

The sizeof operator returns its argument's size in bytes.

The sizeof operator is sometimes called a *compile-time operator*. At compile-time, instead of run-time, the compiler replaces each occurrence of sizeof in your program with an unsigned integer value. But because sizeof is used more in advanced C programming, this operator is better utilized later in the book for performing more advanced programming requirements.

If you use an array as the sizeof argument, C returns the number of bytes you originally reserved for that array. Data inside the array have nothing to do with its returned sizeof value—even if it's only a character array containing a very short string.

Example

Suppose you want to know the size, in bytes, of floating-point variables for your computer. You can determine this by putting the keyword float in parentheses—after sizeof—as shown in the following program.

```
/* Filename: C11SIZE1.C
   Prints the size of floating-point values */
#include <stdio.h>
main()
{
   printf("The size of floating-point variables \n");
   printf("on this computer is %d ", (int) sizeof(float));
   return;
}
```

This program may produce different results on different computers. You can use any valid data type as the sizeof argument. When you directly print sizeof results, as shown here, you should type cast sizeof to an integer in order to print it properly with %d. On PCs, this program very probably produces this output:

```
The size of floating-point variables on this computer is: 4
```

The Comma Operator

Another C operator, sometimes called a *sequence point*, works a little differently. This is the *comma operator (,)*, which does not directly operate on data, but produces a left-to-right evaluation of expressions. This operator enables you to put more than one expression on a single line by separating each one with a comma.

Already you have seen one use of the sequence point comma when you learned how to declare and initialize variables. In the following section of code, the comma separates statements. Because the comma associates from left to right, the first variable, i, is declared and initialized before the second variable.

```
main()
{
   int i=10, j=25;
   /* Rest of program follows */
```

However, the comma is *not* a sequence point when it is used inside function parentheses. Then it is said to *separate* arguments, but it is not a sequence point. Consider the printf() that follows.

```
printf("%d %d %d", i, i++, ++i);
```

You may get one of many results from such a statement. The commas serve only to separate arguments of the printf(), and do not generate the left-to-right sequence that they would otherwise when they aren't used in functions. With the statement shown here, you are not ensured of *any* order! The postfix i++ might possibly be performed before the prefix ++i, even though the precedence table does not explain this. Here, the order of evaluation depends on how your compiler sends these arguments to the printf() function.

> **TIP:** Do not put increment operators or decrement operators in function calls.

Examples

1. You can put more than one expression on a line, using the comma as a sequence point. The following program does this.

```
/* Filename: C11COM1.C
   Illustrates the sequence point */
#include <stdio.h>
main()
{
   int num, sq, cube;
   num = 5;

   /* Calculate the square and cube of the number */
   sq = (num * num), cube = (num * num * num);

   printf("The square of %d is %d, and the cube is %d",
          num, sq, cube);
   return;
}
```

This is not necessarily recommended, however, because it doesn't add anything to the program and actually decreases its readability. In this example, the square and cube are probably better computed on two separate lines.

2. The comma enables some interesting statements. Consider the following section of code.

```
i = 10
j = (i = 12, i + 8);
```

When this code finishes executing, j has the value of 20—even though this is not necessarily clear. In the first statement, i is assigned 10. In the second statement, the comma causes i to be assigned a value of 12, then j is assigned the value of i + 8, or 20.

3. In the following section of code, ans is assigned the value of 12, because the assignment *before* the comma is performed first. Despite this right-to-left associativity of the assignment operator, the comma's sequence point lastly forces the assignment of 12 into x, before x is assigned to ans.

```
ans = (y = 8, x = 12);
```

When this finishes, y contains 8, x contains 12, and ans also contains 12.

Review Questions

Answers to review questions are in Appendix B.

1. What set of statements does the conditional operator replace?

2. Why is the conditional operator called a "ternary" operator?

3. Rewrite the following conditional operator as an if-else statement.

```
ans = (a == b) ? c + 2 : c + 3;
```

4. True or false: The following statements produce the same result.

```
var++;
```

and

```
var = var + 1;
```

5. Why is using the increment and decrement operators more efficient than using the addition and subtraction operators?

6. What is a sequence point?

7. Can the output of the following code section be determined?

```
age = 20;
printf("You are now %d, and will be %d in one year",
        age, age++);
```

8. What is the output of the following program section?

```
char name[20] = "Mike";
printf("The size of name is %d", (int) sizeof(name) );
```

Review Exercises

1. Write a program that prints the numerals from 1 to 10. Use ten different printf()s and only one variable called result to hold the value before each printf(). Use the increment operator to add one to result before each printf().

2. Write a program that asks users for their ages. Using a single printf() that includes a conditional operator, print on-screen the following if the input age is over 21,

   You are not a minor.

   or print this otherwise:

   You are still a minor.

   This printf() may be long, but it helps to illustrate how the conditional operator can work within other statements where if-else logic might not.

3. Use the conditional operator—and *no* if-else statements—to write the following tax-calculation routine: A family pays no tax if its annual salary is less than $5,000. It pays a 10% tax if the salary range begins at $5,000 and ends at $9,999. It pays a 20% tax if the salary range begins at $10,000 and ends at $19,999. Otherwise, the family pays a 30% tax. This is similar to an exercise in Chapter 10, except for the conditional operator.

Summary

Now you have learned almost every operator in the C language. As explained in this chapter, conditional, increment, and decrement are three operators that enable C to stand apart from many other programming languages. You must always be aware of the precedence table whenever you use these, as you must with *all* operators.

The `sizeof` and sequence point operators act unlike most others. The `sizeof` is a compile operator, and it works in a manner similar to the `#define` preprocessor directive in being replaced by its value at compile-time. The sequence point enables you to put multiple statements on the same line—or within a single expression—but you should reserve it only for declaring variables because it may be unclear if it is combined with other expressions.

The next chapter teaches the bitwise operators. They operate on a very low binary level on your computer's variables. Some people have programmed in C for years but have not yet learned the bitwise operators. If you are just learning C, and are not interested in doing bit-level operations, you may want to skim the next chapter and come back to it later when you need these types of operators.

Bitwise Operators

This chapter introduces the *bitwise operators*, which manipulate internal representations of data and not just "values in variables" as the other operators do. These bitwise operators require an understanding of Appendix A's binary numbering system, as well as a computer's memory. If you don't think you're ready to tackle these operators right now, of course, you could always *skim* this chapter and come back to it later.

Some people program in C for years and never learn the bitwise operators. Nevertheless, understanding them can help you improve a program's efficiency and enable you to operate at a deeper level than many other programming languages allow.

This chapter introduces you to the following bitwise operators:

♦ Logical operators

♦ Compound operators

♦ Shift operators

This chapter concludes the discussion on C operators for a while. After you master the bitwise operators, you can perform almost any possible operation on your C variables and constants.

Bitwise Logical Operators

There are four bitwise logical operators, and they are shown in Table 12.1. These operators work on the binary representations of integer data. This enables systems programmers to manipulate internal bits in memory and in variables. The bitwise operators are not just for systems programmers, however. Application programmers also can improve their programs' efficiency in several ways.

Table 12.1. Bitwise logical operators.

Operator	Meaning
&	Bitwise AND
¦	Bitwise inclusive OR
^	Bitwise exclusive OR
~	Bitwise one's complement

Bitwise operators make bit-by-bit comparisons of internal data.

Each of the bitwise operators makes a bit-by-bit comparison of internal data. Bitwise operators apply only to character and integer variables and constants, and not to floating-point data. Because binary numbers consist of 1s and 0s, these 1s and 0s (called *bits*) are compared to each other in order to produce the desired result for each bitwise operator.

Before you study the examples, you should understand Table 12.2. It contains truth tables that describe the action of each bitwise operator upon integer—or character—internal bit patterns.

In bitwise truth tables, you can replace the 1 and 0 with True and False, respectively, if it helps you to understand the result better. For the bitwise AND (&) truth table, both bits being compared by the & operator must be True for the result to be True. In other words, "True AND True results in True."

TIP: By replacing the 1s and 0s with True and False, you might be able to relate the bitwise operators to the regular logical operators, && and ¦¦, that you use for if comparisons.

Table 12.2. Truth tables.

Bitwise AND (&)

```
0 & 0 = 0

0 & 1 = 0

1 & 0 = 0

1 & 1 = 1
```

Bitwise inclusive OR (|)

```
0 | 0 = 0

0 | 1 = 1

1 | 0 = 1

1 | 1 = 1
```

Bitwise exclusive OR (^)

```
0 ^ 0 = 0

0 ^ 1 = 1

1 ^ 0 = 1

1 ^ 1 = 0
```

Bitwise one's complement (~)

```
~0 = 1

~1 = 0
```

The | bitwise operator is sometimes called the *bitwise inclusive OR* operator. If one side of the | operator is 1 (True)—or if both sides are 1—the result is 1 (True).

For bitwise ^, one side or the other—but not both—must be 1.

The ^ operator is called *bitwise exclusive OR*. It means that either side of the ^ operator must be 1 (True) for the result to be 1 (True), but both sides cannot be 1 (True) at the same time.

The ~ operator, called *bitwise one's complement*, reverses each bit to its opposite value.

> **NOTE:** Bitwise 1's complement does *not* negate a number. As Appendix A shows, most computers use a 2's complement to negate numbers. The bitwise 1's complement reverses the bit pattern of numbers, but it doesn't add the additional 1 as the 2's complement requires.

You can test and change individual bits inside variables in order to check for patterns of data. The following examples help to illustrate each of the four bitwise operators.

Examples

1. If you apply the bitwise & operator to numerals 9 and 14, you get a result of 8. Figure 12.1 shows you why this is so. When the binary values of 9 (1001) and 14 (1110) are compared on a bitwise & basis, the resulting bit pattern is 8 (1000).

```
    1   0   0   1   (9)
    ↓   ↓   ↓   ↓
    &   &   &   &
    1   1   1   0   (14)
  ─────────────────
  = 1   0   0   0   (8)
```

Figure 12.1. Performing bitwise & on 9 and 14.

In a C program, you could code this bitwise comparison as follows.

Make `result` *equal to the binary value of 9 (1001) ANDed to the binary value of 14 (1110).*

```
result = 9 & 14;
```

The `result` variable holds 8, which is the result of the bitwise &. The 9 or 14 (or both) could also be stored in variables, with the same results.

2. When you apply the bitwise ¦ operator to the numbers 9 and 14, you get 15. When the binary values of 9 (1001) and 14 (1110) are compared on a bitwise ¦ basis, the resulting bit pattern is 15 (1111) because result's bits are 1 (True) in every position where a bit is 1 in either of the two numbers.

   In a C program, you could code this bitwise comparison as follows:

   ```
   result = 9 ¦ 14;
   ```

   The result variable holds 15, which is the result of the bitwise ¦. The 9 or 14 (or both) could also be stored in variables.

3. The bitwise ^ applied to 9 and 14 produces 7. Bitwise ^ sets the resulting bits to 1 if one number or the other's bit is 1, but not if both of the matching bits are on at the same time.

   In a C program, you could code this bitwise comparison as follows:

   ```
   result = 9 ^ 14;
   ```

   The result variable holds 7 (binary 0111), which is the result of the bitwise ^. The 9 (binary 1001) or 14 (binary 1110)—or both—could also be stored in variables with the same result.

4. The bitwise ~ simply negates each bit. It is a unary bitwise operator because you can apply it to only a single value at any one time. The bitwise ~ applied to 9 results in 6, as shown in Figure 12.2.

```
~ 1  0  0  1   (9)
─────────────
= 0  1  1  0   (6)
```

Figure 12.2. Performing bitwise ~ on the number 9.

In a C program, you could code this bitwise operation like this:

```
result = ~9;
```

The result variable holds 6, which is the result of the bitwise ~. The 9 could have been stored in a variable with the same result.

5. You can take advantage of the bitwise operators to perform tests on data that you could not do as efficiently in other ways.

For example, suppose you want to know if the user typed an odd or even number (assuming integers are being input). You could use the modulus operator (%) to see if the remainder—after dividing the input value by 2—is 0 or 1. If the remainder is 0, the number is even. If the remainder is 1, the number is odd.

The bitwise operators are more efficient than other operators because they directly compare bit patterns without using any mathematical operations. Because a number is even if its bit pattern ends in a 0 and odd if its bit pattern ends in 1, you also can test for odd or even numbers by applying the bitwise & to the data and to a binary 1. This is more efficient than using the modulus operator. The following program informs users if their input value is odd or even, by using this technique.

Identify the file and include the necessary header file. This program will test for odd or even input. We need a place to put the user's number, so declare the input variable as an integer.

Ask the user for the number to be tested. Put the user's answer in input. Use the bitwise operator, &, to test the number. If the rightmost bit in input is 1, tell the user that the number is odd. If the rightmost bit in input is 0, tell the user that the the number is even.

Test if odd or even

```
/* Filename: C12ODEV.C
   Uses a bitwise & to see if a number is odd or even */
#include <stdio.h>
main()
{
   int input;                    /* Will hold user's number */
   printf("What number do you want me to test? ");
   scanf(" %d", &input);

   if (input & 1)                /* True if result is 1;
                                     otherwise it is false (0) */
```

```
        { printf("The number %d is odd", input); }
    else
        { printf("The number %d is even", input); }
    return;
}
```

6. The only difference between the bit patterns for uppercase and lowercase characters is bit number 6 (the third bit from the left, as shown in Appendix A). For lowercase letters, bit 5 is a 1. For uppercase letters, bit 5 is a 0. Figure 12.3 shows how *A* and *B* differ from *a* and *b* by a single bit.

```
                    ASCII  A  is  01000001   (hex 41, decimal 65)
                    ASCII  a  is  01100001   (hex 61, decimal 97)
Only bit 6 is different ────────────────┘

                    ASCII  B  is  01000010   (hex 42, decimal 66)
                    ASCII  b  is  01100010   (hex 62, decimal 98)
Only bit 6 is different ────────────────┘
```

Figure 12.3. Bitwise difference between two uppercase and lowercase ASCII letters.

To convert a character to uppercase, you have to turn off (change to a 0) bit number 5. You can apply a bitwise & to the input character and 223 (which is 11011111 in binary) to turn off bit 5 and convert any input character to its upper-case equivalent. If the number is already in uppercase, this bitwise & does not change it.

The 223 (binary 11011111) is called a *bit mask* because it acts to mask off (just as masking tape masks off areas to be painted) bit 5 so it becomes 0, if it is not already. The following program does this to ensure that users typed uppercase characters when asked for their initials.

Print initials

```
/* Filename: C12UPC61.C
   Converts the input characters to uppercase
   if they aren't already */
#include <stdio.h>
main()
```

```
{
      char first, middle, last;    /* Will hold user's initials */
      int bitmask=223;                    /* 11011111 in binary */

      printf("What is your first initial? ");
      scanf(" %c", &first);
      printf("What is your middle initial? ");
      scanf(" %c", &middle);
      printf("What is your last initial? ");
      scanf(" %c", &last);

      /* Ensure that initials are in uppercase */
      first = first & bitmask;          /* Turn off bit 5 if */
      middle = middle & bitmask;        /* it is not already */
      last = last & bitmask;            /* turned off        */

      printf("Your initials are: %c %c %c", first, middle, last);
      return;
}
```

The next example shows what happens when two of the initials are typed with lowercase letters. The program converts them to uppercase before printing them again. Although there are other ways to convert to lowercase, none are as efficient as using the & bitwise operator.

```
What is your first initial? g
What is your middle initial? M
What is your last initial? p
Your initials are: G M P
```

Bitwise Compound Operators

As with most of the mathematical operators, you can combine the bitwise operators with the equal sign (=) to form *compound bitwise operators*. When you want to update the value of a variable, using a bitwise operator, you can shorten the expression by using the compound bitwise operators shown in Table 12.3.

Table 12.3. Compound bitwise operators.

Operator	Description
&=	Compound bitwise AND assignment
|=	Compound bitwise inclusive OR assignment
^=	Compound bitwise exclusive OR assignment

The previous example that converted initials to their upper-case equivalents could be rewritten using compound bitwise & operations as shown here:

```
/* Filename: C12UPCS2.C
   Converts the input characters to uppercase
   if they aren't already */
#include <stdio.h>
main()
{
    char first, middle, last;    /* Will hold user's initials */
    int bitmask=223;                    /* 11011111 in binary */

    printf("What is your first initial? ");
    scanf(" %c", &first);
    printf("What is your middle initial? ");
    scanf(" %c", &middle);
    printf("What is your last initial? ");
    scanf(" %c", &last);

    /* Use compound bitwise operators to ensure
       that initials are in uppercase */
    first &= bitmask;                   /* Turn off bit 5 if */
    middle &= bitmask;                  /* it is not already */
    last &= bitmask;                    /* turned off        */

    printf("Your initials are: %o %o %c", first, middle, last);
    return;
}
```

Bitwise Shift Operators

The bitwise shift operators are shown in Table 12.4. They shift bits inside a number left or right. The number of bits shifted depends on the value to the right of the bitwise shift operators.

Table 12.4. Bitwise shift operators.

Operator	Description
<<	Bitwise left-shift
>>	Bitwise right-shift

The format of the bitwise shift operators follows:

```
value << numberOfBits
value >> numberOfBits
```

The *value* can be an integer or character variable or constant. The *numberOfBits* determines how many bits are shifted. Figure 12.4 shows what happens when the number 29 (binary 00011101) is left-shifted 3 bits with the bitwise left-shift (<<). Notice that each bit "shifts over" to the left 3 times, and 0s fill in from the right. If this were a bitwise right-shift (>>), the 0s would fill in from the left as the rest of the bits are shifted down 3 times.

Figure 12.4. Shifting the bits in binary 29 to the left.

CAUTION: The results of bitwise shift operators are not consistent when applied to signed values. On many machines the sign bit *propagates* with each shift. That is, for every shift position, the sign bit shifts, but the original sign is retained as well. The end result is that negative numbers fill from the left with 1s, and not with 0s, when a bitwise right-shift is applied to them.

Examples

1. The following program takes two values and shifts them three bits to the left and then three bits to the right. This illustrates how to code the bitwise left-shift and right-shift operators.

```
/* Filename: C12SHFT1.C
   Demonstrates bitwise left and right shift operators */
#include <stdio.h>
main()
{
   int num1=25;                          /* 00011001 binary */
   int num2=102;                         /* 01100110 binary */
   int shift1, shift2;        /* Will hold shifted numbers */

   shift1 = num1 << 3;                  /* Bitwise left shift */
   printf("25 shifted left 3 times is %d \n", shift1);
   shift2 = num2 << 3;                  /* Bitwise left shift */
   printf("102 shifted left 3 times is %d \n", shift2);

   shift1 = num1 >> 3;                  /* Bitwise right shift */
   printf("25 shifted right 3 times is %d \n", shift1);
   shift2 = num2 >> 3;                  /* Bitwise right shift */
   printf("102 shifted right 3 times is %d \n", shift2);

   return;
}
```

The output from this program follows. You may get different results, depending upon your computer's architecture.

```
25 shifted left 3 times is 200
102 shifted left 3 times is 816
25 shifted right 3 times is 3
102 shifted right 3 times is 12
```

2. There is a useful feature of bitwise shifting. If you bitwise left-shift a numeral by a certain number of bit positions, the result is the same as multiplying that number by a power of two. In other words, 15 left-shifted four times results in the same value as 15 times 2^4, or 15 times 16, which equals 240.

If you bitwise right-shift a numeral by a certain number of bit positions, the result is the same as dividing that number by a power of two. In other words, 64 right-shifted two times results in the same value as 64 divided by 2^2, or 64 divided by 4, which equals 16.

If you need to multiply or divide a variable by a power of two, you can do it much faster simply by shifting the number. The following program illustrates this.

```
/* Filename: C12SHFT2.C
   Demonstrates multiplication and division
   by bitwise shifting */
#include <stdio.h>
main()
{
    int num1 = 15;                    /* Numbers to be shifted */
    int num2 = 64;
    int shift1, shift2;

    shift1 = num1 << 4;              /* Multiply num1 by 16 */
    shift2 = num2 >> 2;                /* Divide num2 by 4 */

    printf("15 multiplied by 16 is %d \n", shift1);
    printf("64 divided by 4 is %d \n", shift2);
    return;
}
```

Review Questions

Answers to review questions are in Appendix B.

1. What are the four bitwise logical operators, the three compound bitwise logical operators, and the two bitwise shift operators?

2. What is the result of each of the following bitwise True-False expressions?

   a.   1 ^ 0 & 1 & 1 | 0

   b.   1 & 1 & 1 & 1

c.   1 ^ 1 ^ 1 ^ 1

    d.   ~(1 ^ 0)

3. True or false: 7 (binary 111) can be used as a bitmask to test whether the rightmost three bits in a variable are 1s.

4. What is the difference between the bitwise ~ (1's complement) and 2's complement?

Review Exercises

1. Write a program that converts an entered uppercase letter to a lowercase letter by applying a bitmask and one of the bitwise logical operators. If the character is already in lowercase, do not change it.

2. Write a program that asks users for a number. Multiply that number by every power of 2, from 2^1 to 2^7; and then divide that number by every power of 2, from 2^1 to 2^7. Use only shift operators, no math operators!

Summary

The bitwise operators are not often used in application programs because they work at the bit level. You must be comfortable with the binary numbering system before you can fully understand their operations. However, they offer a very efficient method for changing individual bits, or groups of bits, within variables. By using them, you can test for odd and even numbers, multiply and divide by powers of two, and perform other tasks that you normally would use less-efficient operators and commands to do.

Bitwise operators, despite their efficiency, do not always lend themselves to readable code. Generally, most people reserve bitwise operators for systems-level programming, while using the easier-to-read higher-level operators for data processing.

Part III

C Constructs

The while Loop

The repetitive capabilities of computers make them good tools for processing large amounts of information. The following few chapters introduce you to C constructs, which are the control and looping commands of programming languages. C constructs include powerful, but succinct and efficient, looping commands similar to those of other languages you may already know.

The while loops enable your programs to repeat a series of statements, over and over, as long as a certain condition is always met. Computers do not get "bored" while performing the same tasks repeatedly. This is one reason why they are so important in business data processing.

This chapter teaches you the following:

♦ The while statement

♦ The concept of loops

♦ The do-while loop

♦ Differences between if and while loops

♦ The exit() function

♦ The break statement

♦ Counters and totals

After completing this chapter, you should know the first of several methods C makes available for repeating program sections. This chapter's discussion of loops includes one of the most important uses for looping: creating counter and total variables.

The while Statement

The while statement is one of several C *construct statements*. Each construct (from *construction*) is a programming language statement—or a series of statements—that controls looping. The while, like other such statements, is a *looping statement* that controls the execution of a series of other statements. Looping statements cause parts of a program to execute repeatedly, as long as a certain condition is being met.

The format of the while statement is

```
while (test expression)
   { block of one or more C statements; }
```

While
True

Execute
C statements

The parentheses around *test expression* are required. As long as the *test expression* is True (nonzero), the *block* of one or more C statements executes, repeatedly, until the *test expression* becomes False (evaluates to zero). Braces are required before and after the body of the while loop, unless you want to execute only one statement. Each statement in the body of the while loop requires a semicolon at the end.

The *test expression* usually contains relational, and possibly logical, operators. These operators provide the True-False condition checked in the *test expression*. If the *test expression* is False when the program reaches the while loop for the first time, the body of the while loop does not execute at all. Regardless of whether the body of the while loop executes no times, one time, or many times, the statements following the while loop's closing brace execute if and when the *test expression* becomes False.

The body of a
while loop
executes repeatedly
as long as the *test expression* is
True.

Because the *test expression* determines when the loop finishes, the body of the while loop *must* change the variables used in the *test expression*. Otherwise, the *test expression* never changes and the while loop repeats forever. This is known as an *infinite loop*, and you should avoid it.

> **TIP:** If the body of the while loop contains only one statement, the braces surrounding it are not required. It is a good habit to enclose all while loop statements in braces, however, because if you must add more statements to the body of the while loop later, your braces are already there.

The Concept of Loops

You use the loop concept in everyday life. Any time you need to repeat the same procedure, you are performing a loop—just as your computer does with the while construct. Suppose you are wrapping holiday gifts. The following statements represent the looping steps (in while format) that you go through while gift-wrapping:

while (there are still unwrapped gifts)
  { Get the next gift;
      Cut the wrapping paper;
      Wrap the gift;
      Put a bow on the gift;
      Fill out a name card for the gift;
      Put the wrapped gift with the others; }

Whether you have 3, 15, or 100 gifts to wrap, you would go through this procedure (loop) repeatedly until every gift is wrapped. For an example that might be more easily computerized, suppose you want to total all the checks you wrote last month. You could perform the following loop.

while (there are still checks from the last month to be totaled)
  { Add the amount of the next check to the total; }

The body of this pseudocode while loop has only one statement, but that single statement must be performed until you have added each one of last month's checks. When this loop ends (that is, when no more checks from last month remain to be totaled), you have the total you want.

The body of a while loop can contain one or more C statements, including additional while loops. Your programs will be more readable if you indent the body of a while loop a few spaces to the right. The following examples illustrate this.

Examples

1. Some programs presented earlier in the book require user input with scanf(). If users do not enter appropriate values, these programs display an error message and ask the user to enter another value.

   This is fine, but now that you understand the while loop construct, you should put the error message inside a loop. In this way, users see the message continually until they type proper input values, rather than once.

   The following program is short, but it demonstrates a while loop being used to ensure valid user keyboard input. It asks users if they want to continue. You might want to incorporate this program into a larger one that requires user permission to continue. Put a prompt, such as the one presented here, at the bottom of a screen full of text. The text remains on-screen until the user tells the program to continue executing.

   Identify the file and include the necessary header file. In this program, we want to ensure that the user enters Y or N.
   We need to store the user's answer, so declare the ans variable as a character. Ask the user if they want to continue, and the response. If the user doesn't type Y or N, ask the user for another response.

```
/* Filename: C13WHIL1.C
   Input routine to ensure that user types a
   correct response. This routine might be part
   of a larger program. */
#include <stdio.h>
main()
{
    char ans;
```

Keep asking
while answer
is not yes

```
    printf("Do you want to continue (Y/N)? ");
    scanf(" %c", &ans);                      /* Get user's answer */

    while ((ans != 'Y') && (ans != 'N'))
       { printf("\nYou must type a Y or an N\n");   /* Warn
                                                      and ask */
          printf("Do you want to continue (Y/N)?"); /* again */
          scanf(" %c", &ans); }            /* Body of while loop
                                              ends here */

    return;
}
```

Notice that the two scanf() functions do the same thing. An initial scanf(), outside the while loop, must be done to get an answer that the while loop can check. If users type something other than Y or N, the program prints an error message, asks for another answer, then loops back to check the answer again. This is a more preferred method of data-entry validation than giving users only one additional chance to get it right.

The while loop tests the test expression at the top of the loop. This is why the loop may never execute. If the test is initially False, the loop does not execute even once. The output from this program is shown as follows. The program repeats indefinitely, until the relational test is True (that is, as soon as the user types either Y or N).

```
Do you want to continue (Y/N)? k

You must type a Y or an N
Do you want to continue (Y/N)? c

You must type a Y or an N
Do you want to continue (Y/N)? o

You must type a Y or an N
Do you want to continue (Y/N)? 5
```

```
You must type a Y or an N
Do you want to continue (Y/N)? Y
```

2. The following program is an example of an *invalid* while loop. See if you can find the problem.

```c
/* Filename: C13WHBAD.C
   Bad use of a while loop */
#include <stdio.h>
main()
{
   int a=10, b=20;
   while (a > 5)
      { printf("a is %d, and b is %d \n", a, b);
        b = 20 + a; }
   return;
}
```

This while loop is an example of an infinite loop. It is vital that at least one statement inside the while changes a variable in the test expression (in this example, the variable a); otherwise, the condition is always True. Because the variable a does not change inside the while loop, this program will never end without the user's intervention.

TIP: If you inadvertently write an infinite loop, you must stop the program yourself. If you use a PC, this typically means pressing Ctrl-Break. If you are using a UNIX-based system, your system administrator may have to stop your program's execution.

3. The following program asks users for a first name, then uses a while loop to count the number of characters in the name. This is a *string length program*; that is, it counts characters until it reaches the null zero. Remember that the length of a string is equal to the number of characters in the string up to—but not including—the null zero.

```
/* Filename: C13WHIL2.C
   Counts the number of letters in the user's first name */
#include <stdio.h>
main()
{
   char name[15];           /* Will hold user's first name */
   int count=0;       /* Will hold total characters in name */

   /* Get the user's first name */
   printf("What is your first name? ");
   scanf(" %s", name);

   while (name[count] > 0) /* Loop until null zero reached */
      { count++; }                   /* Add 1 to the count */

   printf("Your name has %d characters", count);
   return;
}
```

The loop continues as long as the value of the next character in the name array is more than zero. Because the last character in the array is a null zero, the test is False on the name's last character and the statement following the body of the loop continues.

NOTE: A built-in string function called strlen() determines the length of strings. You learn about this function in Chapter 22, "Character, String, and Numeric Functions."

4. The previous string length program's while loop is not as efficient as it could be. Because a while loop fails when its test expression is zero, there is no need for the greater-than test. By changing the test expression as the following program shows, you can improve the efficiency of the string length count.

```
/* Filename: C13WHIL3.C
   Counts the number of letters in the user's first name */
#include <stdio.h>
```

```
main()
{
    char name[15];           /* Will hold user's first name */
    int count=0;        /* Will hold total characters in name */

    /* Get the user's first name */
    printf("What is your first name? ");
    scanf(" %s", name);

    while (name[count])  /* Loop until null zero is reached */
        {  count++; }                    /* Add 1 to the count */

    printf("Your name has %d characters", count);
    return;
}
```

The do-while Loop

The body of the do-while executes at least once.

The do-while statement controls the do-while loop, which is similar to the while loop except the relational test occurs at the *bottom* (rather than top) of the loop. This ensures that the body of the loop executes at least once. The do-while tests for a positive relational test; that is, as long as the test is True, the body of the loop continues to execute.

The format of the do-while is

```
do
    { block of one or more C statements; }
while (test expression)
```

The test expression must be enclosed within parentheses, just as it does with a while statement.

Examples

1. The following program is just like the first one you saw with the while loop (C13WHIL1.C), except the do-while is used instead. Notice the placement of the test expression. Because this expression concludes the loop, user input does not need to appear before the loop and then again in its body.

```
/* Filename: C13WHIL4.C
   Input routine to ensure that user types a
   correct response. This routine might be part
   of a larger program. */
#include <stdio.h>
main()
{
   char ans;

   do
    { printf("\nYou must type a Y or an N\n");    /* Warn
                                                     and ask */
      printf("Do you want to continue (Y/N) ?"); /* again */
      scanf(" %c", &ans); }              /* Body of while loop
                                             ends here */
    } while ((ans != 'Y') && (ans != 'N'))

   return;
}
```

2. Suppose you are entering sales amounts into the computer in order to calculate extended totals. You want the computer to print the quantity sold, part number, and extended total (quantity times the price per unit). The following program does that:

Compute extended inventory amount

```
/* Filename: C13INV1.C
   Gets inventory information from user and prints
   an inventory detail listing with extended totals */
#include <stdio.h>
main()
{
   int part_no, quantity;
   float cost, ext_cost;

   printf("*** Inventory Computation ***\n\n");    /* Title */

   /* Get inventory information */
   do
    { printf("What is the next part number (-999 to end)? ");
      scanf(" %d", &part_no);
```

```
          if (part_no != -999)
             { printf("How many were bought? ");
               scanf(" %d", &quantity);
               printf("What is the unit price of this item? ");
               scanf(" %f", &cost);
               ext_cost = cost * quantity;
               printf("\n%d of # %d will cost %.2f", quantity,
                      part_no, ext_cost);
               printf("\n\n\n");        /* Print two blank lines */
             }
      } while (part_no != -999);       /* Loop only if part
                                          number is not -999 */

    printf("End of inventory computation\n");
    return;
}
```

Figure 13.1 shows the output from this program.

```
*** Inventory Computation ***

What is the next part number (-999 to end)? 123
How many were bought? 4
What is the unit price of this item? 5.43

4 of # 123 will cost 21.72


What is the next part number (-999 to end)? 523
How many were bought? 26
What is the unit price of this item? 1.25

26 of # 523 will cost 32.50


What is the next part number (-999 to end)? -999
End of inventory computation
```

Figure 13.1. Displaying extended inventory totals on-screen.

The do-while loop controls the entry of the customer sales information. Notice the "trigger" that ends the loop. If the user enters -999 for the part number, the do-while loop quits because no part numbered –999 exists in the inventory.

However, this program could be improved in several ways. The invoice could be printed to the printer instead of the screen. You learn how to direct your output to a printer in Part 5. Also, the inventory total (the total amount of the entire order) could be computed. You learn how to total such data in the "Counters and Totals" section later in this chapter.

The if Loop Versus the while Loop

Some beginning programmers confuse the if statement with loop constructs. The while and do-while loops repeat a section of code multiple times, depending on the condition being tested. The if statement may or may not execute a section of code; if it does, it executes that section only once.

Use an if statement when you want to conditionally execute a section of code *once,* and use a while or do-while loop if you want it to execute *more than once.* Figure 13.2 shows differences between the if statement and the two while loops.

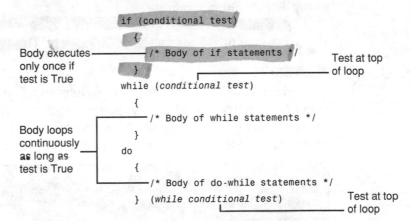

Figure 13.2. Differences between the if statement and the two while loops.

The exit() Function and break Statement

Exit program

C provides the exit() function as a way to leave a program early (before its natural finish). The format of exit() is

```
exit(status);
```

where *status* is an optional integer variable or constant. If you are familiar with your operating system's return codes, *status* enables you to test the results of C programs. In DOS, *status* is sent to the operating system's errorlevel *environment variable*, where it can be tested by batch files.

The exit() function provides an early exit from your program.

Many times, something happens in a program that requires the program's termination. It may be a major problem, such as a disk drive error. Perhaps users indicate that they want to quit the program—you can tell this by giving your users a special value to type in scanf(). The exit() function can be put on a line by itself, or anywhere else that a C statement or function can appear. Typically, exit() is placed in the body of an if statement to end the program early, depending on the result of some relational test.

You should include the stdlib.h header file when you use exit(). This file describes the operation of exit() to your program. Whenever you use a function in a program, you should know its corresponding #include header file, which is usually listed in the compiler's reference manual.

The break statement ends the current loop.

Instead of exiting an entire program, however, you can use the break statement to exit the current loop. The format of break is

```
break;
```

Exit current loop

The break statement can go anywhere in a C program that any other statement can go, but it typically appears in the body of a while or do-while loop in order to leave the loop early. The following examples illustrate the exit() function and the break statement.

> **NOTE:** The break statement exits only the most current loop. If you have a while loop in another while loop, break exits only the internal loop.

Examples

1. Here is a simple program that shows you how the exit() function works. This program looks as though it prints several messages on-screen, but that is misleading. Because exit() appears early in the code, this program quits immediately after main()'s opening brace.

```
/* C13EXIT1.C
   Quits very early due to exit() function */
#include <stdio.h>
#include <stdlib.h>                  /* Required for exit() */
main()
{
    exit(1);               /* Forces program to end here */

    printf("C programming is fun.\n");
    printf("I like learning C by example!\n");
    printf("C is a powerful language that is
    not difficult to learn.");

    return;
}
```

2. The break statement is not intended to be as strong a program exit as the exit() function. Whereas exit() ends the entire program, break quits only the loop that is currently active. In other words, break is usually placed inside a while or do-while loop to make the program think the loop is finished. The statement following the loop executes after a break occurs, but the program does not quit as it does with exit().

The following program appears to print C is fun! until the user enters N to stop it. The message prints only once, however, because the break statement forces an early exit from the loop.

```
/* Filename: C13BRK.C
   Demonstrates the break statement */
#include <stdio.h>
```

```
main()
{
   char user_ans;

   do
     { printf("C is fun! \n");
       break;                        /* Causes early exit */
       printf("Do you want to see the message again (N/Y)? ");
       scanf(" %c", &user_ans);
     } while (user_ans == 'Y');

   printf("That's all for now\n");
   return;
}
```

This program always produces the following output:

```
C is fun!
That's all for now
```

You can tell from this program's output that the break statement does not enable the do-while loop to reach its natural
conclusion, but causes it to finish early. The final printf()
prints because only the current loop—and not the entire
program—exits with the break statement.

3. Unlike the previous program, break is usually placed after an
   if statement. This makes it a *conditional* break, which occurs
   only if the relational test of the if statement is True.

   A good illustration of this is the inventory program you saw
   earlier (C13INV1.C). Even though the users enter –999 when
   they want to quit the program, an additional if test is
   needed inside the do-while. The –999 ends the do-while loop,
   but the body of the do-while still needs an if test, so the
   remaining quantity and cost prompts are not given.

   By inserting a break after testing for the end of the user's
   input, as shown in the following program, the do-while does
   not need the if test. The break quits the do-while as soon as
   the user signals the end of the inventory by entering –999 as
   the part number.

```
/* Filename: C13INV2.C
   Gets inventory information from user and prints
   an inventory detail listing with extended totals */
#include <stdio.h>
main()
{
   int part_no, quantity;
   float cost, ext_cost;

   printf("*** Inventory Computation ***\n\n");   /* Title */

   /* Get inventory information */
   do
    { printf("What is the next part number (-999 to end)? ");
      scanf(" %d", &part_no);
      if (part_no == -999)
        { break; }                      /* Exit the loop if
                                            no more part numbers */
      printf("How many were bought? ");
      scanf(" %d", &quantity);
      printf("What is the unit price of this item? ");
      scanf(" %f", &cost);
      ext_cost = quantity * cost;
      printf("\n%d of # %d will cost %.2f",
             quantity, part_no, ext_cost);
      printf("\n\n\n");                 /* Print two blank lines */
    } while (part_no != -999);          /* Loop only if part
                                            number is not -999 */

   printf("End of inventory computation\n");
   return;
}
```

4. The following program might be used to control two other programs. It illustrates how C can pass information to DOS with exit(). This is your first example of a menu program. Similar to a restaurant menu, a C menu program lists possible user choices. The users decide what they want the computer to do from the menu's available options. The mailing list application in Appendix F uses a menu for its user options.

This program returns either a 1 or a 2 to its operating system, depending on the user's selection. It is then up to the operating system to test the exit value and run the proper program.

```c
/* Filename: C13EXIT2.C
   Asks user for his or her selection and returns
   that selection to the operating system with exit() */
#include <stdio.h>
#include <stdlib.h>
main()
{
   int ans;

   do
     { printf("Do you want to:\n\n");
       printf("\t1. Run the word processor \n\n");
       printf("\t2. Run the database program \n\n");
       printf("What is your selection? ");
       scanf(" %d", &ans);
     } while ((ans != 1) && (ans != 2));   /* Ensures user
                                              enters 1 or 2 */
   exit(ans);  /* Return value to operating system */
   return;
}
```

Counters and Totals

Counting is important for many applications. You may need to know how many customers you have or how many people scored over a certain average in your class. You might want to count how many checks you wrote last month with your computerized checkbook system.

Before you develop C routines to count occurrences, think of how you count in your own mind. If you were adding a total number of something, such as the stamps in your stamp collection or the number of wedding invitations you sent out, you would probably do the following:

Start at 0, and add 1 for each item being counted. When you are finished, you should have the total number (or, the total count).

This is all you do when you count with C: Assign 0 to a variable and add 1 to it every time you process another data value. The increment operator (++) is especially useful for counting.

Examples

1. To illustrate using a counter, the following program prints "Computers are fun!" ten times on the screen. You could write a program that has ten `printf()` functions, but that would not be very elegant. It would also be too cumbersome to have 5000 `printf()` functions, if you wanted to print that same message 5000 times.

   By adding a `while` loop and a counter that stops after a certain total is reached, you can control this printing, as the following program shows:

```
/* Filename: C13CNT1.C
   Program to print a message 10 times */
#include <stdio.h>
main()
{
    int ctr = 0;    /* Holds the number of times printed */

    do
      { printf("Computers are fun!\n");
        ctr++;                      /* Add one to the count,
                                       after each printf() */
      } while (ctr < 10);          /* Print again if fewer
                                       than 10 times        */
    return;
}
```

   The output from this program is shown as follows. Notice that the message prints exactly ten times.

```
Computers are fun!
Computers are fun!
Computers are fun!
```

```
Computers are fun!
Computers are fun!
Computers are fun!
Computers are fun!
Computers are fun!
Computers are fun!
Computers are fun!
```

The heart of the counting process in this program is the statement that follows.

Increment the counter

```
ctr++;
```

You learned earlier that the increment operator adds 1 to a variable. In this program, the counter variable is incremented each time the do-while loops. Because the only operation performed on this line is the increment of ctr, the prefix increment (++ctr) would produce the same results.

2. The previous program not only added to the counter variable, but also performed the loop a specific number of times. This is a common method of conditionally executing parts of a program for a fixed number of times.

The following program is a password program. A password is stored in an integer variable. The user must correctly enter the matching password within three attempts. If the user does not type the correct password in that time, the program ends. This is a common method that dial-up computers use. They enable a caller to try the password a fixed number of times, then hang up the phone if that limit is exceeded. This helps deter people from trying hundreds of different passwords at any one sitting.

If users guess the correct password in three tries, they see the secret message.

```
/* Filename: C13PASS1.C
   Program to prompt for a password and
   check it against an internal one */
#include <stdio.h>
main()
```

```
{
    int stored_pass = 11862;
    int num_tries = 0;       /* Counter for password attempts */
    int user_pass;

    while (num_tries < 3)          .        /* Loop only 3 times */
       { printf("\nWhat is the password (You get 3 tries...)? ");
         scanf(" %d", &user_pass);
         num_tries++;                          /* Add 1 to counter */
         if (user_pass == stored_pass)
            { printf("You entered the correct password.\n");
              printf("The cash safe is behind the picture
              of the ship.\n");
              exit();
            }
         else
            { printf("You entered the wrong password.\n");
             if (num_tries == 3)
             { printf("Sorry, you get no more chances"); }
             else
             { printf("You get %d more tries...\n",
                      3-num_tries); }
          }
       }                                  /* End of while loop */
    return;
}
```

This program gives users three chances—in case they make one or two typing mistakes. But after three unsuccessful attempts, the program quits without displaying the secret message.

3. The following program is a letter guessing game. It includes a message telling users how many tries they made before guessing the correct letter. A counter counts the number of these tries.

```
/* Filename: C13GUES.C
   Letter guessing game */
#include <stdio.h>
main()
```

```
int tries = 0;
char comp_ans, user_guess;

/* Save the computer's letter */
comp_ans = 'T';                      /* Change to a different
                                        letter if desired */

printf("I am thinking of a letter...");
do
   { printf("What is your guess? ");
     scanf(" %c", &user_guess);
     tries++;    /* Add 1 to the guess counting variable */
     if (user_guess > comp_ans)
        { printf("Your guess was too high\n");
          printf("\nTry again...");
        }
     if (user_guess < comp_ans)
        { printf("Your guess was too low\n");
          printf("\nTry again...");
        }
   } while (user_guess != comp_ans); /* Quit when a
                                        match is found */

/* They got it right, let them know */
printf("*** Congratulations!  You got it right! \n");
printf("It took you only %d tries to guess.", tries);
return;
}
```

Figure 13.3 shows a sample output of this program.

Producing Totals

Writing a routine to add values is as easy as counting. Instead of adding 1 to the counter variable, you add a value to the total variable. For instance, if you want to find the total dollar amount of checks you wrote during December, you could start at nothing (0) and add to that the amount of every check written in December. Instead of building a count, you are building a total.

```
I am thinking of a letter...What is your guess? A
Your guess was too low

Try again...What is your guess? Z
Your guess was too high

Try again...What is your guess? N
Your guess was too low

Try again...What is your guess? W
Your guess was too high

Try again...What is your guess? S
Your guess was too low

Try again...What is your guess? T
*** Congratulations!  You got it right!
It took you only 6 tries to guess.
```

Figure 13.3. Counting guesses in a letter guessing game.

When you want C to add values, just initialize a `total` variable to zero, then add each value to the total until you have included all the values.

Examples

1. Suppose you want to write a program that adds your grades for a class you are taking. The teacher has informed you that you earn an A if you can accumulate over 450 points.

   The following program keeps asking you for values until you type –1. The –1 is a signal that you are finished entering grades and now want to see the total. This program also prints a congratulatory message if you have enough points for an A.

Calculate
total grade

```
/* Filename: C13GRAD1.C
   Adds up grades and determines if an A was made */
#include <stdio.h>
main()
{
```

```
float total_grade=0.0;
float grade;                  /* Holds individual grades */

do
{ printf("What is your grade? (-1 to end) ");
  scanf(" %f", &grade);
  if (grade >= 0.0)
    { total_grade += grade; }        /* Add to total */
} while (grade >= 0.0);      /* Quit when -1 entered */

/* Control begins here if no more grades */
printf("\n\nYou made a total of %.1f points\n",
        total_grade);
if (total_grade >= 450.00)
    { printf("** You made an A!!"); }

return;
}
```

Notice that the -1 response does not get added to the total number of points. This program checks for the -1 before adding to total_grade. Figure 13.4 shows the output from this program.

```
What is your grade? (-1 to end) 87
What is your grade? (-1 to end) 89
What is your grade? (-1 to end) 96
What is your grade? (-1 to end) 78
What is your grade? (-1 to end) 99
What is your grade? (-1 to end) 87
What is your grade? (-1 to end) 89
What is your grade? (-1 to end) -1


You made a total of 625.0 points
** You made an A!!
```

Figure 13.4. Computing the total grade.

2. The following program is an extension of the grade calculating program. It not only totals the points, but also computes their average.

The average calculation must know how many grades were entered before it will work. This is a subtle problem because the number of grades to be entered is unknown in advance. Therefore, every time the user enters a valid grade (not –1), the program must add 1 to a counter as well as add that grade to the total variable. This is a combination counting and totaling routine, which is common in many programs.

```c
/* Filename: C13GRAD2.C
   Adds up grades, computes average,
   and determines if an A was made. */
#include <stdio.h>
main()
{
   float total_grade=0.0;
   float grade_avg = 0.0;
   float grade;
   int grade_ctr = 0;

   do
   { printf("What is your grade? (-1 to end) ");
     scanf(" %f", &grade);
     if (grade >= 0.0)
       { total_grade += grade;          /* Add to total */
         grade_ctr ++; }                /* Add to count */
   } while (grade >= 0.0);              /* Quit when -1 entered */

   /* Control begins here if no more grades */
   grade_avg = (total_grade / grade_ctr);        /* Compute
                                                    average */
   printf("\nYou made a total of %.1f points.\n",
           total_grade);
   printf("Your average was %.1f \n", grade_avg);
   if (total_grade >= 450.0)
      { printf("** You made an A!!"); }
   return;
}
```

Figure 13.5 shows the output of this program. Congratulations! You are on your way to becoming a master C programmer.

```
What is your grade? (-1 to end) 88
What is your grade? (-1 to end) 98
What is your grade? (-1 to end) 97
What is your grade? (-1 to end) 87
What is your grade? (-1 to end) 94
What is your grade? (-1 to end) 96
What is your grade? (-1 to end) -1

You made a total of 560.0 points.
Your average was 93.3
** You made an A!!
```

Figure 13.5. Computing total points and the average.

Review Questions

Answers to review questions are in Appendix B.

1. What is the difference between the while loop and the do-while loop?

2. What is the difference between a total variable and a counter variable?

3. Which C operator is most useful for counting?

4. True or false: Braces are not required around the body of while and do-while loops.

5. What is wrong with the following code?

```
while (sales > 50)
   printf("Your sales are very good this month.\n");
   printf("You will get a bonus for your high sales\n");
```

6. What file must you include as a header file if you use `exit()`?

7. How many times does this `printf()` print?

```
int a=0;
do
   { printf("Careful \n");
     a++; }
while (a > 5);
```

8. How can you inform DOS of the program exit status?

9. What is printed to the screen in the following section of code?

```
a = 1;
while (a < 4)
   { printf("This is the outer loop\n");
     a++;
     while (a <= 25)
        { break;
          printf("This prints 25 times\n"); }
   }
```

Review Exercises

1. Write a program with a `do-while` loop that prints the numerals from 10 to 20 (inclusive), with a blank line between each number.

2. Write a weather-calculator program that asks for a list of the previous ten days' temperatures, computes the average, and prints the results. You have to compute the total as the input occurs, then divide that total by 10 to find the average. Use a `while` loop for the ten repetitions.

3. Rewrite the program in Exercise 2 by using a do-while loop.

4. Write a program, similar to the weather calculator in Exercise 2, but make it more general so that it computes the average of any number of days' temperatures. (Hint: You need to count the number of temperatures to compute the final average.)

5. Write a program that produces your own ASCII table on-screen. Don't print the first 31 characters because they are nonprintable. Print the codes numbered 32 through 255 by storing their numbers in integer variables and then printing their ASCII values using the "%c" format code.

Summary

This chapter showed you two ways to produce a C loop: the while loop and the do-while loop. These two variations of while loops differ in where they test their *test condition* statements. The while tests at the top of its loop, and the do-while tests at the bottom. The result is that the body of a do-while loop always executes at least once. You also learned that the exit() function and break statement add flexibility to the while loops. The exit() function terminates the program, and the break statement terminates only the current loop.

This chapter explained two of the most important applications of loops: counters and totals. Your computer can be a wonderful tool for adding and counting, due to the repetitive capabilities offered with while loops.

The next chapter extends your knowledge of loops by showing you how to create a *determinate* loop, called the for loop. This feature is useful when you want a section of code to loop for a specified number of times.

The for Loop

The for loop enables you to repeat sections of your program for a specific number of times. Unlike the while and do-while loops, the for loop is a *determinate loop*. This means when you write your program you can usually determine how many times the loop takes place. The while and do-while loop only until a condition is met. The for loop does this and more: it continues looping until a count (or countdown) is reached.

After the final for loop count is reached, execution continues with the next statement, in sequence. This chapter focuses on the for loop construct by introducing

♦ The for statement

♦ The concept of for loops

♦ Nested for loops

The for loop is a helpful way of looping through a section of code when you want to count, or total, specified amounts, but it does not replace the while and do-while loops.

The for Statement

The for statement encloses one or more C statements that form the body of the loop. These statements in the loop continuously repeat for a certain number of times. You, as the programmer, control the number of loop repetitions.

The format of the for loop is

```
for (start expression; test expression; count expression)
    { Block of one or more C statements; }
```

C evaluates the *start expression* before the loop begins. Typically, the *start expression* is an assignment statement (such as ctr=1;), but it can be any legal expression you specify. C looks at and evaluates *start expression* only once, at the top of the loop.

CAUTION: Do not put a semicolon after the right parenthesis. If you do, the for loop "thinks" the body of the loop is zero statements long! It would continue looping—doing *nothing* each time—until the *test expression* becomes False.

The for loop will loop for a specified number of times.

Every time the body of the loop repeats, the *count expression* executes, usually incrementing or decrementing a variable. The *test expression* evaluates to True (nonzero) or False (zero), then determines if the body of the loop repeats again.

TIP: If only one C statement resides in the for loop's body, braces are not required, but they are recommended. If you add more statements later, the braces are there already, so you cannot inadvertently leave them out.

The Concept of for Loops

You use the concept of for loops throughout your day-to-day life. Any time you need to repeat a certain procedure a specified number of times, that repetition becomes a good candidate for a computerized for loop.

To illustrate the concept of a for loop further, suppose you are putting up ten new shutters on your house. You must do the following steps for each shutter:

1. Move the ladder to the location of the shutter.

2. Take a shutter, hammer, and nails up the ladder.

3. Hammer the shutter to the side of the house.

4. Climb down the ladder.

You must perform each of these four steps exactly ten times, because you have ten shutters. After ten times, you don't put another shutter up because the job is finished. You are looping through a procedure that has several steps (the block of the loop). These steps are the body of the loop. It is not an endless loop because there are a fixed number of shutters; you run out of shutters only after you have gone through all ten of them.

For a less physical example that might be more easily computerized, suppose you need to fill out three tax returns for each of your teenage children. (If you have three teenage children, you probably need more than just a computer to help you get through the day!) For each child, you must perform the following steps:

1. Add up the total income.

2. Add up the total deductions.

3. Fill out a tax return.

4. Put it in an envelope.

5. Mail it.

You then must repeat this entire procedure two more times.

Notice how the sentence before these steps began: *For each child*. This signals an idea similar to the for loop construct.

> **NOTE:** The for loop tests at the top of the loop. If the *test expression* is False when the for loop begins, the body of the loop never executes.

The Choice of Loops

Any loop construct can be written with a for loop, a while loop, or a do-while loop. Generally, you use the for loop when you want to count or loop a specific number of times, and reserve the while and do-while loops for looping until a False condition is met.

Examples

1. To give you a glimpse of the for loop's capabilities, this example shows you two programs: one that uses a for loop and one that does not. The first one is a counting program. Before studying its contents, look at the output. The results basically speak for themselves and illustrate the for loop very well.

Identify the program and include the necessary header file. We need a counter, so make ctr an integer variable.
   1. Add 1 to the counter.
   2. If the counter is less than or equal to 10, print its value and repeat step 1.

The program with a for loop follows:

```c
/* Filename: C14FOR1.C
   Introduces the for loop */
#include <stdio.h>
main()
{
   int ctr;
   for (ctr=1; ctr<=10; ctr++)    /* Start ctr at 1,
                                     increment through loop */
      { printf("%d \n", ctr); }  /* Body of for loop */

   return;
}
```

This program's output is

```
1
2
3
4
5
6
7
8
9
10
```

Here is the same program using a do-while loop:

Identify the program and include the necessary header file. We need a counter, so make ctr an integer variable.
1. *Add 1 to the counter.*
2. *Print the value of the counter.*
3. *If the counter is less than or equal to 10, repeat step 1.*

```c
/* Filename: C14WHI1.C
   Simulating a for loop with a do-while loop */
#include <stdio.h>
main()
{
   int ctr=1;
   do
     { printf("%d \n", ctr); /* Body of do-while loop */
       ctr++; }
   while (ctr <= 10);

   return;
}
```

Notice that the for loop is a cleaner way of controlling the looping process. The for loop does several things that require extra statements in a while loop. With for loops, do you not need to write extra code to initialize variables and increment or decrement them. You can see at a glance (in the expressions in the for statement) exactly how the loop executes, unlike the do-while, which forces you to look at the *bottom* of the loop to see how the loop stops.

2. Both of the following sample programs add the numbers from 100 to 200. The first one uses a for loop, and the second one doesn't. The first example starts with a *start expression* other than 1, starting the loop with a bigger *count expression*.

This program has a for loop:

```
/* Filename: C14FOR2.C
   Demonstrates totaling using a for loop */
#include <stdio.h>
main()
{
   int total, ctr;

   total = 0;                /* Will hold total of 100 to 200 */

   for (ctr=100; ctr<=200; ctr++)      /* ctr is 100, 101,
                                          102,...200      */
      { total += ctr; }  /* Add value of ctr each iteration */

   printf("The total is %d", total);
   return;
}
```

The same program without a for loop follows:

```
/* Filename: C14WHI2.C
   A totaling program using a do-while loop */
#include <stdio.h>
main()
{
   int total=0;           /* Initialize total */
   int num=100;            /* Starting value */

   do
      { total += num;         /* Add to total */
        num++;             /* Increment counter */
      } while (num <= 200);
   printf("The total is %d", total);
```

```
    return;
}
```

Both programs produce this output:

```
The total is 15150
```

The body of the loop in both programs executes 100 times. The starting value is 100, not 1 as in the previous example. Notice that the for loop is less complex than the do-while because the initialization, testing, and incrementing are performed in the single for statement.

> **TIP:** Notice how the body of the for loop is indented. This is a good habit to develop because it makes it easier to see the beginning and ending of the loop's body.

The following is the last example that compares the for loop to an equivalent program without a for loop.

3. The body of the for loop can have more than one statement. The following example requests five pairs of data values, children's first names and their ages. It prints the teacher assigned to each child, based on the child's age. This illustrates a for loop with printf() functions, a scanf() function, and an if statement in its body. Because exactly five children are checked, the for loop ensures that the program ends after the fifth child.

```
/* Filename: C14FOR3.C
   Program that uses a loop to input and print
   the teacher assigned to each child */
#include <stdio.h>
main()
{
    char child[25];        /* Holds child's first name */
    int age;                      /* Holds child's age */
    int ctr;            /* The for loop counter variable */

    for (ctr=1; ctr<=5; ctr++)
```

Get child's
name

Get child's
age

Print
child's
teacher

```
        { printf("What is the next child's name? ");
          scanf(" %s", child);
          printf("What is the child's age? ");
          scanf(" %d", &age);
          if (age <= 5)
             { printf("\n%s has Mrs. Jones for a teacher\n",
                      child);}
          if (age == 6)
             { printf("\n%s has Miss Smith for a teacher\n",
                      child); }
          if (age >= 7)
             { printf("\n%s has Mr. Anderson for a teacher\n",
                      child); }
        }  /* Quits after 5 times */

     return;
}
```

Figure 14.1 shows the output from this program. You can improve this program further, after you learn the switch statement in the next chapter.

```
What is the next child's name? Jim
What is the child's age? 6

Jim has Miss Smith for a teacher

What is the next child's name? Linda
What is the child's age? 3

Linda has Mrs. Jones for a teacher

What is the next child's name? Elizabeth
What is the child's age? 7

Elizabeth has Mr. Anderson for a teacher

What is the next child's name? Bob
What is the child's age? 5

Bob has Mrs. Jones for a teacher

What is the next child's name? Walter
What is the child's age? 3

Walter has Mrs. Jones for a teacher
```

Figure 14.1. Inputting values inside a for loop.

4. The previous examples used an increment as the *count expression*. You can make the for loop increment the loop variable by any value. It does not need to increment by 1.

The following program prints the even numbers from 1 to 20. It then prints the odd numbers from 1 to 20. To do this, 2 is added to the counter variable (instead of 1 as shown in the previous examples) each time the loop executes.

```c
/* Filename: C14EVOD.C
   Prints the even numbers from 1 to 20,
   then the odd numbers from 1 to 20 */
#include <stdio.h>
main()
{
   int num;                        /* The for loop variable */

   printf("Even numbers below 21\n");        /* Title */
   for (num=2; num<=20; num+=2)
     { printf("%d ", num); }  /* Prints every other number */

   printf("\nOdd numbers below 20\n");   /* A second title */
   for (num=1; num<=20; num+=2)
     { printf("%d ", num); }  /* Prints every other number */

   return;
}
```

There are two loops in this program. The body of each one consists of a single printf() function. In the first half of the program, the loop variable, num, is 2 and not 1. If it was 1, the number 1 would print first, as it does in the odd number section.

The two printf() functions that print the titles are not part of either loop. If they were, the program would print a title before each number. The following shows the result of running this program:

```
Even numbers below
2 4 6 8 10 12 14 16 18 20
```

```
Odd numbers below
1 3 5 7 9 11 13 15 17 19
```

5. You can decrement the loop variable as well. If you do, the value is subtracted from the loop variable each time through the loop.

The following example is a rewrite of the counting program. It produces the reverse effect by showing a countdown.

```
/* Filename: C14CNTD1.C
   Countdown to the lift-off */
#include <stdio.h>
main()
{
   int ctr;

   for (ctr=10; ctr!=0; ctr--)
     { printf("%d \n", ctr); }    /* Print ctr as it
                                      counts down */
   printf("*** Blast off! ***");
   return;
}
```

When decrementing a loop variable, the initial value should be larger than the end value being tested. In this example, the loop variable, ctr, counts down from 10 to 1. Each time through the loop (each iteration), ctr is decremented by 1. You can see how easy it is to control a loop by looking at this program's output, as follows.

```
10
 9
 8
 7
 6
 5
 4
 3
 2
 1
*** Blast Off! ***
```

> **TIP:** This program's `for` loop test illustrates a redundancy that you can eliminate thanks to C. The *test expression*, `ctr!=0`; tells the `for` loop to continue looping until `ctr` is not equal to zero. However, if `ctr` becomes zero, that is a False value in itself; there is no reason to add the additional `!=0` except for clarity. The `for` loop can be rewritten
>
> ```
> for (ctr=10; ctr; ctr--)
> ```
>
> without loss of meaning. This is more efficient, and it is such an integral part of C that you should become comfortable with it. There is little loss of clarity once you get used to it.

6. You can also make a `for` loop test for something other than a constant value. The following program combines much of what you have learned so far. It asks for student grades and computes an average. Because there may be a different number of students each semester, the program first asks the user for the number of students. Next, the program loops until the user enters that many scores. It then computes the average based on the total and the number of student grades entered.

```c
/* Filename: C14FOR4.C
   Computes a grade average with a for loop */
#include <stdio.h>
main()
{
   float grade, avg;
   float total=0.0;
   int num;                    /* Total number of grades */
   int loopvar;                /* Used to control for loop */

   printf("\n*** Grade Calculation ***\n\n");  /* Title */
   printf("How many students are there? ");
   scanf(" %d", &num);      /* Get total number to enter */

   for (loopvar=1; loopvar<=num; loopvar++)
      { printf("\nWhat is the next student's grade? ");
        scanf(" %f", &grade);
```

```
                    total += grade;  }      /* Keep a running total */

                avg = total / num;
                printf("\n\nThe average of this class is %.1f", avg);
                return;
            }
```

Due to the `for` loop, the total and the average calculations do not need to be changed if the number of students change.

7. Because characters and integers are so closely associated in C, you can increment character variables in a `for` loop. The following program prints the letters *A* through *Z* with a simple `for` loop.

```
/* Filename: C14FOR5.C
   Prints the alphabet with a simple for loop */
#include <stdio.h>
main()
{
   char letter;

   printf("Here is the alphabet:\n");
   for (letter='A'; letter<='Z'; letter++) /* Loops A to Z */
      { printf("%o ", letter); }

   return;
}
```

This program produces the following output:

```
Here is the alphabet:
A B C D E F G H I J K L M N O P Q R S T U V W X Y Z
```

8. A `for` expression can be blank, or a *null expression*. In the following `for` loop, all the expressions are blank:

```
for (;;)
   { printf("Over and over..."); }
```

This loops forever. Although you should avoid infinite loops, your program might dictate that you make a `for` loop expression blank. If you already initialized the *start expression* earlier in the program, you would be wasting computer time to repeat it in the for loop —and C does not require it.

The following program omits the *start expression* and the *count expression*, leaving only the for loop's *test expression*. Most of the time, you need to omit only one of them. If you use a for loop without two of its expressions, consider replacing it with a while loop or a do-while loop.

```c
/* Filename: C14FOR6.C
   Uses only the test expression in
   the for loop to count by 5s */
#include <stdio.h>
main()
{
   int num=5;                              /* Starting value */

   printf("\nCounting by 5s: \n");              /* Title */
   for (; num<=100;)  /* Contains only the test expression */
     { printf("%d\n", num);
       num+=5;     /* Increment expression outside the loop */
     }                          /* End of the loop's body */

   return;
}
```

The output from this program follows:

```
Counting by 5s:
5
10
15
20
25
30
35
40
45
50
55
60
```

```
65
70
75
80
85
90
95
100
```

Nested for Loops

Any C statement can go inside the body of a for loop—even another for loop! When you put a loop within a loop, you are creating a *nested loop*. The clock in a sporting event works like a nested loop. You might think this is stretching an analogy a little too far, but it truly works. A football game counts down from 15 minutes to 0. It does this four times. The first countdown loops from 15 to 0 (for each minute). That countdown is nested in another that loops from 1 to 4 (for each of the four quarters).

Use nested loops when you want to repeat a loop more than once.

If your program needs to repeat a loop more than one time, it is a good candidate for a nested loop. Figure 14.2 shows two outlines of nested loops. You can think of the inside loop as looping "faster" than the outside loop. In the first example, the inside for loop counts from 1 to 10 before the outside loop (the variable out) can finish its first iteration. When the outside loop finally does iterate a second time, the inside loop starts over.

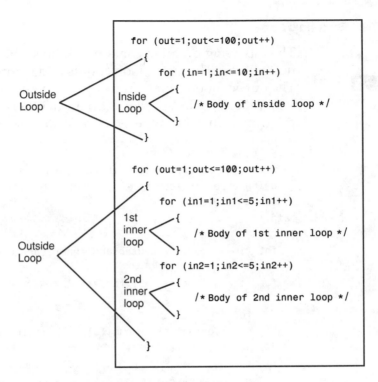

Figure 14.2. Outlines of two nested loops.

The second nested loop outline shows two loops within an outside loop. Both of these loops execute in their entirety before the outside loop finishes its first iteration. When the outside loop starts its second iteration, the two inside loops repeat again.

Notice the order of the braces in each example. The inside loop *always* finishes, and therefore its ending brace must come before the outside loop's ending brace. Indention makes this much clearer because you can "line up" braces of each loop.

Nested loops become important later when you use them for array and table processing.

NOTE: In nested loops, the inside loop (or loops) execute completely before the outside loop's next iteration.

Examples

1. The following program contains a loop within a loop—a nested loop. The inside loop counts and prints from 1 to 5. The outside loop counts from 1 to 3. Therefore, the inside loop repeats, in its entirety, 3 times. In other words, this program prints the values 1 to 5 and does so 3 times.

```
/* Filename: C14NEST1.C
   Print the numbers 1 to 5 three times
   using a nested loop */
#include <stdio.h>
main()
{
    int times, num;   /* Outer and inner for loop variables */

    for (times=1; times<=3; times++)
    {
        for (num=1; num<=5; num++)
            { printf("%d", num); }        /* Inner loop body */
        printf("\n");
    }                                      /* End of outer loop */

    return;
}
```

The indention follows the standard of for loops; every statement in each loop is indented a few spaces. Because the inside loop is already indented, its body is indented another few spaces. The program's output follows:

```
12345
12345
12345
```

2. The outside loop's counter variable changes each time through the loop. If one of the inside loop's control variables is the outside loop's counter variable, you see effects such as that shown in the following program.

```
/* Filename: C14NEST2.C
   An inside loop controlled by the outer loop's
   counter variable */
```

```
#include <stdio.h>
main()
{
   int outer, inner;

   for (outer=5; outer>=1; outer--)
     { for (inner=1; inner<=outer; inner++)
          { printf("%d", inner); }   /* End of inner loop */
     printf("\n");
     }
     return;
}
```

The output from this program follows. The inside loop repeats five times (as outer counts down from 5 to 1) and prints from five numbers to one number.

```
12345
1234
123
12
1
```

The following table traces the two variables through this program. Sometimes you need to "play computer" when learning a new concept such as nested loops. By executing a line at a time, writing down each variable's contents, you produce this table:

The *outer* variable	The *inner* variable
5	1
5	2
5	3
5	4
5	5
4	1
4	2
4	3
4	4
3	1

3	2
3	3
2	1
2	2
1	1

Tip for Mathematicians

The for statement is identical to the mathematical summation symbol. When you write programs to simulate the summation symbol, the for statement is an excellent candidate. A nested for statement is good for double summations.

For example, the following summation

```
i = 30
Σ (i / 3 * 2)
i = 1
```

can be rewritten as

```
total = 0;
for (i=1; i<=30; i++)
{ total += (i / 3 * 2); }
```

4. A factorial is a mathematical number used in probability theory and statistics. A factorial of any number is the multiplied product of every number from 1 to that number.

For instance, the factorial of 4 is 24 because $4 \times 3 \times 2 \times 1 = 24$. The factorial of 6 is 720 because $6 \times 5 \times 4 \times 3 \times 2 \times 1 = 720$. The factorial of 1 is 1 by definition.

Nested loops are good candidates for writing a factorial number generating program. The following program asks the user for a number, then prints every factorial up to, and including, that number.

```
/* Filename: C14FACT.C
   Computes the factorial of numbers through
   the user's number */
```

```
#include <stdio.h>
main()
{
   int outer, num, fact, total;

   printf("What factorial do you want to see? ");
   scanf(" %d", &num);

   for (outer=1; outer <= num; outer++)
     { total = 1;   /* Initialize total for each factorial */
       for (fact=1; fact<= outer; fact++)
          { total *= fact; }       /* Compute each factorial */
     }

   printf("The factorial for %d is %d", num, total);

   return;
}
```

The following shows the first seven factorials. You can run this program, entering different values when asked, and see various factorials. Be careful: factorials multiply quickly. (A factorial of 11 won't fit in an integer variable.)

```
What factorial do you want to see? 7
The factorial for 7 is 5040
```

Review Questions

Answers to review questions are in Appendix B.

1. What is a loop?

2. True or false: The body of a for loop contains at most one statement.

3. What is a nested loop?

4. Why might you want to leave one or more expressions out of the for statement's parentheses?

5. Which loop "moves" fastest: the inner loop or the outer loop?

6. What is the output from the following program?

```
for (ctr=10; ctr>=1; ctr-=3)
   { printf("%d \n", ctr); }
```

7. True or false: A for loop is better to use than a while loop when you know in advance exactly how many iterations a loop requires.

8. What happens when the test expression becomes False in a for statement?

9. True or false: The following program contains a valid nested loop.

```
for (i=1; i<=10; i++);
  { for (j=1; j<=5; j++)
      { printf("%d %d \n". i. j); }
  }
```

10. What is the output of the following section of code?

```
i=1;
start=1;
end=5;
step=1;

for (; start>=end;)
{ printf("%d \n", i);
start+=step;
end--;}
```

Review Exercises

1. Write a program that prints the numbers from 1 to 15 on the screen. Use a for loop to control the printing.

2. Write a program to print the values from 15 to 1 on the screen. Use a for loop to control the printing.

3. Write a program that uses a for loop to print every odd number from 1 to 100.

4. Write a program that asks the user for his or her age. Use a for loop to print "Happy Birthday!" for every year of the user's age.

5. Write a program that uses a for loop to print the ASCII characters from 32 to 255 on the screen. (Hint: Use the %c conversion character to print integer variables.)

6. Using the ASCII table numbers, write a program to print the following output, using a nested for loop. (Hint: The outside loop should loop from 1 to 5, and the inside loop's start variable should be 65, the value of ASCII "A".)

```
A
AB
ABC
ABCD
ABCDE
```

Summary

This chapter taught you how to control loops. Instead of writing extra code around a while loop, you can use the for loop to control the number of iterations at the time you define the loop. All for loops contain three parts: a *start expression*, a *test expression*, and a *count expression*.

You have now seen C's three loop constructs: the while loop, the do-while loop, and the for loop. They are similar, but behave differently in how they test and initialize variables. No loop is better than the others. The programming problem should dictate which loop to use. The next chapter shows you more methods for controlling your loops.

Other Loop Options

Now that you have mastered the looping constructs, you should learn some loop-related statements. This chapter teaches the concepts of *timing loops*, which let you slow down your programs. This can be helpful if you want to display a message for a fixed period of time or write computer games with slower speeds so your users can play them.

You can use two additional looping commands, the break and continue statements, to control the way loops operate. These statements work with while loops and for loops.

This chapter introduces you to the following:

♦ Timing loops

♦ The break statement with for loops

♦ The continue statement with for loops

When you master these concepts, you will be well on your way toward writing powerful programs that process large amounts of data.

Timing Loops

Computers are fast, and at times you probably would like them to be even faster. Sometimes, however, you want to slow down the computer. Often, games need to be slowed down because the computer's speed would make the game unplayable. Other times, you display a message, then clear the screen; if you don't delay the message, it clears too fast for the user to read it.

A nested loop is a perfect place for a *timing loop*, which does nothing except cycles through `for` or `while` loops many times. The larger the end value of the `for` loop, the longer the time in which the loop cycles.

Timing loops make the computer wait.

A nested loop would be good for displaying error messages to your user. If the user requested a report—but had not entered enough data for your program to print the report—you might print a warning message on the screen for a few seconds, telling your users that they cannot request the report yet. After displaying the message for a few seconds, you could clear the message and give the user another chance. (The mailing list program in Appendix F uses timing loops to display error messages.)

There is no way to determine how many iterations a timing loop takes for one second (or minute or hour) of delay because computers run at different speeds. You therefore need to adjust your timing loop's end value to get the delay you want for your computer.

Examples

1. Timing loops are easy to write—simply put an empty `for` loop inside the program. The following program is a rewritten version of the countdown program (C14CNTD1.C) you saw in the preceding chapter. Each number in the countdown is delayed so that the countdown does not appear to take place instantly as soon as you run the program. (Adjust the delay value if this program runs too slowly or too quickly on your computer.)

Identify the program, and include the necessary header file. We need a counter and a delay, so make cd and delay integer variables. Start the counter at 10, and start the delay at 1.

1. If the *delay* is less than or equal to 30,000, add 1 to its value and repeat step 1.

2. Print the value of the counter.

3. If the counter is greater than or equal to 0, subtract 1 from its value and repeat step 1.

Print a blast-off message.

```
/* Filename: C15CNTD1.C
   Countdown to the lift-off with a delay */
#include <stdio.h>
main()
{
    int cd, delay;

    for (cd=10; cd>=0; cd--)
    { { for (delay=1; delay <=30000; delay++); }   /* Delay
                                                       program */
        printf("%d \n", cd);        /* Print countdown value */
    }                               /* End of outer loop */
    printf("Blast off!!!");
    return;
}
```

2. The following program asks users for their ages. If an age is entered that is less than 0, the program beeps (by printing an alarm character, \a), then displays an error message for a few seconds by using a nested timing loop. Because an integer does not hold a large enough value (on many computers) for a long timing loop, you must use a nested timing loop. (Depending on the speed of your computer, adjust the numbers in the loop to display the message slower or faster.)

The program uses a rarely seen printf() conversion character, \r, inside the loop. As you may recall from Chapter 7, "Simple Input and Output," \r is a carriage return character. This conversion character moves the cursor to the beginning of the current line, enabling the program to print blanks on that same line. This overwrites the error message and makes it look as though the error disappears from the screen after a brief pause.

```
/* Filename: C15TIM.C
   Displays an error message for a few seconds */
#include <stdio.h>
main()
{
   int outer, inner, age;

   printf("What is your age? ");
   scanf(" %d", &age);

   while (age <= 0)
     { printf("*** Your age cannot be that small! ***");
       /* Timing loop here */
       for (outer=1; outer<=30000; outer++)
          { for (inner=1; inner<=500; inner++); }
       /* Erase the message */
       printf("\r\n\n");
       printf("What is your age? ");
       scanf(" %d", &age);  /* Ask again */
     }
   printf("\n\nI did not think you would really tell me your age!");
   return;
}
```

NOTE: Notice that the inside loop has a semicolon (;) after the `for` statement—with no loop body. There is no need for a loop body here because the computer is only cycling though the loop to waste a little time.

The break and
for Statements

The `for` loop was designed to execute for a specified number of times. Sometimes, though rarely, the `for` loop should quit before the counting variable has reached its final value. As with `while` loops, you use the `break` statement to quit a `for` loop early.

The break statement goes in the body of the for loop. Programmers rarely put break on a line by itself, and it almost always comes after an if test. If the break were on a line by itself, the loop would always quit early, defeating the purpose of the for loop.

Examples

1. The following program shows what can happen when C encounters an *unconditional* break statement, that is, one not preceded by an if statement.

   Identify the program and include the necessary header files. We need a variable to hold the current number, so make num an integer variable.

   Print a "Here are the numbers" message.

   1. Make num equal to 1. If num is less than or equal to 20, add 1 to it each time through the loop.

   2. Print the value of num.

   3. Break out of the loop.

   Print a goodbye message.

```
/* Filename: C15BRAK1.C
   A for loop defeated by the break statement */
#include <stdio.h>
main()
{
    int num;

    printf("Here are the numbers from 1 to 20\n");
    for(num=1; num<=20; num++)
      { printf("%d \n", num);
        break;  }   /* This exits the for loop immediately */

    printf("That's all, folks!");
    return;
}
```

The following shows you the result of running this program. Notice that the break immediately terminates the for loop. The for loop might as well not be in this program.

```
Here are the numbers from 1 to 20
1
That's all, folks!
```

2. The following program is an improved version of the preceding example. It asks users if they want to see another number. If so, the for loop continues its next iteration. If not, the break statement terminates the for loop.

```c
/* Filename: C15BRAK2.C
   A for loop running at the user's request */
#include <stdio.h>
main()
{
    int num;    /* Loop counter variable */
    char ans;

    printf("Here are the numbers from 1 to 20\n");

    for (num=1; num<=20; num++)
      { printf("%d \n", num);
        printf("Do you want to see another (Y/N)? ");
        scanf(" %c", &ans);
        if ((ans == 'N') || (ans == 'n'))
          { break; }        /* Will exit the for loop
                               if user wants */
      }

    printf("\nThat's all, folks!");
    return;
}
```

The following display shows a sample run of this program. The for loop prints 20 numbers, as long as the user does not answer N to the prompt. Otherwise, the break takes over and terminates the for loop early. The statement after the body of the loop always executes next if the break occurs.

```
Here are the numbers from 1 to 20
1
Do you want to see another (Y/N)? Y
2
Do you want to see another (Y/N)? Y
3
Do you want to see another (Y/N)? Y
4
Do you want to see another (Y/N)? Y
5
Do you want to see another (Y/N)? Y
6
Do you want to see another (Y/N)? Y
7
Do you want to see another (Y/N)? Y
8
Do you want to see another (Y/N)? Y
9
Do you want to see another (Y/N)? Y
10
Do you want to see another (Y/N)? N
That's all, folks!
```

If you nest one loop inside another, the break terminates the "most active" loop, that is, the innermost loop in which the break statement resides.

3. Use the *conditional* break (an if statement followed by a break) when you are missing data. For example, when you process data files, or large amounts of user data-entry, you might expect 100 input numbers and get only 95. You could use a break to terminate the for loop before it cycles through the 96th iteration.

Suppose the teacher using the grade averaging program in the preceding chapter (C14FOR4.C) entered an incorrect total number of students. Maybe she typed 16, but there are only 14 students. The previous for loop looped 16 times, no matter how many students there are, because it relies on the teacher's count.

The following grade averaging program is more sophisticated than that. It asks the teacher for the total number of students, but if the teacher wants, she can enter –99 as a student's score. The –99 does not get averaged; it is used as a trigger value to break out of the for loop before its normal conclusion.

```
/* Filename: C15BRAK3.C
   Computes a grade average with a for loop,
   allowing an early exit with a break statement */
#include <stdio.h>
main()
{
   float grade, avg;
   float total=0.0;
   int num, count=0; /* Total number of grades and counter */
   int loopvar;                    /* Used to control for loop */

   printf("\n*** Grade Calculation ***\n\n");      /* Title */
   printf("How many students are there? ");
   scanf(" %d", &num);          /* Get total number to enter */

   for (loopvar=1; loopvar<=num; loopvar++)
     { printf("\nWhat is the next student's
       grade? (-99 to quit) ");
       scanf(" %f", &grade);
       if (grade < 0.0)              /* A negative number
                                        triggers break */
          { break; }                 /* Leave the loop early */
       count++;
       total += grade;  }            /* Keep a running total */

   avg = total / count;
   printf("\n\nThe average of this class is %.1f", avg);
   return;
}
```

Notice that grade is tested for less than 0, not –99.0. You cannot reliably use floating-point values to compare for equality (due to their bit-level representations). Because no grade is negative, *any* negative number triggers the break statement. The following shows how this program works.

```
*** Grade Calculation ***

How many students are there? 10

What is the next student's grade? (-99 to quit) 87

What is the next student's grade? (-99 to quit) 97

What is the next student's grade? (-99 to quit) 67

What is the next student's grade? (-99 to quit) 89

What is the next student's grade? (-99 to quit) 94

What is the next student's grade? (-99 to quit) -99

The average of this class is 86.8
```

The continue Statement

The *continue* statement causes C to skip all remaining statements in a loop.

Perform another
loop iteration

The break statement exits a loop early, but the continue statement forces the computer to perform another iteration of the loop. If you put a continue statement in the body of a for or a while loop, the computer ignores any statement in the loop that follows continue.

The format of continue is

```
continue;
```

You use the continue statement when data in the body of the loop is bad, out of bounds, or unexpected. Instead of acting on the bad data, you might want to go back to the top of the loop and get another data value. The following examples help illustrate this use of the continue statement.

TIP: The continue statement forces a new iteration of any of the three loop constructs: the for loop, the while loop, and the do-while loop.

Figure 15.1 shows the difference between the break and continue statements.

```
for (i=0;i<=10;i++)
    {
        break;
        Printf("Loop it\n");/*never prints!*/
    }

/*Rest of program */
```

Break terminates loop immediately

```
for (i=0;i<=10;i++)
    {
        continue;
        Printf("Loop it\n");/*never prints!*/
    }

/*Rest of program*/
```

Continue causes loop to perform another iteration

Figure 15.1. The difference between break and continue.

Examples

1. Although the following program appears to print the numbers 1 through 10, each followed by "C Programming," it does not. The continue in the body of the for loop causes an early finish to the loop. The first printf() in the for loop executes, but the second does not—due to the continue.

```
/* Filename: C15CON1.C
   Demonstrates use of continue statement */
#include <stdio.h>
main()
{
    int ctr;

    for (ctr=1; ctr<=10; ctr++)      /* Loop 10 times */
    { printf("%d ", ctr);
        continue;              /* Causes body to end early */
        printf("C Programming\n");
```

```
    }
  return;
}
```

This program produces the following output:

```
1 2 3 4 5 6 7 8 9 10
```

On some compilers, you get a warning message when you compile this type of program. The compiler recognizes that the second printf() is *unreachable* code—it never executes due to the continue statement.

Because of this, most programs do not use a continue, except after an if statement. This makes it a conditional continue statement, which is more useful. The following two examples demonstrate the conditional use of continue.

2. This program asks users for five lowercase letters, one at a time, and prints their uppercase equivalents. It uses the ASCII table (see Appendix C) to ensure that users enter lowercase letters. (These are the letters whose ASCII numbers range from 97 to 122.) If users do not type a lowercase letter, the program ignores this with the continue statement.

```
/* Filename: C15CON2.C
   Prints uppercase equivalents of 5 lowercase letters */
#include <stdio.h>
main()
{
  char letter;
  int ctr;

  for (ctr=1; ctr<=5; ctr++)
    { printf("Please enter a lowercase letter ");
      scanf(" %c", &letter);
      if ((letter < 97) || (letter > 122))   /* See if
                                              out-of-range */
        { continue; }                    /* Go get another */
      letter -= 32;      /* Subtract 32 from ASCII value
                                      to get uppercase */
      printf("The uppercase equivalent is %c \n", letter);
```

```
      }
   return;
}
```

Because of the `continue` statement, only lowercase letters are converted to uppercase.

3. Suppose you want to average the salaries of employees in your company who make over $10,000 a year, but you have only their monthly gross pay figures. The following program might be useful. It prompts for each monthly employee salary, annualizes it (multiplying by 12), and computes an average. The `continue` statement ensures that salaries less than or equal to $10,000 are ignored in the average calculation. It enables the other salaries to "fall through."

If you enter -1 as a monthly salary, the program quits and prints the result of the average.

```
/* Filename: C15CON3.C
   Average salaries over $10,000 */
#include <stdio.h>
main()
{
   float month, year;      /* Monthly and yearly salaries */
   float avg=0.0, total=0.0;
   int count=0;

   do
     { printf("What is the next monthly salary (-1 to quit)? ");
       scanf(" %f", &month);
       if ((year=month*12.00) <= 10000.00)   /* Do not add */
          { continue; }                       /* low salaries */
       if (month < 0.0)
          { break; }              /* Quit if user entered -1 */
       count++;                     /* Add 1 to valid counter */
       total += year;      /* Add yearly salary to total */
     } while (month > 0.0);

   avg = total / (float)count;          /* Compute average */
```

```
    printf("\n\nThe average of high salaries is $%.2f", avg);
    return;
}
```

Notice this program uses both a `continue` and a `break` statement. The program does one of three things, depending on each user's input. It adds to the total, or continues another iteration if the salary is too low, or exits the `while` loop (and the average calculation) if the user types a -1.

The following display is the output from this program:

```
What is the next monthly salary (-1 to quit)? 500.00
What is the next monthly salary (-1 to quit)? 2000.00
What is the next monthly salary (-1 to quit)? 750.00
What is the next monthly salary (-1 to quit)? 4000.00
What is the next monthly salary (-1 to quit)? 5000.00
What is the next monthly salary (-1 to quit)? 1200.00
What is the next monthly salary (-1 to quit)? -1

The average of high salaries is $36600.00
```

Review Questions

Answers to review questions are in Appendix B.

1. What do you use timing loops for?

2. Why would timing loop ranges need to be adjusted for different types of computers?

3. Why do `continue` and `break` statements rarely appear without an `if` statement controlling them?

4. What is the output from the following section of code?

```
for (i=1; i<=10; i++)
   { continue;
     printf("***** \n");
   }
```

5. What is the output from the following section of code?

```
for (i=1; i<=10; i++)
   { printf("***** \n");
     break;
   }
```

6. To perform a very long timing loop, why do you generally need to use a nested loop?

Review Exercises

1. Write a program that prints c is fun on the screen for ten seconds. (Hint: You may need to adjust the timing loop.)

2. Make the program in #1 flash the message c is fun for ten seconds. (Hint: You might need to use several timing loops.)

3. Write a grade averaging program for a class of 20 students. Ignore any grade less than 0 and continue until all 20 student grades are entered, or until the user types -99 to end the program early.

4. Write a program that prints the numerals from 1 to 15 in one column. To the right of the even numbers, print each number's square. To the right of the odd numbers, print each number's cube (the number raised to its third power).

Summary

In this chapter, you learned several additional ways to use and modify your program's loops. By adding timing loops, continue statements, and break statements, you can better control how each loop behaves. Being able to exit early (with the break statement) or continue the next loop iteration early (with the continue statement) gives you more freedom when processing different types of data.

The next chapter shows you a construct of C that does not loop, but relies on the break statement to work properly. This is the switch statement, and it makes your program choices much easier to write.

The switch and goto Statements

This chapter focuses on the switch statement. It improves upon the if and else-if constructs by streamlining the multiple-choice decisions your programs make. The switch statement does not replace the if statement, but it is better to use switch when your programs must perform one of many different actions.

The switch and break statements work together. Almost every switch statement you use includes at least one break statement in the body of the loop. To conclude this chapter—and this part of the book on C constructs—you learn the goto statement for completeness, although it is rarely used.

This chapter introduces the following:

♦ The switch statement used for selection

♦ The goto statement used for branching from one part of your program to another

If you have mastered the if statement, you should have little trouble with the concepts presented here. By learning the switch statement, you should be able to write menus and multiple-choice data-entry programs with ease.

The switch Statement

Use the switch statement when your program makes a multiple-choice selection.

The switch statement is sometimes called the *multiple-choice statement*. The switch statement lets your program choose from several alternatives. The format of the switch statement is a little longer than the format of other statements you have seen. Here is the format of the switch statement:

Select a
block of
statements
based on
a condition

```
switch (expression)
   { case (expression1): { one or more C statements; }
     case (expression2): { one or more C statements; }
     case (expression3): { one or more C statements; }
         .
         .
         .

     default: { one or more C statements; }
   }
```

The *expression* can be an integer expression, a character, a constant, or a variable. The subexpressions *(expression1, expression2, and so on)* can be any other integer expression, character, constant, or variable. The number of case expressions following the switch line is determined by your application. The *one or more C statements* can be any block of C code. If the block is only one statement long, you do not need the braces, but they are recommended.

The default line is optional; most (but not all) switch statements include the default. The default line does not have to be the last line of the switch body.

If *expression* matches *expression1*, the statements to the right of *expression1* execute. If *expression* matches *expression2*, the statements to the right of *expression2* execute. If none of the expressions match that of the switch *expression*, the default case block executes. The case expression does not need parentheses, but they sometimes make the value easier to find.

TIP: Use a break statement after each case block to keep execution from "falling through" to the remaining case statements.

Using the switch statement is easier than its format might lead you to believe. Anywhere an if-else-if combination of statements can go, you can usually put a clearer switch statement instead. The switch statement is much easier to follow than an if-within-an-if-within-an-if, as you have had to write previously.

However, the if and else-if combinations of statements are not bad to use or difficult to follow. When the relational test that determines the choice is complex and contains many && and || operators, the if may be a better candidate. The switch statement is preferred whenever multiple-choice possibilities are based on a single constant, variable, or expression.

> **TIP:** Arrange case statements in the most-often to least-often executed order to improve your program's speed.

The following examples clarify the switch statement. They compare the switch statement to if statements to help you see the difference.

Examples

1. Suppose you are writing a program to teach your child how to count. Your program should ask the child for a number. It then beeps (rings the computer's alarm bell) as many times as necessary to match that number.

   The following program assumes the child presses a number key from 1 to 5. This program uses the if-else-if combination to accomplish this counting-and-beeping teaching method.

   Identify the program and include the necessary header file. We want to sound a beep and move the cursor to the next line, so define a global variable called BEEP that does this. We need a variable to hold the user's answer, so make num an integer variable.

   Ask the user for a number. Get the user's number and assign it to num. If num is 1, call BEEP once. If num is 2, call BEEP twice. If num is 3, call BEEP three times. If num is 4, call BEEP four times. If num is 5, call BEEP five times.

```
/* Filename: C16BEEP1.C
   Beeps a certain number of times */
#include <stdio.h>

/* Define a beep printf() to save repeating printf()s
   throughout the program */
#define BEEP printf("\a \n")
main()
{
    int num;

    /* Get a number from the child (you may have to help) */
    printf("Please enter a number ");
    scanf(" %d", &num);

    /* Use multiple if statements to beep */
    if (num == 1)
      { BEEP; }
    else if (num == 2)
           { BEEP; BEEP; }
        else if (num == 3)
               { BEEP; BEEP; BEEP; }
            else if (num == 4)
                  { BEEP; BEEP; BEEP; BEEP; }
                else if (num == 5)
                     { BEEP; BEEP; BEEP; BEEP; BEEP; }
    return;
}
```

No beeps are sounded if the child enters something other than 1 through 5. This program takes advantage of the #define preprocessor directive to define a shortcut to an alarm print() function. In this case, the BEEP is a little clearer to read, as long as you remember that BEEP is not a command, but gets replaced with the printf() everywhere it appears.

One drawback to this type of if-within-an-if program is its readability. By the time you indent the body of each if and else, the program is shoved too far to the right. There is no room for more than five or six possibilities. More importantly, this type of logic is difficult to follow. Because it involves a multiple-choice selection, a `switch` statement is much better to use, as you can see with the following improved version.

```
/* Filename: C16BEEP2.C
   Beeps a certain number of times using a switch */
#include <stdio.h>

/* Define a beep printf() to save repeating printf()s
   throughout the program */
#define BEEP printf("\a \n")
main()
{
   int num;

   /* Get a number from the child (you may have to help) */
   printf("Please enter a number ");
   scanf(" %d", &num);

   switch (num)
   { case (1): { BEEP;
                 break; }
     case (2): { BEEP; BEEP;
                 break; }
     case (3): { BEEP; BEEP; BEEP;
                 break; }
     case (4): { BEEP; BEEP; BEEP; BEEP;
                 break; }
     case (5): { BEEP; BEEP; BEEP; BEEP; BEEP;
                 break; }
   }
   return;
}
```

This example is much clearer than the previous one. The value of num controls the execution—only the case that matches num executes. The indention helps separate each case.

If the child enters a number other than 1 through 5, no beeps are sounded because there is no case expression to match any other value and there is no default case.

Because the BEEP preprocessor directive is so short, you can put more than one on a single line. This is not a requirement, however. The block of statements following a case can also be more than one statement long.

If more than one case expression is the same, only the first expression executes.

2. If the child does not type a 1, 2, 3, 4, or 5, nothing happens in the last program. What follows is the same program modified to take advantage of the default option. The default block of statements executes if none of the previous cases match.

```
/* Filename: C16BEEP3.C
   Beeps a certain number of times using a switch */
#include <stdio.h>

/* Define a beep printf() to save repeating printf()s
   throughout the program */
#define BEEP printf("\a \n")
main()
{
   int num;

   /* Get a number from the child (you may have to help) */
   printf("Please enter a number ");
   scanf(" %d", &num);

   switch (num)
   { case (1): { BEEP;
                 break; }
     case (2): { BEEP; BEEP;
                 break; }
     case (3): { BEEP; BEEP; BEEP;
                 break; }
     case (4): { BEEP; BEEP; BEEP; BEEP;
                 break; }
     case (5): { BEEP; BEEP; BEEP; BEEP; BEEP;
                 break; }
```

```
    default:  { printf("You must enter a number from 1 to 5\n");
                printf("Please run this program again\n");
                break; }
    }
    return;
}
```

The break at the end of the default case might seem redundant. After all, no other case statements execute by "falling through" from the default case. It is a good habit to put a break after the default case anyway. If you move the default higher in the switch (it doesn't have to be the last switch option), you are more inclined to move the break with it (where it is then needed).

3. To show the importance of using break statements in each case expression, here is the same beeping program without any break statements.

```
/* Filename: C16BEEP4.C
   Incorrectly beeps using a switch */
#include <stdio.h>

/* Define a beep printf() to save repeating printf()s
   throughout the program */
#define BEEP printf("\a \n")
main()
{
   int num;

   /* Get a number from the child (you may have to help) */
   printf("Please enter a number ");
   scanf(" %d", &num);

   switch (num)                       /* Warning! */
   { case (1): { BEEP; }      /* Without a break, this code */
     case (2): { BEEP; BEEP; }     /* falls through to the */
     case (3): { BEEP; BEEP; BEEP; } /* rest of the beeps! */
     case (4): { BEEP; BEEP; BEEP; BEEP;}
```

```
   case (5): { BEEP; BEEP; BEEP; BEEP; BEEP;}
   default:  { printf("You must enter a number from 1 to 5\n");
               printf("Please run this program again\n"); }
}
return;
}
```

If the user types a 1, the program beeps 15 times! The break is not there to stop the execution from falling through to the other cases. Unlike other programming languages, such as Pascal, C's switch statement requires that you insert break statements between each case if you want only one case executed. This is not necessarily a drawback. The trade-off of having to specify break statements gives you more control in how you handle specific cases, as shown in the next example.

4. This program controls the printing of end-of-day sales totals. It first asks for the day of the week. If the day is Monday through Thursday, a daily total is printed. If the day is a Friday, a weekly total and a daily total are printed. If the day happens to be the end of the month, a monthly sales total is printed as well.

In a real application, these totals would come from the disk drive rather than be assigned at the top of the program. Also, instead of individual sales figures being printed, a full daily, weekly, and monthly report of many sales totals would probably be printed. You are on your way to learning more about expanding the power of your C programs. But for now, concentrate on the switch statement and its possibilities.

The daily; daily and weekly; and daily, weekly, and monthly sales figures are handled through a hierarchy of case statements. Because the daily amount is the last case, it is the only report printed if the day of the week is Monday through Thursday. If the day of the week is Friday, the second case prints the weekly sales total and then falls through to the daily total (because Friday's daily total must be printed as well). If it is the end of the month, the first case executes, falling through to the weekly total, then to the daily sales total as well. In this example, the use of a break statement would be harmful. Other languages that do not offer this "fall through" flexibility are more limiting.

```
/* Filename: C16SALE.C
   Prints daily, weekly, and monthly sales totals */
#include <stdio.h>
main()
{
   float daily=2343.34;     /* Later, these figures will */
   float weekly=13432.65;   /* come from a disk file     */
   float monthly=43468.97;  /* instead of being assigned */
                            /* as they are here          */
   char ans;
   int day;          /* Day value to trigger correct case */

   /* Day is assigned 1 through 5 (for Monday through
      Friday) or 6 if it is the end of the month. Assume
      a weekly AND a daily prints if it is the end of the
      month, no matter what the day is. */
   printf("Is this the end of the month? (Y/N) ");
   scanf(" %c", &ans);
   if ((ans=='Y') || (ans=='y'))
     { day=6; }                          /* Month value */
   else
     { printf("What day number, 1 through 5 (for Mon-Fri)
       is it? ");
       scanf(" %d", &day); }

   switch (day)
     { case (6): printf("The monthly total is  $%.2f \n",
                        monthly);
       case (5): printf("The weekly total is  $%.2f \n",
                        weekly);
       default:  printf("The daily total is  $%.2f \n",
                        daily);
     }
   return;
}
```

5. The order of the case statements is not fixed. You can rearrange them to make them more efficient. If only one or two cases are being selected most of the time, put those cases near the top of the switch statement.

For example, asume that most of a company's employees are engineers. By arranging the case statements so that Engineering is at the top, you can speed up this program because C will not have to scan through case expressions that it rarely executes.

```c
/* Filename: C16DEPT2.C
   Prints message depending on the department entered */
#include <stdio.h>
main()
{
   char choice;

   do   /* Display menu and ensure that user enters a
           correct option */
    { printf("\nChoose your department: \n");
      printf("S - Sales \n");
      printf("A - Accounting \n");
      printf("E - Engineering \n");
      printf("P - Payroll \n");
      printf("What is your choice? ");
      scanf(" %c", &choice);
      /* Convert choice to uppercase (if they
         entered lowercase) with the ASCII table */
      if ((choice>=97) && (choice<=122))
        { choice -= 32; }          /* Subtract enough to make
                                      uppercase */
    } while ((choice!='S')&&(choice!='A')&&
            (choice!='E')&&(choice!='P'));

   /* Put Engineering first because it occurs most often */
   switch (choice)
   { case ('E') : { printf("\n Your meeting is at 2:30");
                    break; }
     case ('S') : { printf("\n Your meeting is at 8:30");
                    break; }
     case ('A') : { printf("\n Your meeting is at 10:00");
```

```
                        break; }
        case ('P') : { printf("\n Your meeting has been canceled");
                        break; }
     }
     return;
}
```

The goto Statement

The goto causes execution to jump to a statement other than the next one.

Early programming languages did not offer the flexible constructs that C gives you, such as for loops, while loops, and switch statements. Their only means of looping and comparing was with the goto statement. C still includes a goto, but the other constructs are more powerful, flexible, and easier to follow in a program.

The goto statement causes your program to jump to a different location, rather than execute the next statement in sequence. The format of the goto statement is

goto *statement label*

A *statement label* is named just as variables are (see Chapter 4). A *statement label* cannot have the same name as a C command, a C function, or another variable in the program. If you use a goto statement, there must be a *statement label* elsewhere in the program that the goto branches to. Execution then continues at the statement with the *statement label*.

The *statement label* precedes a line of code. Follow all *statement labels* with a colon (:) so C knows they are labels and doesn't get them confused with variables. You have not seen statement labels in the C programs so far in this book because none of the programs needed them. A *statement label* is optional, unless you have a goto that branches to one.

The following four lines of code each have a different *statement label*. This is not a program, but individual lines that might be included in a program. Notice that the *statement labels* are to the left of the lines.

```
pay: printf("Place checks in the printer \n");
```

```
Again: scanf(" %s", name);
EndIt: printf("That is all the processing. \n");
CALC: amount = (total / .5) * 1.15;
```

The *statement labels* are not intended to replace comments, although their names should reflect the code that follows. Statement labels give goto statements a tag *to go to*. When your program gets to the goto, it branches to the statement labeled by the statement label. The program then continues to execute sequentially until the next goto changes the order again (or until the program ends).

> **TIP:** Use identifying line labels. A repetitive calculation deserves a label such as CalcIt and not x15z. Even though both are allowed, the first one is a better indication of the code's purpose.

Use **goto** Judiciously

The goto is not considered a good programming statement when overused. There is a tendency, especially for beginning programmers, to include too many goto statements in a program. When a program branches all over the place, it becomes difficult to follow. Some people call programs with lots of goto statements "spaghetti code."

To eliminate goto statements and write better structured programs, use the other looping and switch constructs seen in the last few chapters.

But the goto is not necessarily a bad statement—if used judiciously. Starting with the next chapter, you begin to break your programs into smaller modules called functions, and the goto becomes less and less important as you write more and more functions.

For now, become familiar with goto so you can understand programs that use it. Some day, you might be called on to correct the code of someone who used the goto.

Examples

1. The following program has a problem that is a direct result of the goto, but it is still one of the best illustrations of the goto statement. The program consists of an *endless loop* (or an infinite loop). The first three lines (after the opening brace) execute, then the goto in the fourth line causes execution to loop back to the beginning and repeat the first three lines. The goto continues to do this until you press Ctrl-Break or ask your system administrator to cancel the program.

Identify the program and include the necessary header file. We want to print a message, but split it over three lines. We want the message to keep repeating, so label the first line, then use a goto to jump back to that line.

```
/* Filename: C16GOTO1.C
   Program to show use of goto. This program ends
   only when the user presses Ctrl-Break. */
#include <stdio.h>
main()
{
   Again: printf("This message \n");
   printf("\t keeps repeating \n");
   printf("\t\t over and over \n");

   goto Again;    /* Repeat continuously */

   return;
}
```

Notice that the statement label has a colon to separate it from the rest of the line, but you never add the colon to the label at the goto statement. Figure 16.1 shows the result of running this program.

```
              keeps repeating
                      over and over
This message
              keeps repeating
                      over and over
This message
              keeps repeating
      -               over and over
This message
              keeps repeating
                      over and over
This message
              keeps repeating
                      over and over
This message
              keeps repeating
                      over and over
This message
              keeps repeating
                      over and over
This message
              keeps repeating
                      over and over
This message
              keeps repeating
                      over and over
This message
```

Figure 16.1. A repeating printing program.

2. It is sometimes easier to read your program's code when you put the statement labels on lines by themselves. Remember that writing maintainable programs is the goal of every good programmer. Making your programs easier to read should be a prime consideration when you write them. The following program is the same repeating program shown in the previous example, except the statement label is placed on a line by itself.

```c
/* Filename: C16GOTO2.C
   Program to show use of goto. This program ends
   only when the user presses Ctrl-Break. */
#include <stdio.h>
main()
{

Again:
   printf("This message \n");
   printf("\t keeps repeating \n");
   printf("\t\t over and over \n");
```

```
    goto Again;    /* Repeat continuously */
    return;
}
```

The line following the statement label is the one that executes next, after control is passed (by the goto) to the label.

Of course, these are silly examples. You really don't want to write programs with infinite loops. The goto is a statement best preceded with an if, so that the goto eventually stops branching without intervention from the user.

3. The following program is one of the worst-written programs ever! It is the epitome of spaghetti code! However, do your best to follow it and understand its output. By understanding the flow of this output, you can hone your understanding of the goto. You might also appreciate the fact that the rest of this book uses the goto only when needed to make the program clearer.

```
/* Filename: C16GOTO3.C
   This program demonstrates the overuse of goto */
#include <stdio.h>
main()
{
    goto Here;

    First:
    printf("A \n");
    goto Final;

    There:
    printf("B \n");
    goto First;

    Here:
    printf("C \n");
    goto There;

    Final:
    return;
}
```

At first glance, this program appears to print the first three letters of the alphabet, but the goto statements make them print in the reverse order, *C, B, A*. Although the program is not a well-designed program, some indention of the lines without statement labels make it a little more readable. This enables you to quickly separate the statement labels from the rest of the code, as you can see from the following program.

```
/* Filename: C16GOTO4.C
   This program demonstrates the overuse of goto */
#include <stdio.h>
main()
{
    goto Here;

First:
    printf("A \n");
    goto Final;

There:
    printf("B \n");
    goto First;

Here:
    printf("C \n");
    goto There;

Final:
    return;
}
```

This program's listing is slightly easier to follow than the previous one, even though both do the same thing. The remaining programs in this book that use statement labels also use such indention.

You certainly realize that this output would be better produced by the following three lines.

```
printf("C \n");
printf("B \n");
printf("A \n");
```

The goto warning is worth repeating: Use goto sparingly and *only* when its use would make your program more readable and maintainable. Usually, you can use much better commands.

Review Questions

Answers to review questions are in Appendix B.

1. How does goto change the order in which a program normally executes?

2. What statement can substitute for an if-else-if construct?

3. Which statement almost always ends each case statement in a switch?

4. True or false: The order of your case statements has no bearing on the efficiency of your program.

5. Rewrite the following section of code using a switch statement.

```
if (num == 1)
   { printf("Alpha"); }
else if (num == 2)
      { printf("Beta"); }
   else if (num == 3)
         { printf("Gamma"); }
      else
         { printf("Other"); }
```

6. Rewrite the following program using a do-while loop.

```
Ask:
   printf("What is your first name? ");
   scanf(" %s", name);
   if ((name[0] < 'A') || (name[0] > 'Z'))
      { goto Ask; }   /* Keep asking until the user
                           types a valid letter */
```

Review Exercises

1. Write a program using the switch statement that asks users for their age, then prints a message saying "You can vote!" if they are 18, "You can adopt!" if they are 21, or "Are you REALLY that young?" for any other age.

2. Write a program, driven by a menu, for your local TV cable company. Here is how to assess charges: If you are within 20 miles outside the city limits, you pay $12.00 a month; 21 to 30 miles outside the city limits, you pay $23.00 a month; 31 to 50 miles outside the city limits, you pay $34.00. No one outside 50 miles gets the service. Prompt the users with a menu for their residence's distance from the city limits.

3. Write a program that calculates parking fees for a multilevel parking garage. Ask if the driver is in a car or a truck. Charge the driver $2.00 for the first hour, $3.00 for the second, and $5.00 for more than 2 hours. If it is a truck, add $1.00 to the total fee. (Hint: Use one switch and one if statement.)

4. Modify the previous parking problem so the charge depends on the time of day the vehicle is parked. If the vehicle is parked before 8 a.m., charge the fees in exercise #3. If the vehicle is parked after 8 a.m. and before 5 p.m., charge an extra usage fee of 50 cents. If the vehicle is parked after 5 p.m., deduct 50 cents from the computed price. You must prompt users for the starting time in a menu, as follows.

```
1. Before 8 a.m.
2. Before 5 p.m.
3. After 5 p.m.
```

Summary

You now have seen the switch statement and all its options. With it, you can improve the readability of a complicated if-else-if selection. The switch is especially good when several outcomes are possible, based on the user's choice.

The goto statement causes an unconditional branch, and can be difficult to follow at times. The goto statement is not used much these days, and you can almost always use a better construct. However, you should be acquainted with as much C as possible in case you have to work on programs that others have written.

This ends the section on program control. The next section introduces user-written functions. So far, you have been using C's built-in functions, such as printf() and scanf(). Now it's time to write your own.

Part IV

Variable Scope and Modular Programming

Writing C Functions

Computers never get bored. They perform the same input, output, and computations your program requires—for as long as you want them to do it. You can take advantage of their repetitive natures by looking at your programs in a new way: as a series of small routines that execute whenever you need them, however many times you require.

This chapter approaches its subject a little differently than previous chapters. It concentrates on teaching the need for writing your own *functions*, which are *modules* of code that you execute and control from our main() function. So far, all programs in this book have consisted of a single long function called main(). As you learn here, the main() function's primary purpose is to control the execution of other functions that follow it.

This chapter introduces the following:

♦ The need for functions

♦ How to trace functions

♦ How to write functions

♦ How to call and return from functions

This chapter stresses the use of *structured programming*, sometimes called *modular programming*. C was designed to make it easy to write your programs in several modules instead of as one long program. By breaking the program into several smaller routines (*functions*), you can isolate problems, write correct programs faster, and produce programs that are easier to maintain.

Function Basics

When you approach an application that needs to be programmed, it is best not to sit down at the keyboard and start typing. Rather, you should first *think* about the program and what it is supposed to do. One of the best ways to attack a program is to start with the overall goal, then divide this goal into several smaller tasks. You should never lose sight of the overall goal, but you should think also of how individual pieces can fit together to accomplish such a goal.

When you finally do sit down to begin coding the problem, continue to think in terms of those pieces fitting together. Don't approach a program as if it were one giant problem; rather, continue to write those small pieces individually.

This does not mean that you must write separate programs to do everything. You can keep individual pieces of the overall program together—if you know how to write functions. Then you can use the same functions in many different programs.

C programs are not like BASIC or FORTRAN programs. C was designed to force you to think in a modular, or subroutine-like, functional style. Good C programmers write programs that consist of many small functions, even if their programs execute one or more of these functions only once. But those functions work together to produce a program quicker and easier than if the program had to be written from scratch.

C programs should consist of many small functions.

TIP: Rather than code *one* very long program, you should write several smaller routines, called functions. One of those functions must be called main(). The main() function is always the first to execute. It doesn't need to be first in a program, but it usually is.

Breaking Down Problems

If your program does very much, break it into several functions. Each function should do *one* primary task. For example, if you were writing a C program to get a list of characters from the keyboard, alphabetize them, then print them to the screen. You could—but shouldn't—write all that into one big main() function, as the following C *skeleton* (program outline) shows:

```
main()
{
    /* :
       C code to get a list of characters
       :
       C code to alphabetize the characters
       :
       C code to print the alphabetized list on the screen
       : */
    return;
}
```

This skeleton is *not* a good way to write this program. Even though you could type this program in only a few lines of code, it would be much better to get in the habit of breaking up every program into distinct tasks. You should not use main() to do everything—in fact, you should use main() to do little except call each of the functions that do the work.

A better way to organize this program is to write a separate function for each task the program is supposed to do. This doesn't mean that each function should be only one line long. Rather, it means you should make every function a building block that performs only one distinct task in the program.

The following program outline shows you a better way to write the program just described:

```
main()
{
    getletters();    /* Calls a function to get the numbers */
    alphabetize();   /* Calls a function to alphabetize
                        letters */
```

Call 3
functions

```
        printletters(); /* Calls a function to print letters
                              on-screen */
        return;          /* Return to the operating system */
}

getletters()
{
   /* :
      C code to get a list of characters
      :   */
   return;    /* Returns to main() */
}

alphabetize()
{
   /* :
      C code to alphabetize the characters
      :    /*
   return;    /* Returns to main() */
}

printletters()
{
   /* :
      C code to print the alphabetized list on the screen
      :   */
   return;    /* Returns to main() */
}
```

The program outline shows you a much better way of writing this program. It is longer to type, but much better organized. The only thing the main() function does is control the other functions by showing in one place the order in which they are called. Each separate function executes its instructions, then returns to main(), whereupon main() calls the next function until no more functions remain. The main() function then returns control of the computer to the operating system.

> **TIP:** A good rule of thumb is that a function should not be more than one screen in length. If it is longer, you are probably doing too much in that function and should therefore break it into two or more functions.

The first function called `main()` is what you previously used to hold the entire program. From this point, in all but the smallest of programs, `main()` simply controls other functions that do the work.

These listings are not examples of real C programs; instead, they are skeletons, or outlines, of programs. From these outlines, it is easier to develop the actual full program. But before going to the keyboard to write a program such as this, you should know that there will be four distinct sections: a primary function-calling `main()` function, a keyboard data-entry function, an alphabetizing function, and a printing function.

You should never lose sight of the original programming problem and, with the approach just described, you never do! Look again at the `main()` calling routine in the preceding program. Notice that you can glance at `main()` and get a feel for the overall program, without the remaining statements getting in the way. This is a good example of structured, modular programming. A large programming problem has been broken down into distinct, separate modules called functions, and each function performs one primary job in a few C statements.

More Function Basics

Little has been said about naming and writing functions, but you probably understand much of the goals of the previous listing already. C functions generally adhere to the following rules:

1. Every function must have a name.

2. Function names are made up and assigned by the programmer (you!) following the same rules that apply to naming variables: they can contain up to 31 characters, they must begin with a letter, and they can consist of letters, numbers, and the underscore (_) character.

3. All function names have one set of parentheses immediately following them. This helps you (and C) differentiate them from variables. The parentheses may or may not contain something. So far, all such parentheses in this book have been empty.

4. The body of each function, starting immediately after the closing parenthesis of the function name, must be enclosed by braces. This means that a block containing one or more statements makes up the body of each function.

Use meaningful function names. `Calc balance` is more descriptive than `xy3()`.

Although the outline shown in the previous listing is a good example of structured code, it can be further improved—and not only by putting the actual C statements inside the program to make it work. You can improve this program also by using the underscore character (_) in the function names. Do you see how `get_letters()` and `print_letters()` are much easier to read than are `getletters()` and `printletters()`?

CAUTION: Be sure to use the underscore character (_) and not the hyphen (-) when naming functions and variables. If you use a hyphen, C becomes very confused and produces misleading error messages.

All programs must have a `main` function.

The following listing shows you an example of a C function. You can already tell quite a bit about this function. You know, for instance, that it isn't a complete program because it has no `main()` function. (All programs *must* have a `main()` function.) You know also that the function name is `calc_it` because parentheses follow this name. These parentheses happen to have something in them. You know also that the body of the function is enclosed in a block of braces. Inside that block is a *smaller* block, the body of a `while` loop. Finally, you recognize that the `return` statement is the last line of the function.

```
calc_it(int n)
{
    /* Function to print the square of a number */
    int square;
```

```
    while (square <= 250)
      { square = n * n;
        printf("The square of %d is %d \n", n, square);
        n++; }      /* A block within the function */


    return;
}
```

> **TIP:** Not all functions require a `return` statement for their last line, but it is recommended that you always include one because it helps to show your intention to return to the calling function at that point. Later in the book, you learn when the `return` is required. For now, you should just get in the habit of including a `return` statement.

Calling and Returning Functions

A function call is like a temporary program detour.

You have been reading much about "function calling" and "returning control." Although you may already understand these phrases from their context, you can probably learn them better through an illustration of what is meant by a function call.

A function call in C is like a detour on a highway. Imagine you are traveling along the "road" of the primary function called `main()` and then run into a function-calling statement. You must temporarily leave the `main()` function and go execute the function that was called. After that function finishes (its `return` statement is reached), program control reverts to `main()`. In other words, when you finish a detour, you end up back on the "main" route and continue the trip. Control continues as `main()` calls other functions.

> **NOTE:** Generally, the primary function that controls function calls and their order is called a *calling function*. Functions controlled by the calling function are called the *called functions*.

A complete C program, with functions, should make this clear. The following program prints several messages to the screen. Each message printed is determined by the order of the functions. Before worrying too much about what this program does, take a little time to study its structure. You should be able to see three functions defined in the program: main(), next_fun(), and third_fun(). A fourth function is used also, but it is the built-in C printf() function. The three defined functions appear sequentially, one after the other. The body of each is enclosed in braces, and each has a return statement at its end.

```
/* C17FUN1.C
   The following program illustrates function calls */
#include <stdio.h>
main()  /* main() is always the first C function executed */
{
   printf("First function called main() \n");
   next_fun();           /* Second function is called here */
   third_fun();          /* This function is called here */
   printf("main() is completed \n");      /* All control
                                          returns here */
   return;                      /* Control is returned to
                                   the operating system   */
}                               /* This brace concludes main() */


next_fun()                            /* Second function;
                           parentheses always required */
{
   printf("Inside next_fun() \n");    /* No variables are
                                  defined in the program */
   return;          /* Control is now returned to main() */
}


third_fun()                /* Last function in the program */
{
   printf("Inside third_fun() \n");
   return;             /* Always return from all functions */
}
```

The output of this program follows:

```
First function called main()
Inside next_fun()
Inside third_fun()
main() is completed
```

Figure 17.1 shows a tracing of this program's execution. Notice that main() controls which of the other functions is called, as well as the order of the calling. Control *always* returns to the calling function after the called function finishes.

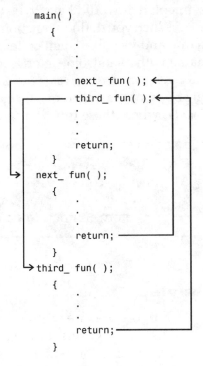

Figure 17.1. Tracing function calls.

To call a function, simply type its name—including the parentheses—and follow it with a semicolon. Remember that semicolons follow all executable statements in C, and a function call (sometimes called a *function invocation*) is an executable statement.

The execution is the function's code being called. Any function can call any other function. It just happens that main() is the only function that calls other functions in this program.

Now you can tell that the following statement is a function call:

```
print_total();
```

Because print_total is not a C command or built-in function name, it must be a variable or a written function's name. Only function names end with the parentheses, so it must be a function call or the start of a function's code. Of the last two possibilities, it must be a call to a function because it ends with a semicolon. If it didn't have a semicolon, it would have to be the start of a function definition.

When you define a function (that is, when you type the function name and its subsequent code inside braces), you *never* follow the name with a semicolon. Notice in the previous program that main(), next_fun(), and third_fun() have no semicolons when they appear in the body of the program. A semicolon follows their names only in main(), where these functions are called.

> **CAUTION:** Never define a function within another function. All function code must be listed sequentially, one after the other, throughout the program. A function's closing brace *must* appear before another function's code can be listed.

Examples

1. Suppose you are writing a program that does the following. First, it asks users for their departments. Then, if they are in accounting, they should receive the accounting department's report. If they are in engineering, they should receive the engineering department's report. And if they are in marketing, they should receive the marketing department's report.

   The skeleton of such a program follows. The code for main() is shown in its entirety, but only a skeleton of the other functions are shown. The switch statement is a perfect function-calling statement for such multiple-choice selections.

```c
/* Skeleton of a departmental report program */
#include <stdio.h>
main()
{
   int choice;

   do
     { printf("Choose your department from the following list\n");
       printf("\t1. Accounting \n");
       printf("\t2. Engineering \n");
       printf("\t3. Marketing \n");
       printf("What is your choice? ");
       scanf(" %d", &choice);
     } while ((choice<1) || (choice>3));   /* Ensure 1, 2,
                                                or 3 */


   switch choice
   { case(1): { acct_report(); /* Call accounting function */
                break; }               /* Don't fall through */
     case(2): { eng_report(); /* Call engineering function */
                break; }
     case(3): { mtg_report();   /* Call marketing function */
                break; }
   }
   return;  /* Program returns to the operating system
                when finished */
}

acct_report()
{
   /* :
      Accounting report code goes here */
      :  */
   return;
}

eng_report()
{
   /* :
      Engineering report code goes here */
```

```
        :   */
    return;
}

mtg_report()  .
{
    /* :
        Marketing report code goes here */
        :   */
    return;
}
```

The bodies of switch statements normally contain function calls. You can tell that these case statements execute functions. For instance, acct_report(); (which is the first line of the first case) is not a variable name or a C command. It is the name of a function defined later in the program. If users enter 1 at the menu, the function called acct_report() executes. When it finishes, control returns to the first case body, whose break statement causes the switch statement to end. The main() function returns to DOS (or to your integrated C environment if you are using one) when its return statement executes.

2. In the previous example, the main() routine is not very modular. It displays the menu, but that should be done in a separate function. Remember that main() should do very little except control the other functions, which do all the work.

Here is a rewrite of this sample program, with a fourth function to print the menu to the screen. This is truly a modular example, with each function performing a single task. Again, the last three functions show only skeleton code because the goal here is simply to illustrate function calling and returning.

```
/* Second skeleton of a departmental report program */
#include <stdio.h>
main()
{
```

```
        int choice;

        do
          {  menu_print();   /* Call function to print the menu */
             scanf(" %d", &choice);
          } while ((choice<1) || (choice>3));    /* Ensure 1, 2,
                                                        or 3 */

        switch choice
        { case(1): { acct_report(); /* Call accounting function */
                     break; }              /* Don't fall through */
           case(2): { eng_report(); /* Call engineering function */
                     break; }
           case(3): { mtg_report();   /* Call marketing function */
                     break; }
        }
        return;  /* Program returns to the operating system
                     when finished */

    }

menu_print()
{
   printf("Choose your department from the following list\n");
   printf("\t1. Accounting \n");
   printf("\t2. Engineering \n");
   printf("\t3. Marketing \n");
   printf("What is your choice? ");
   return;   /* Return to main() */
}

acct_report()
{
   /* :
      Accounting report code goes here */
      :   */
   return;
}

eng_report()
{
```

```
    /* :
       Engineering report code goes here */
       :    */
    return;
}

mtg_report()
{
    /* :
       Marketing report code goes here */
       :    */
    return;
}
```

The menu printing function doesn't have to follow `main()`. Because it's the first function called, however, it seems best to define it there.

3. Readability is the key, so programs broken into separate functions result in better written code. You can write and test each function, one at a time. After you write a general outline of the program, you can list a lot of function calls in `main()`, and define their skeletons after `main()`.

The body of each function initially should consist of a single `return` statement, so that the program compiles in its skeleton format. As you complete each function, you can compile and test the program. This enables you to develop more accurate programs faster. The separate functions let others (who might later modify your program) "zero in" on whatever code they need to change, without affecting the rest of the program.

Another useful habit, popular with many C programmers, is to separate functions from each other with a comment consisting of a line of asterisks (*) or dashes (-). This makes it easy, especially in longer programs, to see where a function begins and ends. What follows is another listing of the previous program, but now with its four functions more clearly separated by this type of comment line.

```
/* Third skeleton of a departmental report program */
#include <stdio.h>
main()
{
   int choice;

   do
     { menu_print();  /* Call function to print the menu */
       scanf(" %d", &choice);
     } while ((choice<1) || (choice>3));  /* Ensure 1, 2,
                                              or 3 */

   switch choice
   { case(1): { acct_report(); /* Call accounting function */
                break; }            /* Don't fall through */
     case(2): { eng_report(); /* Call engineering function */
                break; }
     case(3): { mtg_report();  /* Call marketing function */
                break; }
   }
   return;  /* Program returns to the operating system
               when finished */
}


/*************************************************************/
menu_print()
{
   printf("Choose your department from the following list\n");
   printf("\t1. Accounting \n");
   printf("\t2. Engineering \n");
   printf("\t3. Marketing \n");
   printf("What is your choice? ");
   return;   /* Return to main() */
}


/*************************************************************/
acct_report()
{
   /* :
      Accounting report code goes here */
      :   */
```

```
    return;
}

/************************************************************/
eng_report()
{
    /* :
        Engineering report code goes here */
        :   */
    return;
}

/************************************************************/
mtg_report()
{
    /* :
        Marketing report code goes here */
        :   */
    return;
}
```

Due to space limitations, not all program listings in this book separate the functions in this manner. You might find, however, that your listings are easier to follow if you put these separating comments between your functions. The mailing list application in Appendix F, for example, uses these types of comments to separate its functions.

4. You can execute a function more than once simply by calling it from more than one place in a program. If you put a function call in the body of a loop, the function executes repeatedly until the loop finishes.

The following program prints the message C is Fun! several times on-screen—forward and backward—using functions. Notice that main() does not make every function call. The second function, name_print(), calls the function named reverse_print(). Trace the execution of this program's printf()s. Figure 17.2 shows the program's output to help you trace its execution.

```
/* Filename: C17FUN2.C
   Prints C is fun! several times on the screen */
#include <stdio.h>
main()
{
   int ctr;  /* To control loops */

   for (ctr=1; ctr<=5; ctr++)
     { name_print(); }              /* Calls function 5 times */

   one_per_line();               /* Calls last function once */
   return;
}

/**********************************************************/
name_print()
{
   /* Prints C is Fun! across a line, separated by tabs */
   printf("C is Fun!\tC is Fun!\tC is Fun!\tC is Fun!\n");
   printf("C i s  F u n !\tC  i s  F u n ! \tC  i s  F u n !\n");

   reverse_print();       /* Call next function from here */
   return;                          /* Returns to main() */
}

/**********************************************************/
reverse_print()
{
   /* Prints several C is Fun! messages, */
   /*    in reverse, separated by tabs    */
   printf("!nuF si C\t!nuF si C\t!nuF si C\t\n");

   return;                          /* Returns to name_print() */
}

/**********************************************************/
one_per_line()
{
   /* Prints C is Fun! down the screen */
```

reverse_print

BEGIN

Print
message
backwards

END

```
      printf("C\n \ni\ns\n \nF\nu\nn\n!\n");
      return;    /* Returns to main() */
   }
```

```
C is Fun!       C is Fun!       C is Fun!       C is Fun!
C  is  Fun! C  is  Fun! C  is  Fun!
!nuF si C       !nuf si C       !nuf si C
C is Fun!       C is Fun!       C is Fun!       C is Fun!
C  is  Fun! C  is  Fun! C  is  Fun!
!nuF si C       !nuf si C       !nuf si C
C is Fun!       C is Fun!       C is Fun!       C is Fun!
C  is  Fun! C  is  Fun! C  is  Fun!
!nuF si C       !nuf si C       !nuf si C
C is Fun!       C is Fun!       C is Fun!       C is Fun!
C  is  Fun! C  is  Fun! C  is  Fun!
!nuF si C       !nuf si C       !nuf si C
C is Fun!       C is Fun!       C is Fun!       C is Fun!
C  is  Fun! C  is  Fun! C  is  Fun!
!nuF si C       !nuf si C       !nuf si C
C

i
s

F
u
n
!
```

Figure 17.2. Printing a message several times, forward and backward.

Review Questions

Answers to review questions are in Appendix B.

1. True or false: A function should always include a `return` statement as its last command.

2. What is the name of the first function executed in a C program?

3. Which is better: one long function or several smaller functions? Why?

4. How do function names differ from variable names?

5. How can you use comments to help separate functions visually from each other?

6. What is wrong with the following program section?

```
calc_it()
{
   printf("Getting ready to calculate the square of 25 \n");

   sq_25()
   {
      printf("The square of 25 is %d", (25*25));
      return;
   }

   printf("That is a big number! \n");
   return;
}
```

7. Is the following a variable name, a function call, a function definition, or an expression?

```
scan_names();
```

8. True or false: the following line in a C program is a function call.

```
printf("C is Fun! \n");
```

Summary

You have now been exposed to truly structured programs. Instead of typing a long program, you can break it up into separate functions. This isolates your routines from each other, so that surrounding code doesn't get in the way when you are concentrating on one section of your program.

Functions introduce just a little more complexity, involving the way variable values are recognized by all the program's functions. The next chapter shows you how variables are handled between functions, and helps strengthen your structured programming skills.

Variable Scope

The concept of *variable scope* is most important when you write functions. Variable scope determines which functions recognize certain variables. If a function recognizes a variable, the variable is *visible* to that function. Variable scope protects variables in one function from other functions that might overwrite them. If a function doesn't need access to a variable, that function shouldn't be able to see or change the variable. In other words, the variable should not even be "visible" to that particular function.

This chapter introduces you to

♦ Global and local variables

♦ Passing arguments

♦ Automatic and static variables

♦ Passing parameters

The previous chapter introduced the concept of using a different function for each task. This concept is much more useful when you learn about local and global variable scope.

18

353

Global Versus Local Variables

If you have programmed only in BASIC, the concept of local and global variables may be new to you. In many interpreted versions of BASIC, all variables are *global*. That is, the entire program knows what every variable is and has the capability to change any of them. If you use a variable called SALES at the top of the program, even the last line in the program can use SALES. (If you don't know BASIC, don't despair—there will be one less habit you have to break!)

Global variables can be dangerous. Parts of a program can inadvertently change a variable that shouldn't be changed. For example, suppose you are writing a program that keeps track of a grocery store's inventory. You might keep track of sales percentages, discounts, retail prices, wholesale prices, produce prices, dairy prices, delivered prices, price changes, sales tax percentages, holiday markups, post-holiday markdowns, and so on.

The huge number of prices in such a system is confusing. When writing a program to keep track of each these prices, and it would be easy to mistakenly call both the dairy prices d_prices and the delivered prices d_prices. Either C disallows it (does not let you define the same variable twice) or you overwrite a value used for something else. Whatever happens, keeping track of all of these different—but similarly named—prices make this program confusing to write.

Global variables can be dangerous because code can inadvertently overwrite a variable initialized elsewhere in the program. It is better to make every variable *local* in your programs. Then, only functions that should be able to change the variables can do so.

Global variables are visible across many program functions.

Local variables are visible only in the block where they are defined.

Local variables can be seen (and changed) only from the function they are defined in. Therefore, if a function defines a variable as local, that variable's scope is protected. The variable cannot be used, changed, or erased by any other function—without special programming that you learn about shortly.

If you use only one function, main(), the concept of local and global is academic. But you know from the last chapter that single-function programs are not recommended. It is best to write modular, structured programs made up of many smaller functions. Therefore, you should know how to define variables as local to only those functions that need them.

Defining Variable Scope

When you first learned about variables in Chapter 4, "Variables and Constants," you learned that you can define variables in two places:

♦ After the opening brace of a block of code (usually at the top of a function)

♦ Before a function name, such as main()

All examples in this book so far have declared variables using the first method. You have yet to see an example of the second method. Because most of these programs have consisted entirely of a single main() function, there has been no reason to differentiate the two methods. It is only after you start using several functions in one program that these two variable definition methods become critical.

The following rules, specific to local and global variables, are very important:

♦ A variable is local *if and only if* you define it after the opening brace of a block, usually at the top of a function.

♦ A variable is global *if and only if* you define it outside a function.

All variables you have seen so far have been local. They have all been defined immediately after the opening braces of main(). Therefore, they have been local to main() and only main() can use them. Other functions have no idea these variables even exist because they belong to main() only. When the function (or block) ends, all its local variables are destroyed.

> **TIP:** All local variables disappear (lose their definition) when their block ends.

Global variables are visible ("known") from their point of definition *downward* in the source code. That is, if you define a global variable, *any* line throughout the rest of the program—no matter how many functions and code lines follow it—is able to use that global variable.

Examples

1. The following section of code defines two local variables, i and j.

```
main()
{
    int i, j;                /* Local because they're
                                defined after the brace */
    /* Rest of main() goes here */
}
```

These variables are visible to main() and not to any other function that might follow or be called by main().

2. The following section of code defines two global variables, g and h.

```
#include <stdio.h>
int g, h;                    /* Global because they're
                                defined before a function */
main()
{
    /* main()'s code goes here */
}
```

It really doesn't matter whether your #include lines go before or after global variable declarations.

3. Global variables can appear before any function. In the following program, main() uses no variables. However, both of the two functions after main() can use sales and profit because these variables are global.

```
/* Filename: C18GLO.C
   Program that contains two global variables */
#include <stdio.h>
main()
{
   printf("No variables defined in main() \n\n");
   do_fun();                      /* Call the first function */
   return;
}

float sales, profit;              /* Two global variables */
do_fun()
{
   sales = 20000.00;        /* This variable is visible   */
                            /* from this point down.      */
   profit = 5000.00;        /* So is this one. They are   */
                            /* both global.               */

   printf("The sales in the second function are: %.2f \n",
          sales);
   printf("The profit in the second function is: %.2f \n\n",
          profit);

   third_fun();          /* Call the third function to
                            show that globals are visible */
   return;
}

third_fun()
{
   printf("In the third function: \n");
   printf("The sales in the third function are: %.2f \n",
          sales);
   printf("The profit in the third function is: %.2f \n",
          profit);
   /* If sales and profit were local, they would not be
      visible by more than one function */
   return;
}
```

Note that the main() function can never use sales and profit
because they are not visible to main()—even though they are

global. Remember, global variables are visible only from their point of definition downward in the program. Statements that appear before global variable definitions cannot use those variables. Figure 18.1 shows the result of running this program.

```
No variables defined in main()

The sales in the 2nd function is: 20000.00
The profit in the 2nd function is: 5000.00

In the third function:
The sales in 3rd function is: 20000.00
The profit in 3rd function is: 5000.00
```

Figure 18.1. Demonstrating the visibility of global variables.

TIP: Declare all global variables at the top of your programs. Even though you can define them later (between any two functions), you can spot them faster if you declare them at the top.

4. The following program uses both local and global variables. It should now be obvious to you that j and p are local and i and z are global.

```
/* Filename: C18GLLO.C
   Program with both local and global variables
   Local Variables        Global Variables
      j, p                    i, z              */
```

```
#include <stdio.h>
int i = 0;                      /* Global variable because it's
                                          defined outside main() */
main()
{
   float p ;                             /* Local to main() only */
   p = 9.0;                   /* Put value in global variable */
   printf("%d  %f\n", i, p);           /* Prints global i
                                                 and local p */
   pr_again();                       /* Calls next function */
   return;                               /* Returns to DOS */

}

float z = 9.0;              /* Global variable because it's
                               defined before a function */
pr_again()
{
   int j = 5;                     /* Local to only pr_again() */
   printf("%d %f %d", j, z, i); /* This couldn't print p! */
   return;                              /* Return to main() */
}
```

Even though j is defined in a function that main() calls, main() cannot use j because j is local to pr_again(). When pr_again() finishes, j is no longer defined. The variable z is global from its point of definition down. This is why main() cannot print z. Also, the function pr_again() cannot print p because p is local to main() only.

Make sure you can recognize local and global variables before you continue. A little study here makes the rest of this chapter very easy to understand.

5. Two variables can have the same name, as long as they are local to two different functions. They are distinct variables, even though they are named identically.

   The following short program uses two variables, both named age. They have two different values, and they are considered to be two different variables. The first age is local to main(), and the second age is local to get_age().

```
/* Filename: C18LOC2.C
   Two different local variables with the same name */
#include <stdio.h>
main()
{
    int age;
    printf("What is your age? ");
    scanf(" %d", &age);

    get_age();                      /* Call the second function */
    printf("main()'s age is still: %d", age);

    return;
}

get_age()
{
    int age;                    /* A different age. This one
                                   is local to get+age() */
    printf("What is your age again? ");
    scanf(" %d", &age);
    return;
}
```

Variables local to
main() cannot be
used in another
function that
main() calls.

The output of this program follows. Study this output carefully. Notice that main()'s last printf() does not print the newly changed age. Rather, it prints only the age known to main()—the age that is local to main(). Even though they are named the same, main()'s age has nothing to do with get_age()'s age. They might as well have two different variable names.

```
What is your age? 28
What is your age again? 56
main()'s age is still 28
```

You should be careful when naming variables. Having two variables with the same name is misleading. It would be easy to become confused while changing this program later. If these variables truly need to be separate, name them differently, such as old_age and new_age, or ag1 and ag2. This helps you remember that they are different.

6. There are a few times when overlapping local variable names does not add confusion, but be careful about over-doing it. Programmers often use the same variable name as the counter variable in a for loop. For example, the two local variables in the following program have the same name.

```
/* Filename: C18LOC3.C
   Using two local variables with the same name
   as counting variables */
#include <stdio.h>
main()
{
   int ctr;                              /* Loop counter */
   for (ctr=0; ctr<=10; ctr++)
      { printf("main()'s ctr is %d \n", ctr); }
   do_fun();                    /* Call second function */

   return;
}

do_fun()
{
   int ctr;
   for (ctr=10; ctr>=0; ctr−)
      { printf("do_fun()'s ctr is %d \n", ctr); }
   return;                          /* Return to main() */
}
```

Although this is a nonsense program that simply prints 0 through 10 and then prints 10 through 0, it shows that the use of ctr in both functions is not a problem. These variables do not hold important data that must be processed; rather, they are for loop counting variables. Calling them both ctr leads to little confusion because their use is limited to con-trolling for loops. Because a for loop initializes and incre-ments variables, the functions never rely on the other one's ctr to do anything.

7. Be careful about creating local variables with the same name in the same function. If you define a local variable early in a

function and then define another local variable with the same name inside a new block, C uses only the innermost variable, until its block ends.

The following example helps clarify this confusing problem. The program contains one function with three local variables. See if you can find these three variables.

```
/* Filename: C18MULI.C
   Program with multiple local variables called i */
#include <stdio.h>
main()
{
  int i;                                 /* Outer i */
  i = 10;

  { int i;                               /* New block's i */
    i = 20;                   /* Outer i still holds a 10 */
    printf("%d %d \n", i, i);            /* Prints 20 20 */

    { int i;      /* Another new block and local variable */
      i = 30;                            /* Innermost i only */
      printf("%d %d %d \n", i, i, i); /* Prints 30 30 30 */
    }                  /* Innermost i is now gone forever */

  }        /* Second i is gone forever (its block ended) */

  printf("%d %d %d", i, i, i);          /* Prints 10 10 10 */
  return;
}                   /* main() ends and so do its variables */
```

All local variables are local to the block in which they are defined. This program has three blocks, each one nested within another. Because you can define local variables immediately after an opening brace of a block, there are three distinct i variables in this program.

The local i disappears completely when its block ends (that is, when the closing brace is reached). C always prints the variable that it sees as the most local—the one that resides within the innermost block.

Use Global Variables Sparingly

You may be asking yourself, "Why do I need to know about global and local variables?" At this point, that is an understandable question, especially if you have been programming mostly in BASIC. Here is the bottom line: Global variables can be *dangerous*. Code can inadvertently overwrite a variable that was initialized in another place in the program. It is better to have every variable in your program be *local to the function that needs to access it*.

Read that last sentence again. Even though you now know how to make variables global, you should avoid doing so! Try to never use another global variable. It may seem easier to use global variables when you write programs having more than one function: If you make every variable used by every function global, you never have to worry if one is visible or not to any given function. On the other hand, a function can accidentally change a global variable when it has no right to change it. If you keep variables local only to functions that need them, you protect their values, and you also keep your programs, both the code and all your data, fully modular.

The Need for Passing Variables

You just learned the difference between local and global variables. You saw that by making your variables local, you protect their values because the function that sees the variable is the only one that can modify it.

What do you do, however, if you have a local variable you want to use in *two or more* functions? In other words, you may need a variable to be both inputted from the keyboard in one function and printed in another function. If the variable is local only to the first function, how can the second one access it?

You have two solutions if more than one function needs to share a variable. One, you can declare the variable globally. This is bad because you want *only* those two functions to "see" the variable, but all other functions can "see" it if it is global. The other alternative—and the better one by far—is to *pass* the local variable from one function to another. This has a big advantage: The variable is only known to those two functions. The rest of the program still has no access to it.

> **CAUTION:** Never pass a global variable because C will get confused. There is no reason to pass global variables anyway because they are already visible to all functions.

You pass an argument when you pass one local variable to another function.

When you pass a local variable from one function to another, you *pass an argument* from the first function to the next. You can pass more than one argument (variable) at a time, if you want several local variables sent from one function to another. The receiving function *receive a parameter* (variable) from the function that sends it. You shouldn't worry too much about what you call them—either arguments or parameters. The important thing to remember is that you are sending local variables from one function to another.

> **NOTE:** You have already passed arguments to parameters when you passed data to the `printf()` function. The constants, variables, and expressions in the `printf()` parentheses are arguments. The built-in `printf()` function receives these values (called parameters on the receiving end) and displays them.

A little more terminology is needed before you see some examples. When a function passes an argument, it is called the *passing function*. The function that receives the argument (called a parameter when it is received) is called the *receiving function*. Figure 18.2 explains these terms.

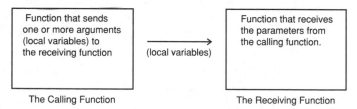

Figure 18.2. The calling and receiving functions.

If a function name has empty parentheses, nothing is being passed to it.

To pass a local variable from one function to another, you must place the local variable in parentheses in both the calling function and the receiving function. For example, the local and global examples presented earlier did not pass local variables from main() to do_fun(). If a function name has empty parentheses, nothing is being passed to it. Given this, the following line passes two variables, total and discount, to a function called do_fun().

```
do_fun(total, discount);
```

It is sometimes said that a variable or function is *defined*. This has *nothing* to do with the #define preprocessor directive, which defines constants. You define variables with statements such as the following:

```
int i, j;
int m=9;
float x;
char ara[] = "Tulsa";
```

These statements tell the program that you need these variables and want them reserved. A function is defined when the C compiler reads the first statement in the function that describes the name and reads also any variables that may have been passed to that function. Never follow a function definition with a semicolon, but always follow the statement that calls a function with a semicolon.

NOTE: To some C purists, a variable is only declared when you write int i; and only truly defined when you assign it a value, such as i=7;. They say that the variable is both declared and defined when you declare the variable and assign it a value at the same time, such as int i=7;.

The following program contains two function definitions, main() and pr_it().

We want to practice passing a variable to a function, so declare i as an integer variable and make it equal to 5. The passing (or calling) function will be main(), and the receiving function will be pr_it(). Pass the i variable to the pr_it() function, then go back to main().

```
main()                      /* The main() function definition */
{
  int i=5;                      /* Define an integer variable */
  pr_it(i);                           /* Calls the pr_it()
                                     function and passes it i */
  return;                   /* Return to the operating system */
}

pr_it(int i)                /* The pr_it() function definition */
{
    printf("%d \n", i);     /* Calls the printf() function */
    return;                             /* Returns to main() */
}
```

Because a passed parameter is treated like a local variable in the receiving function, the `printf()` in `pr_it()` prints a 5, even though the `main()` function initialized this variable.

When you pass arguments to a function, the receiving function has no idea about the data types of the incoming variables. Therefore, you must include each parameter's data type in front of the parameter's name. In the previous example, the definition of `pr_it()` (the first line of the function) contains the type, `int`, of the incoming variable `i`. Notice that the `main()` calling function does not need to indicate the variable type. In this example, `main()` already knows the type of variable `i` (an integer); only `pr_it()` needs to know that `i` is an integer.

> **TIP:** Always declare the parameter types in the receiving function. Precede each parameter in the function's parentheses with `int`, `float`, or whatever each passed variable's data type happens to be.

Examples

1. Here is a `main()` function that contains three local variables. `main()` passes one of these variables to the first function and two of them to the second function.

```
/* Filename: C18LOC4.C
   Pass three local variables to functions */
#include <stdio.h>
main()
{
   char initial;            /* 3 variables local to main() */
   int age;
   float salary;

   /* Fill these variables in main() */
   printf("What is your initial? ");
   scanf(" %c", &initial);
   printf("What is your age? ");
   scanf(" %d", &age);
   printf("What is your salary? ");
   scanf(" %f", &salary);

   pr_init(initial);                /* Call pr_init() and
                                       pass it initial */
   pr_other(age, salary);       /* Call pr_other() and pass
                                   it age and salary  */

   return;
}

pr_init(char initial)         /* Never put a semicolon in
                                 the function definition */
{
   printf("Your initial is really %c? \n", initial);
   return;                       /* Return to main() */
}

pr_other(int age, float salary)          /* Must type both
                                            parameters */
{
   printf("You look young for %d \n", age);
   printf("And $%.2f is a LOT of money!", salary);
   return;                       /* Return to main() */
}
```

2. A receiving function can contain its own local variables. As long as the names are not the same, these local variables do not conflict with the passed ones. In the following program, the second function receives a passed variable from `main()` and also defines its own local variable called `price_per`.

```
/* Filename: C18LOC5.C
   Second function has its own local variable */
#include <stdio.h>
main()
{
   int gallons;

   printf("Richard's Paint Service \n");
   printf("How many gallons of paint did you buy? ");
   scanf(" %d", &gallons);        /* Get gallons in main() */

   compute_sale(gallons);    /* Compute total in function */
   return;
}


compute_sale(int gallons)
{
   float price_per = 12.45;    /* Local to compute_sale() */

   printf("The total is: $%.2f \n",
           (price_per*(float)gallons) );
      /* Had to type cast gallons because it was integer */
   return;                            /* Return to main() */
}
```

3. The following sample code lines test your skill at recognizing calling functions and receiving functions. Being able to recognize the difference is half the battle of understanding them.

```
do_it()
```

This must be the first line of a new function because it does not end with a semicolon.

```
do_it2(sales);
```

This calls a function called `do_it2()`. The calling function passes the variable called `sales` to `do_it2()`.

```
pr_it(float total)
```

This is the first line of a function that receives a floating-point variable from another function that called it. All receiving functions must specify the type of each variable being passed.

```
pr_them(float total, int number)
```

This is the first line of a function that receives two variables—one is a floating-point variable and the other is an integer. This line cannot be calling the function `pr_them` because there is no semicolon at the end of the line.

Automatic Versus Static Variables

The terms *automatic* and *static* describe what happens to local variables when a function returns to the calling procedure. By default, all local variables are automatic, meaning that they are erased when their function ends. To declare a variable as an automatic variable, prefix its definition with the term `auto`. The `auto` keyword is optional with local variables because they are automatic be default.

The two statements after `main()`'s opening brace declare automatic local variables:

```
main()
{
   int i;
   auto float x;
   /* Rest of main() goes here */
```

Because `auto` is the default, we did not need to include the term `auto` with `x`.

NOTE: C programmers rarely use the auto keyword with local variables because they are automatic by default.

Automatic variables are local and disappear when their function ends.

The opposite of an automatic variable is a static variable. All global variables are static and, as mentioned, all static variables retain their values. Therefore, if a local variable is static, it too retains its value when its function ends—in case the function is called a second time. To declare a variable as static, place the static keyword in front of the variable when you define it. The following code section defines three variables, i, j, and k. The variable i is automatic, but j and k are static.

```
my_fun()              /* Start of new function definition */
{
    int i;
    static j=25;    /* Both j and k are static variables */
    static k=30;
```

If local variables are static, their values remain in case the function is called again.

Always assign an initial value to a static variable when you declare it, as shown here in the last two lines. This initial value is placed in the static variable only the first time my_fun() executes. If you don't assign a static variable an initial value, C initializes it to zero.

TIP: Static variables are good to use when you write functions that keep track of a count or add to a total when called. If the counting or total variables were local and automatic, their values would disappear when the function finished—destroying the totals.

Examples

1. Consider this program:

```
/* Filename: C18STA1.C
   Tries to use a static variable
   without a static declaration */
#include <stdio.h>
main()
{
   int ctr;                     /* Used in the for loop to
                                   call a function 25 times */
   for (ctr=1; ctr<=25; ctr++)
     { triple_it(ctr); }        /* Pass ctr to a function
                                    called triple_it() */
   return;
}


triple_it(int ctr)
{
   int total, ans;            /* Local automatic variables */
   /* Triples whatever value is passed to it
      and adds the total */

   total=0;     /* Will hold total of all numbers tripled */

   ans = ctr * 3;                    /* Triple number passed */
   total += ans;  /* Add triple numbers as this is called */

   printf("The number %d, multiplied by 3 is: %d \n",
         ctr, ans);

   if (total > 300)
     { printf("The total of the triple numbers is
       over 300 \n"); }
   return;
}
```

> **Automatic and Static Rules for Local Variables**
>
> Local automatic variables disappear when their block ends. All local variables are automatic by default. You can prefix a variable (when you define it) with the auto keyword, or you can omit it; the variable is still automatic and its value is destroyed when the block it is local to ends.
>
> Local static variables do not lose their values when their function ends. They remain local to that function. When the function is called after the first time, the static variable's value is still in place. You declare a static variable by placing the static keyword before the variable's definition.

This is a nonsense program that doesn't do much, yet you may sense something is wrong. The program passes numbers from 1 to 25 to the function called triple_it. The function triples the number and prints it.

The variable called total is initially set to 0. The idea here is to add each tripled number and print a message when the total is larger than 300. However, the printf() *never* executes. For each of the 25 times that this subroutine is called, total is reset to 0. The total variable is an automatic variable whose value is erased and initialized every time its procedure is called. The next example corrects this.

2. If you want total to retain its value after the procedure ends, you must make it static. Because local variables are automatic by default, you need to include the static keyword to override this default. Then the value of the total variable is retained each time the subroutine is called.

The following corrects the mistake in the previous program.

```
/* Filename: C18STA2.C
   Uses a static variable with the static declaration */
#include <stdio.h>
main()
{
```

```
        int ctr;                        /* Used in the for loop to
                                           call a function 25 times */
        for (ctr=1; ctr<=25; ctr++)
          { triple_it(ctr); }           /* Pass ctr to a function
                                                 called triple_it() */


        return;
    }

    triple_it(int ctr)
    {
        static int total=0;                 /* Local and static */
        int ans;                        /* Local and automatic */
        /* total will be set to 0 only the first time this
           function is called. */

        /* Triples whatever value is passed to it and add
           the total */

        total=0;     /* Will hold total of all numbers tripled */

        ans = ctr * 3;                      /* Triple number passed */
        total += ans;  /* Add triple numbers as this is called */

        printf("The number %d, multiplied by 3 is: %d \n",
               ctr, ans);

        if (total > 300)
          { printf("The total of the triple numbers is
            over 300 \n"); }
        return;
    }
```

Figure 18.3 shows this program's output. Notice that the
function's printf() is triggered, even though total is a local
variable. Because total is static, its value is not erased when
the function finishes. When the function is called a second
time by main(), total's previous value (when you left the
routine) is still there.

```
The number 1, multiplied by 3 is: 3
The number 2, multiplied by 3 is: 6
The number 3, multiplied by 3 is: 9
The number 4, multiplied by 3 is: 12
The number 5, multiplied by 3 is: 15
The number 6, multiplied by 3 is: 18
The number 7, multiplied by 3 is: 21
The number 8, multiplied by 3 is: 24
The number 9, multiplied by 3 is: 27
The number 10, multiplied by 3 is: 30
The number 11, multiplied by 3 is: 33
The number 12, multiplied by 3 is: 36
The number 13, multiplied by 3 is: 39
The number 14, multiplied by 3 is: 42
The number 15, multiplied by 3 is: 45
The number 16, multiplied by 3 is: 48
The number 17, multiplied by 3 is: 51
The number 18, multiplied by 3 is: 54
The number 19, multiplied by 3 is: 57
The number 20, multiplied by 3 is: 60
The number 21, multiplied by 3 is: 63
The number 22, multiplied by 3 is: 66
The number 23, multiplied by 3 is: 69
The number 24, multiplied by 3 is: 72
The number 25, multiplied by 3 is: 75
```

Figure 18.3. Using a static variable to retain a value.

This does not mean that local static variables become global. The main program cannot refer, use, print, or change total because it is local to the second function. Static simply means that the local variable's value is still there if the program calls the function again.

Three Issues of Parameter Passing

To have a complete understanding of programs with several functions, you need to learn three additional concepts:

♦ Passing arguments (variables) by value (also called "by copy")

♦ Passing arguments (variables) by address (also called "by reference")

♦ Returning values from functions

The first two concepts deal with the way local variables are passed and received. The third concept describes how receiving functions send values back to the calling functions. The next chapter concludes this discussion by explaining these three methods for passing parameters and returning values.

Review Questions

Answers to review questions are in Appendix B.

1. True or false: A function should always include a `return` statement as its last command, even though `return` is not required.

2. When a local variable is passed, is it called an argument or a parameter?

3. True or false: A function that is passed variables from another function cannot also have its own local variables.

4. What must appear inside the receiving function's parentheses, besides the variables passed to it?

5. If a function keeps track of a total or count every time it is called, should the counting or totaling variable be automatic or static?

6. When would you pass a global variable to a function? (Be careful—this may be a trick question!)

7. How many arguments are there in the following statement?

   ```
   printf("The rain has fallen %d inches.", rainf);
   ```

Review Exercises

1. Write a program that asks, in `main()`, for the age of the user's dog. Write a second function called `people()` that computes the dog's age in human years (by multiplying the dog's age by 7).

2. Write a function that counts the number of times it is called. Name the function count_it(). Do not pass it anything. In the body of count_it(), print the following message:

```
The number of times this function has been called is: ##
```

where ## is the number. (Hint: Because the variable must be local, make it static and initialize it to zero when you first define it.)

3. The following program contains several problems. Some of these problems produce errors. One problem is not an error, but a bad location for a variable declaration. (Hint: Find all global variables.) See if you can spot some of the problems, and rewrite the program so that it works better.

```c
/* Filename: C18BAD.C
   Program with bad uses of variable declarations */
#include <stdio.h>
#define NUM 10

char city[] = "Miami";
int count;

main()
{
   int abc;

   count = NUM;
   abc = 5;
   do_var_fun();

   printf("%d %d %d %c", abc, count, pgm_var, xyz);
   return;
}

int pgm_var = 7;

do_var_fun()
{
   char xyz = 'A';
```

```
    xyz = 'b';
    printf("%c %d %d %s", xyz, pgm_var, abc, city);
    return;
}
```

Summary

Parameter passing is necessary because local variables are better than global. Local variables are protected in their own routines, but sometimes they must be shared with other routines. If local data is to remain in those variables (in case the function is called again in the same program), the variables should be static because otherwise their automatic values would disappear.

Most of the information in this chapter should become more obvious as you use functions in your own programs. The next chapter goes into more detail on the actual passing of parameters and shows you two different ways to do it.

Passing Values

C passes variables between functions using two different methods. The one you use depends on how you want the passed variables to be changed. This chapter explores these two methods. The concepts discussed here are not new to the C language. Other programming languages, such as Pascal, FORTRAN, and QBasic, pass parameters using similar techniques. A computer language must have the capability to pass information between functions, before it can be called truly structured.

This chapter introduces you to the following:

♦ Passing variables by value

♦ Passing arrays by address

♦ Passing nonarrays by address

Pay close attention because most of the programs in the remainder of the book rely on the methods described in this chapter.

Passing by Value (by Copy)

The two wordings "passing by value" and "passing by copy" mean the same thing in computer terms. Some textbooks and C programmers say that arguments are passed *by value*, and some say they are passed *by copy*. Both of these phrases describe one of the two methods by which arguments are passed to receiving functions. (The other method is called "by address," or "by reference." This method is covered later in the chapter.)

When an argument (local variable) is passed by value, a copy of the variable's value is sent to—and is assigned to—the receiving function's parameter. If more than one variable is passed by value, a copy of each of their values is sent to—and is assigned to—the receiving function's parameters.

When you pass by value, a copy of the variable's value is passed to the receiving function.

Figure 19.1 shows the *passing by copy* in action. The value of i— not the variable itself—is passed to the called function, which receives it as a variable i. There are two variables called i, not one. The first is local to main(), and the second is local to pr_it(). They both have the same names, but because they are local to their respective functions, there is no conflict. The variable does not have to be called i in both functions, and because the value of i is sent to the receiving function, it does not matter what the receiving function calls the variable that receives this value.

Figure 19.1. Passing the variable i by value.

In this case, when passing and receiving variables between functions, it is wisest to retain the *same* names. Even though they are not the same variables, they hold the same value. In this example, the value 5 is passed from main()'s i to pr_it()'s i.

Because a copy of i's value (and not the variable itself) is passed to the receiving function, if pr_it() changed i, it would be changing only its copy of i and not main()'s i. This makes for true separation of functions and variables. You now have the technique for passing a copy of a variable to a receiving function, with the receiving function being unable to modify the calling function's variable.

All of C's nonarray variables that you have seen so far are passed by value. You do not have to do anything special to pass variables by value, except to pass them in the calling function's argument list and receive them in the receiving function's parameter list.

> **NOTE:** The default method for passing parameters is by value, as just described, unless you pass arrays. Arrays are always passed by the other method, by address, as described later in this chapter.

Examples

1. The following program asks users for their weight. It then passes that weight to a function that calculates the equivalent weight on the moon. Notice that the second function uses the passed value, and calculates with it. After the weight is passed to the second function, that function can treat it as though it were a local variable.

Identify the program and include the necessary header file. We want to calculate the user's weight on the moon. Because we need to hold the user's weight somewhere, declare the variable weight *as an integer. We also need a function that will do the calculations, so create a function called* moon().

Ask the user how much he or she weighs. Get the user's answer and put it in weight. *Now pass the user's weight to the* moon() *function, which will divide the weight by 6 to get the equivalent weight on the moon. Display the user's weight on the moon. We're finished, so leave the* moon() *function, then leave the* main() *function.*

```
/* Filename: C19PASS1.C
   Calculate the user's weight in a second function */
#include <stdio.h>
main()
{
```

```
    int weight;                     /* main()'s local weight */
    printf("How many pounds do you weigh? ");
    scanf(" %d", &weight);

    moon(weight);            /* Call the moon() function and
                                          pass it the weight */
    return;                  /* Return to the operating system */
}

moon(int weight)            /* Declare the passed parameter */
{
    /* Moon weights are 1/6th earth's weights */
    weight /= 6;                    /* Divide the weight by 6 */

    printf("You weigh only %d pounds on the moon!", weight);
    return;                          /* Return to main() */
}
```

The output of this program follows:

```
How many pounds do you weigh? 120
You weigh only 20 pounds on the moon!
```

2. You can rename passed variables in the receiving function. They are distinct from the passing function's variable. The following is the same program as in #1, except the receiving function calls the passed variable earth_weight. A new variable, called moon_weight, is local to the called function and is used for the moon's equivalent weight.

Compute
weight
on moon

```
/* Filename: C19PASS2.C
   Calculate the user's weight in a second function */
#include <stdio.h>
main()
{
    int weight;                     /* main()'s local weight */
    printf("How many pounds do you weigh? ");
    scanf(" %d", &weight);

    moon(weight);            /* Call the moon() function and
                                          pass it the weight */
```

```
    return;                 /* Return to the operating system */
}

moon(int earth_weight)    /* Declare the passed parameter */
{
    int moon_weight;            /* Local to this function */

    /* Moon weights are 1/6th earth's weights */
    moon_weight = earth_weight / 6;   /* Divide weight by 6 */

    printf("You only weigh %d pounds on the moon!",
            moon_weight);
    return;                         /* Return to main() */
}
```

The resulting output is identical to that of the previous program. Renaming the passed variable changes nothing.

3. The next example passes three variables—of three different types—to the called function. In the receiving function's parameter list, each of these variable types must be declared.

This program prompts users for three values in the `main()` function. The `main()` function then passes these variables to the receiving function, which calculates and prints values related to those passed variables. When the called function modifies a variable passed to the function, notice again that this does *not* affect the calling function's variable. When variables are passed by value, the value—not the variable itself—is passed.

```
/* Filename: C19PASS3.C
   Get grade information for a student */
#include <stdio.h>
main()
{
    char lgrade;                        /* Letter grade */
    int  tests;             /* Number of tests not yet taken */
    float average; /* Student's average based on 4.0 scale */

    printf("What letter grade do you want? ");
    scanf(" %c", &lgrade);
```

```
        printf("What is your current test average? ");
        scanf(" %f", &average);
        printf("How many tests do you have left? ");
        scanf(" %d", &tests);

        check_grade(lgrade, average, tests);  /* Call function
                              and pass three variables by value */
        return;
}

check_grade(char lgrade, float average, int tests)
{
    switch (tests)
    {
        case (0): { printf("You will get your current grade
                      of %c", lgrade);
                    break; }
        case (1): { printf("You still have time to bring
                      your average ");
                    printf("of %.1f up. Study hard!", average);
                    break; }
        default:  { printf("Relax. You still have plenty of
                      time.");
                    break; }
    }
    return;
}
```

Passing by Address (by Reference)

The two phrases "by address" and "by reference" mean the same thing. The previous section described passing arguments by value (or by copy). This section describes how to pass arguments by address.

When you pass by address, the address of the variable is passed to the receiving function.

When you pass an argument (local variable) *by address*, the variable's address is sent to—and is assigned to—the receiving function's parameter. (If you pass more than one variable by address, each of their addresses is sent to—and is assigned to—the receiving function's parameters.)

Variable Addresses

All variables in memory (RAM) are stored at memory addresses. See Figure 19.2. If you want more information on the internal representation of memory, you should refer to Appendix A.

```
Memory      Address

              0        (If you have 640K of RAM, as many
              1        microcomputers do, you have exactly
              2        655,360 characters of RAM.
              .        Each of those memory locations has a
              .        separate address, just as each house
              .        and building have separate
              .        addresses.)
            655,358
            655,359
            655,360
```

Figure 19.2. **Memory addresses.**

When you tell C to define a variable (such as int i;), you are requesting C to find an unused place in memory and assign that place (or memory address) to i. When your program uses the variable called i, C knows to go to i's address and use whatever is there.

If you define five variables as follows:

```
int i;
float x=9.8;
char ara[2] = {'A', 'B'};
int j=8, k=3;
```

C might arbitrarily place them in memory at the addresses shown in Figure 19.3.

You don't know what is contained in the variable called i because you haven't put anything in it yet. Before you use i, you should initialize it with a value. (All variables—except character variables—usually take up more than one byte of memory.)

Figure 19.3. Storing variables in memory.

Sample Program

All C arrays are
passed by address.

The address of the variable, not its value, is copied to the receiving function when you pass a variable by address. In C, *all arrays are passed by address*. (Actually, a copy of their address is passed, but you will understand this better when you learn more about arrays and pointers.) The following important rule holds true for programs that pass by address:

> Every time you pass a variable by address, if the receiving function changes the variable, it is changed also in the calling function.

Therefore, if you pass an array to a function and the function changes the array, those changes are still with the array when it returns to the calling function. Unlike passing by value, passing by address gives you the ability to change a variable in the *called* function and keep those changes in effect in the *calling* function. The following sample program should help to illustrate this concept.

```
/* Filename: C19ADD1.C
   Passing by address example */
#include <stdio.h>
main()
{
```

```
    char name[4]="ABC";

    change_it(name);              /* Passes by address because
                                              it is an array */
    printf("%s \n", name);        /* Called function can
                                              change array */

    return;
}

change_it(char c[4])        /* You must tell the function
                                      that c is an array */

{
    printf("%s \n", c);          /* Print as it is passed */
    strcpy(c, "USA");            /* Change the array, both
                                      here and in main() */

    return;
}
```

Here is the output from this program:

```
ABC
USA
```

At this point, you should have no trouble understanding that the array is passed from main() to the function called change_it(). Even though change_it() calls the array c, it refers to the same array passed by the main() function (name).

Figure 19.4 shows how the array is passed. Although the address of the array—and not its value—is passed from name to c, both arrays are the same.

Figure 19.4. Passing an array by address.

Before going any further, a few additional comments are in order. Because the address of name is passed to the function—even though the array is called c in the receiving function—it is still the same array as name. Figure 19.5 shows how C accomplishes this at the memory-address level.

	Memory	Address	
Variable Name			
	·	·	
	·	·	
	·	·	
name[0]--c[0]->	U	41,324	(Keep in mind that the
name[1]--c[1]->	S	41,325	actual address will depend
name[2]--c[2]->	A	41,326	on where your C compiler
	·	·	puts the variables.)
	·	·	
	·	·	

Figure 19.5. The array being passed is the same array in both functions.

The variable array is referred to as name in main() and as c in change_it(). Because the address of name is copied to the receiving function, the variable gets changed no matter what it is called in either function. Because change_it() changes the array, the array is changed also in main().

Examples

1. You can now use a function to fill an array with user input. The following function asks users for their first name in the function called get_name(). As users type the name in the array, it is also entered in main()'s array. The main() function then passes the array to pr_name(), where it is printed. (If arrays were passed by value, this program would not work. Only the array value would be passed to the called functions.)

```
/* Filename: C19ADD2.C
   Get a name in an array, then print it using
   separate functions */
#include <stdio.h>
main()
{
```

```
        char name[25];
        get_name(name);                       /* Get the user's name */
        print_name(name);                     /* Print the user's name */
        return;
    }
```

```
    get_name(char name[25])        /* Pass the array by address */
    {
        printf("What is your first name? ");
        scanf(" %s", name);
        return;
    }

    print_name(char name[25])
    {
        printf("\n\n Here it is: %s", name);
        return;
    }
```

When you pass an array, be sure to specify the array's type in the receiving function's parameter list. If the previous program declared the passed array with

```
get_name(char name)
```

the function `get_name()` would think it is being passed a single character variable, *not* a character array. You never need to put the array size in brackets. The following statement would also work as the first line of `get_name()`.

```
get_name(char name[])
```

Most C programmers put the array size in the brackets even though the size is not needed.

2. Many programmers pass character arrays to functions in order to erase them. Here is a function called `clear_it()`. It expects two parameters: a character array and the total number of elements declared for that array. The array is passed by address (as are all arrays) and the number of elements, `num_els`, is passed by value (as are all nonarrays). When the function finishes, the array is cleared (that is, all its elements are reset to null zero). Subsequent functions that use it can then have an empty array.

Clear
all elements
in array

```
clear_it(char ara[10], int num_els)
{
    int ctr;
    for (ctr=0; ctr<num_els; ctr++)
      { ara[ctr] = '\0'; }
    return;
}
```

The brackets after ara do not need to contain a number, as described in the previous example. The 10 in this example is simply a placeholder for the brackets. Any value (or no value) would work as well.

Passing Nonarrays by Address

You can pass nonarrays by address as well.

You now should see the difference between passing variables by address and by value. Arrays can be passed by address, and nonarrays can be passed by value. You can override the *by value* default for nonarrays. This is helpful sometimes, but it is not always recommended because the called function can damage values in the called function.

If you want a nonarray variable changed in a receiving function and also want the changes kept in the calling function, you must override the default and pass the variable by address. (You should understand this section better after you learn how arrays and pointers relate.) To pass a nonarray by address, you must do the following:

1. Precede the variable in the calling function with an ampersand (&).

2. Precede the variable in the receiving function with an asterisk (*), everywhere the variable appears.

This might sound strange to you (and it is, at this point). Few C programmers override the default of passing by address. When you learn about pointers later, you should have little need for this. Most C programmers don't like to clutter their code with these extra ampersands and asterisks, but they know they can do this if necessary.

The following examples demonstrate how to pass nonarray variables by address.

Examples

1. The following program passes a variable by address from main() to a function. The function changes it and returns to main(). Because the variable is passed by address, main() recognizes the new value.

```
/* Filename: C19ADD3.C
   Demonstrate passing nonarrays by address */
#include <stdio.h>
main()
{
   int amt;

   amt = 100;                /* Assign a value in main() */
   printf("In main(), amt is %d \n", amt);

   do_fun(&amt);            /* The & means pass it by address */
   printf("After return, amt is %d in main() \n", amt);
   return;
}

do_fun(int *amt)                        /* Inform function of
                                           passing by address */
{
   *amt = 85;                /* Assign new value to amt */
   printf("In do_fun(), amt is %d \n", *amt);
   return;
}
```

The output from this program follows:

```
In main(), amt is 100
In do_fun(), amt is 85
After return, amt is 85 in main()
```

Notice that amt changed in the called function. Because it was passed by address, it gets changed also in the calling function.

How `scanf()` Passes Values

You can now understand some of the strangeness of the built-in `scanf()` function. The `scanf()` function passes arguments to its internal code. The arguments are control strings and variables that fill up with keyboard input.

Recall that you must put an ampersand (`&`) before each nonarray variable in the `scanf()` list. For example, to input three integers from the keyboard, you have to code `scanf()` as follows:

```
scanf("%d %d %d", &i1, &i2, &i3);
```

Think about what is happening. If you did not force these variables to be passed by address, the calling function would not be able to access the values typed from the keyboard! When a user types in values, the `scanf()` function fills its parameters with those typed values because you pass the variables by address. The calling program also recognizes those values because they get changed in both places.

No ampersand is needed in front of `scanf()` array variables. To get a name from the keyboard, you would type the following `scanf()` statement:

```
soanf(name);
```

The ampersand is not needed because all arrays are automatically passed by address. When `scanf()` gets the keyboard values into the array, the calling program (your program) recognizes them because the array is changed in both places.

2. You can use a function to get the user's keyboard values. The `main()` function recognizes those values as long as you pass them by address. The following program calculates the cubic feet in a swimming pool. In one function, it requests the width, length, and depth. In another function, it calculates the cubic feet of water. Finally, in a third function, it prints the answer. The `main()` function is clearly a controlling function, passing variables between these functions by address.

Calculate pool's cubic feet

```c
/* Filename: C19POOL.C
   Calculate the cubic feet in a swimming pool */
#include <stdio.h>
main()
{
   int length, width, depth, cubic;

   get_values(&length, &width, &depth);
   calc_cubic(&length, &width, &depth, &cubic);
   print_cubic(&cubic);

   return;
}

get_values(int *length, int *width, int *depth)
{
   printf("What is the pool's length? ");
   scanf(" %d", &*length);
   printf("What is the pool's width? ");
   scanf(" %d", &*width);
   printf("What is the pool's average depth? ");
   scanf(" %d", &*depth);
   return;
}

calc_cubic(int *length, int *width, int *depth, int *cubic)
{
   /* This may look confusing, but you must
      precede each variable with an asterisk */
   *cubic = (*length) * (*width) * (*depth);
   return;
}

print_cubic(int *cubic)
{
   printf("\nThe pool has %d cubic feet\n", *cubic);
   return;
}
```

```
What is the pool's length? 16
What is the pool's width? 32
What is the pool's average depth? 6
The pool has 3072 cubic feet
```

Notice the strange scanf() parameters. All variables in a function must be preceded with an asterisk if they are to be passed by address. Because scanf() requires an ampersand before its nonarray variables, this technique adds confusion to the scanf() statement. As you learn in a later chapter, & and * cancel each other. If you find yourself using scanf() in functions (on nonarray variables passed by address), you can omit &*. For example, the first scanf() could be rewritten as follows without any change in the program's output:

```
scanf(" %d", length);
```

Review Questions

Answers to review questions are in Appendix B.

1. What kind of variables are always passed by address?

2. What kind of variables are always passed by value?

3. True or false: If a variable is passed by value, it is passed also by copy.

4. If a variable is passed to a function by value and the function changes the variable, is it changed in the called function?

5. If a variable is passed to a function by address and the function changes the variable, is it changed in the called function?

6. What is wrong with the following function?

```
do_fun(x, y, z)
{
    printf("The variables are: %d, %d, and %d", x, y, z);
    return;
}
```

7. Suppose you pass a nonarray variable and an array to a function at the same time. What is the default?

   a. Both are passed by address

   b. Both are passed by value

   c. One is passed by address and the other is passed by value

Review Exercises

1. Write a `main()` function and a second function that `main()` calls. Ask users for their annual income in `main()`. Pass the income to the second function and print a congratulatory message if the user makes more than $50,000 or an encouragement message if the user makes less.

2. Write a three-function program, consisting of the following functions:

```
main()
fun1()
fun2()
```

   Declare a 10-element character array in `main()`, fill it with the letters A through J in `fun1()`, then print that array backwards in `fun2()`.

3. Write a program whose `main()` function passes a number to a function called `print_aster()`. The `print_aster()` function prints that many asterisks on a line, across the screen. If `print_aster()` is passed a number greater than 80, display an error because most screens cannot print more than 80 characters on the same line. When execution is finished, return control to `main()` and then return to the operating system.

4. Write a function that is passed two integer values by address. The function should declare a third local variable. Use the third variable as an intermediate variable and swap the values of both integers passed. For example, suppose the calling function passes it `old_pay` and `new_pay` as in

```
swap_it(old_pay, new_pay);
```

The `swap_it()` function should reverse the two values so that, when control is returned to the calling function, the values of `old_pay` and `new_pay` are swapped.

Summary

You now have a complete understanding of the various methods for passing data to functions. Because you will be using local variables as much as possible, you need to know how to pass local variables between functions but also keep the variables away from functions that don't need them.

You can pass data in two ways: by value and by address. When you pass data by value, which is the default method for nonarrays, only a copy of the variable's contents are passed. If the called function modifies its parameters, those variables are not modified in the calling function. When you pass data by address, as is done with arrays and nonarray variables preceded by an ampersand, the receiving function can change the data in both functions.

Whenever you pass values, you must ensure that they match in number and type. If you don't match them, you could have problems. For example, suppose you pass an array and a floating-point variable, but in the receiving function, you receive a floating-point variable followed by an array. The data is not getting to the receiving function properly because the parameter data types do not match the variables being passed. The next chapter shows you how to protect against such disasters by prototyping all your functions.

Function Return Values and Prototypes

So far, you have passed variables to functions in only one direction—a calling function passed data to a receiving function. You have yet to see how data is passed back *from* the receiving function to the calling function. When you pass variables by address, the data gets changed in both functions—but this is different from passing data back. This chapter focuses on writing function return values that improve your programming power.

After you learn to pass and return values, you need to *prototype* the functions you write—as well as C's built-in functions, such as printf() and scanf(). By prototyping your functions, you ensure the accuracy of passed and returned values.

This chapter introduces you to the following:

♦ Returning values from functions

♦ Prototyping functions

♦ Understanding header files

This chapter concludes the coverage on functions. After this chapter, your programs will be truly modular. You should write better, more powerful, and more accurate programs after you finalize your understanding of functions and how to use them.

Function Return Values

Until now, all functions in this book have been *subroutines* or *subfunctions*. A C subroutine is a function that is called from another function, but it does not return any values. The difference between subroutines and functions is not as critical in C as it is in other languages. All functions, whether they are subroutines or functions that return values, are defined in the same way. You can pass variables to each of them, as you have seen throughout Part 4.

Put the return value at the end of the `return` statement.

Functions that return values offer you a new approach to programming. In addition to passing data one-way, from calling to receiving function, you can pass data back from a receiving function to its calling function. When you want to return a value from a function to its calling function, put the return value after the `return` statement. To make the return value clearer, many programmers put parentheses around the return value, as shown in the following syntax:

```
return (return value);
```

> **CAUTION:** Do not return global variables. There is no need to do it because their values are already known throughout the code.

The calling function must have a use for the return value. For example, suppose you wrote a function that calculated the average of any three integer variables passed to it. If you return the average, the calling function has to receive that return value. The following sample program helps to illustrate this principle.

Calculate average

```
/* Filename: C20AVG.C
   Calculates the average of three input values */
#include <stdio.h>
main()
```

```
{
    int num1, num2, num3;
    int avg;                    /* Will hold the return value */

    printf("Please type three numbers (such as 23, 54, 85) ");
    scanf(" %d, %d, %d", &num1, &num2, &num3);

    /* Call the function, passing the numbers,
       and accept the return value */
    avg = calc_av(num1, num2, num3);

    printf("\n\nThe average is %d", avg);       /* Print the
                                                   return value */
    return;
}

int calc_av(int num1, int num2, int num3)
{
    int local_avg;   /* Holds the average for these numbers */
    local_avg = (num1+num2+num3) / 3;

    return (local_avg);
}
```

Here is a sample output from the program:

```
Please type three numbers (such as 23, 54, 85) 30, 40, 50
The average is 40
```

Study this program carefully. It is similar to many you have seen, but a few additional points should be considered now that the function returns a value. It may help to walk through this program a few lines at a time.

The first part of main() is similar to many programs you have seen. It declares its local variables: three for user input and one for the calculated average. The printf() and scanf() are familiar to you. The function call to calc_av() is also familiar; it passes three variables (num1, num2, and num3) by value to calc_av(). (If it passed them by address, an ampersand (&) would have to precede each argument, as discussed in the previous chapter.)

Put the function's return type before its name.

The receiving function, `calc_av()`, seems similar to others you have seen, except the first line, the function's definition line, has one addition—the `int` before its name. This is the *type* of the return value. You must always precede a function name with its return data type. If you do not specify a type, C assumes a type of `int`. Therefore, if this example had no return type, it would work just as well because an `int` return type would be assumed.

Because the variable being returned from `calc_av()` is an integer, the `int` return type was placed before `calc_av()`'s name.

You can also see that the return statement of `calc_av()` includes the return value, `local_avg`. This is the variable being sent back to the calling function, `main()`. You can return only a single variable to a calling function.

This introduces a rule for returning variables. Even though a function can receive more than one parameter, it can return only a single value to the calling function. If a receiving function will be modifying more than one value from the calling function, you must pass the parameters by address; you cannot return multiple values using a `return` statement.

After the receiving function, `calc_av()`, returns the value, `main()` must do something with that returned value. So far, you have seen function calls on lines by themselves. Notice in `main()` that the function call appears on the right side of the following assignment statement:

```
avg = calc_av(num1, num2, num3);
```

When the `calc_av()` function returns its value—the average of the three numbers—that value *replaces* the function call. If the average computed in `calc_av()` is 40, the C compiler "sees" the following statement in place of the function call:

```
avg = 40;
```

You typed a function call to the right of the equal sign, but the program replaces a function call with its return value when the `return` takes place. In other words, a function that returns a value *becomes* that value. You *must* put such a function anywhere you would put any variable or constant, usually to the right of an equal sign, or in an expression, or in `printf()`. The following is an *incorrect* way of calling `calc_av()`.

```
calc_av(num1, num2, num3);
```

If you did this, C would have nowhere to put the return value of 40 (or whatever it happens to be).

> **CAUTION:** Function calls that return values seldom appear on lines by themselves. Because the function call is replaced by the return value, you should do something with that return value (such as assign it to a variable or use it in a expression). Return values can be ignored, but doing so usually defeats the purpose of using them.

Examples

1. The following program passes a number to a function called `doub()`. The function doubles the number and returns the result.

```
/* Filename: C20DOUB.C
   Doubles the user's number */
#include <stdio.h>
main()
{
    int number;                     /* Holds user's input */
    int d_number;      /* Will hold double the user's input */
    printf("What number do you want doubled? ");
    scanf(" %d", &number);

    d_number = doub(number);        /* Assign return value */
    printf("%d doubled is %d", number, d_number);
    return;
}
```

```
int doub(int num)
{
    int d_num;
    d_num = num * 2;                /* Double the number */
    return (d_num);                 /* Return the result */
}
```

The program produces output such as this:

```
What number do you want doubled? 5
5 doubled is 10
```

2. Function return values can be used *anywhere* constants, variables, and expressions can be used. The following program is similar to the last. The difference is in main().

The function call is performed not on a line by itself, but from a printf(). This is a nested function call. You call the built-in function printf() using the return value from one of the program's functions named doub(). Because the call to doub() is replaced by its return value, the printf() has enough information to proceed as soon as doub() returns. This gives main() less overhead because it no longer needs a variable called d_number, although you must use your own judgment as to whether this program is easier to maintain. Sometimes it is wise to include function calls within other expressions; other times it is clearer to call the function and assign its return value to a variable before using it.

```c
/* Filename: C20DOUB2.C
   Doubles the user's number */
#inolude <stdio.h>
main()
{
    int number;                         /* Holds user's input */
    printf("What number do you want doubled? ");
    scanf(" %d", &number);

    /* The third printf() parameter is
       replaced with a return value */
    printf("%d doubled is %d", number, doub(number));

    return;
}

int doub(int num)
{
    int d_num;
```

```
   d_num = num * 2;                    /* Double the number */
   return (d_num);                     /* Return the result */
}
```

3. The following program asks the user for a number. That number is then passed to a function called `sum()`, which adds the numbers from 1 to that number. In other words, if the user types a 6, the function returns the result of the following calculation:

   ```
   1 + 2 + 3 + 4 + 5 + 6
   ```

   This is known as the *sum of the digits* calculation, and it is sometimes used for depreciation in accounting.

```
/* Filename: C20SUMD.C
   Compute the sum of the digits */
#include <stdio.h>
main()
{
   int num, sumd;

   printf("Please type a number: ");
   scanf(" %d", &num);

   sumd = sum(num);
   printf("The sum of the digits is %d", sumd);
   return;
}

int sum(int num)
{
   int ctr;                            /* Local loop counter */
   int sumd=0;                         /* Local to this function */
   if (num <= 0)   /* Check whether parameter is too small */
     { sumd = num; }     /* Returns parameter if too small */
   else
     { for (ctr=1; ctr<=num; ctr++)
          { sumd += ctr; }
     }
   return(sumd);
}
```

Following is a sample output from this program:

```
Please type a number: 6
The sum of the digits is 21
```

4. The following program contains two functions that return values. The first function, maximum(), returns the larger of two numbers entered by the user. The second one, minimum(), returns the smaller.

```
/* Filename: C20MINMX.C
   Finds minimum and maximum values in functions */
#include <stdio.h>
main()
{
    int num1, num2;                  /* User's two numbers */
    int min, max;

    printf("Please type two numbers (such as 46, 75) ");
    scanf(" %d, %d", &num1, &num2);

    max = maximum(num1, num2);    /* Assign the return    */
    min = minimum(num1, num2);    /* value of each        */
                                  /* function to variables */

    printf("The minimum number is %d \n", min);
    printf("The maximum number is %d \n", max);
    return;
}

int maximum(int num1, int num2)
{
    int max;               /* Local to this function only */
    max = (num1 > num2) ? (num1) : (num2);
    return (max);
}

int minimum(int num1, int num2)
{
    int min;               /* Local to this function only */
    min = (num1 < num2) ? (num1) : (num2);
    return (min);
}
```

Here is a sample output from this program:

```
Please type two numbers (such as 46, 75) 72, 55
The minimum number is 55
The maximum number is 72
```

If the user types the same number, minimum and maximum are the same.

These two functions can be passed any two integer values. In such a simple example as this one, the user already knows which number is lower or higher. The point of such an example is to show how to code return values. You might want to use similar functions in a more useful application, such as finding the highest paid employee from a payroll disk file.

Function Prototypes

The word *prototype* is sometimes defined as a model. In C, a function prototype models the actual function. Before completing your study of functions, parameters, and return values, you must understand how to prototype each function in your program.

You should prototype each function in your program. By prototyping, you inform C of the function's parameter types and its return value, if any. You do not always need to prototype functions, but it is recommended. Sometimes, a prototype is mandatory before your functions can work properly.

A simple example should help to clarify the need for prototyping. The following simple program asks the user for a temperature in Celsius, then converts it to Fahrenheit. The parameter and the return type are both floating-point. You know the return type is floating-point due to the word float before the convert() function's definition. See if you can follow this program. Other than the Celsius calculation, it is similar to others you have seen.

```
/* Filename: C20TEMP.C
   Converts Celsius temperature to Fahrenheit */
#include <stdio.h>
main()
```

```
{
    float c_temp;                    /* Holds Celsius temperature
                                                    from the user */
    float f_temp;                /* Holds converted temperature */
    printf("What is the Celsius temperature to convert? ");
    scanf(" %f", &c_temp);

    f_temp = convert(c_temp);    /* Convert the temperature */

    printf("The Fahrenheit equivalent is %.1f", f_temp);
    return;
}

float convert(float c_temp) /* The return var and parameter are
                                    both floating-point values */
{
    float f_temp;                            /* Local variable */
    f_temp = c_temp * (9.0 / 5.0) + 32.0;
    return (f_temp);
}
```

You must prototype all functions that return a data type other than `int`.

If you run this program, your C compiler will refuse to compile it or you will get incorrect results, at best. Yet this program seems similar to many you have seen previously. The primary difference is the return type; when you return a data type that is not `int`, you must prototype the function to ensure that it works.

Although prototyping is not required for functions that return integers, you should prototype them as well. Taking this one step further, you should prototype *all* functions, whether they return a value or not.

To prototype a function, copy the function's definition line to the top of your program (immediately before or after the `#include <stdio.h>` line is fine). Place a semicolon at the end of it, and you have the prototype. The definition line (the function's first line) contains the return type, the function name, and the type of each argument, so the function prototype serves as a model of the function that will follow.

If a function does not return a value, or if that function has no arguments passed to it, you should still prototype it. Place the keyword `void` in place of the return type or the parameters. Even `main()` can be prototyped. The following listing shows the corrected version of the previous program—now with the prototype lines. Because there are two functions, main() and convert(), there are two prototypes.

```
/* Filename: C20TEMP2.C
   Converts Celsius to Fahrenheit */
#include <stdio.h>
void main(void);                        /* main()'s prototype */
float convert(float c_type);     /* convert()'s prototype */

void main(void)                 /* The function must match
                                              its prototype */
{
   float c_temp;               /* Holds Celsius temperature
                                              from the user */
   float f_temp;               /* Holds converted temperature */
   printf("What is the Celsius temperature to convert? ");
   scanf(" %f", &c_temp);

   f_temp = convert(c_temp);   /* Convert the temperature */

   printf("The Fahrenheit equivalent is %.1f", f_temp);
   return;
}

float convert(float c_temp)       /* The return var and
                                        parameter are both
                                        floating-point values */

{
   float f_temp;                         /* Local variable */
   f_temp = c_temp * (9.0 / 5.0) + 32.0;
   return (f_temp);
}
```

All functions must match their prototypes. Because main()'s prototype includes the two void keywords, which means there are no return types and no arguments to main(), the first line of main() must also have voids. But you have to list only the data types of each parameter—not the individual parameter names—in the parentheses of the function's prototype.

You can look at a statement and tell whether it is a prototype or a function definition (the function's first line) by the semicolon at the end.

Prototype for Safety

Prototyping protects you from programming mistakes. Suppose you write a function that expects two arguments: an integer followed by a floating-point value. Here is the definition line of such a function:

```
my_fun(int num, float amount)
```

What if you passed incorrect data types to my_fun()? If you were to call this function by passing it two constants, a floating-point followed by an integer, as in

```
my_fun(23.43, 5);        /* Call the my_fun() function */
```

the function would *not* receive correct parameters. It is expecting an integer followed by a floating-point, but you did the opposite and sent it a floating-point followed by an integer.

Despite the power of your C compiler, *you don't get an error* if you do this. C lets you pass such incorrect values if you don't prototype first. By prototyping such a function at the top of the program, such as

Prototyping protects your programs from function programming errors.

```
void my_fun(int num, float amount);      /* Prototype */
```

you tell the compiler to check this function for accuracy. You inform the compiler to expect nothing after the return statement (due to the void keyword) and to expect an integer followed by a floating-point in the parentheses.

If you break any of the prototype's rules, the compiler informs you of the problem and you can correct it. Without the prototype, the program would compile but the results would be wrong. Such a program would be difficult to debug, at best.

Prototype All Functions

You should prototype every function in your program, even main() as the previous example shows. As just described, the prototype defines (for the rest of the program) which functions follow, their return types, and their parameter types. You should also prototype C's built-in functions, such as `printf()` and `scanf()`.

Think about how you would prototype `printf()`. You don't always pass it the same types of parameters because you print different data with each `printf()`. Prototyping functions that you write is easy: The prototype is basically the first line in the function. Prototyping functions that you do not write may seem difficult, but it isn't—you have already done it with every program in this book!

The designers of C realized that all functions should be prototyped. They realized also that you cannot prototype built-in functions, so they did it for you and placed the prototypes in header files on your disk. You have been including the `printf()` and `scanf()` prototypes in each program with the following statement:

> Header files contain built-in function prototypes.

```
#include <stdio.h>
```

Inside the `stdio.h` file is a prototype of many of C's input and output functions. By having prototypes of these functions, you ensure that they cannot be passed bad values. If someone attempts to pass incorrect values, C catches the problem.

Prototyping is the primary reason why you should always include the matching header file when you use C's built-in functions. The `strcpy()` function you saw in previous chapters requires the following line:

```
#include <string.h>
```

This is the header file for the `strcpy()` function. Without it, the program may or may not work, depending on how careful you are with the data you pass to `strcpy()`. It is best to be safe and prototype. If you want values other than `int` to be returned from a function, a prototype is required.

Examples

1. You should prototype all programs, even those with only a single `main()` function. The following program includes two prototypes: one for `main()` and an included header file for `printf()` and `scanf()`.

```
/* Filename: C20PRO1.C
```

```
                    Calculates sales tax on a sale */
#include <stdio.h>              /* Prototype built-in functions */
void main(void);                        /* Prototype main() */
void main(void)
{

    float total_sale;
    float tax_rate = .07;            /* Assume 7% tax rate */

    printf("What is the total sale? ");
    scanf(" %f", &total_sale);

    total_sale += (tax_rate * total_sale);
    printf("The total sale is %.2f", total_sale);
    return;
}
```

2. The following program asks the user for a number in main(),
   and passes that number to ascii(). The ascii() function
   returns the ASCII character that matches the user's number.
   This illustrates a character return type. Functions can return
   any data type.

```
/* Filename: C20ASC.C
    Prints the ASCII character of the user's number */
/* Prototypes follow */
#include <stdio.h>
char ascii(int num);

main()
{
    int num;
    char asc_char;

    printf("Enter an ASCII number? ");
    scanf(" %d", &num);

    asc_char = ascii(num);
    printf("The ASCII character for %d is %c", num, asc_char);
    return;
}

char ascii(int num)
```

BEGIN

Get ASCII
number

Call
ascii()
conversion
function

Print
ASCII
character

END

ascii() — BEGIN

Convert
ASCII
number

END

```
{
    char asc_char;
    asc_char = (char)num;
    return (asc_char);
}
```

The output from this program follows:

```
Enter an ASCII number? 67
The ASCII character for 67 is C
```

3. Suppose you need to calculate net pay for a company. You find yourself multiplying the hours worked by the hourly pay, then deducting taxes to compute the net pay. The following program includes a function that does this for you. It requires three arguments: the hours worked, the hourly pay, and the tax rate (as a floating-point decimal, such as .30 for 30%). The function returns the net pay. The main() calling program tests the function by sending three different payroll values to the function and printing the three return values.

```
/* Filename: C20NPAY.C
   Defines a function that computes net pay */
#include <stdio.h>
void main(void);
float netpayfun(float hours, float rate, float taxrate);

void main(void)
{
    float net_pay;

    net_pay = netpayfun(40.0, 3.50, .20);
    printf("The pay for 40 hours at $3.50/hr., and a 20%
    tax rate is:");
    printf("$%.2f", net_pay);

    net_pay = netpayfun(50.0, 10.00, .30);
    printf("The pay for 50 hours at $10.00/hr., and a 30%
            tax rate is:");
    printf("$%.2f", net_pay);
```

```
    net_pay = netpayfun(10.0, 5.00, .10);
    printf("The pay for 10 hours at $5.00/hr., and a 10%
    tax rate is:");
    printf("$%.2f", net_pay);

    return;
}

float netpayfun(float hours, float rate, float taxrate)
{
    float gross_pay, taxes, net_pay;
    gross_pay = (hours * rate);
    taxes = (taxrate * gross_pay);
    net_pay = (gross_pay - taxes);
    return (net_pay);
}
```

Review Questions

Answers to review questions are in Appendix B.

1. How do you declare function return types?

2. What is the maximum number of return values a function can return?

3. What are header files for?

4. What is the default function return type?

5. True or false: A function that returns a value can be passed only a single parameter.

6. How do prototypes protect the programmer from bugs?

7. Why don't you need to return global variables?

8. What is the return type, given the following function prototype?

```
float my_fun(char a, int b, float c);
```

How many parameters are passed to `my_fun()`? What are their types?

Review Exercises

1. Write a program that contains two functions. The first function returns the square of the integer passed to it, and the second function returns the cube. As with all programs from this point on, be sure to prototype all functions, including `main()`.

2. Write a function that returns the double-precision area of a circle, given that a double-precision radius is passed to it. The formula for calculating the area of a circle is

   ```
   area = 3.14159 * radius * radius
   ```

3. Write a function that returns the value of a polynomial given this formula:

   $$9x^4 + 15x^2 + x^1$$

   Assume that x is passed from `main()` and that it is supplied by the user.

Summary

You learned how to build your own collection of functions. When you write a function, you might want to use it in more than one program—there is no need to reinvent the wheel. Many programmers write useful functions and use them in more than one program.

You understand the importance of prototyping functions. You should prototype all your own functions and include the appropriate header file when you use one of C's built-in functions. Furthermore, when a function returns a value other than an integer, you must prototype for C to recognize the noninteger return value.

The rest of this book incorporates concepts presented in this part to take advantage of separate, modular functions and local data. You are ready to learn more about how C performs input and output. The next chapter teaches you the theory behind I/O in C and introduces more built-in functions.

Part V

Character Input, Output, and Library Functions

Device and Character I/O

Unlike many programming languages, C contains no input or output commands. C is an extremely *portable* language, meaning that a C program compiled and run on one computer can compile and run also on another computer. Most incompatibilities between computers reside in their input/output (I/O) mechanics. Each different device requires a different method of performing I/O.

By putting all I/O capabilities in common functions supplied with each computer's compiler—and not in C statements—the designers of C ensured that programs were not tied to specific hardware for input and output. A compiler must be modified for every computer for which it is written. This ensures that the compiler works with any specific computer and all of its devices. The compiler programmers write input/output functions for each machine. When your C program writes a character to the screen, the program works whether you have a color PC screen or a UNIX X/Windows terminal.

This chapter shows you additional ways to perform data input and output, besides using the scanf() and printf() functions you have seen throughout the book. By providing character-based I/O functions, C gives you the basic I/O functions you need to write powerful data entry and printing routines.

This chapter introduces you to

◆ Stream and character I/O

◆ Buffered and nonbuffered I/O

◆ Standard device I/O

◆ Redirecting I/O from MS-DOS and UNIX

◆ Printing formatted output

By the time you finish this chapter, you should understand the standard built-in I/O functions available in C. Performing character input and output, one character at a time, may sound like a slow method of handling data I/O. You soon learn, however, that character I/O gives you the ability to create more powerful I/O functions than you can by using `scanf()` or `printf()`.

Character Stream I/O

C views input and output from all devices as a stream of characters.

C views all input and output as streams of characters. Whether your program gets input from the keyboard, a disk file, a modem, or a mouse, C sees only a stream of characters. C does not "know" or "care" what type of device is supplying the input. C lets the operating system take care of the device specifics. The designers of C want your programs to operate on characters of data without regard to whatever physical method is taking place.

This stream I/O means that the functions you use to get input from the keyboard can be used to get input also from the modem or any other input device. You can use the same functions to write to a disk file, a printer, or the screen. You must have some way of routing that stream input or output to the proper device, but each program's I/O functions work in a similar manner. Figure 21.1 illustrates this concept.

Figure 21.1. I/O consists of streams of characters.

The Newline Character: \n

Portability is the key to C's success. Few companies have the resources to rewrite every program they use when they change computer equipment. They need a programming language that works on many platforms (hardware combinations). C achieves true portability better than almost all other programming languages.

It is because of portability that C uses the generic newline character, \n, instead of the specific carriage return and line feed sequences that other languages use. This is also why C uses \t for tab and all the other control characters utilized in I/O functions.

If C relied on a specific ASCII code to represent these special characters, your programs would not be portable. Suppose you wrote a C program on one computer and used a carriage return value such as 12—12 may not be the carriage return value on another type of computer. By using the newline character and the other control characters available in C, you ensure that your program works on any computer on which it is compiled. The specific compilers substitute their computer's actual codes for the control codes in your programs.

Standard Devices

Table 21.1 shows a listing of standard I/O devices. C always assumes that input comes from stdin, or the *standard input device*. This is usually the keyboard, although you can reroute this default. C assumes that all output goes to stdout, or the *standard output device*. There is nothing magic in the words *stdin* and *stdout*, but many people see these words for the first time in the C language.

Table 21.1. Standard I/O devices in C.

I/O Device	C Name	MS-DOS Name	UNIX Name
Screen	stdout	CON:	stdout
Keyboard	stdin	CON:	stdin
Printer	stdprn	PRN: or LPT1:	lpr
Serial port	stdaux	AUX: or COM1:	machine dependent
Error messages	stderr	CON:	stderr
Disk files	none	filename	filename

Take a moment to study Table 21.1. MS-DOS users might think it is confusing that three devices are named CON:. MS-DOS knows the difference between the screen device called CON: (which stands for *console*) and the keyboard device called CON: from the context of the data stream. If you send an output stream (a stream of characters) to CON:, MS-DOS routes it to the screen. If you request input from CON:, MS-DOS gets it from the keyboard. (These defaults hold true as long as you have not redirected these devices.) MS-DOS sends all error messages to the screen (CON:) as well.

> **NOTE:** If you want to route I/O to a second printer or serial port, read Chapter 30, "Sequential Files."

UNIX users may understand the standard C device names already because many of these names are the same as their equivalent UNIX device names. If you use a print spooler, your UNIX printing device may be different from lpr.

If you program on a mainframe, you must use *JCL* (Job Control Language) to route C's standard devices, such as stdin and stdout, to your preferred local or remote I/O devices. If you are new to programming, you may have to contact your system administrator to help you with setting up a JCL file that connects C programs to the appropriate I/O devices.

Redirecting Devices from MS-DOS and UNIX

The operating system gives you control over devices.

The reason `printf()` goes to the screen is simply because `stdout` is routed to the screen by default on most computers. The reason `scanf()` gets input from the keyboard is because most computers consider the keyboard to be the standard input device, `stdin`. After compiling your program, C does *not* send data to the screen or get it from the keyboard. Instead, the program sends output to `stdout` and gets input from `stdin`. The operating system routes the data to the appropriate device.

Most PC- and UNIX-based operating systems let you reroute I/O from their default locations to other devices through the use of the *output redirection symbol,* >, and the *input redirection symbol,* <. The goal of this book is certainly not to delve into operating system redirection. You might want to get a good book on your operating system (such as *Using MS-DOS 5* or *Using UNIX*) to learn more about how your operating system handles I/O.

Basically, the output redirection symbol informs the operating system that you want standard output to go to a device other than the default (the screen). The input redirection symbol routes input away from the keyboard to another input device. The following examples illustrate how to do this in MS-DOS.

Examples

1. Suppose you write a program that uses only `scanf()` and `printf()` for input and output. You want the program to get input from a file called MYDATA, instead of from the keyboard. Because `scanf()` receives input from `stdin`, you must redirect `stdin`. After compiling the program to a file called MYPGM.EXE, you can redirect its input away from the keyboard with the following DOS command:

```
C:>MYPGM < MYDATA
```

You can include a full path name before either the program name or the file name. There is a danger, however, in redirecting all output such as this. *All* output, including screen prompts for keyboard input, goes to MYDATA. This is probably unacceptable in most cases; you will still want prompts and some messages to go the screen. In the next section, you read how to separate I/O, sending some output to one device such as the screen and the rest to another device such as a file or a printer.

2. You can route the program's output to the printer by typing the following line:

```
C:>MYPGM > PRN:
```

This uses the DOS device name for the printer. UNIX users must use 1pr or the print spooler's device name in place of PRN: in these examples.

3. If the program requires lots of input, and that input is stored in a file called ANSWERS, you can override the keyboard default device that scanf() uses, as follows.

When scanf() requires input, have the program read from the file named ANSWERS.

```
C:>MYPGM < ANSWERS
```

4. You can also combine redirection symbols. To get input from the ANSWERS disk file and send the output to the printer, you can use the following code:

```
C:>MYPGM < ANSWERS > PRN:
```

TIP: MS-DOS users can reroute output to a serial printer or a second parallel printer port by substituting COM1: or LPT2: in place of PRN: in these examples.

Printing Formatted Output

The fprintf() function enables your program to write to the printer.

Print data to a device

It is easy to send program output to the printer using the fprintf() function. The format of fprintf() follows:

```
fprintf(device, control_string [, one or more values]);
```

You might notice that the format of fprintf() is similar to that of printf(). The only difference between fprintf() and printf() (besides the names) is that fprintf() requires a *device* as its first argument. Usually, this device is the standard printer, stdprn. In Chapter 30, "Sequential Files," you learn how to write formatted data to a disk file by using fprintf().

The following examples show how you can combine printf() and fprintf() to write to both the screen and the printer.

> **CAUTION:** Some compilers, despite being compatible with ANSI C, do not let fprintf() print to a printer using the stdprn device. If yours does not, you need to learn more about file I/O. See Part 7, "Structures and File I/O," to learn how to route output to the printer using a file pointer.

Example

The fprintf() function uses the stdio.h header file.

The following program asks users for their first and last names. It then prints the full name—last name first—to the printer.

```c
/* Filename: C21FPR1.C
   Prints a name on the printer */
#include <stdio.h>
main()
{
   char first[20];
   char last[20];

   printf("What is your first name? ");
   scanf(" %s", first);
```

```
printf("What is your last name? ");
scanf(" %s", last);

/* Send names to the printer */
fprintf(stdprn, "In a phone book, your name");
fprint(" looks like this: \n");
fprintf(stdprn, " %s, %s", last, first);
return;
}
```

Character I/O Functions

Because all I/O is actually character I/O, C provides many functions that perform character input and output. The printf() and scanf() functions, however, are not character I/O functions. The printf() and scanf() functions are called *formatted I/O functions* because they give you formatting control (using conversion characters) over your input and output.

There is nothing wrong with using printf() for formatted output, but scanf() has many problems, some of which you have seen. In this section, you learn how to write your own character input routines that replace scanf(). To prepare you for the upcoming chapters on disk files, you also learn how to use character output functions. These functions are generally easier to use than scanf() and printf() because they don't require formatting codes.

The getc() and putc() Functions

The getc() and putc() functions handle character I/O with any standard device.

The most fundamental character I/O functions are getc() and putc(). The putc() function writes a single character to the standard output device, which is the screen, unless you redirect it from your operating system. The getc() function inputs a single character from the standard input device, which is the keyboard, unless you redirect it.

The format for `getc()` follows:

```
int_var = getc(device);
```

Assign device input to a variable

Don't let the integer `int_var` confuse you. Even though `getc()` is a character function, you use an integer variable to store the `getc()` input value. `getc()` returns a –1 when an end-of-file condition occurs. If you are using `getc()` to read information from a disk file, the –1 is read when the end of the file is reached. If you used a character variable, the –1 would be interpreted as 255. You learn more about end-of-file conditions in Chapter 30, "Sequential Files." As with all integer variables, you can use the integer input value as though it were a character.

The `getc()` *device* can be any C standard input device. If you are getting character input from the keyboard, use `stdin` as the *device*. If you initialize your modem and want to receive characters from it, use `stdaux` for the *device*.

The format of `putc()` follows:

```
putc(int_val, device);
```

Send character to a device

The `int_val` can be an integer variable, expression, or constant. You output character data with `putc()`. The *device* can be any standard output C device. To write a character to your printer, use `stdprn` for the *device*.

> **NOTE:** Most of the character I/O functions, including `getc()` and `putc()`, are actually called *macros*. These are not true functions, but rather a form of preprocessor directives. Most C programmers program for years and never notice the difference, and you probably won't either. As a precaution, however, be sure you do not include an expression in `putc()`, such as `putc(mychar++);`. A macro may not evaluate this properly.

Examples

1. The following program asks users for their initials, one character at a time. Notice that the program uses both `printf()` and `putc()`. The `printf()` is still useful for formatted output, such as messages to the user. Writing individual characters is best achieved with `putc()`.

   The program must call two `getc()` functions for each character typed. When you answer a `getc()` prompt, by typing a character followed by an Enter keypress, C sees that input as a stream of two characters. The `getc()` first gets the letter you typed, then it gets the \n (newline, supplied to C when you press Enter). Examples that follow correct this double-`getc()` problem.

```
/* Filename: C21CH1.C
   Introduces getc() and putc() */
#include <stdio.h>
main()
{
   int in_char;                /* Holds incoming initial */
   char first, last;            /* Holds converted first
                                   and last initial */

   printf("What is your first name initial? ");
   in_char = getc(stdin);      /* Wait for first initial */
   first = in_char;
   in_char = getc(stdin);          /* Ignore newline */

   printf("What is your last name initial? ");

   in_char = getc(stdin);          /* Wait for last initial */
   last = in_char;
   in_char = getc(stdin);          /* Ignore newline */

   printf("\nHere they are: \n");
   putc(first, stdout);
   putc(last, stdout);
   return;
}
```

Here is the output from this program:

```
What is your first name initial? G
What is your last name initial? P

Here they are:
GP
```

2. You can add carriage returns to better space the output. To print the two initials on two separate lines, use putc() to send a newline character to stdout. The following program does this.

```c
/* Filename: C21CH2.C
   Introduces getc() and putc() and uses
   putc() to output newline */
#include <stdio.h>
main()
{
    int in_char;                /* Holds incoming initial */
    char first, last;           /* Holds converted first
                                          and last initial */

    printf("What is your first name initial? ");
    in_char = getc(stdin);      /* Wait for first initial */
    first = in_char;
    in_char = getc(stdin);         /* Ignore newline */

    printf("What is your last name initial? ");

    in_char = getc(stdin);      /* Wait for last initial */
    last = in_char;
    in_char = getc(stdin);         /* Ignore newline */

    printf("\nHere they are: \n");
    putc(first, stdout);
    putc('\n', stdout);            /* A newline is output */
    putc(last, stdout);
    return;
}
```

3. It may be clearer to define the newline character as a constant. At the top of the program, you could have

```
#define NEWLINE '\n'
```

The `putc()` could then read

```
putc(NEWLINE, stdout);
```

Some programmers prefer to define their character formatting constants and refer to them by name. You can decide whether you think this is clearer or whether you want to continue using the \n character constant in `putc()`.

The getchar() and putchar() Functions

Both `getchar()` and `putchar()` use `stdin` and `stdout` as their target devices.

When you perform character I/O, the `getchar()` and `putchar()` functions are easier to use than `getc()` and `putc()`. The `getchar()` and `putchar()` functions are identical to `getc()` and `putc()`, except you do not specify a device because they assume the standard input and output devices, `stdin` and `stdout` (typically, the screen and the keyboard) will be used. In the following:

```
in_char=getc(stdin);
```

is identical to

```
in_char=getchar();
```

and

```
putc(var, stdout);
```

is identical to

```
putchar(var);
```

The `getchar()` and `putchar()` functions are two of the most frequently used character I/O functions in C. Most I/O is performed on the keyboard and screen, and these two devices are generally routed to `stdin` and `stdout` by the operating system, unless you redirect them.

The getchar() and the getc() functions are both *buffered* input functions. That is, as you type characters, the data goes to a buffer rather than immediately to your program. The buffer is a section of memory managed by C (and has nothing to do with some computers' *typeahead buffers*).

Figure 21.2 shows you how this works. When your program gets to a getc() or a getchar(), the program temporarily waits as you type the input. The program does not see the characters because they are going to the buffer in memory. There is no limit to the size of the buffer; it keeps filling up with input until you press Enter. The Enter keypress signals the computer to release the buffer to your program.

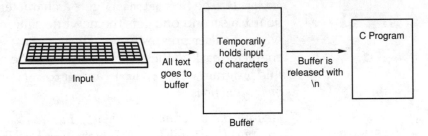

Figure 21.2. The getc() and getchar() input goes to a buffer, where it is held until you press Enter.

Both getchar() and putchar() use the stdio.h header file.

Most multiuser computers will buffer all input. Most PCs allow either buffered or nonbuffered input. The getch() function (shown later in this chapter) is nonbuffered. With getc() and getchar(), all input is buffered, and this affects the timing of your program's input. Your program receives no characters from a getchar() or getc() until you press Enter. Suppose that you ask a question such as the following:

```
Do you want to see the report again (Y/N)?
```

and use getchar() for input. If the user presses a Y, the program does not know this until the user presses Enter too. Then the Y and Enter keypresses are sent, one character at a time, to the program, where the input is processed. If you want immediate response to a user's typing (such as INKEY$ does, if you are familiar with BASIC), you must use getch().

> **TIP:** By using buffered input, the user can type a string of characters in response to repeated `getc()` requests, and correct the input with the Backspace key before pressing Enter. If the input is nonbuffered, the Backspace becomes just one more character of data.

Examples

1. The following sample program illustrates `getchar()` and `putchar()`. The first `getchar()` gets a character from the keyboard; a second one gets the newline character produced when the user presses Enter. The `putchar()` echoes the typed character back to the screen. You might be able to see from this program why `getchar()` and `putchar()` are called *mirror-image functions*.

Identify the program and include the necessary header file. This program will get a character from the user. Declare an integer variable called my_char, and use it to hold the character that the user types. Ask the user to type a character. Use the get_char function to store the typed character in the my_char variable. Call get_char again for the user's Enter keypress. Tell the user what they typed, by displaying the contents of my_char.

```
/* Filename: C21GPC.C
   Illustrates simple getchar() and putchar() */
#include <stdio.h>
main()
{
    int my_char;                            /* Must be integer */

    printf("Please type a character... ");
    my_char = getchar();             /* Get the character */
    getchar();                       /* Discard the newline */
```

```
    printf("You typed this: ");
    putchar(my_char);
    return;
}
```

When you get
characters, you may
need to discard the
newline keypress.

This program must discard the newline character. It could have done so by assigning the input character—from `getchar()`—to an extra variable, as previous examples have done. Because we know that the user must press Enter after typing a character, we can ignore the second return value by not assigning `getchar()` to anything. You know the user must press Enter (to end the input), so it is all right to discard it with an unused `getchar()` function call.

2. The `scanf()` function has limited use when inputting strings such as names and sentences. The `scanf()` function allows only one word to be entered at a time. If you ask users for their full names with these lines:

```
printf("What are your first and last names? ");
scanf(" %s", names);                /* Get the name into the
                                       names character array */
```

the array called `names` would receive only the first name; `scanf()` ignores all data to the right of the first space.

Using `getchar()`, you can build an input function that does not have a single-word limitation. When you want to get a string of characters from users, such as their first and last names, you can call the `get_in_str()` function shown in the next program.

```
/* Filename: C21IN.C
   Program that builds an input string array
   using getchar() */
#include <stdio.h>
#define MAX 25                          /* Size of character
                                           array to be typed in */

void main(void);
void get_in_str(char str[], int len);

void main(void)
```

```
{
    char input_str[MAX];   /* Keyboard input will fill this */
    printf("What is your full name? ");
    get_in_str(input_str, MAX);     /* String from keyboard */
    printf("After return, your name is %s", input_str);
    return;
}


/*************************************************************
The following function requires that a string and the maximum
length of the string be passed to it. It accepts input from
the keyboard, and sends keyboard input into the string. Upon
return, the calling routine has access to the string.
**************************************************************/
void get_in_str(char str[], int len)
{
    int i=0, input_char;        /* Index and character typed */
    input_char = getchar(); /* Get next character in string */
    while (i<(len-1) && (input_char!='\n'))
      {
        str[i] = input_char;        /* Build the string, one
                                        character at a time */

        i++;
        input_char = getchar();          /* Get the next
                                        character in the string */
      }
    str[i]='\0';        /* Make the char array into a string */
    return;
}
```

The main() function defines an array and prompts the user for a name. After the prompt, the program calls the get_in_str() function and uses getchar() to build the input array, one character at a time. The function keeps looping, using the while loop, until the user presses Enter (signaled by the newline character, \n) or the maximum number of characters are typed.

You might want to use this function in your own programs.

Be sure to pass it a character array and an integer that holds the maximum array size (you don't want the input string to be longer than the character array that holds the string). When control returns to main()—or to whichever function called get_in_str()—the array has the user's full input, spaces and all.

> **NOTE:** The loop checks for len-1 to save room for the null terminating zero at the end of the input string.

3. Because the getchar() function is used frequently for building strings (as the last example showed), many programmers have chosen to insert it directly inside the while test.

   Here is a rewritten version of the get_in_str() function shown in the last example. Notice that by putting the getchar() directly inside the while conditional test, you streamline the function. The while conditional test takes a little more room, but the improved efficiency is worth it. This is a common input procedure, and you should become familiar with seeing getchar() inside tests such as this. At first it may seem awkward and cumbersome, but many C programmers choose to use it because it gives them greater control over user input.

```
void get_in_str(char str[], int len)
{
    int i=0, input_char;        /* Index and character typed */
    /* Get next character in string */
    while (i<(len-1) && ((input_char=getchar()) != '\n') )
      {
        str[i] = input_char;       /* Build the string, one
                                             character at a time */
        i++;
      }
    str[i]='\0';       /* Make the char array into a string */
    return;
}
```

The getch() and putch() Functions

Both getch() and putch() use the conio.h header file.

The getch() and putch() functions are slightly different from the previous character I/O functions. Their formats are similar to getchar() and putchar(); they both assume that stdin and stdout are the standard input and output devices, and you cannot specify other devices (unless you redirect them with your operating system). The format of getch() and putch() follows:

```
int_var = getch();
```

and

```
putch(int_var);
```

Both getch() and putch() offer nonbuffered I/O that "grabs" characters immediately after they are typed.

The getch() and putch() functions are not ANSI C standard functions, but they are available on a large number of compilers and well worth mentioning. getch() and putch() are nonbuffered functions. However, many multiuser computer systems buffer getch(), even though the function was not designed for buffered input. The putch() character output function is a mirror-image of getch(); it is a nonbuffered output function. Because almost every output device (except screens and modems) are inherently buffered, putch() effectively does the same thing as putc().

Characters input with getch() are not echoed to the screen as they are typed.

Another difference between getch() and the other character input functions is that getch() does not echo the input characters on-screen as it receives them. When you type characters in response to getchar(), you see the characters as you type them (as they are sent to the buffer). If you want to display on-screen the characters received by getch(), you must follow getch() with putch(). It is handy to echo the characters on-screen so that users can verify what they typed.

Both getch() and putch() assume that stdin and stdout are the standard input and output devices. When you want your program to respond immediately to keyboard input, use getch(). Some programmers want to make users press Enter after answering a prompt or selecting from a menu. They feel that buffered input gives users more time to decide if they really want to give that answer; users can press Backspace and correct the input before pressing Enter.

Other programmers like to "grab" the user's single-character answer (such as a menu response) and act on it immediately. They feel that pressing Enter is an added and unneeded burden for the user. The choice is yours. You should understand both buffered and nonbuffered input, so you can use either one.

> **TIP:** Although getche() is not an ANSI C standard function, you can use it on most computer systems. The getche() function is a nonbuffered input function identical to getch(), except the input characters are echoed (displayed) to the screen as the user types them. Using getche() instead of getch() sometimes keeps you from having to echo the user's input to the screen.

Example

The following program uses the getch() and putch() functions. The user is asked to enter five letters. These five letters are added to the character array named letters using a for loop. As you run this program, notice that the characters are not echoed to the screen as you type them. As you type the characters, the program receives each character, adds it to the array, and loops again, because getch() is unbuffered. (If this were buffered input, the program would not loop through the five iterations until you pressed Enter.)

A second loop uses putch() to print the five letters. A third loop uses putc() to print the five letters to the printer.

```
/* Filename: C21GCH1.C
   Uses getch() and putch() for input and output */
#include <stdio.h>
#include <conio.h>
main()
{
   int ctr;                      /* The for loop counter */
   char letters[5];    /* Holds five input characters. No
                          room is needed for the null zero
                          because this array will never be
                          treated like a string.          */
```

```
printf("Please type five letters... \n");
for (ctr=0; ctr<5; ctr++)
    {
        letters[ctr] = getch();        /* Add input to array */
    }
for (ctr=0; ctr<5; ctr++)   /* Print them to the screen */
    {
        putch(letters[ctr]);
    }
for (ctr=0; ctr<5; ctr++)  /* Print them to the printer */
    {
        putc(letters[ctr], stdprn);
    }
return;
}
```

When you run this program, don't press Enter after typing the five letters. The loop ends automatically after the fifth letter (due to the for loop). This is possible only because of the nonbuffered input allowed with getch().

Review Questions

Answers to review questions are in Appendix B.

1. Why are there no input or output commands in C?

2. True or false: If you use the character I/O functions to send output to stdout, the output always goes to the screen.

3. What is the difference between getc() and getchar()?

4. What is the difference between getch() and getchar()?

5. What function sends formatted output to devices other than the screen?

6. What are the MS-DOS and UNIX redirection symbols?

7. What nonstandard function, most similar to getch(), echoes the input character to the screen as the user types it?

8. True or false: When you use `getchar()`, the program receives your input as you type it.

9. Which keypress releases buffered input to the program?

10. True or false: Using devices and functions described in this chapter, you could write one program that sends some output to the screen, some output to the printer, and some output to the modem.

Review Exercises

1. Write a program that asks users for five letters and prints them backwards, first to the screen and then to the printer. (Note: If your compiler does not let you send output to the printer using `fprintf()`, ignore the last part of this exercise.)

2. Write a miniature typewriter program, using `getc()` and `putc()`. Loop to get a line of user input (until the user presses Enter), then write that line of characters to the printer. Because `getc()` is buffered, nothing goes to the printer until the user presses Enter at the end of each line of text. (Use the string-building input function shown in C21IN.C.)

3. Add a `putch()` inside the first loop of C21GCH1.C to echo the characters to the screen as the user types them. (This simulates the nonstandard `getche()` function offered with some C compilers.)

4. A *palindrome* is a word or phrase spelled (but not necessarily punctuated) the same way forward and backward. Here are two examples:

```
Madam, I'm Adam
Golf? No sir, prefer prison flog!
```

Write a C program that asks the user for a phrase. Build the input, one character at a time, using a character input function such as `getchar()`. After you have the full string (store it in a character array), test the phrase to see if it is a palindrome. You need to filter out special nonalphabetic characters, storing only alphabetic characters to a second character array. You must also convert the characters—as you store them—to uppercase. The first palindrome would become

```
MADAMIMADAM
```

Using one or more `for` or `while` loops, you can now test the phrase to see if it is a palindrome. Print the result of the test to the printer. Sample output should appear as follows:

```
"Madam, I'm Adam" is a palindrome.
```

Summary

You now should understand the generic method that C programs use for input and output. By writing to standard I/O devices, C achieves portability. If you write a program for one computer, it will work on another. If C were to write directly to specific hardware, programs could not work on every computer.

If you still want to use formatted I/O functions, such as `printf()`, you can do so. The `fprintf()` function enables you to write formatted output to any device, including the printer.

Although the methods of character I/O are primitive, their flexibility allows you to build on them and create your own input functions. One of the most often used C functions, a string-building character I/O function, was demonstrated in this chapter (the C21IN.C program).

The next two chapters introduce many character and string functions, including string I/O functions. The string I/O functions build on the principles presented here. You may be surprised at the extensive character and string manipulation functions available in the C language.

Character, String, and Numeric Functions

C provides many built-in functions in addition to the `printf()`, `scanf()`, and `strcpy()` functions you have seen so far throughout the book. These built-in functions increase your productivity and save you programming time. You don't need to write as much code because the built-in functions perform many useful tasks for you.

This chapter introduces you to the following:

- Character conversion functions
- Character and string testing functions
- String manipulation functions
- String I/O functions
- Mathematic, trigonometric, and logarithmic functions
- Random-number processing

Character Functions

This section explores many of the character functions available in ANSI C. Generally, you pass character arguments to the functions, and the functions return values that you can store or print. By using these functions, you off-load much of your work to C and let it perform the more tedious manipulations of character and string data.

Character Testing Functions

The character functions return True or False results based on characters you pass to them.

Several functions test for certain characteristics of your character data. You can test to see if your character data is alphabetic, digital, uppercase, lowercase, and much more. You must pass a character variable or constant argument to the function (by placing the argument in the function parentheses) when you call it. These functions all return a True or False result, so you can test their return values inside an `if` statement or a `while` loop.

NOTE: All character functions presented in this section are prototyped in the ctype.h header file. Be sure to include ctype.h at the top of any program that uses them.

Alphabetic and Digital Testing

The following functions test for alphabetic conditions:

◆ `isalpha(c)`: Returns True (nonzero) if *c* is an uppercase or lowercase letter. Returns False (zero) if *c* is not a letter.

◆ `islower(c)`: Returns True (nonzero) if *c* is a lowercase letter. Returns False (zero) if *c* is not a lowercase letter.

◆ `isupper(c)`: Returns True (nonzero) if *c* is an uppercase letter. Returns False (zero) if *c* is not an uppercase letter.

Remember that any nonzero value is True in C, and zero is always False. If you use the return values of these functions in a relational test, the True return value is not always 1 (it can be any nonzero value), but it is always considered True for the test.

The following functions test for digits:

♦ `isdigit(c)`: Returns True (nonzero) if *c* is a digit 0 through 9. Returns False (zero) if *c* is not a digit.

> **NOTE:** Although some character functions test for digits, the arguments are still character data and cannot be used in mathematical calculations, unless you calculate using the ASCII values of characters.

♦ `isxdigit(c)`: Returns True (nonzero) if *c* is any of the hexadecimal digits 0 through 9 or A, B, C, D, E, F, a, b, c, d, e, or f. Returns False (zero) if *c* is anything else. (See Appendix A for more information on the hexadecimal numbering system.)

The following function tests for numeric or alphabetical arguments:

♦ `isalnum(c)`: Returns True (nonzero) if *c* is a digit 0 through 9 or an alphabetic character (either uppercase or lowercase). Returns False (zero) if *c* is not a digit or a letter.

> **CAUTION:** You can pass to these functions only a character value or an integer value holding the ASCII value of a character. You cannot pass an entire character array to character functions. If you want to test the elements of a character array, you must pass the array one element at a time.

Example

The following program asks users for their initials. If a user types anything but alphabetic characters, the program displays an error and asks again.

Identify the program and include the necessary header files. The program will ask the user for his or her first initial, so declare the character variable initial *to hold the user's answer.*

1. Ask the user for his or her first initial, and get the user's answer.

2. If the answer was not an alphabetic character, tell the user this and repeat step 1.

Print a thank-you message on-screen.

```
/* Filename: C22INI.C
   Asks for first initial and tests
   to ensure that it is correct */
#include <stdio.h>
#include <ctype.h>
main()
{
   char initial;
   printf("What is your first initial? ");
   scanf(" %c", &initial);

   while (! isalpha(initial))
     {
        printf("\nThat was not a valid initial! \n");
        printf("\nWhat is your first initial? ");
        scanf(" %c", &initial);
     }

   printf("\nThanks!");
   return;
}
```

This use of the not operator (!) is quite clear. The program continues to loop while the entered character is *not* alphabetic.

Special Character Testing Functions

A few character functions become useful when you need to read from a disk file, a modem, or another operating system device that you route input from. These functions are not used as much as the character functions you saw in the last section, but they can be useful for testing specific characters for readability.

The remaining character testing functions follow:

The character testing functions do not change characters.

♦ `iscntrl(c)`: Returns True (nonzero) if *c* is a *control character* (any character from the ASCII table numbered 0 through 31). Returns False (zero) if *c* is not a control character.

♦ `isgraph(c)`: Returns True (nonzero) if *c* is any printable character (a noncontrol character) except a space. Returns False (zero) if *c* is a space or anything other than a printable character.

♦ `isprint(c)`: Returns True (nonzero) if *c* is a printable character (a noncontrol character) from ASCII 32 to ASCII 127, including a space. Returns False (zero) if *c* is not a printable character.

♦ `ispunct(c)`: Returns True (nonzero) if *c* is any punctuation character (any printable character other than a space, a letter, or a digit). Returns False (zero) if *c* is not a punctuation character.

♦ `isspace(c)`: Returns True (nonzero) if *c* is a space, newline (\n), carriage return (\r), tab (\t), or vertical tab (\v) character. Returns False (zero) if *c* is anything else.

Character Conversion Functions

Both `tolower()` and `toupper()` return lowercase or uppercase arguments.

Two remaining character functions can be very handy. Rather than test characters, these functions change characters to their lowercase or uppercase equivalents.

♦ `tolower(c)`: Converts *c* to lowercase. Nothing is changed if you pass `tolower()` a lowercase letter or a nonalphabetic character.

♦ `toupper(c)`: Converts *c* to uppercase. Nothing is changed if you pass `toupper()` an uppercase letter or a nonalphabetic character.

These functions return their changed character values.

These functions are very useful for user input. Suppose you are asking users a yes-or-no question, such as the following:

```
Do you want to print the checks (Y/N)?
```

Before knowing `toupper()` and `tolower()`, you would need to check for both a *Y* and a *y* before printing the checks. Instead of testing for both conditions, you can convert the character to uppercase, and test for a *Y*.

Example

Here is a program that prints an appropriate message if the user is a girl or a boy. The program tests for *G* and *B* after converting the user's input to uppercase. No check for lowercase needs to be done.

Identify the program and include the necessary header files. The program will ask the user a question requiring an alphabetic answer, so declare the character variable ans to hold the user's response.

Ask whether the user is a girl or a boy, and store the user's answer in ans. *The user must press Enter, so get and then discard the Enter keypress. Change the value of* ans *to uppercase. If the answer is G, print a message. If the answer is B, print a different message. If the answer is something else, print another message.*

```c
/* Filename: C22GB.C
   Tests whether the user typed a G or a B */
#include <stdio.h>
#include <ctype.h>
main()
{
    char ans;                        /* Holds user's response */
    printf("Are you a girl or a boy (G/B)? ");
    ans=getchar();                            /* Get answer */
    getchar();                            /* Discard newline */

    ans = toupper(ans);      /* Convert answer to uppercase */
    switch (ans)
```

```
{   case ('G'): { printf("You look pretty today!\n");
                  break; }
    case ('B'): { printf("You look handsome today!\n");
                  break; }
    default :   { printf("Your answer makes no sense!\n");
                  break; }
  }
  return;
}
```

Here is the output from the program:

```
Are you a girl or a boy (G/B)? B
You look handsome today!
```

String Functions

Some of the most powerful built-in C functions are the string functions. They perform much of the tedious work for which you have been writing code so far, such as inputting strings from the keyboard and comparing strings.

As with the character functions, there is no need to "reinvent the wheel" by writing code when built-in functions do the same task. Use these functions as much as possible.

Now that you have a good grasp of the foundations of C, you can master the string functions. They enable you to concentrate on your program's primary purpose, rather than spend time coding your own string functions.

Useful String Functions

You can use a handful of useful string functions for string testing and conversion. You have already seen (in earlier chapters) the strcpy() string function, which copies a string of characters into a character array.

NOTE: All string functions in this section are prototyped in the string.h header file. Be sure to include string.h at the top of any program that uses the string functions.

The string functions work on character arrays that contain strings or on string constants.

Some string functions that test or manipulate strings follow:

♦ strcat(*s1*, *s2*): Concatenates (merges) the *s2* string to the end of the *s1* character array. The *s1* array must have enough reserved elements to hold both strings.

♦ strcmp(*s1*, *s2*): Compares the *s1* string with the *s2* string on an alphabetical, element-by-element basis. If *s1* alphabetizes before *s2*, strcmp() returns a negative value. If *s1* and *s2* are the same strings, strcmp() returns 0. If *s1* alphabetizes after *s2*, strcmp() returns a positive value.

♦ strlen(*s1*): Returns the length of *s1*. Remember, the length of a string is the number of characters up to—but not including—the null zero. The number of characters defined for the character array has nothing to do with the length of the string.

TIP: Before using strcat() to concatenate strings, use strlen() to ensure that the target string (the string being concatenated to) is large enough to hold both strings.

String I/O Functions

In the previous few chapters, you have used a character input function, getchar(), to build input strings. Now you can begin to use the string input and output functions. Although the goal of the string-building functions has been to teach you the specifics of the language, these string I/O functions are much easier to use than writing a character input function.

The string input and output functions are listed as follows:

♦ gets(*s*): Stores input from stdin (usually directed to the keyboard) into the string named *s*.

♦ puts(*s*): Outputs the *s* string to stdout (usually directed to the screen by the operating system).

♦ fgets(*s*, *len*, *dev*): Stores input from the standard device specified by *dev* (such as stdin or stdaux) in the *s* string. If more than *len* characters are input, fgets() discards them.

♦ fputs(*s*, *dev*): Outputs the *s* string to the standard device specified by *dev*.

Both **gets()** and **puts()** input and output strings.

These four functions make the input and output of strings easy. They work in pairs. That is, strings input with gets() are usually output with puts(). Strings input with fgets() are usually output with fputs().

> **TIP:** gets() replaces the string-building input function you saw in earlier chapters.

Terminate gets() or fgets() input by pressing Enter. Each of these functions handles string-terminating characters in a slightly different manner, as follows:

gets()	A newline input becomes a null zero (\0)
puts()	A null at the end of the string becomes a newline character (\n)
fgets()	A newline input stays, and a null zero is added after it
fputs()	The null zero is dropped, and a newline character is not added

Therefore, when you enter strings with gets(), C places a string-terminating character in the string at the point where you press Enter. This creates the input string. (Without the null zero, the input would not be a string.) When you output a string, the null zero at the end of the string becomes a newline character. This is good because you typically prefer a newline at the end of a line of output (to put the cursor on the next line).

Because `fgets()` and `fputs()` can input and output strings from devices such as disk files and telephone modems, it may be critical that the incoming newline characters are retained for the data's integrity. When outputting strings to these devices, you do not want C inserting extra newline characters.

> **CAUTION:** Neither `gets()` nor `fgets()` ensures that its input strings are large enough to hold the incoming data. It is up to you to make sure enough space is reserved in the character array to hold the complete input.

One final function is worth noting, although it is not a string function. It is the `fflush()` function, which flushes (empties) whatever standard device is listed in its parentheses. To flush the keyboard of all its input, you would code as follows:

Empty input stream

```
fflush(stdin);
```

When doing string input and output, sometimes an extra newline character gets into the keyboard buffer. A previous answer to `gets()` or `getc()` might have an extra newline you forgot to discard. When a program seems to ignore `gets()`, you might have to insert `fflush(stdin)` before `gets()`.

Flushing the standard input device causes no harm, and using it can clear the input stream so that your next `gets()` works properly. You can also flush standard output devices with `fflush()` to clear the output stream of any characters you may have sent into it.

> **NOTE:** The header file for `fflush()` is in stdio.h.

Example

The following program shows you how easy it is to use `gets()` and `puts()`. The program requests the name of a book from the user using a single gets() function call, then prints the book title with puts().

Identify the program and include the necessary header files. The program will ask the user for the name of a book. Declare the character array book *with 30 elements to hold the user's answer.*

Ask the user for the book's title, and store the user's response in the book *array. Display the string stored in* book *to an output device, probably your screen. Print a thank-you message.*

```
/* Filename: C22GPS1.C
   Gets and puts strings */
#include <stdio.h>
#include <string.h>
main()
{
    char book[30];

    printf("What is the book title? ");
    gets(book);                    /* Get an input string */
    puts(book);                    /* Display the string */
    printf("Thanks for the book!\n");
    return;

}
```

The output of the program follows:

```
What is the book title? Mary and Her Lambs
Mary and Her Lambs
Thanks for the book!
```

Converting Strings to Numbers

Sometimes you need to convert numbers stored in character strings to a numeric data type. ANSI C provides three functions that let you do this:

♦ atoi(*s*): Converts *s* to an integer. The name stands for *alphabetic to integer*.

♦ atol(s): Converts s to a long integer. The name stands for *a*lphabetic *to* *l*ong integer.

♦ atof(s): Converts s to a floating-point number. The name stands for *a*lphabetic *to* *f*loating-point.

> **NOTE:** These three ato() functions are prototyped in the stdlib.h header file. Be sure to include stdlib.h at the top of any program that uses the ato() functions.

The string must contain a valid number. Here is a string that can be converted to an integer:

"1232"

The string must hold a string of digits short enough to fit in the target numeric data type. The following string could not be converted to an integer with the atoi() function:

"-1232495.654"

However, it could be converted to a floating-point number with the atof() function.

C cannot perform any mathematical calculation with such strings, even if the strings contain digits that represent numbers. Therefore, you must convert any string into its numeric equivalent before performing any arithmetic with it.

> **NOTE:** If you pass a string to an ato() function and the string does not contain a valid representation of a number, the ato() function returns 0.

These functions become more useful to you later, after you learn about disk files, pointers, and command-line arguments.

Numeric Functions

This section presents many of the built-in C numeric functions. As with the string functions, these functions save you time by converting and calculating numbers instead of you having to write functions that do the same thing. Many of these are trigonometric and advanced math functions. You may use some of these numeric functions only rarely, but they are there if you need them.

This section concludes the discussion of C's standard built-in functions. After mastering the concepts in this chapter, you are ready to learn more about arrays and pointers. As you develop more skills in C, you may find yourself relying on these numeric, string, and character functions when you write more powerful programs.

Useful Mathematical Functions

Several built-in numeric functions return results based on numeric variables and constants passed to them. Even if you write only a few science and engineering programs, some of these functions may be useful.

NOTE: All mathematical and trigonometric functions are prototyped in the math.h header file. Be sure to include math.h at the top of any program that uses the numeric functions.

These numeric functions return double-precision values.

Here are the functions listed with their descriptions:

◆ `ceil(x)`: The `ceil()`, or *ceiling*, function rounds numbers up to the nearest integer.

◆ `fabs(x)`: Returns the absolute value of *x*. The absolute value of a number is its positive equivalent.

TIP: Absolute value is used for distances (which are always positive), accuracy measurements, age differences, and other calculations that require a positive result.

- `floor(x)`: The `floor()` function rounds numbers down to the nearest integer.

- `fmod(x, y)`: Returns the floating-point remainder of (*x*/*y*), with the same sign as *x*; *y* cannot be zero. Because the modulus operator (`%`) works only with integers, this function is supplied to find the remainder of floating-point number divisions.

- `pow(x, y)`: Returns *x* raised to the *y* power, or x^y. If *x* is less than or equal to zero, *y* must be an integer. If *x* equals zero, *y* cannot be negative.

- `sqrt(x)`: Returns the square root of *x*; *x* must be greater than or equal to zero.

The *n*th Root

No function returns the *n*th root of a number, only the square root. In other words, you cannot call a function that gives you the 4th root of 65,536. (By the way, 16 is the 4th root of 65,536, because 16 times 16 times 16 times 16 = 65,536.)

You can use a mathematical trick to simulate the *n*th root, however. Because C lets you raise a number to a fractional power—with the `pow()` function—you can raise a number to the *n*th root by raising it to the (1/*n*) power. For example, to find the 4th root of 65,536, you could type this:

```
root = pow(65536.0, (1.0/4.0));
```

Note that the decimal point keeps the numbers in floating-point format. If you leave them as integers, such as

```
root = pow(65536, (1,4));
```

C produces incorrect results. The `pow()` function and most other mathematical functions require floating-point values as arguments.

To store the 7th root of 78,125 in a variable called `root`, for example, you would type

```
root = pow(78125.0, (1.0/7.0));
```

This stores 5.0 in root because 5⁷ equals 78,125.

Knowing how to compute the nth root comes in handy in scientific programs and also in financial applications, such as time value of money problems.

Example

The following program uses the fabs() function to compute the difference between two ages.

```c
/* Filename: C22ABS.C
   Prints the difference between two ages */
#include <stdio.h>
#include <math.h>
main()
{
   float age1, age2, diff;
   printf("\nWhat is the first child's age? ");
   scanf(" %f", &age1);
   printf("What is the second child's age? ");
   scanf(" %f", &age2);

   /* Calculate the positive difference */
   diff = age1 - age2;
   diff = fabs(diff);     /* Determine the absolute value */

   printf("\nThey are %.0f years apart.", diff);
   return;
}
```

The output from this program follows. Because of fabs(), the order of the ages doesn't matter. Without absolute value, this program would produce a negative age difference if the first age was less than the second. Because the ages are relatively small, floating-point variables are used in this example. C automatically converts floating-point arguments to double precision when passing them to fabs().

```
What is the first child's age? 10
What is the second child's age? 12

They are 2 years apart.
```

Trigonometric Functions

The following functions are available for trigonometric applications:

◆ `cos(x)`: Returns the cosine of the angle x, expressed in radians.

◆ `sin(x)`: Returns the sine of the angle x, expressed in radians.

◆ `tan(x)`: Returns the tangent of the angle x, expressed in radians.

These are probably the least-used functions. This is not to belittle the work of scientific and mathematical programmers who need them, however. Certainly they are grateful that C supplies these functions! Otherwise, programmers would have to write their own functions to perform these three basic trigonometric calculations.

Most C compilers supply additional trigonometric functions, including hyperbolic equivalents of these three functions.

TIP: If you need to pass an angle that is expressed in degrees to these functions, convert the angle's degrees to radians by multiplying the degrees by $\pi/180.0$ (π equals approximately 3.14159).

Logarithmic Functions

Three highly mathematical functions are sometimes used in business and mathematics. They are listed as follows:

♦ `exp(x)`: Returns the base of natural logarithm (*e*) raised to a power specified by *x* (e^x); *e* is the mathematical expression for the approximate value of 2.718282.

♦ `log(x)`: Returns the natural logarithm of the argument *x*, mathematically written as `ln(x)`. *x* must be positive.

♦ `log10(x)`: Returns the base-10 logarithm of argument *x*, mathematically written as `log10(x)`. *x* must be positive.

Random-Number Processing

Random events happen every day. You wake up and it might be sunny or rainy. You might have a good day or a bad day. You might get a phone call or you might not. Your stock portfolio might go up or down in value.

Random events are especially important in games. Part of the fun in games is your luck with rolling dice or drawing cards, combined with your playing skills.

Simulating random events is an important task for computers. Computers, however, are finite machines; that is, given the same input, they *always* produce the same output. This can cause them to give you some very boring games!

The designers of C knew this, and found a way to overcome it. They wrote a random-number generating function called `rand()`. You can use `rand()` to compute a dice roll or draw a card, for example.

To call the `rand()` function and assign the returned random number to test, you use the following syntax:

The `rand()` function produces random integer numbers.

Generate a random number

```
test = rand();
```

The `rand()` function returns an integer from 0 to 32767. Never use an argument in the `rand()` parentheses.

Every time you call `rand()` in the same program, you get a different number. If you run the *same* program over and over, however, `rand()` returns the *same* set of random numbers. One way to get a different set of random numbers is to call the `srand()` function. The format of `srand()` follows:

```
srand(seed);
```

where *seed* is an integer variable or constant. If you don't call `srand()`, C assumes a *seed* value of 1.

> **NOTE:** The `rand()` and `srand()` functions are prototyped in the stdlib.h header file. Be sure to include stdlib.h at the top of any program that uses `rand()` or `srand()`.

The *seed* value reseeds, or resets, the random-number generator, so the *next* random number is based on the new *seed* value. If you call `srand()` with a different *seed* value at the top of a program, `rand()` returns a different random number each time you run the program.

Why Do They Make Us Do This?

There is considerable debate among C programmers concerning the random-number generator. Many think that the random numbers should be *truly* random, and that they should not have to seed the generator themselves. They think that C should do its own internal seeding when you ask for a random number.

However, many applications would no longer work if the random-number generator were randomized for you. Computers are used all the time in business, engineering, and research to simulate the pattern of real-world events. Researchers need to be able to duplicate these simulations, over and over. Even though the events inside the simulations might be random from each other, the running of the simulations cannot be random if researchers are to study several different effects. Mathematicians and statisticians also need to repeat random-number patterns for their analyses, especially when they work with risk, probability, and gaming theory.

Because so many computer users need to repeat their random-number patterns, the designers of C have wisely chosen to give you, the programmer, the option of keeping the same random patterns or changing them. The advantages far outweigh the disadvantage of including an extra `srand()` function call.

If you want to produce a different set of random numbers every time your program runs, you must find how your C compiler reads the computer's system clock. You can use the seconds count from the clock to seed the random-number generator so that it seems truly random.

Review Questions

Answers to review questions are in Appendix B.

1. How do the character testing functions differ from the character conversion functions?

2. What are the two string input functions?

3. What is the difference between `floor()` and `ceil()`?

4. What does the following nested function return?

```
isalpha(islower('s'));
```

5. If the character array `str1` contains the string `Peter` and the character array `str2` contains `Parker`, what does `str2` contain after the following line of code executes?

```
strcat(s2, s1);
```

6. What is the output of the following `printf()`?

```
printf("%d %d", floor(8.5), ceil(8.5) );
```

7. True or false: The `isxdigit()` and `isgraph()` functions could return the same value, depending on the character passed to them.

8. Assume you declare a character array with the following statement:

```
char ara[5];
```

Now suppose the user types `Programming` in response to the following statement:

```
fgets(ara, 5, stdin);
```

Would `ara` contain `Prog`, `Progr`, or `Programming`?

9. True or false: The following statements print the same results.

```
printf("%f", pow(64.0, (1.0/2.0) );
printf("%f", sqrt(64.0) );
```

Review Exercises

1. Write a program that asks users for their ages. If a user types anything other than two digits, display an error message.

2. Write a program that stores a password in a character array called pass. Ask users for the password. Use strcmp() to let users know if they typed the proper password. Use the string I/O functions for all of the program's input and output.

3. Write a program that rounds up and rounds down the numbers –10.5, –5.75, and 2.75.

4. Ask users for their names. Print every name in reverse case; that is, print the first letter of each name in lowercase and the rest of the name in uppercase.

5. Write a program that asks users for five movie titles. Print the longest title. Use only the string I/O and manipulation functions presented in this chapter.

6. Write a program that computes the square root, cube root, and fourth root of the numbers from 10 to 25, inclusive.

7. Ask users for the titles of their favorite songs. Discard all the special characters in each title. Print the words in the title, one per line. For example, if they enter My True Love Is Mine, Oh, Mine!, you should output the following:

```
My
True
Love
```

```
Is
Mine
Oh
Mine
```

8. Ask users for the first names of ten children. Using `strcmp()` on each name, write a program to print the name that comes first in the alphabet.

Summary

You have learned the character, string, and numeric functions that C provides. By including the ctype.h header file, you can test and convert characters that a user types. These functions have many useful purposes, such as converting a user's response to uppercase. This makes it easier for you to test user input.

The string I/O functions give you more control over both string and numeric input. You can get a string of digits from the keyboard and convert them to a number with the `ato()` functions. The string comparison and concatenation functions enable you to test and change the contents of more than one string.

Functions save you programming time because they take over some of your computing tasks, leaving you free to concentrate on your programs. C's numeric functions round and manipulate numbers, produce trigonometric and logarithmic results, and produce random numbers.

Now that you have learned most of C's built-in functions, you are ready to improve your ability to work with arrays. The following chapter extends your knowledge of character arrays and shows you how to produce arrays of any data type.

Part VI

Arrays and Pointers

Introducing Arrays

This chapter discusses different types of arrays. You are already familiar with character arrays, which are the only method for storing character strings in the C language. A character array isn't the only kind of array you can use, however. There is an array for every data type in C. By learning how to process arrays, you greatly improve the power and efficiency of your programs.

This chapter introduces

- Array basics of names, data types, and subscripts
- Initializing an array at declaration time
- Initializing an array during program execution
- Selecting elements from arrays

The sample programs in these next few chapters are some of the most advanced that you have seen in this book. Arrays are not difficult to use, but their power makes them well-suited to more advanced programming.

Array Basics

An array is a list of more than one variable having the same name.

Although you have seen a special use of arrays as character strings, you still need a review of arrays in general. An array is a *list* of more than one variable having the same name. Not all lists of variables are arrays. The following list of four variables, for example, does not qualify as an array.

```
sales      bonus_92      first_initial      ctr
```

This is a list of variables (four of them), but they don't make up an array because they each have different names. You might wonder how more than one variable can have the same name; this seems to violate the rules for variables. If two variables have the same name, how can C know which one you mean whenever you use that name?

Array variables, or array elements, are differentiated by a *subscript*, which is a number inside brackets. Suppose you want to store a person's name in a character array called name. You know you can do this with

```
char name[] = "Ray Krebbs";
```

or

```
char name[11] = "Ray Krebbs";
```

Because C knows to reserve an extra element for the null zero at the end of every string, you don't need to specify the 11 as long as you initialize the array with a value. The variable name is an array because brackets follow its name. The array has a single name called name, and it contains 11 elements. The array is stored in memory, as shown in Figure 23.1. Each element is a character.

> **NOTE:** All array subscripts begin with 0.

You can manipulate individual elements in the array by their subscripts. For instance, the following printf() function prints Ray's initials.

	name
[0]	R
[1]	a
[2]	y
[3]	
[4]	K
[5]	r
[6]	e
[7]	b
[8]	b
[9]	s
[10]	\0

Figure 23.1. Storing the name character array in memory.

Print the first and fifth elements of the array called name.

```
printf("%c. %c", name[0], name[4]);
```

You can define an array as any data type in C. You can have integer arrays, long integer arrays, double floating-point arrays, short integer arrays, and so on. C recognizes that you are defining an array, and not a single nonarray variable, when you put brackets, [ ], after the array name.

The following line defines an array called ages, consisting of 5 integers:

```
int ages[5];
```

The first element in the ages array is ages[0]. The second element is ages[1], and the last one is ages[4]. This declaration of ages does not assign values to the elements, so you don't know what is *in* ages and your program cannot assume that it contains zeros or anything else.

Here are some more array definitions:

```
int weights[25], sizes[100]; /* Declare two integer arrays */
float salaries[8];      /* Declare a floating-point array */
double temps[50];       /* Declare a double floating-point array */
char letters[15];            /* Declare an array of letters */
```

When you declare an array, you instruct C to reserve a specific number of memory locations for that array. C protects those elements. In the previous lines of code, if you assign a value to letters[2] you don't overwrite any data in weights, sizes, salaries, or temps. Also, if you assign a value to sizes[94], you don't overwrite data stored in weights, salaries, temps, or letters.

Each element in an array occupies the same amount of storage as a nonarray variable of the same data type. In other words, each element in a character array occupies one byte. Each element in an integer array occupies two or more bytes of memory—depending on the computer's internal architecture. The same is true for every other data type.

Your program may reference elements by using formulas for subscripts. As long as the subscript can evaluate to an integer, you can use a constant, a variable, or an expression for the subscript. All of the following are references to individual array elements:

Array elements follow each other in memory, with nothing between them.

```
ara[4]
sales[ctr+1]
bonus[month]
salary[month[i]*2]
```

All array elements are stored in a contiguous, back-to-back fashion. This is important to remember, especially as you write more advanced programs. You can *always* count on an array's first element preceding the second. The second element is always placed immediately before the third, and so on. Memory is not "padded"; that is, C ensures and guarantees there is no extra space between array elements. This is true for character arrays, integer arrays, floating-point arrays, and every other type of array. If a floating-point value occupies four bytes of memory on your computer, the *next* element in a floating-point array *always* begins exactly four bytes after that previous element.

The Size of Arrays

The `sizeof()` function returns the number of bytes needed to hold its argument. If you request the size of an array name, `sizeof()` returns the number of bytes *reserved* for the entire array.

For example, suppose you declare an integer array of 100 elements called `scores`. If you were to find the size of the array, as in the following:

```
n = sizeof(scores);
```

n holds either 200 or 400, depending on the integer size of your computer. The `sizeof()` function always returns the reserved amount of storage, no matter what data is in the array. Therefore, a character array's contents—even if it holds a very short string—does *not* affect the size of the array that was originally reserved in memory.

If you request the size of an individual array element, however, as in the following:

```
n = sizeof(scores[6]);
```

n holds either 2 or 4, depending on the integer size of your computer.

You must never go out-of-bounds of any array. For example, suppose you want to keep track of the exemptions and salary codes of five employees. You could reserve two arrays to hold such data like this:

```
int exemptions[5];   /* Holds up to 5 employee exemptions */
char sal_codes[5];     /* Holds up to 5 employee codes */
```

Figure 23.2 shows how C reserves memory for these arrays. The figure assumes a two-byte integer size, although this may differ on some computers. Notice that C "knows" to reserve five elements for `exemptions` from the array declaration. C starts reserving memory for `sal_codes` *after* it reserves all five elements for `exemptions`. If you declare several *more* variables—either locally or globally—after these two lines, C always protects these reserved five elements for `exemptions` and `sal_codes`.

Figure 23.2. **Locating two arrays in memory.**

C protects only as many array elements as you specify.

Because C does its part to protect the data in the array, so must you. If you reserve five elements for `exemptions`, you have five integer array elements referred to as `exemptions[0]`, `exemptions[1]`, `exemptions[2]`, `exemptions[3]`, and `exemptions[4]`. C *does not* protect more than five elements for `exemptions`! Suppose that you put a value into an `exemptions` element that you did not reserve:

```
exemptions[6] = 4; /* Assign a value to an out-of-range element */
```

C lets you do this—but the results are damaging! C overwrites *other* data (in this case, `sal_codes[2]` and `sal_codes[3]` because they are reserved where the sixth element of `exemptions` has to be placed). Figure 23.3 shows the damaging results of assigning a value to an out-of-range element.

> **CAUTION:** Unlike most programming languages, ANSI C lets you assign values to out-of-range (nonreserved) subscripts. You must be very careful *not* to do this; otherwise, you start overwriting your other data or code.

Figure 23.3. The arrays in memory after overwriting part of sal_codes.

Although you can define an array of any data type, you cannot declare an array of strings. A *string* is not a C variable data type. You learn how to hold multiple strings in an array-like structure in Chapter 27, "Pointers and Arrays."

Initializing Arrays

You must assign values to array elements before using them. Here are the two ways to initialize elements in an array:

♦ Initialize the elements at declaration time

♦ Initialize the elements in the program

> **NOTE:** C automatically initializes global arrays to null zeros. Therefore, global character array elements are all null, and numeric array elements all contain zero. You should limit your use of global arrays. If you use global arrays, explicitly initialize them to zero, even though C does this for you, to clarify your intentions.

Initializing Elements at Declaration Time

You already know how to initialize character arrays that hold strings when you define the arrays: You simply assign them a string.

For example, the following declaration reserves six elements in a character array called `city`:

```
char city[6];                      /* Reserve space for city */
```

If you also want to initialize `city` with a value, you could do it like this:

Initialize arrays

```
char city[6] = "Tulsa";           /* Reserve space and
                                      initialize city */
```

The `6` is optional because C counts the elements needed to hold `Tulsa`, plus an extra element for the null zero at the end of the quoted string.

You can also reserve a character array and initialize it—a single character at a time—by using braces around the character data. The following line of code declares an array called `initials` and initializes it with eight characters:

```
char initials[8] = {'Q', 'K', 'P', 'G', 'V', 'M', 'U', 'S'};
```

The array `initials` is *not a string!* Its data does not end in a null zero. There is nothing wrong with defining an array of characters such as this one, but you must remember that you cannot treat the array as if it were a string. Do not use string functions with it or attempt to print the array with the `%s printf()` format code.

By using braces, you can initialize any type of array. For example, if you want to initialize an integer array that holds your five children's ages, you could do it with the following declaration:

```
int child_ages[5] = {2, 5, 6, 8, 12};    /* Declare and
                                             initialize array */
```

In another example, if you want to keep track of the last three years' total sales, you could declare an array and initialize it at the same time with the following:

```
double sales[] = {454323.43, 122355.32, 343324.96};
```

As with character arrays, you do not need to state explicitly the array size when you declare and initialize an array of any type. C would know, in this case, to reserve three double floating-point array elements for `sales`. Figure 23.4 shows the representation of `child_ages` and `sales` in memory.

Figure 23.4. In-memory representation of two different types of arrays.

NOTE: You cannot initialize an array, using the assignment operator and braces, *after* you declare it. You can initialize arrays in this manner only when you declare them. If you want to fill an array with data after you declare the array, you must do so element-by-element or by using functions as described in the next section.

C zeros all array values that you do not define explicitly at declaration time.

Although C does not automatically zero-out (or initialize to *any* value) array elements, if you initialize some but not all of the elements when you declare the array, C finishes the job for you by assigning the remainder to zero.

TIP: To initialize every element of a large array to zero at the same time, declare the entire array and initialize its first value to zero. C finishes filling in the rest of the array to zero.

For instance, suppose you need to reserve array storage for profit figures of the three previous months as well as the three months to follow. You need to reserve six elements of storage, but you know values for only the first three of them. You can initialize the array as follows:

```
double profit[6] = {67654.43, 46472.34, 63451.93};
```

Because you explicitly initialized three of the elements, C initializes the rest to zero. If you use an appropriate `printf()` to print the entire array, one element per line, you would get

```
67654.43
46472.34
63451.93
00000.00
00000.00
00000.00
```

CAUTION: Always declare an array with the maximum number of subscripts, unless you initialize the array at the same time. The following array declaration is illegal:

```
int count[];              /* Bad array declaration! */
```

C does not know how many elements to reserve for `count`, so it reserves *none*. If you then assign values to `count`'s nonreserved elements, you may (and probably would) overwrite other data.

The only time you can leave the brackets empty is if you also assign values to the array, such as the following:

```
int count[] = {15, 9, 22, -8, 12}; /* Good definition */
```

C can tell, from the list of values, how many elements to reserve. In this case, C reserves five elements for `count`.

Examples

1. Suppose you want to track the stock market averages for the last 90 days. Instead of storing them in 90 different variables, it is much easier to store them in an array. You could declare the array like this:

```
float stock[90];
```

The rest of the program could assign values to the averages.

2. Suppose that you just finished taking classes at a local university and want to average your six class scores. The following program initializes one array for the school name and another for the six classes. The body of the program averages each of the six scores.

```c
/* Filename: C23ARA1.C
   Averages six test scores */
#include <stdio.h>
main()
{
    char s_name[] = "Tri Star University";
    float scores[6] = {88.7, 90.4, 76.0, 97.0, 100.0, 86.7};
    float average=0.0;
    int ctr;

    /* Compute total of scores */
    for (ctr=0; ctr<6; ctr++)
        { average += scores[ctr]; }

    /* Compute the average */
    average /= (float)6;

    printf("At %s, your class average is %.1f.", s_name,
        average);
    return;
}
```

The output follows:

```
At Tri Star University, your class average is 89.8.
```

Notice that using arrays makes processing lists of information much easier. Instead of averaging six differently named variables, you can use a for loop to step through each array element. If you had to average 1000 numbers, you could still do so with a simple for loop, as in this example. If the 1000 variables were not in an array, but were individually named, you would need to write a considerable amount of code just to add them.

3. The following program is an expanded version of the previous one. It prints the six scores before computing the

average. Notice that you must print array elements individually; you cannot print an entire array in a single printf(). (You can print an entire character array with %s, but only if it holds a null-terminated string of characters.)

```c
/* Filename: C23ARA2.C
   Prints and averages six test scores */
#include <stdio.h>
void main(void);
void pr_scores(float scores[]);

void main(void)
{
   char s_name[] = "Tri Star University";
   float scores[6] = {88.7, 90.4, 76.0, 97.0, 100.0, 86.7};
   float average=0.0;
   int ctr;

   /* Call function to print scores */
   pr_scores(scores);

   /* Compute total of scores */
   for (ctr=0; ctr<6; ctr++)
      { average += scores[ctr]; }

   /* Compute the average */
   average /= (float)6;

   printf("At %s, your class average is %.1f.",
          s_name, average);
   return;
}

void pr_scores(float scores[6])
{
   /* Prints the six scores */
   int ctr;

   printf("Here are your scores:\n");            /* Title */
   for (ctr=0; ctr<6; ctr++)
      printf("%.1f\n", scores[ctr]);
   return;
}
```

To pass an array to a function, you need to specify only its name. In the receiving function's parameter list, you must state the array type and include its brackets, which tell the function that it is an array. (You do not explicitly need to state the array size in the receiving parameter list as shown in the prototype.)

4. To improve the maintainability of your programs, define all array sizes with the #define preprocessor directive. What if you took four classes next semester but still wanted to use the same program? You could modify it by changing all the 6s to 4s, but if you had defined the array size with a defined constant, you would have to change only one line in order to change the program's subscript limits. Notice how the following program uses a defined constant for the number of classes.

```
/* Filename: C23ARA3.C
   Prints and averages six test scores */
#include <stdio.h>
void main(void);
void pr_scores(float scores[]);
#define CLASS_NUM 6

void main(void)
{
    char s_name[] = "Tri Star University";
    float scores[CLASS_NUM] = {88.7, 90.4, 76.0, 97.0,
                               100.0, 86.7};
    float average=0.0;
    int ctr;

    /* Call function to print scores */
    pr_scores(scores);

    /* Compute total of scores */
    for (ctr=0; ctr<CLASS_NUM; ctr++)
       { average += scores[ctr]; }

    /* Compute the average */
    average /= (float)CLASS_NUM;
```

```
          printf("At %s, your class average is %.1f.",
                 s_name, average);
          return;
   }


   void pr_scores(float scores[CLASS_NUM])
   {
      /* Prints the six scores */
      int ctr;

      printf("Here are your scores:\n");               /* Title */
      for (ctr=0; ctr<CLASS_NUM; ctr++)
        printf("%.1f\n", scores[ctr]);
      return;
   }
```

For such a simple example, using a defined constant for the maximum subscript may not seem like a big advantage. If you were writing a larger program that processed several arrays, however, changing the defined constant at the top of the program is much easier than searching the program for each occurrence of that array reference.

Using defined constants for array sizes has the added advantage of protecting you from going out of the subscript bounds. You do not have to remember the subscript when looping through arrays; you can use the defined constant instead.

Initializing Elements in the Program

Rarely do you know the contents of arrays when you declare them. Usually, you fill an array with user input or a disk file's data. The for loop is a perfect tool for looping through arrays when you fill them with values.

> **CAUTION:** An array name cannot appear on the left side of an assignment statement.

You cannot assign one array to another. Suppose you want to copy an array called total_sales to a second array called saved_sales. You *cannot* do so with the following assignment statement:

```
saved_sales = total_sales;                    /* Invalid! */
```

Rather, you have to copy the arrays one element at a time, using a loop, such as the following section of code does.

We want to copy one array to another. We have to do so one element at a time, so we need a counter. Initialize a variable called ctr to 0; the value of ctr will represent a position in the array.

1. *Assign the element that occupies the position in the first array represented by the value of ctr to the same position in the second array.*
2. *If the counter is less than the size of the array, add 1 to the counter. Repeat step 1.*

```
for (ctr=0; ctr<ARRAY_SIZE; ctr++)
   { saved_sales[ctr] = total_sales[ctr]; }
```

The following examples illustrate methods for initializing arrays in a program. After learning about disk processing later in the book, you learn to read array values from a disk file.

Examples

1. The following program uses the assignment operator to assign ten temperatures to an array.

```
/* Filename: C23ARA4.C
   Fill an array with ten temperature values */
#include <stdio.h>
#define NUM_TEMPS 10
main()
{
   float temps[NUM_TEMPS];
   int ctr;
```

```
temps[0] = 78.6;          /* Subscripts always begin at 0 */
temps[1] = 82.1;
temps[2] = 79.5;
temps[3] = 75.0;
temps[4] = 75.4;
temps[5] = 71.8;
temps[6] = 73.3;
temps[7] = 69.5;
temps[8] = 74.1;
temps[9] = 75.7;

/* Print the temps */
printf("Daily temperatures for the last %d days:\n",
       NUM_TEMPS);
for (ctr=0; ctr<NUM_TEMPS; ctr++)
   { printf("%.1f \n", temps[ctr]); }

return;
}
```

2. The following program uses a for loop and scanf() to assign
   eight integers entered individually by the user. The program
   then prints a total of all the numbers.

```
/* Filename: C23TOT.C
   Totals eight input values from the user */
#include <stdio.h>
#define NUM 8
main()
{
   int nums[NUM];
   int total = 0;        /* Holds total of user's 8 numbers */

   for (ctr=0; ctr<NUM; ctr++)
     { printf("Please enter the next number...");
       scanf("%d", &nums[ctr]);
       total += nums[ctr]; }

   printf("The total of the numbers is %d", total);
   return;
}
```

3. You don't have to access an array in the same order as you initialized it. The next chapter, "Array Processing," shows you how to change the order of an array. You also can use the subscript to select items from an array of values.

The following program requests sales data for the preceding twelve months. Users can then type a month they want to see. That month's sales figure is then printed, without figures from other months getting in the way. This is how you begin to build a search program to find requested data: You store the data in an array (or in a disk file that can be read into an array, as you learn later), then wait for a user's request to see specific pieces of the data.

```
/* Filename: C23SAL.C
   Stores twelve months of sales and
   prints selected ones */
#include <stdio.h>
#include <ctype.h>
#define NUM 12
main()
{
   float sales[NUM];
   int ctr, ans;
   int req_month;                     /* Holds user's request */

   /* Fill the array */
   printf("Please enter the twelve monthly sales values\n");
   for (ctr=0; ctr<NUM; ctr++)
     { printf("What are sales for month number %d\n", ctr+1);
       scanf("%f", &sales[ctr]); }

   /* Wait for a requested month */
   for (ctr=0; ctr<25; ctr++)
     { printf("\n"); }                 /* Clear the screen */

   printf("*** Sales Printing Program ***\n");
   printf("Prints any sales from the last %d months\n\n",
           NUM);
   do
     { printf("What month (1-%d) do you want to see a");
       printf(" sales value for?",NUM);
```

```
            scanf("%d", &req_month);
            /* Adjust for zero-based subscript */
            printf("\nMonth %d's sales are %.2f",req_month,
                    sales[req_month-1]);
            printf("\nDo you want to see another (Y/N)? ");
            ans=getch();
            ans=toupper(ans);
        } while (ans == 'Y');
    return;
}
```

Notice the helpful screen-clearing routine that prints 23 newline characters. This scrolls the screen until it is blank. (Most compilers come with a better built-in screen-clearing function, but the ANSI C standard does not offer one because the compiler would be too closely linked with specific hardware.)

Figure 23.5 shows the second screen from this program. After the twelve sales values are entered into the array, any or all of them can be requested, one at a time, simply by supplying the month's number (that is, the number of the subscript).

```
*** Sales Printing Program ***
Prints any sales from the last 12 months


What month (1-12) do you want to see a sales value for?1

Month 1's sales are 3233.45
Do you want to see another (Y/N)?
What month (1-12) do you want to see a sales value for?5

Month 5's sales are 6535.64
Do you want to see another (Y/N)?
What month (1-12) do you want to see a sales value for?2

Month 2's sales are 6434.67
Do you want to see another (Y/N)?
What month (1-12) do you want to see a sales value for?8

Month 8's sales are 4598.79
Do you want to see another (Y/N)?
```

Figure 23.5. Printing individually requested values from an array.

Review Questions

Answers to review questions are in Appendix B.

1. True or false: A single array can hold several values of different data types.

2. How do C programs tell one array element from another if all elements have identical names?

3. Why must you initialize an array before using it?

4. Given the following definition of an array, called `weights`, what is the value of `weights[5]`?

```
int weights[10] = {5, 2, 4};
```

5. If you pass an integer array to a function and change it, does the array get changed also in the calling function? (Hint: Remember how character arrays are passed to functions.)

6. How does C initialize global array elements?

Review Exercises

1. Write a program to store the ages of six of your friends in a single array. Store each of the six ages using the assignment operator. Print the ages on-screen.

2. Modify the program in #1 to print the ages backwards.

3. Write a simple data program to track a radio station's ratings (1, 2, 3, 4, or 5) for the previous 18 months. Use `scanf()` to initialize the array with the ratings. Print the ratings on-screen with an appropriate title.

4. Write a program to store the numbers from 1 to 100 in an array of 100 integer elements. (Hint: The subscripts should begin at 0 and end at 99.)

5. Write a program that a small business owner could use to track customers. Assign each customer a number (starting at 0). Whenever a customer purchases something, store the sale in the element that matches the customer's number (that is,

the next unused array element). When the store owner signals the end of the day, print a report consisting of each customer number with its matching sales, a total sales figure, and an average sales figure per customer.

Summary

You now know how to declare and initialize arrays consisting of various data types. You can initialize an array either when you declare it or in the body of your program. Array elements are much easier to process than many variables that each have a different name.

C has powerful sorting and searching techniques that make your programs even more serviceable. The next chapter introduces these techniques and shows you still other ways to access array elements.

Array Processing

C provides many ways to access arrays. If you have programmed in other computer languages, you will find that some of C's array indexing techniques are different. Arrays in the C language are closely linked with *pointers*. Chapter 26, "Pointers," describes the many ways pointers and arrays interact. Because pointers are so powerful, and because learning arrays well provides a good foundation for learning about pointers, this chapter attempts to describe in detail how to reference arrays.

This chapter discusses the different types of array processing. You will learn how to search an array for one or more values, find the highest and lowest values in an array, and sort an array into numerical or alphabetical order.

This chapter introduces the following concepts:

♦ Searching arrays

♦ Finding the highest and lowest values in arrays

♦ Sorting arrays

♦ Advanced subscripting with arrays

Many programmers see arrays as a turning point. Gaining an understanding of array processing will make your programs more accurate and allow for more powerful programming.

Searching Arrays

Array elements do not always appear in the order in which they are needed.

Arrays are one of the primary means by which data is stored in C programs. Many types of programs lend themselves to processing lists (arrays) of data, such as an employee payroll program, a scientific research of several chemicals, or customer account processing. As mentioned in the previous chapter, array data usually is read from a disk file. Later chapters describe disk file processing. For now, you should understand how to manipulate arrays so that you see the data exactly the way you want to see it.

Chapter 23, "Introducing Arrays," shows how to print arrays in the same order that you entered the data. This is sometimes done, but it is not always the most appropriate method of looking at data.

For instance, suppose that a high school used C programs for its grade reports. Suppose also that the school wanted to see a list of the top 10 grade-point averages. You could not print the first 10 grade-point averages in the list of student averages because the top 10 GPAs might not (and probably will not) appear as the first 10 array elements. Because the GPAs would not be in any sequence, the program would have to sort the array into numeric order, from high GPAs to low, or else search the array for the 10 highest GPAs.

You need a method for putting arrays in a specific order. This is called *sorting* an array. When you sort an array, you put that array in a specific order, such as in alphabetical or numerical order. A dictionary is in sorted order, and so is a phone book.

When you reverse the order of a sort, it is called a *descending sort*. For instance, if you wanted to look at a list of all employees in descending salary order, the highest-paid employees would be printed first.

Figure 24.1 shows a list of eight numbers in an array called unsorted. The middle list of numbers is an ascending sorted version of unsorted. The third list of numbers is a descending sorted version of unsorted.

Unsorted	Ascending order	Descending order
6	1	8
1	2	7
2	3	6
4	4	5
7	5	4
8	6	3
3	7	2
5	8	1

Figure 24.1. A list of unsorted numbers sorted into an ascending and a descending order.

Before you learn to sort, it would be helpful to learn how to search an array for a value. This is a preliminary step in learning to sort. What if one of those students received a grade change? The computer must be able to access that specific student's grade to change it (without affecting the others). As the next section shows, programs can search for specific array elements.

NOTE: C provides a method for sorting and searching lists of strings, but you cannot understand how to do this until you learn about pointers, starting in Chapter 26, "Pointers." The sorting and searching examples and algorithms presented in this chapter demonstrate sorting and searching arrays of numbers. The same concepts will apply (and will actually be much more usable for "real-world" applications) when you learn how to store lists of names in C.

Searching for Values

You do not need to know any new commands to search an array for a value. Basically, the if and for loop statements are all you need.

You do not have to sort an array to find its extreme values.

To search an array for a specific value, look at each element in that array, comparing with the if statement to see whether they match. If they do not, you keep searching down the array. If you run out of array elements before finding the value, it is not in the array.

You can perform several different kinds of searches. You might need to find the highest or the lowest value in a list of numbers. This is informative when you have much data and want to know the extremes of the data (such as the highest and lowest sales region in your division). You also can search an array to see whether it contains a matching value. For example, you can see whether an item is already in an inventory by searching a part number array for a match.

The following programs illustrate some of these array-searching techniques.

Examples

1. To find the highest number in an array, compare each element with the first one. If you find a higher value, it becomes the basis for the rest of the array. Continue until you reach the end of the array and you will have the highest value, as the following program shows.

Identify the program and include the I/O header file. We want to find the highest value in an array, so define the array size as a constant, then initialize the array.

Loop through the array, comparing each element to the highest value. If an element is higher than the highest value saved, store the element as the new high value. Print the highest value found in the array.

```
/* Filename: C24HIGH.C
   Finds the highest value in the array */
#include <stdio.h>
#define SIZE 15
main()
{
   /* Puts some numbers in the array */
   int ara[SIZE]={5,2,7,8,36,4,2,86,11,43,22,12,45,6,85};
   int high_val, ctr;
```

```
    high_val = ara[0];              /* Initializes with first
                                            array element */
    for (ctr=1; ctr<SIZE; ctr++)
      {                        /* Stores current value if it is
                                  higher than the highest so far */
        if (ara[ctr] > high_val)
          { high_val = ara[ctr]; }
      }

    printf("The highest number in the list is %d.", high_val);
    return;
}
```

The output of the program is the following:

```
The highest number in the list is 86.
```

You have to save the element if and only if it is higher than the one you are comparing. Finding the smallest number in an array is just as easy, except that you compare to see whether each succeeding array element is less than the lowest value found so far.

2. The following example expands on the previous one by finding the highest and the lowest value. First, store the first array element in *both* the highest and the lowest variable to begin the search. This ensures that each element after that one is tested to see whether it is higher or lower than the first.

This example also uses the rand() function from Chapter 22, "Character, String, and Numeric Functions," to fill the array with random values from 0 to 99 by applying the modulus operator (%) and 100 against whatever value rand() produces. The program prints the entire array before starting the search for the highest and the lowest.

```
/* Filename: C24HILO.C
   Finds the highest and the lowest value in the array */
#include <stdio.h>
#include <stdlib.h>
#define SIZE 15
```

Find array's
highest value

```
main()
{
   int ara[SIZE];
   int high_val, low_val, ctr;

   /* Fills array with random numbers from 0 to 99 */
   for (ctr=0; ctr<SIZE; ctr++)
     { ara[ctr] = rand() % 100; }

   /* Prints the array to the screen */
   printf("Here are the %d random numbers:\n",
          SIZE);                                 /* Title */
   for (ctr=0; ctr<SIZE; ctr++)
     { printf("%4d\n", ara[ctr]); }

   printf("\n\n");                    /* Prints a blank line */

   high_val = ara[0];    /* Initializes first element to
                             both high and low */
   low_val  = ara[0];

   for (ctr=1; ctr<SIZE; ctr++)
      {                   /* Stores current value if it is
                              higher than the highest so far */
        if (ara[ctr] > high_val)
          { high_val = ara[ctr]; }
        if (ara[ctr] < low_val)
          { low_val = ara[ctr]; }
      }

   printf("The highest number in the list is %d.\n",
          high_val);
   printf("The lowest number in the list is %d.\n",
          low_val);
   return;
}
```

Figure 24.2 shows the output from this program.

```
Here are the 15 random numbers:
   46
   30
   82
   90
   56
   17
   95
   15
   48
   26
    4
   58
   71
   79
   92


The highest number in the list is 95.
The lowest number in the list is 4.
```

Figure 24.2. Printing the highest and the lowest values in a list of random numbers.

3. The next program fills an array with part numbers from an inventory. You must use your imagination, because the inventory array normally would fill more of the array, would be initialized from a disk file, and would be part of a larger set of arrays that hold descriptions, quantities, costs, selling prices, and so on. For this example, assignment statements initialize the array. The important idea from this program is not the array initialization, but the method for searching the array.

NOTE: If the newly entered part number is already on file, the program tells the user. Otherwise, the part number is added to the end of the array.

```
/* Filename: C24SERCH.C
   Searches a part number array for the input value. If
   the entered part number is not in the array, it is
   added. If the part number is in the array, a message
   is printed. */
```

```c
#include <stdio.h>
#define MAX 100
void main(void);
void fill_parts(long int parts[MAX]);

void main(void)
{
   long int search_part;              /* Holds user request */
   long int parts[MAX];
   int ctr;
   int num_parts=5;              /* Beginning inventory count */

   fill_parts(parts);     /* Fills the first five elements */
   do
   {
     printf("\n\nPlease type a part number...")
     printf("(-9999 ends program) ");
     scanf("%ld", &search_part);
     if (search_part == -9999)
       { break; }                /* Exits loop if user wants */
     /* Scan array to see whether part is in inventory */
     for (ctr=0; ctr<num_parts; ctr++) /* Checks each item */
     { if (search_part == parts[ctr])        /* If it is in
                                                inventory...*/
         { printf("\nPart %ld is already in inventory",
                 search_part);
           break;
         }
       else
        { if (ctr == (num_parts-1) )       /* If not there,
                                                adds it */
          { parts[num_parts] = search_part;    /* Adds to
                                              end of array */
            num_parts++;
            printf("\n%ld was added to inventory\n",
                  search_part);
            break;
          }
       }
   }
```

```
        } while (search_part != -9999);      /* Loops until user
                                                        signals end */

        return;
    }

    void fill_parts(long int parts[MAX])
    {
        /* Assigns five part numbers to array for testing */
        parts[0] = 12345;
        parts[1] = 24724;
        parts[2] = 54154;
        parts[3] = 73496;
        parts[4] = 83925;
        return;
    }
```

Figure 24.3 shows the output from this program.

```
Please type a part number...(-9999 ends program) 25432

25432 was added to inventory


Please type a part number...(-9999 ends program) 12345

Part 12345 is already in inventory

Please type a part number...(-9999 ends program) 65468

65468 was added to inventory


Please type a part number...(-9999 ends program) 25432

Part 25432 is already in inventory

Please type a part number...(-9999 ends program) 43234
```

Figure 24.3. Searching a table of part numbers.

Sorting Arrays

There are many times when you need to sort one or more arrays. Suppose that you were to take a list of numbers, write each number on a separate piece of paper, and throw all the pieces of paper into the air. The steps you would take—shuffling and changing the order of the pieces of paper, trying to put them in order—would be similar to what your computer goes through to sort numbers or character data into a sorted order.

Because sorting arrays requires exchanging values of elements back and forth, it helps if you first learn the technique for swapping variables. Suppose that you had two variables named score1 and score2. What if you wanted to reverse their values (putting score2 into the score1 variable, and vice versa)? You could not do this:

```
score1 = score2;    /* Does not swap the two values */
score2 = score1;
```

Why doesn't this work? In the first line, the value of score1 gets replaced with score2's value. When the first line finishes, both score1 and score2 contain the same value. Therefore, the second line cannot work as desired.

To swap two variables, you need to use a third variable to hold the intermediate result. (This is the only function of this third variable.) For instance, to swap score1 and score2, use a third variable (called hold_score in this code), as in

```
hold_score = score1;    /* These three lines properly */
score1 = score2;        /* swap score1 and score2      */
score2 = hold_score;
```

This exchanges the two values in the two variables.

There are several different ways to sort arrays. These methods include the *bubble sort*, the *quicksort*, and the *shell sort*. The basic goal of each method is to compare each array element to another array element and swap them if the higher one is less than the other.

The theory behind these sorts is beyond the scope of this book; however, the bubble sort is one of the easiest to understand. Values in the array are compared to each other, a pair at a time, and swapped if they are not in back-to-back order. The lowest value eventually "floats" to the top of the array, like a bubble in a glass of soda.

Figure 24.4 shows a list of numbers before, during, and after a bubble sort. The bubble sort steps through the array, comparing

The lowest values in a list "float" to the top with the bubble sort algorithm.

pairs of numbers, to see whether they need to be swapped. Several passes might have to be made through the array before it is finally sorted (no more passes are needed). Other types of sorts improve on the bubble sort. The bubble sort procedure is easy to program, but it is slower compared to many of the other methods.

First Pass

3	2	2	2
2	3	3	3
5	5	1	1
1	1	5	4
4	4	4	5

Second Pass

2	2
3	1
1	3
4	4
5	5

Third Pass

2	1
1	2
3	3
4	4
5	5

Fourth Pass

1
2
3
4
5

Figure 24.4. Sorting a list of numbers using the bubble sort.

The following programs show the bubble sort in action.

Examples

1. The following program assigns 10 random numbers between 0 and 99 to an array, then sorts the array. A nested `for` loop is perfect for sorting numbers in the array (as shown in the `sort_array()` function). Nested `for` loops provide a nice mechanism for working on pairs of values, swapping them if needed. As the outside loop counts down the list, referencing each element, the inside loop compares each of the remaining values to those array elements.

```c
/* Filename: C24SORT1.C
    Sorts and prints a list of numbers */
#define MAX 10
#include <stdio.h>
#include <stdlib.h>
void fill_array(int ara[MAX]);
void print_array(int ara[MAX]);
void main(void);
void sort_array(int ara[MAX]);

void main(void)
{
    int ara[MAX];

    fill_array(ara);     /* Puts random numbers in the array */

    printf("Here are the unsorted numbers:\n");
    print_array(ara);              /* Prints the unsorted array */

    sort_array(ara);                       /* Sorts the array */

    printf("\n\nHere are the sorted numbers:\n");
    print_array(ara);      /* Prints the newly sorted array */
    return;
}


void fill_array(int ara[MAX])
```

```
{
   /* Puts random numbers in the array */
   int ctr;
   for (ctr=0; ctr<MAX; ctr++)
      { ara[ctr] = (rand() % 100); }    /* Forces number to
                                                0-99 range */

   return;
}

void print_array(int ara[MAX])
{
   /* Prints the array */
   int ctr;
   for (ctr=0; ctr<MAX; ctr++)
      { printf("%d\n", ara[ctr]); }
   return;
}

void sort_array(int ara[MAX])
{
   /* Sorts the array */
   int temp;            /* Temporary variable to swap with */
   int ctr1, ctr2;              /* Need two loop counters to */
                               /*   swap pairs of numbers    */
   for (ctr1=0; ctr1<(MAX-1); ctr1++)
      { for (ctr2=(ctr1+1); ctr2<MAX; ctr2++)/* Test pairs */
         { if (ara[ctr1] > ara[ctr2])    /* Swap if this */
            { temp = ara[ctr1]; /* pair is not in order */
              ara[ctr1] = ara[ctr2];
              ara[ctr2] = temp;   /* "float" the lowest
                                         to the highest */
            }
         }
      }
   return;
}
```

Figure 24.5 shows the output from this program. If any two randomly generated numbers were the same, the bubble sort would work properly, placing them next to each other in the list.

```
Here are the unsorted numbers:
46
30
82
90
56
17
95
15
48
26


Here are the sorted numbers:
15
17
26
30
46
48
56
82
90
95
```

Figure 24.5. Searching a table of part numbers.

To produce a descending sort, use the less-than (<) logical operator when swapping array elements.

2. The following program is just like the last, except it prints the list of numbers in descending order.

A descending sort is as easy to write as an ascending sort. With the ascending sort (from low to high values), you compare pairs of values, testing to see whether the first is greater than the second. With a descending sort, you test to see whether the first is less than the second one.

```c
/* Filename: C24SORT2.C
   Sorts and prints a list of numbers in reverse
   and descending order */
#define MAX 10
#include <stdio.h>
#include <stdlib.h>
void fill_array(int ara[MAX]);
void print_array(int ara[MAX]);
void main(void);
void sort_array(int ara[MAX]);

void main(void)
{
```

```
      int ara[MAX];

      fill_array(ara);     /* Puts random numbers in the array */

      printf("Here are the unsorted numbers:\n");
      print_array(ara);              /* Prints the unsorted array */

      sort_array(ara);                      /* Sorts the array */

      printf("\n\nHere are the sorted numbers:\n");
      print_array(ara);       /* Prints the newly sorted array */
      return;
   }

void fill_array(int ara[MAX])
{
   /* Puts random numbers in the array */
   int ctr;
   for (ctr=0; ctr<MAX; ctr++)
      { ara[ctr] = (rand() % 100); }        /* Forces number
                                                to 0-99 range */

   return;
}

void print_array(int ara[MAX])
{
   /* Prints the array */
   int ctr;
   for (ctr=0; ctr<MAX; ctr++)
      { printf("%d\n", ara[ctr]); }
   return;
}

void sort_array(int ara[MAX])
{
   /* Sorts the array */
   int temp;             /* Temporary variable to swap with */
   int ctr1, ctr2;             /* Need two loop counters      */
                               /*   to swap pairs of numbers */
   for (ctr1=0; ctr1<(MAX-1); ctr1++)
      { for (ctr2=(ctr1+1); ctr2<MAX; ctr2++)/* Test pairs */
```

```
                            /* Notice the difference in descending (here)
                               and ascending */
                          { if (ara[ctr1] < ara[ctr2]) /* Swap if this     */
                              { temp = ara[ctr1]; /* pair is not in order */
                                ara[ctr1] = ara[ctr2];
                                ara[ctr2] = temp;  /* "float" the lowest
                                                          to the highest   */
                              }
                          }
                      }
                return;
          }
```

TIP: You can save the previous programs' sort functions in two separate files named sort_ascend and sort_descend. When you need to sort two different arrays, #include these files inside your own programs. Even better, compile each of these routines separately and link the one you need to your program. (You must check your compiler's manual to learn how to do this.)

You can sort character arrays just as easily as you sort numeric arrays. C uses the ASCII table for its sorting comparisons. If you look at the ASCII table in Appendix C, you will see that numbers sort before letters and that uppercase letters sort before lowercase letters.

Advanced Referencing of Arrays

The array notation you have seen so far is common in computer programming languages. Most languages use subscripts inside brackets (or parentheses) to refer to individual array elements. For instance, you know that the following array references describe the first and fifth elements of the array called sales (remember that the starting subscript is always 0):

```
sales[0]
sales[4]
```

C provides another approach to referencing arrays. Even though the title of this section includes the word "advanced," this array-referencing method is not difficult. It is very different, however, especially if you are familiar with another programming language's approach.

An array name is the address of the starting element of the array.

There is nothing wrong with referring to array elements in the manner you have seen so far. However, the second approach, unique to C, will be helpful when you learn about pointers in upcoming chapters. Actually, C programmers who have programmed for several years rarely use the subscript notation you have seen.

In C, an array's name is not just a label for you to use in programs. To C, the array name is the actual address where the first element begins in memory. Suppose that you define an array called amounts with the following statement:

```
int amounts[6] = {4, 1, 3, 7, 9, 2};
```

Figure 24.6 shows how this array is stored in memory. The figure shows the array beginning at address 405,332. (The actual addresses of variables are determined by the computer when you load and run your compiled program.) Notice that the name of the array, amounts, is located somewhere in memory and contains the address of amounts[0], or 405,332.

You can refer to an array by its regular subscript notation, or by modifying the address of the array. The following both refer to the third element of amounts:

amounts[3] and (amounts + 3)[0]

Because C considers the array name to be an address in memory that contains the location of the first array element, nothing keeps you from using a different address as the starting address and referencing from there. Taking this one step further, *each* of the following also refers to the third element of amounts:

(amounts+0)[3] and (amounts+2)[1] and (amounts-2)[5]

(1+amounts)[2] and (3+amounts)[0] and (amounts+1)[2]

You can print any of these array elements with a printf() function using the standard integer %d control code.

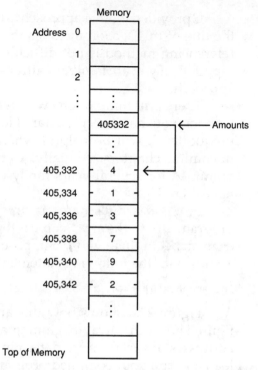

Figure 24.6. **The array name** amounts **holds the address of** amounts[0].

When you print strings inside character arrays, referencing the arrays by their modified addresses is more useful than with integers. Suppose that you stored three strings in a single character array. You could initialize this array with the following statement:

```
char names[]={'T','e','d','\0','E','v','a','\0','S',
            'a','m','\0'};
```

Figure 24.7 shows how this array might look in memory. The array name, names, contains the address of the first element, names[0] (the letter T).

CAUTION: The hierarchy table in Appendix D shows that array subscripts have precedence over addition and subtraction. Therefore, you must enclose array names in parentheses if you want to modify the name as shown in these examples. The following are not equivalent:

`(2+amounts)[1]` and `2+amounts[1]`

The second example takes the value of `amounts[1]` (which is 1 in this example array) and adds 2 to it (resulting in a value of 3).

This second method of array referencing might seem like more trouble than it is worth, but learning to reference arrays in this fashion will make your transition to pointers much easier. An array name is actually a pointer itself, because the array contains the address of the first array element (it "points" to the start of the array).

names	[0]	T
	[1]	e
	[2]	d
	[3]	\0
	[4]	E
	[5]	v
	[6]	a
	[7]	\0
	[8]	S
	[9]	a
	[10]	m
	[11]	\0

Figure 24.7. Storing more than one string in a single character array.

You have yet to see a character array that holds more than one string, but C allows it. The problem with such an array is how you reference, especially how you print, the second and third strings. If you were to print this array using the %d string control code (as you have been doing) with the following printf():

```
printf("%s", names);
```

C would print the following:

```
Ted
```

The %s control code prints characters starting at the array's address until it reaches null zero.

As mentioned in Chapter 7, "Simple Input and Output" (where this book introduces control codes), the %s control code prints the string starting at the address of the specified array. Without a different way to reference the array, you would have no way to print the three strings inside the single array (without resorting to printing them one element at a time).

Because the %s control code requires a starting address, you can print the three strings with the following printf() function calls:

```
printf("%s", names);        /* Prints Ted */
printf("%s", (names+4));    /* Prints Eva */
printf("%s", (names+8));    /* Prints Sam */
```

To test your understanding, what will the following printf() function calls print?

```
printf("%s", (names+1));
printf("%s", (names+6));
```

The first printf() prints ed. The %s prints the string starting at the address specified. The characters ed begin at (names+1) and the %s stops printing when it gets to the null zero. The second printf() prints a. Adding 6 to the address at names produces the address where the a is located. The "string" is only one character long because the null zero appears in the array immediately after the a.

To sum up character arrays, the following refer to individual array elements (single characters):

names[2] and (names+1)[1]

and with such, you can print them with the %c control code, but not with %s. The following refer to addresses only, and as such, you can print them with the %s control code

    names and (names+4)

but *not* with %c.

> **CAUTION:** Never use %c to print an address reference, even if that address contains a character. Print strings by specifying an address with %s, and single characters by specifying the character element with %c.

The following examples are a little different from most you have seen. They do not perform "real-world" work, but they are study examples for you to familiarize yourself with this new method of array referencing. The next few chapters expand on these methods.

Examples

1. The following program stores the numbers from 100 to 600 in an array, then prints elements using the new method of array subscripting.

```
/* Filename: C24REF1.C
   Print elements of an integer array in different ways */
#include <stdio.h>
main()
{
   int num[6] = {100, 200, 300, 400, 500, 600};

   printf("num[0] is \t%d \n", num[0]);
   printf("(num+0)[0] is \t%d \n", (num+0)[0]);
   printf("(num-2)[2] is \t%d \n\n", (num-2)[2]);

   printf("num[1] is \t%d \n", num[1]);
   printf("(num+1)[0] is \t%d \n", (num+1)[0]);
   printf("(num-5)[4] is \t%d \n\n", (num-5)[4]);
```

```
        printf("num[5] is \t%d \n", num[5]);
        printf("(num+5)[0] is \t%d \n", (num+5)[0]);
        printf("(num+2)[3] is \t%d \n\n", (num+2)[3]);

        printf("(3+num)[1] is \t%d \n", (3+num)[1]);
        printf("3+num[1] is \t%d \n", 3+num[1]);
        return;
}
```

Figure 24.8 shows the output of this program.

```
num[0] is       100
(num+0)[0] is   100
(num-2)[2] is   100

num[1] is       200
(num+1)[0] is   200
(num-5)[4] is   200

num[5] is       600
(num+5)[0] is   600
(num+2)[3] is   600

(3+num)[1] is   500
3+num[1] is     203
```

Figure 24.8. The output of various array references.

2. The following program prints strings and characters from a
   character array. The printf()s use %s and %c properly; you
   could not interchange any %s for %c (or %c for %s) and get
   correct output.

```
/* Filename: C24REF2.C
   Prints elements and strings from an array */
#include <stdio.h>
main()
{
    char names[]={'T','e','d','\0','E','v','a','\0','S',
                  'a','m','\0'};

    /* Must use extra percent (%) to print %s and %c */
    printf("names with \%s: %s\n", names);
    printf("names+0 with \%s: %s\n", names+0);
    printf("names+1 with \%s: %s\n", names+1);
```

```
    printf("names+2 with \%s: %s\n", names+2);
    printf("names+3 with \%s: %s\n", names+3);
    printf("names+5 with \%s: %s\n", names+5);
    printf("names+8 with \%s: %s\n\n", names+8);

    printf("(names+0)[0] with \%c: %c\n", (names+0)[0]);
    printf("(names+0)[1] with \%c: %c\n", (names+0)[1]);
    printf("(names+0)[2] with \%c: %c\n", (names+0)[2]);
    printf("(names+0)[3] with \%c: %c\n", (names+0)[3]);
    printf("(names+0)[4] with \%c: %c\n", (names+0)[4]);
    printf("(names+0)[5] with \%c: %c\n\n", (names+0)[5]);

    printf("(names+2)[0] with \%c: %c\n", (names+2)[0]);
    printf("(names+2)[1] with \%c: %c\n", (names+2)[1]);
    printf("(names+1)[4] with \%c: %c\n\n", (names+1)[4]);

    printf("(names-4)[6] with \%c: %c\n", (names-4)[6]);
    printf("(names-6)[11] with \%c: %c\n", (names-6)[11]);
    return;
}
```

Study the output shown in Figure 24.9 by comparing it to the program. You will learn more about strings, characters, and character array referencing from studying this one example than from 20 pages of textual description.

```
names with %s: Ted
names+0 with %s: Ted
names+1 with %s: ed
names+2 with %s: d
names+3 with %s:
names+5 with %s: va
names+8 with %s: Sam

(names+0)[0] with %c: T
(names+0)[1] with %c: e
(names+0)[2] with %c: d
(names+0)[3] with %c:
(names+0)[4] with %c: E
(names+0)[5] with %c: v

(names+2)[0] with %c: d
(names+2)[1] with %c:
(names+1)[4] with %c: v

(names-4)[6] with %c: d
(names-6)[11] with %c: v
```

Figure 24.9. The output of various character array references.

Review Questions

Answers to review questions are in Appendix B.

1. True or false: You must access an array in the same order that you initialized it.

2. Where did the bubble sort get its name?

3. Are the following values sorted in ascending or descending order?

   33   55   78   78   90   102   435   859
   976   4092

4. How does C use the name of an array?

5. Given the following array definition:

```
char teams[] = {'E','a','g','l','e','s','\0','R',
                'a','m','s','\0'};
```

what is printed with each of these statements? (Answer "invalid" if the printf() is illegal.)

   a.   printf("%s", teams);

   b.   printf("%s", teams+7);

   c.   printf("%s", (teams+3);

   d.   printf("%s", teams[0]);

   e.   printf("%c", (teams+0)[0]);

   f.   printf("%c", (teams+5));

   g.   printf("%c", (teams-200)[202]);

Review Exercises

1. Write a program to store six of your friends' ages in a single array. Assign the ages in random order. Print the ages, from low to high, on the screen.

2. Modify the program in Exercise 1 to print the ages in descending order.

3. Using the new approach of subscripting arrays, rewrite the programs in Exercises 1 and 2. Always put a 0 in the subscript brackets, modifying the address instead (use (ages+3)[0] rather than ages[3]).

4. Sometimes, *parallel arrays* are used in programs that must track more than one list of values that are related. For instance, suppose that you had to maintain an inventory, tracking the integer part numbers, prices, and quantities of each item. This would require three arrays: an integer part number array, a floating-point price array, and an integer quantity array. Each array would have the same number of elements (the total number of parts in the inventory). Write a program to maintain such an inventory, and reserve enough elements for 100 parts in the inventory. Present the user with an input screen. When the user enters a part number, search the part number array. As soon as you locate the position of the part, print the corresponding price and quantity. If the part does not exist, let the user add it to the inventory, along with the matching price and quantity.

Summary

You are beginning to see the true power of programming languages. Arrays give you the ability to search and sort lists of values. Sorting and searching are what computers do best; computers can quickly scan through hundreds and even thousands of values, looking for a match. Scanning through files of paper by hand, looking for just the right number, takes much more time. By stepping through arrays, your program can quickly scan, print, sort, and calculate a list of values. You now have the tools to sort lists of numbers, as well as search for values in a list.

You will use the concepts learned here for sorting and searching lists of character string data as well, as soon as you learn a little more about the way C manipulates strings and pointers. To help build a solid foundation for this and more advanced material, you now know how to reference array elements without using conventional subscripts.

Now that you have mastered this chapter, the next one will be easy. Chapter 25, "Multidimensional Arrays," shows you how you can keep track of arrays in a different format called a *matrix*. Not all lists of data lend themselves to matrices, but you should be prepared for when you need them.

Multidimensional Arrays

Some data fits into lists, such as the data discussed in the previous two chapters, and other data is better suited for tables of information. This chapter takes arrays one step further. The previous chapters introduced single-dimensional arrays; that is, arrays that have only one subscript, which represent lists of values.

This chapter introduces arrays of more than one dimension, which are called *multidimensional arrays*. Multidimensional arrays, sometimes called *tables* or *matrices*, have at least two dimensions—rows and columns—and sometimes they have even more dimensions.

This chapter introduces the following concepts:

♦ What multidimensional arrays are

♦ Reserving storage for multidimensional arrays

♦ Putting data into multidimensional arrays

♦ Using nested `for` loops to process multidimensional arrays

If you understand single-dimensional arrays, you should have no trouble understanding arrays that have more than one dimension.

Multidimensional Array Basics

A multidimensional array has more than one subscript.

A multidimensional array is an array with more than one subscript. Whereas a single-dimensional array is a list of values, a multidimensional array simulates a table of values, or even multiple tables of values. The most commonly used table is a two-dimensional table (an array with two subscripts).

Suppose that a softball team wanted to keep track of its players' batting record. The team played 10 games, and there are 15 players on the team. Table 25.1 shows the team's batting record.

Table 25.1. A softball team's batting record.

Player Name	Game 1	Game 2	Game 3	Game 4	Game 5	Game 6	Game 7	Game 8	Game 9	Game 10
Adams	2	1	0	0	2	3	3	1	1	2
Berryhill	1	0	3	2	5	1	2	2	1	0
Downing	1	0	2	1	0	0	0	0	2	0
Edwards	0	3	6	4	6	4	5	3	6	3
Franks	2	2	3	2	1	0	2	3	1	0
Grady	1	3	2	0	1	5	2	1	2	1
Howard	3	1	1	1	2	0	1	0	4	3
Jones	2	2	1	2	4	1	0	7	1	0
Martin	5	4	5	1	1	0	2	4	1	5
Powers	2	2	3	1	0	2	1	3	1	2
Smith	1	1	2	1	3	4	1	0	3	2
Smithtown	1	0	1	2	1	0	3	4	1	2
Townsend	0	0	0	0	0	0	1	0	0	0
Ulmer	2	2	2	2	2	1	1	3	1	3
Williams	2	3	1	0	1	2	1	2	0	3

Do you see that the softball table is a two-dimensional table? It has rows (the first dimension) and columns (the second dimension). Therefore, you would call this a two-dimensional table with 15 rows and 10 columns. (Generally, the number of rows is specified first.)

Each row has a player's name, and each column has a game number associated with it, but these are not part of the actual data. The data consists of only 150 values (15 rows by 10 columns equals 150 data values). The data in a two-dimensional table, just as with arrays, always is the same type of data; in this case, every value is an integer. If it were a table of salaries, every element would be floating-point.

A three-dimensional table has three dimensions: depth, rows, and columns.

The number of dimensions, in this case two of them, corresponds to the dimensions in the physical world. The single-dimensioned array is a line, or list of values. Two dimensions represent both length and width. You write on a piece of paper in two dimensions; two dimensions represent a flat surface. Three dimensions represent width, length, and depth. You have seen 3-D movies. Not only do the images have width and height, but they also appear to have depth. Figure 25.1 shows what a three-dimensional array looks like if it has a depth of four, six rows, and three columns. Notice that a three-dimensional table resembles a cube.

It is difficult to visualize more than three dimensions. However, you can think of each dimension after three as another occurrence. In other words, a list of one player's season batting record could be stored in an array. The team's batting record (as shown in Table 25.1) is two-dimensional. The league, made of up several teams' batting records, would represent a three-dimensional table. Each team (the depth of the table) would have rows and columns of batting data. If there is more than one league, that could be another dimension (another set of data).

C enables you to store several dimensions, although "real-world" data rarely requires more than two or three.

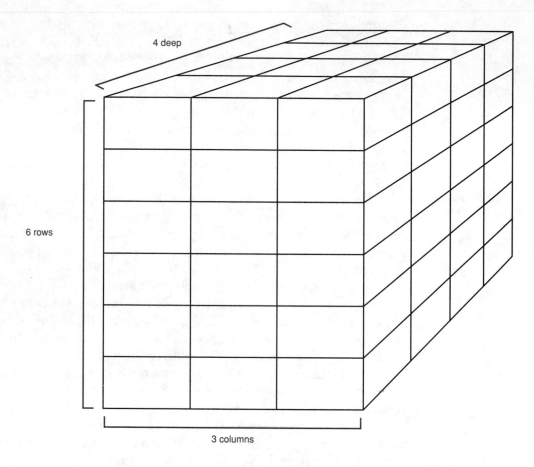

Figure 25.1. Representing a three-dimensional table (a cube).

Reserving Multidimensional Arrays

When you reserve a multidimensional array, you must let C know that the array has more than one dimension. Put more than one subscript in brackets after the array name. You must put a different number, in brackets, for each dimension in the table. For example, to reserve the team data from Table 25.1, you would use the following multidimensional array declaration.

Declare an integer array called teams *with 15 rows and 10 columns.*

```
int teams[15][10];  /* Reserves a two-dimensional table */
```

> **CAUTION:** Unlike other programming languages, C requires you to enclose each dimension in brackets. Do not reserve multidimensional array storage like this:
>
> ```
> int teams[15,10];   /* Invalid table declaration */
> ```

Properly reserving the teams table produces a table with 150 elements. Figure 25.2 shows what each element's subscript looks like.

If you needed to track three teams, and each team had 15 players and played 10 games, you could dimension it as follows:

```
int teams[3][15][10]; /* Reserves a three-dimensional table */
```

The far-right dimension always represents columns, the next represents rows, and so on.

Figure 25.2 shows this dimension's three occurrences of the teams table.

When dimensioning a two-dimensional table, always put the maximum number of rows first, and the maximum number of columns second. C always uses 0 as the starting subscript of each dimension. The last element, the lower-right element of the teams table, would be teams[2][14][9].

Examples

1. Suppose that you wanted to keep track of utility bills for the year. You could store 12 months of four utilities in a two-dimensional table of floating-point amounts, as the following array declaration demonstrates:

```
float utilities[12][4];        /* Reserve 48 elements */
```

You can compute the total number of elements in a multi-dimensional array by multiplying the subscripts. Because 12 times 4 is 48, there are 48 elements in this array (12 rows, 4 columns). Each of these elements is a floating-point data type.

Columns

[0] [0]	[0] [1]	[0] [2]	[0] [3]	[0] [4]	[0] [5]	[0] [6]	[0] [7]	[0] [8]	[0] [9]
[1] [0]	[1] [1]	[1] [2]	[1] [3]	[1] [4]	[1] [5]	[1] [6]	[1] [7]	[1] [8]	[1] [9]
[2] [0]	[2] [1]	[2] [2]	[2] [3]	[2] [4]	[2] [5]	[2] [6]	[2] [7]	[2] [8]	[2] [9]
[3] [0]	[3] [1]	[3] [2]	[3] [3]	[3] [4]	[3] [5]	[3] [6]	[3] [7]	[3] [8]	[3] [9]
[4] [0]	[4] [1]	[4] [2]	[4] [3]	[4] [4]	[4] [5]	[4] [6]	[4] [7]	[4] [8]	[4] [9]
[5] [0]	[5] [1]	[5] [2]	[5] [3]	[5] [4]	[5] [5]	[5] [6]	[5] [7]	[5] [8]	[5] [9]
[6] [0]	[6] [1]	[6] [2]	[6] [3]	[6] [4]	[6] [5]	[6] [6]	[6] [7]	[6] [8]	[6] [9]
[7] [0]	[7] [1]	[7] [2]	[7] [3]	[7] [4]	[7] [5]	[7] [6]	[7] [7]	[7] [8]	[7] [9]
[8] [0]	[8] [1]	[8] [2]	[8] [3]	[8] [4]	[8] [5]	[8] [6]	[8] [7]	[8] [8]	[8] [9]
[9] [0]	[9] [1]	[9] [2]	[9] [3]	[9] [4]	[9] [5]	[9] [6]	[9] [7]	[9] [8]	[9] [9]
[10] [0]	[10] [1]	[10] [2]	[10] [3]	[10] [4]	[10] [5]	[10] [6]	[10] [7]	[10] [8]	[10] [9]
[11] [0]	[11] [1]	[11] [2]	[11] [3]	[11] [4]	[11] [5]	[11] [6]	[11] [7]	[11] [8]	[11] [9]
[12] [0]	[12] [1]	[12] [2]	[12] [3]	[12] [4]	[12] [5]	[12] [6]	[12] [7]	[12] [8]	[12] [9]
[13] [0]	[13] [1]	[13] [2]	[13] [3]	[13] [4]	[13] [5]	[13] [6]	[13] [7]	[13] [8]	[13] [9]
[14] [0]	[14] [1]	[14] [2]	[14] [3]	[14] [4]	[14] [5]	[14] [6]	[14] [7]	[14] [8]	[14] [9]

Rows

Figure 25.2. Subscripts for the softball team table.

2. If you were keeping track of five years' worth of utilities, you would have to add an extra dimension. The first dimension would be the years, the second would be the months, and the last would be the individual utilities. Here is how you would reserve storage:

```
float utilities[5][12][4];      /* Reserve 240 elements */
```

Mapping Arrays to Memory

C approaches multidimensional arrays a little differently than most programming languages do. When you use subscripts, you do not have to understand the internal representation of multidimensional arrays. However, most C programmers feel that a deeper understanding of these arrays is important, especially when programming advanced applications.

A two-dimensional array is actually an *array of arrays*. You program multidimensional arrays as though they were tables with rows and columns. A two-dimensional array is really a single-dimensional array, and each of its elements is not an integer, floating-point, or character, but another array.

Knowing that a multidimensional array is an array of other arrays is critical primarily when passing and receiving such arrays. C passes all arrays, including multidimensional arrays, by address. Suppose that you were using an integer array called scores, reserved as a 5 by 6 table. You can pass scores to a function called print_it() as follows:

```
print_it(scores);          /* Pass table to a function */
```

The function print_it() has to know the type of parameter being passed to it. The print_it() function must also know that the parameter is an array. If table were one-dimensional, you could receive it as

```
print_it(int scores[])     /* Works only if scores
                              are one-dimensional   */
```

or

```
print_it(int scores[10])   /* Assuming that scores
                              have 10 elements      */
```

If scores were a multidimensional table, you would have to designate each pair of brackets and put the maximum number of subscripts in its brackets, as in

```
print_it(int scores[5][6])   /* Let print_it() know
                                about dimensions     */
```

or

```
print_it(int scores[][6])        /* Let print_it() know
                                    about dimensions    */
```

Notice that you do *not* have to state explicitly the maximum subscript on the first dimension when receiving multidimensional arrays, but you must designate the second. If scores were a three-dimensional table, dimensioned as 10 by 5 by 6, you would receive it in print_it() as

```
print_it(int scores[][5][6])      /* Only first dimension
                                     is optional        */
```

or

```
print_it(int scores[10][5][6])      /* Let print_it() know
                                       about dimensions */
```

C stores multi-dimensional arrays in row order.

You should not need to worry too much about the way tables are physically stored. Even though a two-dimensional table is actually an array of arrays (and each of those arrays would contain another array if it were a three-dimensional table), you can use subscripts to program multidimensional arrays as if they were stored in row and column order.

Multidimensional arrays are stored in *row order*. Suppose that you want to keep track of a 3 by 4 table. The top of Figure 25.3 shows how that table (and its subscripts) could be visualized. Despite the two-dimensional table organization, your memory is still sequential storage. C has to map multidimensional arrays to single-dimensional memory, and it does so in row order.

Each row fills memory before the next row is stored. Figure 25.3 shows how a 4 by 4 table is mapped to memory. The entire first row (table[0][0] through table[0][3]) is stored first in memory before any of the second row. A table is really an array of arrays, and, as you learned in previous chapters, array elements are always stored sequentially in memory. Therefore, the first row (array) completely fills memory before the second row. Figure 25.3 shows how two-dimensional arrays map to memory.

Figure 25.3. Mapping a two-dimensional table to memory.

Defining Multidimensional Arrays

C is not picky about the way you define a multidimensional array when you initialize it at declaration time. As with single-dimensional arrays, you initialize multidimensional arrays with braces that designate dimensions. Because a multidimensional array is an array of arrays, you can nest braces when you initialize them.

The following three array definitions fill the three arrays ara1, ara2, and ara3, as shown in Figure 25.4:

```
int ara1[5] = {8, 5, 3, 25, 41};  /* One-dimensional array */
int ara2[2][4]={{4, 3, 2, 1},{1, 2, 3, 4}};
int ara3[3][4]={{1, 2, 3, 4},{5, 6, 7, 8},{9, 10, 11, 12}};
```

ara1

[0]	[1]	[2]	[3]	[4]
8	5	3	25	41

ara2

Columns

	0	1	2	3
0	4	3	2	1
1	1	2	3	4

Rows

ara3

Columns

	0	1	2	3
0	1	2	3	4
1	5	6	7	8
2	9	10	11	12

Rows

Figure 25.4. After initializing a table.

Notice that the multidimensional arrays are stored in row order. In ara3, the first row gets the first four elements of the definition (1, 2, 3, and 4).

> **TIP:** To make a multidimensional array initialization match the array's subscripts, some programmers like to show how arrays are filled. Because C programs are free-form, you can initialize ara2 and ara3 as
>
> ```
> int ara2[2][4]={{4, 3, 2, 1},  /* Does exactly the same */
>                 {1, 2, 3, 4}}; /* thing as before       */
>
> int ara3[4][4]={{1, 2, 3, 4},
>                 {5, 6, 7, 8},
>                 {9, 10, 11, 12},
>                 {13, 14, 15, 16}}; /* Visually more obvious */
> ```

C does not mind if you initialize a multidimensional array as if it were single-dimensional. You must keep track of the row order if you do this. For instance, the following two definitions also reserve storage for and initialize ara2 and ara3:

```
int ara2[2][4]={4, 3, 2, 1, 1, 2, 3, 4};
int ara3[3][4]={1, 2, 3, 4, 5, 6, 7, 8, 9, 10, 11, 12, 13,
                14, 15, 16};
```

There is no difference in initializing ara2 and ara3 with and without the nested braces. The nested braces seem to show the dimensions and how C fills them a little better, but the choice of using nested braces is yours.

One last point to consider is how multidimensional arrays are viewed by your compiler. Many people program in C for years, but never understand how tables are really stored internally. As long as you use subscripts, a table's internal representation should not matter. As soon as you learn about pointer variables, however, you might want to know how C stores your tables in case you want to reference them using pointers (as shown in the next few chapters).

> **TIP:** Multidimensional arrays (unless they are global) are *not* initialized to specific values unless you assign them values at declaration time or in the program. As with single-dimensional arrays, if you initialize one or more of the elements, but not all of them, C fills the rest with zeros. If you want to zero-out an entire multidimensional array, you can do so with the following:
>
> ```
> float  sales[3][4][7][2]  =  {0};     /*  Fills  all  of  sales
>                                          with zeros */
> ```

Figure 25.5 shows the way C stores a 3 by 4 table in memory. Unlike single-dimensional arrays, each element is stored contiguously, but notice how C views the data. Because a table is an array of arrays, the array name contains the address of the start of the primary array. Each of those elements points to the arrays they contain (the data in each row). This coverage of table storage is for your information only, at this point. As you become more proficient in C, and write more powerful programs that manipulate internal memory, you might want to review this method C uses for table storage.

Tables and for Loops

As the following examples show, nested for loops are useful when you want to loop through every element of a multidimensional table.

For instance, the section of code

```
for (row=0; row<2; row++)
   { for (col=0; col<3; col++)
       { printf("%d  %d\n", row, col); }
   }
```

produces the following output:

```
0    0
0    1
0    2
1    0
1    1
1    2
```

These are exactly the subscripts, in row order, for a two-row by three-column table that is dimensioned with

```
int table[2][3];
```

Nested loops work well with multidimensional arrays.

Notice that there are as many `for` loops as there are subscripts in the array (two). The outside loop represents the first subscript (the rows), and the inside loop represents the second subscript (the columns). The nested `for` loop steps through each element of the table.

You can use `scanf()`, `gets()`, `getc()`, and other input functions to fill a table, and you also can assign values to the elements when declaring the table. More often, the data comes from data files on the disk. Regardless of what method actually stores values in multi-dimensional arrays, nested `for` loops are excellent control statements to step through the subscripts. The following examples demonstrate how nested `for` loops work with multidimensional arrays.

Examples

1. The following statements reserve enough memory elements for a television station's ratings (A through D) for one week:

```
char ratings[7][48];
```

These statements reserve enough elements to hold seven days (the rows) of ratings for each 30-minute time slot (48 of them in a day).

Every element in a table is always the same type. In this case, each element is a character variable. Some could be initialized with the following assignment statements:

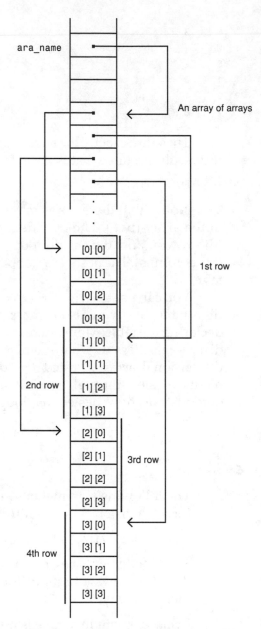

Figure 25.5. Internal representation of a two-dimensional table.

```
shows[3][12] = 'B';   /* Store B in 4th row, 13th column */
shows[1][5] = 'A' ;   /* Store C in 2nd row, 6th column */
shows[6][20] = getchar();
```

2. A computer company sells two sizes of disks: 3 1/2-inch and 5 1/4-inch. Each disk comes in one of four capacities: single-sided double-density, double-sided double-density, single-sided high-density, and double-sided high-density.

The disk inventory is well-suited for a two-dimensional table. The company determined that the disks have the following retail prices:

Disk Size	Double Density		High Density	
	Single-Sided	Double-Sided	Single-Sided	Double-Sided
3 1/2"	2.30	2.75	3.20	3.50
5 1/4"	1.75	2.10	2.60	2.95

The company wants to store the price of each disk in a table for easy access. The following program does that with assignment statements.

```
/* Filename: C25DISK1.C
   Assigns disk prices to a table */
#include <stdio.h>
main()
{
    float disks[2][4];  /* Table of disk prices */
    int row, col;

    disks[0][0] = 2.30;     /* Row 1, column 1 */
    disks[0][1] = 2.75;     /* Row 1, column 2 */
    disks[0][2] = 3.20;     /* Row 1, column 3 */
    disks[0][3] = 3.50;     /* Row 1, column 4 */
    disks[1][0] = 1.75;     /* Row 2, column 1 */
    disks[1][1] = 2.10;     /* Row 2, column 2 */
    disks[1][2] = 2.60;     /* Row 2, column 3 */
    disks[1][3] = 2.95;     /* Row 2, column 4 */
```

BEGIN

Fill disk
inventory
table

Print
table to
screen

END

```
/* Print the prices */
for (row=0; row<2; row++)
   { for (col=0; col<4; col++)
      { printf("$%.2f \n", disks[row][col]); }
   }

   return;
}
```

This program displays the prices as follows:

```
$2.30
$2.75
$3.20
$3.50
$1.75
$2.10
$2.60
$2.95
```

It prints them one line at a time, without any descriptive titles. Although the output is not labeled, it illustrates how you can use assignment statements to initialize a table, and how nested `for` loops can print the elements.

3. The preceding disk inventory would be displayed better if the output had descriptive titles. Before you add titles, it is helpful for you to see how to print a table in its native row and column format.

Typically, you use a nested `for` loop, such as the one in the previous example, to print rows and columns. You should not output a newline character with every `printf()`, however. If you do, you see one value per line, as in the previous program's output, which is not the row and column format of the table.

You do not want to see every disk price on one line, but you want each row of the table printed on a separate line. You must insert a `printf("\n");` to send the cursor to the next line each time the row number changes. Inserting newlines after each row prints the table in its row and column format, as this program shows:

```
/* Filename: C25DISK2.C
   Assigns disk prices to a table
   and prints them in a table format */
#include <stdio.h>
main()
{
    float disks[2][4];   /* Table of disk prices */
    int row, col;

    disks[0][0] = 2.30;        /* Row 1, column 1 */
    disks[0][1] = 2.75;        /* Row 1, column 2 */
    disks[0][2] = 3.20;        /* Row 1, column 3 */
    disks[0][3] = 3.50;        /* Row 1, column 4 */
    disks[1][0] = 1.75;        /* Row 2, column 1 */
    disks[1][1] = 2.10;        /* Row 2, column 2 */
    disks[1][2] = 2.60;        /* Row 2, column 3 */
    disks[1][3] = 2.95;        /* Row 2, column 4 */

    /* Print the prices */
    for (row=0; row<2; row++)
       { for (col=0; col<4; col++)
         { printf("$%.2f\t", disks[row][col]);
         }
         printf("\n");  /* Prints a new line each row */
       }

    return;
}
```

Here is the output of the disk prices in their native table order:

$2.30	$2.75	$3.20	$3.50
$1.75	$2.10	$2.60	$2.95

4. To add the titles, simply print a row of titles before the first row of values, then print a new column title before each column, as shown in the following program:

```
/* Filename: C25DISK3.C
   Assigns disk prices to a table
   and prints them in a table format with titles */
```

```
#include <stdio.h>
main()
{
    float disks[2][4];  /* Table of disk prices */
    int row, col;

    disks[0][0] = 2.30;        /* Row 1, column 1 */
    disks[0][1] = 2.75;        /* Row 1, column 2 */
    disks[0][2] = 3.20;        /* Row 1, column 3 */
    disks[0][3] = 3.50;        /* Row 1, column 4 */
    disks[1][0] = 1.75;        /* Row 2, column 1 */
    disks[1][1] = 2.10;        /* Row 2, column 2 */
    disks[1][2] = 2.60;        /* Row 2, column 3 */
    disks[1][3] = 2.95;        /* Row 2, column 4 */

    /* Print the top titles */
    printf("\tSingle-sided,\tDouble-sided,\tSingle-sided,
\tDouble-sided\n");
    printf("\tDouble-density\tDouble-density\tHigh-density
\tHigh-density\n");

    /* Print the prices */
    for (row=0; row<2; row++)
      { if (row == 0)
        { printf("3-1/2\"\t"); }              /* Need \" to
                                              print quotation */
      else
        { printf("5-1/4\"\t"); }
      for (col=0; col<4; col++)     /* Print the current row */
      { printf("$%.2f\t\t", disks[row][col]);
        }
        printf("\n");            /* Prints a new line each row */
      }

    return;
}
```

Figure 25.6 shows the output from this program.

	Single-sided, Double-density	Double-sided, Double-density	Single-sided, High-density	Double-sided High-density
3-1/2"	$2.30	$2.75	$3.20	$3.50
5-1/4"	$1.75	$2.10	$2.60	$2.95

Figure 25.6. The table of disk prices with titles.

Review Questions

Answers to the review questions are in Appendix B.

1. What statement reserves a two-dimensional table of integers called scores with five rows and six columns?

2. What statement reserves a three-dimensional table of four character arrays called initials with 10 rows and 20 columns?

3. In the following statement, which subscript (first or second) represents rows and which represents columns?

   ```
   int weights[5][10];
   ```

4. How many elements are reserved with the following statement?

   ```
   int ara[5][6];
   ```

5. The following table of integers is called ara:

4	1	3	5	9
10	2	12	1	6
25	42	2	91	8

What values do the following elements contain?

a.   `ara[2][2]`

b.   `ara[0][1]`

c.   `ara[2][3]`

d.   `ara[2][4]`

6. What control statement is best for stepping through multi-dimensional arrays?

7. Note the following section of a program:

```
int grades[3][5] = {80,90,96,73,65,67,90,68,92,84,70,
                    55,95,78,100};
```

What are the values of the following:

a.   `grades[2][3]`

b.   `grades[2][4]`

c.   `grades[0][1]`

Review Exercises

1. Write a program that stores and prints the numbers from 1 to 21 in a 3 by 7 table. (Hint: Remember that C begins subscripts at 0.)

2. Write a program that reserves storage for three years' worth of sales data for five salespeople. Use assignment statements to fill the table with data, then print it, one value per line.

3. Instead of using assignment statements, use the scanf() function to fill the salespeople data from Exercise 2.

4. Write a program that tracks the grades for five classes, each having 10 students. Input the data using the scanf() function. Print the table in its native row and column format.

Summary

You now know how to create, initialize, and process multi-dimensional arrays. Although not all data fits in the compact format of tables, much does. Using nested for loops makes stepping through a multidimensional array straightforward.

One of the limitations of a multidimensional array is that each element must be the same data type. This keeps you from being able to store several kinds of data in tables. Subsequent chapters show you how to store data in different ways to overcome this limitation of tables.

Pointers

C reveals its true power through *pointer variables*. Pointer variables (or *pointers*, as they generally are called) are variables that contain addresses of other variables. All variables you have seen so far have held data values. You understand that variables hold various data types: character, integer, floating-point, and so on. Pointer variables contain the location of regular data variables; they in effect *point* to the data because they hold the address of the data.

When first learning C, students of the language tend to shy away from pointers, thinking that pointers will be difficult. Pointers do not have to be difficult. In fact, after you work with them for a while, you will find that they are easier to use than arrays (and much more flexible).

This chapter introduces the following concepts:

♦ What pointers are

♦ Pointers of different data types

♦ The "address of" (&) operator

♦ The dereferencing (*) operator

♦ Arrays of pointers

Pointers offer a highly efficient means of accessing and changing data. Because pointers contain the actual address of your data, your compiler has less work to do when finding that data in memory. Pointers do not have to link data to specific variable names. A pointer can point to an unnamed data value. With pointers, you gain a "different view" of your data.

Introduction to Pointer Variables

Pointers are variables. They follow all the normal naming rules of regular, nonpointer variables. As with regular variables, you must declare pointer variables before using them. There is a type of pointer for every data type in C; there are integer pointers, character pointers, floating-point pointers, and so on. You can declare global pointers or local pointers, depending on where you declare them.

Pointers contain addresses of other variables.

About the only difference between pointer variables and regular variables is the data they hold. Pointers do not contain data in the usual sense of the word. Pointers contain addresses of data. If you need a quick review of addresses and memory, see Appendix A, "Memory Addressing, Binary, and Hexadecimal Review."

There are two pointer operators in C:

&   The "address of" operator

*   The dereferencing operator

Don't let these operators throw you; you have seen them before! The & is the bitwise AND operator (from Chapter 12, "Bitwise Operators") and the * means, of course, multiplication. These are called *overloaded* operators. They perform more than one function, depending on how you use them in your programs. C does not confuse * for multiplication when you use it as a dereferencing operator with pointers.

Any time you see the & used with pointers, think of the words "address of." The & operator always produces the memory address of whatever it precedes. The * operator, when used with pointers, either declares a pointer or dereferences the pointer's value. The next section explains each of these operators.

Declaring Pointers

Because you must declare all pointers before using them, the best way to begin learning about pointers is to understand how to declare and define them. Actually, declaring pointers is almost as easy as declaring regular variables. After all, pointers are variables.

If you need to declare a variable that will hold your age, you could do so with the following variable declaration:

```
int age=30;       /* Declare a variable to hold my age */
```

Declaring age like this does several things. C now knows that you will need a variable called age, so C reserves storage for that variable. C also knows that you will store only integers in age, not floating-point or double floating-point data. The declaration also requests that C store the value of 30 in age after it reserves storage for age.

Where did C store age in memory? As the programmer, you do not really care where C decided to store age. You do not need to know the variable's address because you will never refer to age by its address. If you want to calculate or print with age, you will call it by its name, age.

> **TIP:** Make your pointer variable names meaningful. The name file_ptr makes more sense than x13 for a file-pointing variable, although either name is allowed.

Suppose that you want to declare a pointer variable. This pointer variable will not hold your age, but it will point to age, the variable that holds your age. (Why you would want to do this is explained in this and the next few chapters.) p_age might be a good name for the pointer variable. Figure 26.1 illustrates what you want to do. The figure assumes that C stored age at the address 350,606; however, your C compiler arbitrarily determines the address of age, so it could be anything.

Figure 26.1. p_age contains the address of age; p_age points to the age variable.

The name p_age by itself has nothing to do with pointers, except that is the name you made up for the pointer to age. You could just as easily have given p_age the name house, x43344, space_trek, or whatever else you wanted to call it, just as you can name variables anything (as long as the name follows the legal naming rules of variables). This reinforces the idea that a pointer is just a variable that you must reserve in your program. Make up meaningful variable names, even for pointer variables. p_age is a good name for a variable that points to age (as would be ptr_age and ptr_to_age).

To declare the p_age pointer variable, you must do the following:

```
int * p_age;          /* Declare an integer pointer */
```

Similar to the declaration for age, this declaration reserves a variable called p_age. The p_age variable is not a normal integer variable, however. Because of the dereferencing operator, *, C knows that this is to be a pointer variable. Some C programmers prefer to declare such a variable without a space after the *, as follows:

```
int *p_age;               /* Declare an integer pointer */
```

Either method is okay, but you must remember that the * is *not* part of the name. When you later use p_age, you will not always prefix the name with the *, unless you are dereferencing it at the time (as later examples show).

> **TIP:** Whenever the dereferencing operator, *, appears in a variable definition, the variable being declared is *always* a pointer variable.

Consider the declaration for p_age if the asterisk were not there: C would think you were declaring a regular integer variable. The * is important, because it tells C to interpret p_age as a pointer variable, not as a normal, data variable.

Assigning Values to Pointers

Pointers can point only to data of their own type.

p_age is an integer pointer. This is very important. p_age can point only to integer values, never to floating-point, double floating-point, or even character variables. If you needed to point to a floating-point variable, you might do so with a pointer declared as

```
float *point;      /* Declares a floating-point pointer */
```

As with any automatic variable, C does not initialize pointers when you declare them. If you declared p_age as previously described, and you wanted p_age to point to age, you would have to explicitly assign p_age to the address of age. The following statement does this:

```
p_age = &age;      /* Assign the address of age to p_age */
```

What value is now in p_age? You do not know exactly, but you know it is the address of age, wherever that is. Instead of assigning the address of age to p_age with an assignment operator, you can declare and initialize pointers at the same time. These lines declare and initialize both age and p_age:

```
int age=30;        /* Declares a regular integer
                      variable, putting 30 in it       */
int *p_age=&age;   /* Declares an integer pointer,
                      initializing it with the address
                      of p_age                         */
```

These two lines produce the variables described in Figure 26.1.

If you wanted to print the value of age, you could do so with the following printf():

```
printf("%d", age);            /* Prints the value of age */
```

You also can print the value of age like this:

Print value that pointer points to

```
printf("%d", *p_age);                /* Dereferences p_age */
```

The dereference operator produces a value that tells the pointer where to point. Without the *, the last printf() would print an address (the address of age). With the *, the printf() prints the value at that address.

You can assign a different value to age with the following statement:

```
age=41;                      /* Assign a new value to age */
```

You also can assign a value to age like this:

```
*p_age=41;
```

This declaration assigns 41 to the value to which p_age points.

> **TIP:** The * appears before a pointer variable in only two places—when you declare a pointer variable, and when you dereference a pointer variable (to find the data it points to).

Pointers and Parameters

Now that you understand the pointer's * and & operators, you can finally see why scanf()'s requirements were not really as strict as they first appeared. While passing a regular variable to scanf(), you had to prefix the variable with the & operator. For instance, the following scanf() gets three integer values from the user:

```
scanf(" %d %d %d", &num1, &num2, &num3);
```

This scanf() does not pass the three variables, but passes the *addresses* of the three variables. Because scanf() knows the exact locations of these parameters in memory (because their addresses were passed), it goes to those addresses and puts the keyboard input values into those addresses.

This is the only way scanf() could work. If you passed these variables by copy, without putting the "address of" operator (&) before them, scanf() would get the keyboard input and fill a *copy* of the variables, but not the actual variables num1, num2, and num3. When scanf() then returned control to your program, you would not have the input values.

You might recall from Chapter 19, "Passing Values," that you can pass by address and override C's normal default of passing by copy (or "by value"). To pass by address, pass a variable preceded by an & and put an asterisk before the parameter everywhere it appears in the receiving function. The following function call passes tries by address to the receiving function called pr_it():

```
pr_it(&tries);   /* Pass integer tries to pr_it() by
                    address (tries would normally pass
                    by copy)                         */
```

The following function, pr_it(), receives the address of tries, in effect receiving tries by address:

```
pr_it(int *tries)        /* Receive tries by address
                            (dereference its value)  */
{
*tries++;           /* This changes tries in calling
                       and receiving functions      */
    return;
}
```

Now that you understand the & and * operators, you can completely understand the passing of nonarray parameters by address to functions. (Arrays default to passing by address without requiring that you use & and *.)

Examples

1. The following section of a program declares three regular variables of three different data types, and pointers that point to those variables:

```
char initial= 'Q';      /* Declares three regular variables */
int num=40;             /* of three different types        */
float sales=2321.59;

char *p_initial=&initial;   /* Declares three pointers.   */
int * ptr_num=&num;         /* Pointer names and spacing  */
float * sales_add = &sales; /* after * are not critical.   */
```

2. You can initialize pointers, just as with regular variables, with assignment statements. You do not have to initialize them when you declare them. The next few lines of code are equivalent to the code in Example 1:

```
char initial;       /* Declares three regular variables */
int num;            /* of three different types          */
float sales;

char *p_initial;    /* Declares three pointers but does */
int * ptr_num;      /* not initialize them yet           */
float * sales_add;

initial='Q';        /* Initializes the regular variables */
num=40;             /* with values                        */
sales=2321.59;

p_initial=&initial;    /* Initializes the pointers with */
ptr_num=&num;          /* the addresses of their         */
sales_add=&sales;      /* corresponding variables        */
```

Notice that you do not put the * operator before the pointer variable names when assigning them values. You would prefix a pointer variable with the * only if you were dereferencing it.

NOTE: In this example, the pointer variables could have been assigned the addresses of the regular variables before the regular variables were assigned values. There would be no difference in the operation. The pointers are assigned the addresses of the regular variables regardless of the data in the regular variables.

Keep the data type of each pointer consistent. Do *not* assign a floating-point variable to an integer's address. For instance, you cannot make the following assignment statement:

```
p_initial = &sales;        /* Invalid pointer assignment */
```

because p_initial can point only to character data, not to floating-point data.

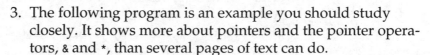

3. The following program is an example you should study closely. It shows more about pointers and the pointer operators, & and *, than several pages of text can do.

```
/* Filename: C26POINT.C
Demonstrates the use of pointer declarations
and operators */
#include <stdio.h>
main()
{
    int num=123;                /* A regular integer variable */
    int *p_num;                 /* Declares an integer pointer */

    printf("num is %d\n", num);       /* Prints value of num */
    printf("The address of num is %ld \n", &num); /* Prints
                                    num's location */
    p_num = &num;               /* Puts address of num in p_num,
                                   in effect making p_num point
                                   to num                       */
                                /* No * in front of p_num)      */
    printf("*p_num is %d \n", *p_num);  /* Prints value of
                                            num       */
    printf("p_num is %ld \n", p_num);   /* Prints location
                                            of num    */
    return;
}
```

Here is the output from this program:

```
num is 123
The address of num is 65522
*p_num is 123
p_num is 65522
```

If you run this program, you probably will get different results for the value of p_num because your compiler will place num at a different location, depending on your memory setup. The actual address is moot, however. Because the pointer p_num always contains the address of num, and because you can dereference p_num to get num's value, the actual address is not critical.

4. The following program includes a function that swaps the values of any two integers passed to it. You might recall that a function can return only a single value. Therefore, before now, you could not write a function that changed two different values and returned both values to the calling function.

To swap two variables (reversing their values for sorting, as you saw in Chapter 24, "Array Processing") you need the ability to pass both variables by address. Then, when the function reverses the variables, the calling function's variables also are swapped.

Notice the function's use of dereferencing operators before each occurrence of num1 and num2. You do not care which address num1 and num2 is stored at, but you must make sure that you dereference whatever addresses were passed to the function.

Be sure to pass arguments with the prefix & to functions that receive by address, as done here in main().

Identify the program and include the I/O header file. This program will swap two integers, so initialize two integer variables in main(). Pass the variables to the swapping function, called swap_them, then switch their values. Print the results of the swap in main().

Reverse
two
variables

```
/* Filename: C26SWAP.C
      Program that includes a function that swaps
      any two integers passed to it */
#include <stdio.h>
void swap_them(int *num1, int *num2);
void main(void);
```

```
void main(void)
{
    int i=10, j=20;
    printf("\n\nBefore swap, i is %d and j is %d\n\n",
            i, j);
    swap_them(&i, &j);
    printf("\n\nAfter swap, i is %d and j is %d\n\n",
            i, j);
    return;
}
void swap_them(int *num1, int *num2)
{
int temp;                /* Variable that holds
                            in-between swapped value.    */
temp = *num1;            /* The asterisks ensure that the  */
*num1 = *num2;           /* calling function's variables   */
*num2 = temp;            /* (and not copies of them) are   */
                         /* worked on in this function.    */

    return;
}
```

Arrays of Pointers

If you need to reserve many pointers for many different values, you might want to declare an array of pointers. You know that you can reserve an array of characters, integers, long integers, and floating-point values, as well as an array of every other data type available. You also can reserve an array of pointers, with each pointer being a pointer to a specific data type.

The following reserves an array of 10 integer pointer variables:

```
int *iptr[10]; /* Reserves an array of 10 integer pointers */
```

Figure 26.2 shows how C views this array. Each element holds an address (after being assigned values) that points to other values in memory. Each value pointed to must be an integer. You can assign an element from iptr an address just as you would for nonarray pointer variables. You can make iptr[4] point to the address of an integer variable named age by assigning it like this:

```
iptr[4] = &age;     /* Make iptr[4] point to address of age */
```

Figure 26.2. An array of 10 integer pointers.

The following reserves an array of 20 character pointer variables:

```
char *cpoint[20];        /* Array of 20 character pointers */
```

Again, the asterisk is not part of the array name. The asterisk lets C know that this is an array of integer pointers and not just an array of integers.

Some beginning C students get confused when they see such a declaration. Pointers are one thing, but reserving storage for arrays of pointers tends to bog novices down. However, reserving storage for arrays of pointers is easy to understand. Remove the asterisk from the last declaration as follows

```
char cpoint[20];
```

and what do you have? You have just reserved a simple array of 20 characters. Adding the asterisk tells C to go one step further: rather than an array of character variables, you want an array of character pointing variables. Instead of having each element be a character variable, you have each element hold an address that points to characters.

Reserving arrays of pointers will be much more meaningful after you learn about structures in the next few chapters. As with regular, nonpointing variables, an array makes processing several variables much easier. You can use a subscript to reference each variable (element) without having to use a different variable name for each value.

Review Questions

Answers to review questions are in Appendix B.

1. What kind of variable is reserved in each of the following?

    a.   `int *a;`

    b.   `char * cp;`

    c.   `float * dp;`

2. What words should come to mind when you see the & operator?

3. What is the dereferencing operator?

4. How would you assign the address of the floating-point variable `salary` to a pointer called `pt_sal`?

5. True or false: You must define a pointer with an initial value when declaring it.

6. In both of the following sections of code

```
int i;
int * pti;
i=56;
pti = &i;
```

and

```
int i;
int * pti;
pti = &i;        /* These two lines are reversed */
i=56;            /* from the preceding example   */
```

is the value of `pti` the same after the fourth line of each section?

7. In the following section of code:

```
float pay;
float *ptr_pay;
pay=2313.54;
ptr_pay = &pay;
```

Determine the value of each of the following (answer "invalid" if it cannot be determined):

a.   pay

b.   *ptr_pay

c.   *pay

d.   &pay

8. What does the following declare?

```
double *ara[4][6];
```

a.   An array of double floating-point values

b.   An array of double floating-point pointer variables

c.   An invalid declaration statement

NOTE: Because this is a theory-oriented chapter, review exercises are saved until you master Chapter 27, "Pointers and Arrays."

Summary

Declaring and using pointers might seem like a lot of trouble at this point. Why assign *p_num a value when it is easier (and clearer) to assign a value directly to num? If you are asking yourself that question, you probably understand everything you should from this chapter and are ready to begin seeing the true power of pointers: combining pointers and array processing.

27

Pointers and Arrays

Arrays and pointers are closely related in the C programming language. You can address arrays as if they were pointers and address pointers as if they were arrays. Being able to store and access pointers and arrays gives you the ability to store strings of data in array elements. Without pointers, you could not store strings of data in arrays because there is no fundamental string data type in C (no string variables, only string constants).

This chapter introduces the following concepts:

♦ Array names and pointers

♦ Character pointers

♦ Pointer arithmetic

♦ Ragged-edge arrays of string data

This chapter introduces concepts you will use for much of your future programming in C. Pointer manipulation is very important to the C programming language.

Array Names as Pointers

An array name is just a pointer, nothing more. To prove this, suppose that you have the following array declaration:

```
int ara[5] = {10, 20, 30, 40, 50};
```

An array name is a pointer.

If you printed ara[0], you would see 10. Because you now fully understand arrays, this is the value you would expect.

But what if you were to print *ara? Would *ara print anything? If so, what? If you thought an error message would print because ara is not a pointer but an array, you would be wrong. An array name is a pointer. If you print *ara, you also would see 10.

Recall how arrays are stored in memory. Figure 27.1 shows how ara would be mapped in memory. The array name, ara, is nothing more than a pointer that points to the first element of the array. Therefore, if you dereference that pointer, you dereference the value stored at the first element of the array, which is 10. Dereferencing ara is exactly the same thing as referring to ara[0], because they both produce the same value.

Figure 27.1. Storing the array called ara in memory.

You now see that you can reference an array with subscripts or with pointer dereferencing. Can you use pointer notation to print the third element of ara? Yes, and you already have the tools to do so. The following printf() prints ara[2] (the third element of ara) without using a subscript:

```
printf("%d",C1 *(ara+2) );                /* Prints ara[2] */
```

The expression `*(ara+2)` is not vague at all, if you remember that an array name is just a pointer that always points to the array's first element. `*(ara+2)` takes the address stored in `ara`, adds 2 to the address, and dereferences that location. The following holds true:

ara+0 points to ara[0]

ara+1 points to ara[1]

ara+2 points to ara[2]

ara+3 points to ara[3]

ara+4 points to ara[4]

Therefore, to print, store, or calculate with an array element, you can use either the subscript notation or the pointer notation. Because an array name contains the address of the array's first element, you must dereference the pointer to get the element's value.

Internal Locations

C knows the internal data size requirements of characters, integers, floating-points, and the other data types on your computer. Therefore, because `ara` is an integer array, and because each element in an integer array consumes 2 to 4 bytes of storage, depending on the computer, C adds 2 or 4 bytes to the address if you reference arrays as just shown.

If you write `*(ara+3)` to refer to ara[3], C would add 6 or 12 bytes to the address of `ara` to get the third element. C does not add an actual 3. You do not have to worry about this, because C handles these internals. When you write `*(ara+3)`, you are actually requesting that C add three integer addresses to the address of `ara`. If `ara` were a floating-point array, C would add three floating-point addresses to `ara`.

Pointer Advantages

An array name is a pointer constant.

Although arrays are really pointers in disguise, they are special types of pointers. An array name is a *pointer constant*, not a pointer variable. You cannot change the value of an array name, because you cannot change constants. This explains why you cannot assign an array new values during a program's execution. For instance, even if cname is a character array, the following is not valid in C:

```
cname = "Christine Chambers";  /* Invalid array assignment */
```

The array name, cname, cannot be changed because it is a constant. You would not attempt the following

```
5 = 4 + 8 * 21;                    /* Invalid assignment */
```

because you cannot change the constant 5 to any other value. C knows that you cannot assign anything to 5, and C will print an error message if you attempt to change 5. C also knows that an array name is a constant and that you cannot change an array to another value. (You can assign values to an array only at declaration time, one element at a time during execution, or by using functions such as strcpy().)

This brings you to the most important reason to learn pointers: pointers (except arrays referenced as pointers) are variables. You *can* change a pointer variable, and being able to do so makes processing virtually any data, including arrays, much more powerful and flexible.

Examples

1. By changing pointers, you make them point to different values in memory. The following program demonstrates how to change pointers. The program first defines two floating-point values. A floating-point pointer points to the first variable, v1, and is used in the printf(). The pointer is then changed so that it points to the second floating-point variable, v2.

```
/* Filename: C27PTRCH.C
   Changes the value of a pointer variable */
#include <stdio.h>
main()
{
   float v1=676.54;                         /* Defines two */
   float v2=900.18;                /* floating-point variables */
   float * p_v;          /* Defines a floating-point pointer */

   p_v = &v1;                  /* Makes pointer point to v1 */
   printf("The first value is %.2f \n", *p_v);  /* Prints
                                          676.54  */

   p_v = &v2;              /* Changes the pointer so that it
                             points to v2                 */
   printf("The second value is %.2f \n", *p_v);  /* Prints
                                          900.18 */

   return;
}
```

Because they can change pointers, most C programmers use pointers rather than arrays. Because arrays are easy to declare, C programmers sometimes declare arrays and then use pointers to reference those arrays. If the array data changes, the pointer helps to change it.

2. You can use pointer notation and reference pointers as arrays with array notation. The following program declares an integer array and an integer pointer that points to the start of the array. The array and pointer values are printed using subscript notation. Afterward, the program uses array notation to print the array and pointer values.

Study this program carefully. You will see the inner workings of arrays and pointer notation.

```
/* Filename: C27ARPTR.C
   References arrays like pointers and
   pointers like arrays */
#include <stdio.h>
main()
{
   int ctr;
   int iara[5] = {10, 20, 30, 40, 50};
```

```
         int *iptr;

         iptr = iara;          /* Make iptr point to array's first
                                  element. This would work also:
                                  iptr = &iara[0];                 */

     printf("Using array subscripts:\n");
     printf("iara\tiptr\n");
     for (ctr=0; ctr<5; ctr++)
        { printf("%d\t%d \n", iara[ctr], iptr[ctr]);   }

     printf("\nUsing pointer notation:\n");
     printf("iara\tiptr\n");
     for (ctr=0; ctr<5; ctr++)
        { printf("%d\t%d \n", *(iara+ctr), *(iptr+ctr));   }

  return;
  }
```

Here is the program's output:

```
Using array subscripts:
iara    iptr
10      10
20      20
30      30
40      40
50      50

Using pointer notation:
iara    iptr
10      10
20      20
30      30
40      40
50      50
```

Using Character Pointers

The ability to change pointers is best seen when working with character strings in memory. You can store strings in character arrays, or point to them with character pointers. Consider the following two string definitions:

```
char cara[] = "C Is fun";    /* An array holding a string */
char *cptr = "C by Example";  /* A pointer to the string */
```

Figure 27.2 shows how C stores these two strings in memory. C stores both in basically the same way. You are familiar with the array definition. When assigning a string to a character pointer, C finds enough free memory to hold the string and assigns the address of the first character to the pointer. The previous two string definition statements do almost exactly the same thing; the only difference between them is the changeability of the two pointers (the array name and the character pointers).

Because the %s control code prints strings, starting at the array or pointer name until the null zero is reached, you can print each of these strings with the following printf() statements:

```
printf("String 1: %s \n", cara);
printf("String 2: %s \n", cptr);
```

Notice that you print strings in arrays and strings pointed to in the same way. You might wonder what advantage one method of storing strings has over the other. The seemingly minor difference between these stored strings makes a big difference when you change them.

Suppose that you want to store the string Hello in the two strings. You *cannot* assign the string to the array like this:

```
cara = "Hello";                           /* Invalid */
```

Because you cannot change the array name, you cannot assign it a new value. The only way to change the contents of the array is by assigning the array characters from the string an element at a time, or by using a built-in function such as strcpy(). You can, however, make the character array point to the new string like this:

```
cptr = "Hello";        /* Change the pointer so that
                          it points to the new string */
```

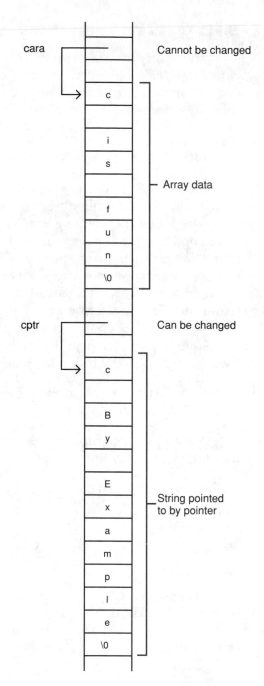

Figure 27.2. **Storing two strings: one in an array and one pointed to.**

> **TIP:** If you want to store user input in a string pointed to by a pointer, first you must reserve enough storage for that input string. The easiest way to do this is to reserve a character array, then assign a character pointer to the beginning element of that array like this:
>
> ```
> char input[81];    /* Holds a string as long as 80 characters */
>
> char *iptr=input;    /*  Could also have done this:
>                          char *iptr=&input[0];    */
> ```
>
> Now you can input a string by using the pointer:
>
> ```
> gets(iptr);            /*  Make sure that iptr points to
>                            the string typed by the user */
> ```
>
> You can use pointer manipulation, arithmetic, and modification on the input string.

Examples

1. Suppose that you want to store your sister's full name and print it. Instead of using arrays, you can use a character pointer. The following program does just that.

```
/* Filename: C27CP1.C
   Stores a name in a character pointer */
#include <stdio.h>
main()
{
   char *c="Bettye Lou Horn";

   printf("My sister's name is %s", c);
   return;
}
```

This prints the following:

```
My sister's name is Bettye Lou Horn
```

2. Suppose that you need to change a string pointed to by a character pointer. If your sister changed her last name to Henderson by marriage, your program could show both strings in the following manner:

Identify the program and include the I/O header file. This program uses a character pointer to point to a string literal in memory. We'll call the character pointer c. Point to the string literal, then print the string. Make the character pointer point to a new string literal, then print the new string.

```
/* Filename: C27CP2.C
    Illustrates changing a character string */
#include <stdio.h>
main()
{
    char *c="Bettye Lou Horn";

    printf("My sister's maiden name was %s \n", c);

    c = "Bettye Lou Henderson";  /* Assigns new string to c */

    printf("My sister's married name is %s \n", c);
    return;
}
```

The output is as follows:

```
My sister's maiden name was Bettye Lou Horn
My sister's married name is Bettye Lou Henderson
```

3. Do not use character pointers to change string constants. Doing so can confuse the compiler, and you probably will not get the results you expect. The following program is similar to those you just saw. Instead of making the character pointer point to a new string, this example attempts to change the contents of the original string.

```
/* Filename: C27CP3.C
    Illustrates changing a character string improperly */
#include <stdio.h>
```

```
main()
{
    char *c="Bettye Lou Horn";

    printf("My sister's maiden name was %s \n", c);

    c += 11; /* Makes c point to the last name (the 12th character)*/
    c = "Henderson";          /* Assigns a new string to c */

    printf("My sister's married name is %s \n", c);
    return;
}
```

The program seems to change the last name from Horn to Henderson, but it does not. Here is the output of this program:

```
My sister's maiden name was Bettye Lou Horn
My sister's married name is Henderson
```

Why didn't the full string print? Because the address pointed to by c was incremented by 11, c still points to Henderson, so that was all that printed.

4. You might guess at a way to fix the last program. Instead of printing the string stored at c after assigning it to Henderson, you might want to decrement it by 11 so that it points to its original location, the start of the name. The code to do this follows, but it does not work as expected. Study the program before reading the explanation.

```
/* Filename: C27CP4.C
   Illustrates changing a character string improperly */
#include <stdio.h>
main()
{
    char *c="Bettye Lou Horn";

    printf("My sister's maiden name was %s \n", c);

    c += 11;                  /* Makes c point to the last
                                 name (the 12th character) */
```

```
    c = "Henderson";            /* Assigns a new string to c */
    c -= 11;                        /* Makes c point to its
                                    original location (???) */

    printf("My sister's married name is %s \n", c);
    return;
}
```

This program produces garbage at the second `printf()`. There are actually two string constants in this program. When you first assign c to Bettye Lou Horn, C reserves space in memory for the constant string and puts the starting address of the string in c.

When the program then assigns c to Henderson, C finds room for *another* character constant, as shown in Figure 27.3. If you subtract 11 from the location of c, after it points to the new string Henderson, c points to an area of memory that your program is not using. There is no guarantee that printable data appears before the string constant Henderson. If you want to manipulate parts of the string, you must do so an element at a time, just as you must with arrays.

Pointer Arithmetic

You saw an example of pointer arithmetic when you accessed array elements with pointer notation. By now you should be comfortable with the fact that both of these array or pointer references are identical:

    ara[sub] and *(ara + sub)

You can increment or decrement a pointer. If you increment a pointer, the address inside the pointer variable increments. The pointer does not always increment by 1, however.

Suppose that f_ptr is a floating-point pointer that points to the first element of an array of floating-point numbers. You could initialize f_ptr as follows:

```
float fara[] = {100.5, 201.45, 321.54, 389.76, 691.34};
f_ptr = fara;
```

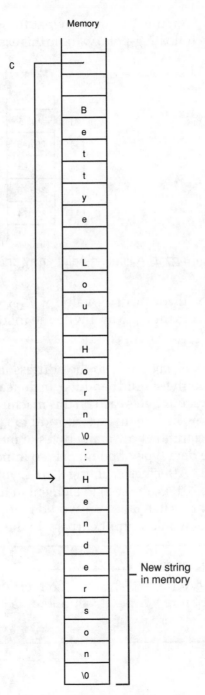

Figure 27.3. Two string constants appear in memory because two string constants are used in the program.

Figure 27.4 shows what these variables look like in memory. Each floating-point value in this example takes four bytes of memory.

Figure 27.4. A floating-point array and a pointer.

Incrementing a pointer can add more than one byte to the pointer.

If you print the value of *f_ptr, you see 100.5. Suppose that you increment f_ptr by 1 with the following statement:

```
f_ptr++;
```

C does *not* add 1 to the address in f_ptr, even though it seems as though 1 should be added. In this case, because floating-point values take four bytes each on this machine, C adds 4 to f_ptr. How does C know how many bytes to add to f_ptr? C knows from the pointer's declaration how many bytes of memory pointers take. This is why the data type of pointers is so important.

After incrementing f_ptr, if you were to print *f_ptr, you would see 201.45, the second element in the array. If C added only 1 to the address in f_ptr, f_ptr would point only to the second byte of 100.5. This would output garbage to the screen.

> **NOTE:** When you increment a pointer, C adds one data type size (in bytes) to the pointer, not 1. When you decrement a pointer, C subtracts one data type size (in bytes) from the pointer.

Examples

1. The following program defines an array with five values. An integer pointer is then initialized to point to the first element in the array. The rest of the program prints the dereferenced value of the pointer, then increments the pointer so that it points to the next integer in the array.

   Just to show you what is going on, the size of integer values is printed at the bottom of the program. Because (in this case) integers take two bytes, C increments the pointer by 2 so that it points to the next integer. (The integers are two bytes apart from each other.)

```c
/* Filename: C27PTI.C
   Increments a pointer through an integer array */
#include <stdio.h>
main()
{
    int iara[] = {10,20,30,40,50};
    int *ip = iara;                  /* The pointer points to
                                        the start of the array */

    printf("%d \n", *ip);
    ip++;                            /* 2 is actually added */
    printf("%d \n", *ip);
    ip++;                            /* 2 is actually added */
    printf("%d \n", *ip);
    ip++;                            /* 2 is actually added */
    printf("%d \n", *ip);
    ip++;                            /* 2 is actually added */
    printf("%d \n\n", *ip);
    printf("The integer size is %d ",sizeof(int));
    printf("bytes on this machine");
    return;
}
```

Here is the output from the program:

```
10
20
30
40
50
The integer size is 2 bytes on this machine
```

2. Here is the same program using a character array and a character pointer. Because a character takes only one byte of storage, incrementing a character pointer actually adds just 1 to the pointer; only 1 is needed because the characters are only one byte apart from each other.

```c
/* Filename: C27PTC.C
   Increments a pointer through a character array */
#include <stdio.h>
main()
{
    char cara[] = {'a', 'b', 'c', 'd', 'e'};
    char *cp = cara;                /* The pointers points to
                                       the start of the array */
    printf("%c \n", *cp);
    cp++;                           /* 1 is actually added */
    printf("%c \n", *cp);
    cp++;                           /* 1 is actually added */
    printf("%c \n", *cp);
    cp++;                           /* 1 is actually added */
    printf("%c \n", *cp);
    cp++;                           /* 1 is actually added */
    printf("%c \n\n", *cp);
    printf("The character size is %d ",sizeof(char));
    printf("bytes on this machine");
    return;
}
```

3. The next program shows the many ways you can add to, subtract from, and reference arrays and pointers. The program defines a floating-point array and a floating-point pointer. The body of the program prints the values from the array using array and pointer notation.

```c
/* Filename: C27ARPT2.C
   Comprehensive reference of arrays and pointers */
```

```c
#include <stdio.h>
main()
{
   float ara[] = {100.0, 200.0, 300.0, 400.0, 500.0};
   float *fptr;                    /* Floating-point pointer */

   /* Make pointer point to array's first value */
   fptr = &ara[0];           /* Could also have been this:
                                 fptr = ara; */


   printf("%.1f \n", *fptr);             /* Prints 100.0 */
   fptr++;       /* Points to next floating-point value */
   printf("%.1f \n", *fptr);             /* Prints 200.0 */
   fptr++;       /* Points to next floating-point value */
   printf("%.1f \n", *fptr);             /* Prints 300.0 */
   fptr++;       /* Points to next floating-point value */
   printf("%.1f \n", *fptr);             /* Prints 400.0 */
   fptr++;       /* Points to next floating-point value */
   printf("%.1f \n", *fptr);             /* Prints 500.0 */

   fptr = ara;          /* Points to first element again */
   printf("%.1f \n", *(fptr+2) );    /* Prints 300.00 but
                                   does not change fptr */

   /* References both array and pointer using subscripts  */
   printf("%.1f  %.1f \n", (fptr+0)[0],
          (ara+0)[0]);                /* 100.0   100.0 */
   printf("%.1f  %.1f \n", (fptr+1)[0],
          (ara+1)[0]);                /* 200.0   200.0 */
   printf("%.1f  %.1f \n", (fptr+4)[0],
          (ara+4)[0]);                /* 500.0   500.0 */

   /* References both array and pointer using subscripts.
      Notice that subscripts are based from addresses that
      begin before the data in the array and the pointer. */
   printf("%.1f  %.1f \n", (fptr-1)[2],
          (ara-1)[2]);                /* 200.0   200.0 */
   printf("%.1f  %.1f \n", (fptr-20)[23],
          (ara-20)[23]);              /* 400.0   400.0 */
   return;
}
```

The following is the output from this program:

```
100.0
200.0
300.0
400.0
500.0
300.0
100.0   100.0
200.0   200.0
500.0   500.0
200.0   200.0
400.0   400.0
```

Arrays of Strings

An array that a character pointer defines is a ragged-edge array.

You now are ready for one of the most useful applications of character pointers: storing arrays of strings. Actually, you cannot store an array of strings, but you can store an array of character pointers, and each character pointer can point to a string in memory.

By defining an array of character pointers, you define a *ragged-edge array*. A ragged-edge array is similar to two-dimensional tables, except that instead of each row being the same length (the same number of elements), each row contains a different number of characters.

The word *ragged-edge* derives from the use of word processors. A word processor typically can print text fully justified or with a ragged-right margin. The columns of this paragraph are fully justified, because both the left and the right columns align evenly. Letters you write by hand and type on typewriters (remember what a typewriter is?) generally have ragged-right margins. It is very difficult to type so that each line ends in exactly the same right column.

All two-dimensional tables you have seen so far have been fully justified. For example, if you declared a character table with five rows and 20 columns, each row would contain the same number of characters. You could define the table with the following statement:

```
char names[5][20]={ {"George"},
                    {"Michelle"},
                    {"Joe"},
                    {"Marcus"},
                    {"Stephanie"} };
```

This table is shown in Figure 27.5. Notice that much of the table is wasted space. Each row takes 20 characters, even though the data in each row takes far fewer characters. The unfilled elements contain null zeros because C zeros out all elements you do not initialize in arrays. This type of table uses too much memory.

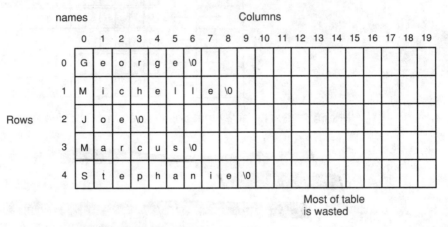

Figure 27.5. A fully justified table.

To fix the memory-wasting problem of fully justified tables, you should declare a single-dimensional array of character pointers. Each pointer points to a string in memory, and the strings do *not* have to be the same length.

Here is the definition for such an array:

```
char *names[5]={ {"George"},
                 {"Michelle"},
                 {"Joe"},
                 {"Marcus"},
                 {"Stephanie"} };
```

This array is single-dimensional. The definition should not confuse you, although it is something you have not seen. The asterisk before names makes this an array of pointers. The type of pointers is character. The strings are *not* being assigned to the array elements, but they are being *pointed to* by the array elements. Figure 27.6 shows this array of pointers. The strings are stored elsewhere in memory. Their actual locations are not critical because each pointer points to the starting character. The strings waste no data. Each string takes only as much memory as needed by the string and its terminating zero. This gives the data its ragged-right appearance.

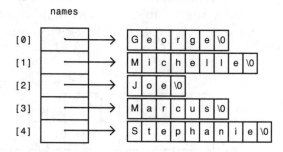

Figure 27.6. The array that points to each of the five strings.

To print the first string, you would use this printf():

```
printf("%s", *names);            /* Prints George */
```

To print the second string, you would use this printf():

```
printf("%s", *(names+1));        /* Prints Michelle */
```

Whenever you dereference any pointer element with the * dereferencing operator, you access one of the strings in the array. You can use a dereferenced element any place you would use a string constant or character array (with strcpy(), strcmp(), and so on).

> **TIP:** Working with pointers to strings is *much* more efficient than working with the strings. For instance, sorting a list of strings takes a lot of time if they are stored as a fully justified table. Sorting strings pointed to by a pointer array is much faster. You swap only pointers during the sort, not entire strings.

Examples

1. Here is a full program that uses the pointer array with five names. The `for` loop controls the `printf()` function, printing each name in the string data. Now you can see why learning about pointer notation for arrays pays off!

```c
/* Filename: C27PTST1.C
   Prints strings pointed to by an array */
#include <stdio.h>
main()
{
    char *name[5]={ {"George"},     /* Defines a ragged-edge */
                    {"Michelle"},   /* array of pointers to  */
                    {"Joe"},        /* strings               */
                    {"Marcus"},
                    {"Stephanie"} };
    int ctr;

    for (ctr=0; ctr<5; ctr++)
        { printf("String #%d is %s \n", (ctr+1), *(name+ctr));
}

    return;
}
```

The following is the output from this program:

```
String #1 is George
String #2 is Michelle
String #3 is Joe
String #4 is Marcus
String #5 is Stephanie
```

2. The following program stores the days of the week in an array. When the user types a number from 1 to 7, the day of the week that matches that number (with Sunday being 1) displays by dereferencing the pointer that points to that string.

```
/* Filename: C27PTST2.C
   Prints the day of the week based on an input value */
#include <stdio.h>
main()
{
    char *days[] = {"Sunday",     /* The seven separate sets */
                "Monday",         /* of braces are optional. */
                "Tuesday",
                "Wednesday",
                "Thursday",
                "Friday",
                "Saturday"};
    int day_num;

    do
      { printf("What is a day number (from 1 to 7)? ");
        scanf(" %d", &day_num);
      } while ((day_num<1) || (day_num>7));     /* Ensures
                                          an accurate number */



    day_num--;                      /* Adjusts for subscript */
    printf("The day is %s\n", *(days+day_num));
    return;
}
```

Review Questions

Answers to review questions are in Appendix B.

1. What is the difference between an array name and a pointer?

2. Assume that `ipointer` points to integers that take four bytes of memory. If you performed the following statement

   ```
   ipointer += 2;
   ```

   how many bytes are added to `ipointer`?

3. Which of the following are equivalent, assuming that `iary` is an integer array and `iptr` is an integer pointer that points to the start of the array?

    a.   `iary` and `iptr`

    b.   `iary[1]` and `*iptr+1`

    c.   `iary[3]` and `*(iptr + 3)`

    d.   `(iary-4)[9]` and `iary[5]`

    e.   `*iary` and `iary[0]`

    f.   `iary[4]` and `*iptr+4`

4. Why is it more efficient to sort a ragged-edge character array than a fully justified string array?

5. Given the following array and pointer definition

```
int ara[] = {1, 2, 3, 4, 5, 6, 7, 8, 9, 10};
int *ip1, *ip2;
```

which of the following is allowed?

    a.   `ip1 = ara;`

    b.   `ip2 = ip1 = &ara[3];`

    c.   `ara = 15;`

    d.   `*(ip2 + 2) = 15;   /* Assuming ip2 and ara are equal */`

Review Exercises

1. Write a program to store your family members' names in a character array of pointers. Print the names.

2. Write a program that asks the user for 15 daily stock market averages and stores those averages in a floating-point array. Using only pointer notation, print the array forward and backward. Using only pointer notation, print the highest and lowest stock market quote in the list.

3. Modify the bubble sort shown in Chapter 24, "Array Processing," so that it sorts using pointer notation. Add this bubble sort to the program in Exercise 2 to print the stock market averages in ascending order.

4. Write a program that requests 10 song titles from the user. Store the titles in an array of character pointers (a ragged-edge array). Print the original titles, print the alphabetized titles, and print the titles in backwards alphabetical order (from Z to A).

Summary

You deserve a break! You now understand the foundation of C's pointers and array notation. As soon as you have mastered this section, you are on your way to thinking in C as you design your programs. C programmers know that C's arrays are pointers in disguise, and they program them accordingly.

Being able to use ragged-edge arrays offers two advantages: You can hold arrays of string data without wasting extra space, and you can quickly change the pointers without having to move the string data around in memory.

As you progress into advanced C concepts, you will appreciate the time you spend mastering pointer notation. The next chapter introduces a new topic called *structures*. Structures enable you to store data in a more unified manner than simple variables have allowed.

Part VII

Structures and File I/O

28

Structures

Using structures, you have the ability to group data and work with that data as a whole. Business data processing uses the concepts of structures in almost every program. Being able to manipulate several variables as a single group makes your programs easier to manage.

This chapter introduces the following concepts:

♦ Structure definitions

♦ Initializing structures

♦ The dot operator (.)

♦ Structure assignment

♦ Nested structures

This chapter is one of the last in the book to present brand-new concepts. The rest of the book builds on the structure concepts you will learn in this chapter.

Introduction to Structures

Structures can have members of different data types.

A *structure* is a collection of one or more variable types. As you know, each element in an array must be the same data type, and you must refer to the entire array by its name. Each element (called a *member*) in a structure can be a different data type.

Suppose you wanted to keep track of your CD music collection. You might want to track the following pieces of information about each CD:

Title

Artist

Number of songs

Cost

Date bought

There would be five members in this CD structure.

TIP: If you have programmed in other computer languages, or if you have ever used a database program, C structures are analogous to file records, and members are analogous to fields in those records.

After deciding on the members, you must decide what data type each member is. The title and artist would both be character arrays, the number of songs would be integer, the cost would be floating-point, and the date would be another character array. This information would be represented like this:

Member Name	Data Type
Title	Character array of 25 characters
Artist	Character array of 20 characters
Number of songs	Integer
Cost	Floating-point
Date bought	Character array of eight characters

Each structure you define can have an associated structure name called a *structure tag*. Structure tags are not required in most cases, but it is generally best to define one for each structure in your program. The structure tag is *not* a variable name. Unlike array names that reference the array as variables, a structure tag is just a label for the structure's format.

You name structure tags yourself, using the same naming rules for variables. If you give the CD structure a structure tag named `cd_collection`, you are telling C that the tag called `cd_collection` looks like two character arrays, followed by an integer, a floating-point value, and a final character array.

A structure tag is actually a newly defined data type that you, the programmer, define. When you want to store an integer, you do not have to define to C what an integer is. C already knows what an integer is. When you want to store a CD collection's data, however, C does not know what format your CD collection will take. You have to tell C (using the example being described here) that you need a new data type. That data type will be your structure tag, called `cd_collection` in this example, and it will look like the structure previously described (two character arrays, integer, floating-point, and character array).

A structure tag is a label for the structure's format.

NOTE: No memory is reserved for structure tags. A structure tag is your own data type. C does not reserve memory for the integer data type until you declare an integer variable. C does not reserve memory for a structure until you declare a structure variable.

Figure 28.1 shows the CD structure, graphically representing the data types within the structure. Notice that there are five members and that each member is a different data type. The entire structure is called `cd collection` because that is the structure tag.

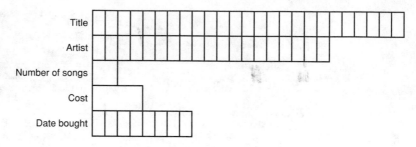

Figure 28.1. The layout of the `cd_collection` structure.

> **NOTE:** The mailing-list application in Appendix F uses a structure to hold people's names, addresses, cities, states, and ZIP codes.

Examples

1. Suppose you were asked to write a program for a company's inventory system. The company had been using a card-file inventory system that tracked the following items:

   Item name
   Quantity in stock
   Quantity on order
   Retail price
   Wholesale price

   This would be a perfect use for a structure containing five members. Before defining the structure, you would have to determine the data types of each member. After asking questions about the range of data (you must know the largest item name, and the most quantity that would ever be on order to ensure your data types will hold the data), you decide to use the following structure tag and data types:

Structure tag: inventory	
Member	Data Type
Item name	Character array of 20 characters
Quantity in stock	`long int`
Quantity on order	`long int`
Retail price	`double`
Wholesale price	`double`

2. Suppose the same company also wanted you to write a program that kept track of their monthly and annual salaries, printing a report at the end of the year that showed each month's individual salary and the total salary at the end of the year.

What would the structure look like? Be careful! This type of data probably does not need a structure. Because all the monthly salaries will be the same data type, a floating-point or a double floating-point array will hold the monthly salaries nicely without the complexity of a structure.

Structures are very useful for keeping track of data that must be grouped, such as inventory data, a customer's name and address data, or an employee data file.

Defining Structures

To define a structure, you must use the `struct` statement. The `struct` statement defines a new data type, with more than one member, for your program. The format of the `struct` statement is this:

```
struct [structure tag]
   {
      member definition;
      member definition;
         :
      member definition;
   } [one or more structure variables];
```

As mentioned earlier, the *structure tag* is optional (hence the brackets in the format). Each *member definition* is a normal variable definition, such as `int i;` or `float sales[20];` or any other valid variable definition, including variable pointers if the structure requires a pointer as a member. At the end of the structure's definition, before the final semicolon, you can specify one or more structure variables.

If you specify a structure variable, you request C to reserve space for that variable. C knows that the variable is not integer, character, or any other internal data type; C knows the variable will be a type that looks like the structure. It might seem strange that the members themselves do not reserve storage, but they don't. The structure variables do. This is made very clear in the examples that follow.

Here is the way you would declare the CD structure:

```
struct cd_collection
  {
    char title[25];
    char artist[20];
    int num_songs;
    float price;
    char date_bought[9];
  } cd1, cd2, cd3;
```

Before going any further, you should be able to answer the following questions about this structure:

♦ What is the structure tag?

♦ How many members are there?

♦ What are the member data types?

♦ What are the member names?

♦ How many structure variables are there?

♦ What are their names?

The structure tag is called `cd_collection`. There are five members, two character arrays, an integer, a floating-point, and a character array. The member names are `title`, `artist`, `num_songs`, `price`, and `date_bought`. There are three structure variables—`cd1`, `cd2`, and `cd3`.

> **TIP:** Many times, you can visualize structure variables as looking like a card-file inventory system. Figure 28.2 shows how you might keep your CD collection in a 3 by 5 card file. Each CD takes one card (representing each structure variable), and the information about each CD (the structure members) is on each card.

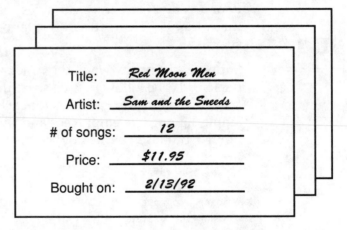

Figure 28.2. Using a card-file CD inventory system.

If you had 1000 CDs, you would have to declare 1000 structure variables. Obviously, you would not want to list that many structure variables at the end of a structure definition. To help define structures for a large number of occurrences, you must define an *array of structures*. Chapter 29, "Arrays of Structures," shows you how to do that. For now, concentrate on familiarizing yourself with structure definitions.

Examples

1. Here is a structure definition of the inventory application described earlier in this chapter.

```
struct inventory
{
    char item_name[20];
    long int in_stock;
    long int order_qty;
    float retail;
    float wholesale;
} item1, item2, item3, item4;
```

Four inventory structure variables are defined. Each structure variable—item1, item2, item3, and item4—looks like the structure.

2. Suppose a company wanted to track its customers and personnel. The following two structure definitions would create five structure variables for each structure. This example, having five employees and five customers, is very limited, but it serves to show how structures can be defined.

```
struct employees
{
    char emp_name[25];              /* Employee's full name */
    char address[30];              /* Employee's address */
    char city[10];
    char state[2];
    long int zip;
    double salary;                    /* Annual salary */
} emp1, emp2, emp3, emp4, emp5;

struct customers
{
    char cust_name[25];             /* Customer's full name */
    char address[30];               /* Customer's address */
    char city[10];
    char state[2];
    long int zip;
    double balance;           /* Balance owed to company */
} cust1, cust2, cust3, cust4, cust5;
```

Each structure has very similar data. A little later in this chapter, you learn how to consolidate similar member definitions by creating nested structures.

> **TIP:** Put comments to the right of members to document the purpose of the members.

Initializing Structure Data

You can define a structure's data when you declare the structure.

There are two ways to initialize members of a structure. You can initialize members when you declare a structure, and you can initialize a structure within the body of the program. Most programs lend themselves to the latter method, because you do not always know structure data when you write your program.

Here is an example of a structure declared and initialized at the same time:

```
struct cd_collection
   {
   char title[25];
   char artist[20];
   int num_songs;
   float price;
   char date_bought[9];
   } cd1 = {"Red Moon Men", "Sam and the Sneeds",
            12, 11.95, "02/13/92"};
```

When first learning about structures, you might be tempted to initialize members individually inside the structure, such as

```
char artist[20]="Sam and the Sneeds";        /* Invalid */
```

You cannot initialize individual members because they are *not* variables. You can assign only values to variables. The only structure variable in this structure is cd1. The braces must enclose the data you initialize in the structure variables, just as they enclose data when you initialize arrays.

This method of initializing structure variables gets tedious when there are several structure variables (as there usually are). Putting the data into several variables, each set of data enclosed in braces, gets messy and takes too much space in your code.

More importantly, you usually will not even know the contents of the structure variables. Generally, the user enters data to be stored in structures, or you read them from a disk file.

Use the dot operator to initialize members of structures.

A better approach to initializing structures is to use the *dot operator* (.). The dot operator is one way to initialize individual members of a structure variable within the body of your program. With the dot operator, you can treat each structure member almost as if it were a regular nonstructure variable.

The format of the dot operator is

```
structure_variable_name.member_name
```

A structure variable name must *always* precede the dot operator, and a member name must always appear after the dot operator. Using the dot operator is very easy, as the following examples show.

Examples

1. Here is a simple program that uses the CD collection structure and the dot operator to initialize the structure. Notice that the program treats members as if they were regular variables when combined with the dot operator.

Identify the program and include the necessary header file. Define a CD structure variable with five members. Fill the CD structure variable with data, then print it.

BEGIN

Define a CD structure

Assign data to structure members

Print structure members

END

```
/* Filename: C28ST1.C
   Structure initialization with the CD collection */
#include <stdio.h>
#include <string.h>
main()
{
    struct cd_collection
    {
      char title[25];
      char artist[20];
      int num_songs;
      float price;
      char date_bought[9];
    } cd1;
```

```
        /* Initialize members here */
        strcpy(cd1.title, "Red Moon Men");
        strcpy(cd1.artist, "Sam and the Sneeds");
        cd1.num_songs=12;
        cd1.price=11.95;
        strcpy(cd1.date_bought, "02/13/92");

        /* Print the data to the screen */
        printf("Here is the CD information:\n\n");
        printf("Title: %s \n", cd1.title);
        printf("Artist: %s \n", cd1.artist);
        printf("Songs: %d \n", cd1.num_songs);
        printf("Price: %.2f \n", cd1.price);
        printf("Date bought: %s \n", cd1.date_bought);

        return;
}
```

Here is the output from this program:

```
Here is the CD information:

Title: Red Moon Men
Artist: Sam and the Sneeds
Songs: 12
Price: 11.95
Date bought: 02/13/92
```

2. By using the dot operator, you can get structure data from the keyboard with any of the data-input functions you know, such as scanf(), gets(), and getchar().

The following program asks the user for student information. To keep the example reasonably short, only two students are defined in the program.

```
/* Filename: C28ST2.C
   Structure input with student data */
#include <stdio.h>
#include <string.h>
main()
{
   struct students
```

```
{
  char name[25];
  int age;
  float average;
} student1, student2;

/* Get data for two students */
printf("What is first student's name? ");
gets(student1.name);
printf("What is the first student's age? ");
scanf(" %d", &student1.age);
printf("What is the first student's average? ");
scanf(" %f", &student1.average);

fflush(stdin);    /* Clear input buffer for next input */

printf("\nWhat is second student's name? ");
gets(student2.name);
printf("What is the second student's age? ");
scanf(" %d", &student2.age);
printf("What is the second student's average? ");
scanf(" %f", &student2.average);

/* Print the data */
printf("\n\nHere is the student information you
entered:\n\n");
printf("Student #1:\n");
printf("Name:    %s\n", student1.name);
printf("Age:     %d\n", student1.age);
printf("Average: %.1f\n", student1.average);

printf("\nStudent #2:\n");
printf("Name:    %s\n", student2.name);
printf("Age:     %d\n", student2.age);
printf("Average: %.1f\n", student2.average);

return;
}
```

Figure 28.3 shows the output from this program.

```
What is first student's name? Joe Sanders
What is the first student's age? 13
What is the first student's average? 78.4

What is second student's name? Mary Reynolds
What is the second student's age? 12
What is the second student's average? 98.9


Here is the student information you entered:

Student #1:
Name:    Joe Sanders
Age:     13
Average: 78.4

Student #2:
Name:    Mary Reynolds
Age:     12
Average: 98.9
```

Figure 28.3. The user is filling structure variables with values.

Define structures globally and structure variables locally.

3. Structure variables are passed by copy, not by address as with arrays. Therefore, if you fill a structure in a function, you must return it to the calling function in order for the calling function to recognize it, or use global structure variables, which is generally not recommended.

A good solution to the local/global structure problem is this: Define your structures globally without *any* structure variables. Define all your structure variables locally to the functions that need them. As long as your structure definition is global, you can declare local structure variables from that structure. All subsequent examples in this book use this method.

This is where structure tag plays an important role. Use the structure tag to define local structure variables. The following program is similar to the previous one. Notice that the student structure is defined globally with *no structure variables.* In each function, local structure variables are declared by referring to the structure tag. The structure tag keeps you from having to redefine the structure members every time you define a new structure variable.

```
/* Filename: C28ST3.C
   Structure input with student data passed to functions */
#include <stdio.h>
#include <string.h>
struct students fill_structs(struct students student_var);
void pr_students(struct students student_var);
void main(void);

struct students                          /* A global structure */
   {
     char name[25];
     int age;
     float average;
   };                              /* No memory reserved yet */

void main(void)
{
   struct students student1, student2;    /* Defines two
                                             local variables */

   /* Call function to fill structure variables */
   student1 = fill_structs(student1);           /* student1
                     is passed by copy, so it must be
                     returned for main() to recognize it */
   student2 = fill_structs(student2);

   /* Print the data */
   printf("\n\nHere is the student information you");
   printf(" entered:\n\n");
   pr_students(student1);    /* Print first student's data */
   pr_students(student2);    /* Print second student's data */

   return;
}

struct students fill_structs(struct students student_var)
{
   /* Get student's data */
   fflush(stdin);     /* Clear input buffer for next input */
   printf("What is student's name? ");
   gets(student_var.name);
   printf("What is the student's age? ");
```

```
    scanf(" %d", &student_var.age);
    printf("What is the student's average? ");
    scanf(" %f", &student_var.average);

    return (student_var);
}

void pr_students(struct students student_var)
{
    printf("Name:    %s\n", student_var.name);
    printf("Age:     %d\n", student_var.age);
    printf("Average: %.1f\n", student_var.average);
    return;
}
```

The prototype and definition of the `fill_structs()` function might seem complicated, but it follows the same pattern you have seen throughout this book. Before a function name, you must declare `void` or put the return data type if the function returns a value. `fill_structs()` does return a value, and the type of value it returns is `struct students`.

4. Because structure data is nothing more than regular variables grouped together, feel free to calculate using structure members. As long as you use the dot operator, you can treat structure members just as you would other variables.

The following example asks for a customer's balance and uses a discount rate, included in the customer's structure, to calculate a new balance. To keep the example short, the structure's data is initialized at variable declaration time.

This program does not actually require structures because only one customer is used. Individual variables could have been used, but they would not illustrate calculating with structures.

```
/* Filename: C28CUST.C
   Updates a customer balance in a structure */
#include <stdio.h>

struct customer_rec
    {
```

```
        char cust_name[25];
        double balance;
        float dis_rate;
    } ;

main()
{
    struct customer_rec customer = {"Steve Thompson",
                                    2431.23, .25};

    printf("Before the update, %s", customer.cust_name);
    printf(" has a balance of $%.2f\n", customer.balance);

    /* Update the balance */
    customer.balance *= (1.0-customer.dis_rate);

    printf("After the update, %s", customer.cust_name);
    printf(" has a balance of $%.2f\n", customer.balance);
    return;
}
```

5. You can copy the members of one structure variable to the members of another as long as both structures have the same format. Some older versions of C require you to copy each member individually when you want to copy one structure variable to another, but ANSI C makes duplicating structure variables easy.

   Being able to copy one structure variable to another will seem more meaningful when you read Chapter 29, "Arrays of Structures."

   The following program declares three structure variables, but initializes only the first one with data. The other two are then initialized by assigning the first structure variable to them.

```
/* Filename: C28STCPY.C
   Demonstrates assigning one structure to another */
#include <stdio.h>

struct student
{
```

```
    char st_name[25];
    char grade;
    int age;
    float average;
};

main()
{
    struct student std1 = {"Joe Brown", 'A', 13, 91.4};
    struct student std2, std3;          /* Not initialized */

    std2 = std1;                /* Copies each member of std1 */
    std3 = std1;                /* to std2 and std3           */


    printf("The contents of std2:\n");
    printf("%s, %c, ", std2.st_name, std2.grade);
    printf("%d, %.1f\n\n", std2.age, std2.average);

    printf("The contents of std3:\n");
    printf("%s, %c, ", std3.st_name, std3.grade);
    printf("%d, %.1f\n", std3.age, std3.average);
    return;
}
```

Copy members
of one structure
to another

Here is the output from the program:

```
The contents of std2
Joe Brown, A, 13, 91.4

The contents of std3
Joe Brown, A, 13, 91.4
```

Notice that each member of std1 was assigned to std2 and std3 with two single assignments.

Nested Structures

C gives you the ability to nest one structure definition within another. This saves time when you are writing programs that use similar structures. You have to define the common members only once in their own structure and then use that structure as a member in another structure.

The following two structure definitions illustrate this point:

```
struct employees
{
   char emp_name[25];              /* Employee's full name */
   char address[30];               /* Employee's address */
   char city[10];
   char state[2];
   long int zip;
   double salary;                     /* Annual salary */
};

struct customers
{
   char cust_name[25];             /* Customer's full name */
   char address[30];               /* Customer's address */
   char city[10];
   char state[2];
   long int zip;
   double balance;             /* Balance owed to company */
};
```

These structures hold different data. One structure is for employee data and the other holds customer data. Even though the data should be kept separate (you don't want to send a customer a paycheck!), the structure definitions have a lot of overlap and can be consolidated by creating a third structure.

Suppose you created the following structure:

```
struct address_info
{
   char address[30];          /* Common address information */
   char city[10];
   char state[2];
   long int zip;
```

```
};
```
This structure could then be used *as a member* in the other structures like this:

```
struct employees
{
    char emp_name[25];          /* Employee's full name */
    struct address_info e_address;   /* Employee's address */
    double salary;                   /* Annual salary */
};

struct customers
{
    char cust_name[25];         /* Customer's full name */
    struct address_info c_address;   /* Customer's address */
    double balance;             /* Balance owed to company */
};
```

It is important to realize that there is a total of three structures, and that they have the tags address_info, employees, and customers. How many members does the employees structure have? If you answered three, you are correct. There are three members in both employees and customers. The employees structure has the structure of a character array, followed by the address_info structure, followed by the double floating-point member salary. Figure 28.4 shows how these structures look.

As soon as you define a structure, that structure is then a new data type in the program and can be used anywhere a data type (such as int, float, and so on) can appear.

You can assign members values using the dot operator. To assign the customer balance a number, you can type something like this:

```
customer.balance = 5643.24;
```

The nested structure might seem to pose a problem. How can you assign a value to one of the nested members? By using the dot operator, you must nest the dot operator just as you nest the structure definitions. You would assign a value to the customer's ZIP code like this:

```
customer.c_address.zip = 34312;
```

employees:

customers:

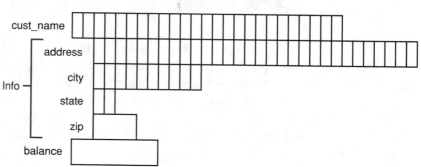

Figure 28.4. Defining a nested structure.

To assign a value to the employee's ZIP code, you would do this:

```
employee.e_address.zip = 59823;
```

Review Questions

Answers to review questions are in Appendix B.

1. What is the difference between structures and arrays?

2. What are the individual elements of a structure called?

3. What are the two ways to initialize members of a structure?

4. Do you pass structures by copy or by address?

5. True or false: The following structure definition reserves storage in memory:

```
struct crec
   { char name[25];
     int age;
     float sales[5];
     long int num;
   }
```

6. Should you declare a structure globally or locally?

7. Should you declare a structure variable globally or locally?

8. How many members does the following structure declaration contain?

```
struct item
   {
     int quantity;
     struct part_rec item_desc;
     float price;
     char date_bought[8];
   };
```

Review Exercises

1. Write a structure a video store can use in a program that tracks their video tape inventory. Make sure the structure includes the tape title, the length of the tape (in minutes), the cost of the tape, the rental price of the tape, and the date of the movie's release.

2. Write a program that uses the structure you declared in Exercise 1. Define three structure variables and initialize them *when you declare the variables* with data. Print the data to the screen.

3. Write a teacher's program that keeps track of 10 students' names, ages, letter grades, and IQs. Use 10 different structure variable names and get the data for the students in a `for` loop from the keyboard. Print the data on the printer when the teacher finishes entering the information for all the students.

Summary

With structures you have the ability to group data in more flexible ways than arrays allow. Your structures can contain members of different data types. You can initialize the structures either at declaration time or during the program with the dot operator.

Structures become even more powerful when you declare arrays of structure variables. Chapter 29, "Arrays of Structures," shows you how to declare several structure variables without giving them each a different name. This lets you step through structures much quicker with loop constructs.

Arrays of Structures

This chapter builds on the previous one by showing you how to create many structures for your data. After creating an array of structures, you can store many occurrences of your data values.

Arrays of structures are good for storing a complete employee file, inventory file, or any other set of data that fits within the structure format. Whereas arrays provide a handy way to store several values that are the same type, with arrays of structures you can store several values of different types together, grouped as structures.

This chapter introduces the following concepts:

- ♦ Creating arrays of structures
- ♦ Initializing arrays of structures
- ♦ Referencing elements from a structure array
- ♦ Arrays as members

Many C programmers use arrays of structures as a prelude to storing their data in a disk file. You can input and calculate your disk data in arrays of structures, and then store those structures in memory. Arrays of structures also provide a means of holding data you read from the disk.

Declaring Arrays of Structures

It is very easy to declare an array of structures. Specify the number of reserved structures, inside array brackets, when you declare the structure variable. Consider the following structure definition:

```
struct stores
    { int employees;
        int registers;
        double sales;
    } store1, store2, store3, store4, store5;
```

This structure should pose no problem for you to understand because there are no new commands used in the structure declaration. This structure declaration creates five structure variables. Figure 29.1 shows how C stores these five structures in memory. Each of the structure variables has three members—two integers followed by a double floating-point value.

Figure 29.1. The structure of store1, store2, store3, store4, and store5.

If the fourth store increased its employee count by three, you could update the store's employee number with the following assignment statement:

```
store4.employees += 3;          /* Add 3 to this store's
                                   employee count */
```

Suppose that the fifth store just opened and you want to initialize its members with data. If the stores are a chain and the new store is similar to one of the others, you might begin initializing the store's data by assigning each of its members the same data as another store's like this:

```
store5 = store2;                /* Define initial values
                                   for the store5 members */
```

Arrays of structures make working with large numbers of structure variables manageable.

Such structure declarations are fine for a small number of structures, but if the stores were a national chain, five structure variables would not be enough. Suppose there were 1000 stores. You would not want to create 1000 different store variables and work with each one individually. It would be much easier to create an array of store structures.

Consider the following structure declaration:

```
struct stores
    { int employees;
        int registers;
        double sales;
    } store[1000];
```

In one quick declaration, this code creates 1000 store structures, each one containing three members. Figure 29.2 shows how these structure variables appear in memory. Notice the name of each individual structure variable: `store[0]`, `store[1]`, `store[2]`, and so on.

CAUTION: Be careful that your computer does not run out of memory when you create a large number of structures. Arrays of structures quickly consume valuable memory. You might have to create fewer structures, storing more data in disk files and less data in memory.

Figure 29.2. **An array of the** store **structures.**

The element store[2] is an array element. This array element, unlike the others you have seen, is a structure variable. Therefore, it contains three members, each of which you can reference with the dot operator.

The dot operator works the same way for structure array elements as it does for regular structure variables. If the number of employees for the fifth store (store[4]) increased by three, you could update the structure variable like this:

```
store[4].employees += 3;      /* Add 3 to this store's
                                 employee count */
```

You can assign complete structures to one another using array notation also. To assign all the members of the 20th store to the 45th store, you would do this:

```
store[44] = store[19];      /* Copy all members from the
                               20th store to the 45th */
```

The rules of arrays are still in force here. Each element of the array called store is the *very same data type*. The data type of store is struct stores. As with any array, each element must be the same data type; you cannot mix data types within the same array. This array's data type happens to be a structure you created containing three members. The data type for store[316] is the same for store[981] and store[74].

The name of the array, store, is a pointer constant to the starting element of the array, store[0]. Therefore, you can use pointer notation to reference the stores. To assign `store[60]` the same value as `store[23]`, you can reference the two elements like this:

```
*(store+60) = *(store+23);
```

You also can mix array and pointer notation, such as

```
store[60] = *(store+23);
```

and get the same results.

You can increase the sales of `store[8]` by 40 percent using pointer or subscript notation as well, as in

Increase
sales
by 40%

```
store[8].sales = (*(store+8)).sales * 1.40;
```

The extra pair of parentheses are required because the dot operator has precedence over the dereferencing symbol in C's hierarchy of operators (see Appendix D). Of course, in this case, the code is not helped by the pointer notation. The following is a much clearer way to increase the `sales` by 40 percent:

```
store[8].sales *= 1.40;
```

Keep Your Array Notation Straight

You would never access the member `sales` like this:

```
store.sales[8] = 3234.54;          /* Invalid */
```

Array subscripts follow only array elements. `sales` is not an array; it was declared as being a double floating-point number. `store` can never be used *without* a subscript (unless you are using pointer notation).

Here is a corrected version of the previous assignment statement:

```
store[8].sales=3234.54;            /* Correctly assigns
                                      the value          */
```

The following examples build an inventory data-entry system for a mail-order firm using an array of structures. There is very little new you have to know when working with arrays of structures. Concentrate on the notation used when accessing arrays of structures and their members to get comfortable with the arrays of structures notation.

Examples

1. Suppose you work for a mail-order company that sells disk drives. You are given the task of writing a tracking program for the 125 different drives you sell. You must keep track of the following information:

   Storage capacity in megabytes
   Access time in milliseconds
   Vendor code (A, B, C, or D)
   Cost
   Price

   Because there are 125 different disk drives in the inventory, the data will fit nicely into an array of structures. Each array element is a structure containing the five members described in the list.

   The following structure definition defines the inventory:

```
struct inventory
{
     long int storage;
     int access_time;
     char vendor_code;
     double code;
     double price;
} drive[125];  /* Defines 125 occurrences of the structure */
```

2. When working with a large array of structures, your first concern should be how the data will be input into the array elements. The application determines the best method of data-entry.

   For instance, if you are converting from an older computerized inventory system, you will have to write a conversion program that reads the inventory file in its native format and saves it to a new file in the format needed by your C programs. This is no easy task. It requires that you have extensive knowledge of the system from which you are converting.

   If you are writing a computerized inventory system for the first time, your job is a little easier because you do not need to worry about converting the old files. You still must realize that someone has to type the data into the computer. You will have to write a data-entry program that receives each inventory item from the keyboard and saves it to a disk file. You should give the user a chance to edit inventory data to correct any data that he or she originally might have typed incorrectly.

One of the reasons this book waits until the last chapters to introduce disk files is that disk file formats and structures share a common bond. As soon as you store data in a structure, or more often, in an array of structures, you can very easily write that data to a disk file using straightforward disk I/O commands.

The following program takes the array of disk drive structures shown in the previous example and adds a data-entry function so that the user can enter data into the array of structures. The program is menu-driven. The user has a choice, when starting the program, to add data, print data to the screen, or exit the program. Because you have yet to see disk I/O commands, the data in the array of structures goes away when the program ends. As mentioned earlier, saving those structures to disk is an easy task after you learn C's disk I/O commands. For now, concentrate on the manipulation of the structures.

This program is longer than many you have seen in this book, but if you have followed the discussion of structures and the dot operator, you should have little trouble following the code.

Identify the program and include the necessary header files. Define a structure that describes the format of each inventory item. Create an array of structures called disk.

Display a menu that gives the user the choice of entering new inventory data, displaying the data on-screen, or quitting the program. If the user wants to enter new inventory items, prompt the user for each item and store the data into the array of structures. If the user wants to see the inventory, loop through each inventory item in the array, displaying each one on-screen.

```
/* Filename: C29DSINV.C
   Data-entry program for a disk drive company */
#include <stdio.h>
#include <stdlib.h>

struct inventory              /* Global structure definition */
{
   long int storage;
   int access_time;
   char vendor_code;
   float cost;
   float price;
};              /* No structure variables defined globally */

void disp_menu(void);
struct inventory enter_data();
void see_data(struct inventory disk[125], int num_items);
void main(void);

void main(void)
{
struct inventory disk[125];   /* Local array of structures */
   int ans;
   int num_items=0;                    /* Number of total items
                                          in the inventory */

   do
     {
        do
         { disp_menu();   /* Display menu of user choices */
           scanf(" %d", &ans);       /* Get user's request */
         } while ((ans<1) || (ans>3));

         switch (ans)
     { case (1): { disk[num_items] = enter_data(); /* Enter
                                           disk data */
                num_items++; /* Increment number of items */
                break; }
         case (2): { see_data(disk, num_items);  /* Display
                                           disk data */
                break; }
         default : { break; }
```

```
        }
        } while (ans!=3);              /* Quit program
                                          when user is through */

    return;
}

void disp_menu(void)
{

    printf("\n\n*** Disk Drive Inventory System ***\n\n");
    printf("Do you want to:\n\n");
    printf("\t1. Enter new item in inventory\n\n");
    printf("\t2. See inventory data\n\n");
    printf("\t3. Exit the program\n\n");
    printf("What is your choice? ");
    return;
}

struct inventory enter_data()
{
    struct inventory disk_item;    /* Local variable to fill
                                      with input */

    printf("\n\nWhat is the next drive's storage in bytes? ");
    scanf(" %ld", &disk_item.storage);
    printf("What is the drive's access time in ms? ");
    scanf(" %d", &disk_item.access_time);
    printf("What is the drive's vendor code (A, B, C, or D)? ");
    fflush(stdin);   /* Discard input buffer
                        before getting character */
    disk_item.vendor_code = getchar();
    getchar();   /* Discard carriage return */
    printf("What is the drive's cost? ");
    scanf(" %f", &disk_item.cost);
    printf("What is the drive's price? ");
    scanf(" %f", &disk_item.price);

    return (disk_item);
}

void see_data(struct inventory disk[125], int num_items)
```

```
{
    int ctr;
    printf("\n\nHere is the inventory listing:\n\n");
    for (ctr=0;ctr<num_items;ctr++)
        {
        printf("Storage: %ld\t", disk[ctr].storage);
        printf("Access time: %d\n", disk[ctr].access_time);
        printf("Vendor code: %c\t", disk[ctr].vendor_code);
        printf("Cost: $%.2f\t", disk[ctr].cost);
        printf("Price: $%.2f\n", disk[ctr].price);
        }
    return;
}
```

Figure 29.3 shows an item being entered into the inventory
file. Figure 29.4 shows the inventory listing being displayed
to the screen. There are many features and error-checking
functions you can add, but this program is the foundation of
a more comprehensive inventory system. You can easily
adapt it to a different type of inventory, a video tape collection, a coin collection, or any other tracking system just by
changing the structure definition and the member names
throughout the program.

```
*** Disk Drive Inventory System ***

Do you want to:

        1. Enter new item in inventory

        2. See inventory data

        3. Exit the program

What is your choice? 1


What is the next drive's storage in bytes? 120000
What is the drive's access time in ms? 17
What is the drive's vendor code (A, B, C, or D)? A
What is the drive's cost? 121.56
What is the drive's price? 240.00
```

Figure 29.3. Entering inventory information.

```
What is your choice? 2

Here is the inventory listing:

Storage: 120000 Access time: 17
Vendor code: A  Cost: $121.56    Price: $240.00
Storage: 320000 Access time: 21
Vendor code: D  Cost: $230.85    Price: $409.57
Storage: 280000 Access time: 19
Vendor code: C  Cost: $210.84    Price: $398.67


*** Disk Drive Inventory System ***

Do you want to:

        1. Enter new item in inventory

        2. See inventory data

        3. Exit the program

What is your choice? 3
```

Figure 29.4. Displaying the inventory data.

Arrays as Members

Members of structures themselves can be arrays. Array members pose no new problems, but you have to be careful when you access individual array elements. Keeping track of arrays of structures that contain array members might seem like a great deal of work on your part, but there is really nothing to it.

Consider the following structure definition. This statement declares an array of 100 structures, each structure holding payroll information for a company. Two of the members, name and department, are arrays.

```
struct payroll
  { char name[25];                /* Employee name array */
    int dependents;
    char department[10];          /* Department name array */
    float salary;
  } employee[100];                /* An array of 100 employees */
```

Figure 29.5 shows what these structures look like. The first and third members are arrays. name is an array of 25 characters, and department is an array of 10 characters.

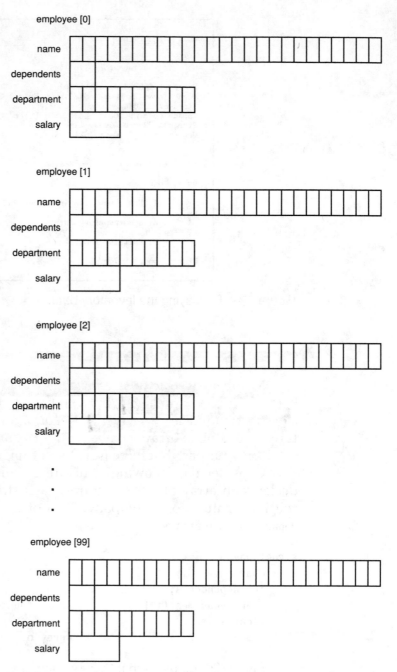

Figure 29.5. The payroll data.

Suppose that you need to save the 25th employee's initial in a character variable. Assuming that `initial` is already declared as a character variable, the following statement assigns the employee's initial to `initial`:

```
initial = employee[24].name[0];
```

The double subscripts might look confusing, but the dot operator requires a structure variable on its left (`employee[24]`) and a member on its right (`name`'s first array element). Being able to refer to member arrays makes the processing of character data in structures simple.

Examples

1. Suppose that an employee got married and wanted her name changed in the payroll file. (She happens to be the 45th employee in the array of structures.) Given the payroll structure described in the previous section, this would assign a new name to her structure:

```
strcpy(employee[44].name, "Mary Larson");   /* Assign
                                                a new name */
```

When you refer to a structure variable using the dot operator, you can use regular commands and functions to process the data in the structures.

2. A bookstore wants to catalog its inventory of books. The following program creates an array of 100 structures. Each structure contains several types of variables, including arrays. This program is the data-entry portion of a larger inventory system. Study the references to the members to see how member arrays are used.

```
/* Filename: C29BOOK.C
   Bookstore data-entry program */
#include <stdio.h>

struct inventory
  { char title[25];                       /* Book's title      */
```

```
        char pub_date[19];              /* Publication date */
        char author[20];               /* Author's name   */
        int num;                        /* Number in stock */
        int on_order;                   /* Number on order */
        float retail;                   /* Retail price    */
    };

main()
{
    struct inventory book[100];
    int total=0;                /* Total books in inventory */
    int ans;

    do     /* This program enters data into the structures */
      { printf("Book #%d:\n", (total+1));
      printf("What is the title? ");
      gets(book[total].title);
      printf("What is the publication date? ");
      gets(book[total].pub_date);
      printf("Who is the author? ");
      gets(book[total].author);
      printf("How many books of this title are there? ");
      scanf(" %d", &book[total].num);
      printf("How many are on order? ");
      scanf(" %d", &book[total].on_order);
      printf("What is the retail price? ");
      scanf(" %f", &book[total].retail);
      fflush(stdin);
      printf("\nAre there more books? (Y/N) ");
      ans=getchar();
      fflush(stdin);              /* Discard carriage return */
      ans=toupper(ans);              /* Convert to uppercase */
      if (ans=='Y')
        { total++;
          continue; }
      } while (ans=='Y');
    return;
}
```

Much more is needed to make this a usable inventory program. An exercise at the end of this chapter recommends
ways you can improve on this program by adding a printing

routine and a title and author search. One of the first things you should do is put the data-entry routine in a separate function to make the code more modular. Because this example is so short, and because the program performs only one task (data-entry), there was no advantage to putting the data-entry task into a separate function.

3. Here is a very comprehensive example of the steps you might go through to write a C program. You are getting to the point where you understand enough of the C language to start writing some advanced programs. Sadly, this book is coming to an end. I hope it is fulfilling its goal of introducing the C language in a conversational style with many examples along the way.

Assume that you have been hired by a local bookstore to write a magazine inventory system. You need to track the following:

> Magazine title (at most, 25 characters)
> Publisher (at most, 20 characters)
> Month (1, 2, 3,...12)
> Publication year
> Number of copies in stock
> Number of copies on order
> Price of magazine (dollars and cents)

Suppose that there is a projected maximum of 1000 magazine titles that the store will ever carry. This means that you need 1000 occurrences of the structure, not 1000 magazines total. Here is a good structure definition for such an inventory:

```
struct mag_info
   { char title[25];
     char pub[25];
     int month;
     int year;
     int stock_copies;
     int order_copies;
     float price;
   } mags[1000];            /* Define 1000 occurrences */
```

Because this program will consist of more than one function, it will be best to declare the structure globally, and the structure variables locally within the functions that need them.

This program needs three basic functions: a `main()` controlling function, a data-entry function, and a data printing function. You can add much more, but this is a good start for an inventory system. To keep the length of this example reasonable, assume that the user will want to enter several magazines, then print them. (To make the program more "usable," you would want to add a menu so that the user can control when he or she adds and prints the information, as well as add more error-checking and editing capabilities.)

Here is an example of the complete data-entry and printing program with prototypes. The arrays of structures are passed between the functions from `main()`.

```
/* Filename: C29MAG.C
   Magazine inventory program for adding and displaying
   a bookstore's magazines */
#include <stdio.h>
#include <ctype.h>

struct mag_info
   { char title[25];
     char pub[25];
     int month;
     int year;
     int stock_copies;
     int order_copies;
     float price;
   };

struct mag_info fill_mags(struct mag_info mag);
void print_mags(struct mag_info mags[], int mag_ctr);
void main(void);

void main(void)
{
```

Print every member of every structure in the array

```
    struct mag_info mags[1000];
    int mag_ctr=0;              /* Number of magazine titles */
    char ans;

    do
    {                           /* Assumes that there will be
                                   at least one magazine filled */
      mags[mag_ctr] = fill_mags(mags[mag_ctr]);
      printf("Do you want to enter another magazine? ");
      fflush(stdin);
      ans = getchar();
      fflush(stdin);            /* Discard carriage return */
      if (toupper(ans) == 'Y')
        { mag_ctr++; }
        } while (toupper(ans) == 'Y');
      print_mags(mags, mag_ctr);
      return;                   /* Return to operating system */
}

void print_mags(struct mag_info mags[], int mag_ctr)
{
   int i;
   for (i=0; i<=mag_ctr; i++)
     { printf("\n\nMagazine %d:\n", i+1);   /* Adjust for
                                                subscript */
       printf("\nTitle: %s \n", mags[i].title);
       printf("\tPublisher: %s \n", mags[i].pub);
       printf("\tPub. Month: %d \n", mags[i].month);
       printf("\tPub. Year: %d \n", mags[i].year);
       printf("\tIn-stock: %d \n", mags[i].stock_copies);
       printf("\tOn order: %d \n", mags[i].order_copies);
       printf("\tPrice: %.2f \n", mags[i].price);
     }
   return;
}

struct mag_info fill_mags(struct mag_info mag)
{
   puts("\n\nWhat is the title? ");
   gets(mag.title);
   puts("Who is the publisher? ");
   gets(mag.pub);
```

```
        puts("What is the month (1, 2, ..., 12)? ");
        scanf(" %d", &mag.month);
        puts("What is the year? ");
        scanf(" %d", &mag.year);
        puts("How many copies in stock? ");
        scanf(" %d", &mag.stock_copies);
        puts("How many copies on order? ");
        scanf(" %d", &mag.order_copies);
        puts("How much is the magazine? ");
        scanf(" %f", &mag.price);
        return (mag);
    }
```

Review Questions

Answers to review questions are in Appendix B.

1. True or false: Each element in an array of structures must be the same type.

2. What is the advantage of creating an array of structures instead of using individual variable names for each structure variable?

3. Given the following structure declaration:

```
struct item
    { char part_no[8];
      char descr[20];
      float price;
      int in_stock;
    } inventory[100];
```

a. How would you assign a price of 12.33 to the 33rd item's in-stock quantity?

b. How would you assign the first character of the 12th item's part number the value of X?

c. How would you assign the 97th inventory item the same values as the 63rd?

4. Given the following structure declaration:

```
struct item
  { char desc[20];
    int num;
    float cost;
  } inventory[25];
```

a. What is wrong with the following statement?

```
item[1].cost = 92.32;
```

b. What is wrong with the following statement?

```
strcpy(inventory.desc, "Widgets");
```

c. What is wrong with the following statement?

```
inventory.cost[10] = 32.12;
```

Review Exercises

1. Write a program that stores an array of friends' names, phone numbers, and addresses and prints them two ways: with their full name and address, or with just their name and phone number for a phone listing.

2. Add a sort function to the program in Exercise 1 so that you can print your friends' names in alphabetical order. (Hint: You have to make the member holding the names a character pointer.)

3. Expand on the book data-entry program C29BOOK.C by adding features to make it more usable (such as search book by author, by title, and be able to print an inventory of books on order).

Summary

You have mastered structures and arrays of structures. Many useful inventory and tracking programs are ready to be written using structures. By being able to create arrays of structures, you can now create several occurrences of data.

The next step in the process of learning C is to save those structures and other data to disk files. The next two chapters explore the concepts of disk file processing.

Sequential Files

So far, every example in this book has processed data that resided inside the program listing or came from the keyboard. You assigned constants and variables to other variables and created new data values from expressions. The programs also received input with scanf(), gets(), and the character input functions.

The data that is created by the user and assigned to variables with assignment statements is sufficient for some applications. With the large volumes of data that most real-world applications need to process, however, you need a better way of storing that data. For all but the smallest computer programs, disk files offer the solution.

After storing data on the disk, the computer helps you enter, find, change, and delete the data. The computer and C are simply tools to help you manage and process data. This chapter focuses on disk and file processing concepts and teaches you the first of two methods of disk access, *sequential file access*.

This chapter introduces you to the following concepts:

♦ An overview of disk files

♦ The types of files

♦ Processing data on the disk

♦ Sequential file access

♦ File I/O functions

After this chapter, you will be ready to tackle the more advanced random file access methods covered in Chapter 31, "Random Access Files." If you have programmed computerized data files with another programming language, you might be surprised at how C borrows from other programming languages, especially BASIC, when working with disk files. If you are new to disk file processing, be assured that disk files are simple to create and read.

Why Use a Disk?

The typical computer system has much less memory storage than hard disk storage. Your disk drive holds much more data than can fit in your computer's RAM. This is the primary reason for using the disk for your data. The disk memory, because it is nonvolatile, also lasts longer. When you power-off your computer, the disk memory is not erased, but RAM is erased. Also, when your data changes, you (or more important, your users) do not have to edit the program and look for a set of assignment statements. Instead, the users run previously-written programs that make changes to the disk data.

This makes programming more difficult at first because programs have to be written to change the data on the disk. However, nonprogrammers then can use the programs and modify the data without knowing how to program.

Disks hold more data than computer memory.

The capacity of your disk makes it a perfect place to store your data as well as your programs. Think about what would happen if all data had to be stored with a program's assignment statements. What if the Social Security office in Washington, D.C., asked you to write a C program to compute, average, filter, sort, and print the name and address of each person in their office's computer data files? Would you want your program to include millions of assignment statements? Not only would you not want the program to hold that much data, but it could not do so because only relatively small amounts of data fit in a program before you run out of RAM.

By storing data on your disk, you are much less limited because you have more storage. Your disk can hold as much data as you have disk capacity. Also, if your disk requirements grow, you usually can increase your disk space, whereas you cannot always add more RAM to your computer.

> **NOTE:** ANSI C cannot access the special extended memory or expanded memory that some computers have.

When working with disk files, C does not have to access much RAM because C reads data from your disk drive and processes the data only parts at a time. Not all your disk data has to reside in RAM for C to process it. C reads some data, processes it, and then reads some more. If C requires disk data a second time, it rereads that place on the disk.

Types of Disk File Access

Your programs can access files two ways: through sequential access or random access. Your application determines the method you should choose. The access mode of a file determines how you read, write, change, and delete data from the file. Some of your files can be accessed in both ways, sequentially and randomly, as long as your programs are written properly and the data lends itself to both types of file access.

A sequential file must be accessed in the same order the file was written. This is analogous to cassette tapes: You play music in the same order it was recorded. (You can quickly fast-forward or rewind through songs that you do not want to listen to, but the order of the songs dictates what you do to play the song you want.) It is difficult, and sometimes impossible, to insert data in the middle of a sequential file. How easy is it to insert a new song in the middle of two other songs on a tape? The only way to truly add or delete records from the middle of a sequential file is to create a completely new file that combines both old and new records.

It might seem that sequential files are limiting, but it turns out that many applications lend themselves to sequential file processing.

Unlike with sequential files, you can access random access files in any order you want. Think of data in a random access file as you would think of songs on a compact disc or a record; you can go directly to any song you want without having to play or fast-forward through the other songs. If you want to play the first song, the sixth song, and then the fourth song, you can do so. The order of play has nothing to do with the order in which the songs appear on the recording. Random file access sometimes takes more programming but rewards that effort with a more flexible file access method. Chapter 31, "Random Access Files," discusses how to program for random access files.

Sequential File Concepts

There are three operations you can perform on sequential disk files. You can

◆ Create disk files

◆ Add to disk files

◆ Read from disk files

Your application determines what you need to do. If you are creating a disk file for the first time, you must create the file and write the initial data to it. Suppose that you wanted to create a customer data file. You would create a new file and write your current customers to that file. The customer data might originally be in arrays, arrays of structures, pointed to with pointers, or typed into regular variables by the user.

Over time, as your customer base grows, you can add new customers to the file. When you add to the end of a file, you *append* to that file. As your customers entered your store, you would read their information from the customer data file.

Customer disk processing brings up one disadvantage of sequential files, however. Suppose that a customer moves and wants you to change his or her address in your files. Sequential access files do not lend themselves well to changing data stored in them. It is also difficult to remove information from sequential files. Random files, described in the next chapter, provide a much easier approach to changing and removing data. The primary approach to changing or removing data from a sequential access file is to create a new one from the old one with the updated data. Because of the updating ease provided with random access files, this chapter concentrates on creating, reading, and adding to sequential files.

> **NOTE:** All file functions described in this chapter use the stdio.h header file.

Opening and Closing Files

Before you can create, write to, or read from a disk file, you must open the file. This is analogous to opening a file cabinet before working with a file stored in the cabinet. As soon as you are done with a cabinet's file, you close the file door. You must also close a disk file when you finish with it.

When you open a disk file, you must inform C only of the filename and what you want to do (write to, add to, or read from). C and your operating system work together to make sure that the disk is ready, and they create an entry in your file directory (if you are creating a file) for the filename. When you close a file, C writes any remaining data to the file, releases the file from the program, and updates the file directory to reflect the file's new size.

> **CAUTION:** If you use a PC, you must ensure that the FILES= statement in your CONFIG.SYS file is large enough to hold the maximum number of disk files you will have open, with one left over for your C program itself. If you are unsure of how to do this, check your DOS reference manual or a beginner's book about DOS.

To open a file, you must call the fopen() function (for "file open"). To close a file, call the fclose() function. Here is the format of these two function calls:

Prepare a file for access

```
file_ptr = fopen(file_name, access);
```

and

```
fclose(file_ptr);
```

The file_ptr is a special type of pointer that points only to files, not to data variables. You must define a file pointer with FILE *, a definition in the stdio.h header file. The examples that follow show you how to define a file pointer.

Your operating system handles the exact location of your data in the disk file. You do not want to worry about the exact track and sector number of your data on the disk. Therefore, you let the file_ptr point to the data you are reading and writing. Your program only has to generically manage the file_ptr while C and the operating system take care of locating the actual physical data.

The file_name is a string (or a character pointer that points to a string) containing a valid filename for your computer. If you are using a PC or a UNIX-based computer, the file_name can contain a complete disk and directory pathname. If you are using a mainframe, you must use the complete dataset name in the file_name string. Generally, you can specify the filename in uppercase or lowercase letters, as long as your operating system does not have a preference.

> **CAUTION:** Typically, UNIX is the only operating system that specifies that a lowercase filename is different from an uppercase (or mixed case) filename. Therefore, if a file is named UNIXfile.Dat, your fopen() command must use UNIXfile.Dat, not unixfile.dat, UNIXFILE.DAT, or any other combination of upper- or lowercase.

The access can be one of the mode values from Table 30.1. The updating access modes (those with a plus sign) are not discussed here. Rather, file updating is saved for random access files in the next chapter.

Table 30.1. Possible access modes.

Mode	Description
"r"	Opens a file for reading
"w"	Opens a file for writing (creating it)
"a"	Opens a file for appending (adding to it)
"r+"	Opens a file for update (reading and writing)

Mode	Description
`"w+"`	Opens a file for update (create it, then allow reading and writing)
`"a+"`	Opens a file for update (read the entire file, or write to the end of it)

Sometimes you see programs that contain a *t* or a *b* in the access mode, such as `"rt"` or `"wb+"`. The *t* means *text file* and is the default mode; each of the access modes listed in Table 30.1 is equivalent to using *t* after the access mode letter (`"rt"` is identical to `"r"`, and so on). A text file is an ASCII file, compatible with most other programming languages and applications. Text files do not always contain text, in the word processing sense of the word. Any data you need to store can go in a text file. Programs that read ASCII files can read data you create as C text files. The *b* in the access mode means *binary mode*. See the "Binary Modes" box that follows for a discussion of the binary file modes.

Binary Modes

If you specify *b* inside the access mode rather than *t*, C creates or reads the file in a binary format. Binary data files are "squeezed"—that is, they take less space than text files. The disadvantage of using binary files is that other programs cannot always read the data files. Only C programs written to access binary files (using the *b* access mode) can read and write to them. The advantage of binary files is that you save disk space because your data files are more compact. Other than the access mode in the `fopen()` function, you use no additional commands to access binary files with your C programs.

The binary format is a system-specific file format. In other words, not all computers can read a binary file created on another computer.

Here is a complete list of binary file access modes:

`"rb" "wb" "ab" "ab+" "a+b" "wb+" "w+b" "ab+" "a+b"`

If you open a file for writing (using access modes of "w", "wt", "wb", or "w+"), C creates the file. If a file by that name already exists, C overwrites the old file with no warning. When opening files, you must be careful that you do not overwrite existing data you want to save.

If an error occurs during the opening of a file, C does not return a valid file pointer. Instead, C returns a file pointer equal to the value NULL. NULL is defined in stdio.h. For example, if you open a file for output, but use a disk name that is invalid, C cannot open the file and will make the file pointer point to NULL. Always check the file pointer when writing disk file programs to ensure that the file opened properly.

> **TIP:** Beginning programmers like to open all files at the beginning of their programs and close them at the end. This is not always best. Open files immediately before you access them and close them when you are done with them. This protects the files, keeping them open only as long as needed. A closed file is more likely to be protected in the unlikely (but possible) event of a power failure or a computer breakdown.

This section has contained much file access theory. The following examples help illustrate these concepts.

Examples

1. Suppose that you want to create a file for storing your house payment records for the last year. Here are the first few lines in the program that would create a file called house.dat on your disk.

Include the stdio.h header file. Start the program with the main() function. Declare the file_ptr variable with FILE, found in stdio.h. Open the house.dat file for writing and creating.

```
#include <stdio.h>

main()
{
```

```
FILE *file_ptr;                 /* Declares a file pointer */
file_ptr = fopen("house.dat", "w"); /* Creates the file */
```

The rest of the program writes data to the file. The program never has to refer to the filename again. The program uses the file_ptr variable to refer to the file. Examples in the next few sections illustrate how. There is nothing special about file_ptr, other than its name (although the name is meaningful in this case). You can name file pointer variables XYZ or a908973 if you like, but these names are not meaningful.

You must include the stdio.h header file because it contains the definition for the FILE *declaration. You do not have to worry about the physical FILE's specifics. The file_ptr "points" to data in the file as you write it. Put the FILE *declarations in your programs where you declare other variables and arrays.

> **TIP:** Because files are not part of your program, you might find it useful to declare file pointers globally. Unlike data in variables, there is rarely a reason to keep file pointers local.

Before finishing with the program, you should close the file. The following fclose() function closes the house file:

```
fclose(file_ptr);               /* Closes the house payment file */
```

2. If you like, you can put the complete pathname in the filename. The following opens the household payment file in a subdirectory on the D disk drive:

```
file_ptr = fopen("d:\mydata\house.dat", "w"); /* Creates
                                                  the file */
```

3. If you like, you can store a filename in a character array or point to it with a character pointer. Each of the following sections of code is equivalent:

```
char fn[] = "house.dat";    /* Filename in character array */
file_ptr = fopen(fn, "w");              /* Creates the file */
```

```
char *myfile="house.dat";              /* Filename pointed to */
file_ptr = fopen(myfile, "w");             /* Creates the file */
/* Let the user enter the filename */
printf("What is the name of the household file? ");
gets(filename);                    /* Filename must be an
                                    array or character pointer */
file_ptr = fopen(filename, "w");      /* Creates the file */
```

No matter how you specify the filename when opening the file, close the file with the file pointer. This `fclose()` function closes the open file, no matter which method you used to open the file:

```
fclose(file_ptr);          /* Closes the house payment file */
```

4. You should check the return value from `fopen()` to ensure that the file opened properly. Here is code after `fopen()` that checks for an error:

Check to see if an error occurred

```
#include <stdio.h>

main()
{
   FILE *file_ptr;                 /* Declares a file pointer */
   file_ptr = fopen("house.dat", "w"); /* Creates the file */
   if (file_ptr == NULL)
      { printf("Error opening file.\n"); }
   else
      { /* Rest of output commands go here */ }
```

5. You can open and write to several files in the same program. Suppose that you wanted to read data from a payroll file and create a backup payroll data file. You would have to open the current payroll file using the `"r"` reading mode, and the backup file in the output `"w"` mode.

For each open file in your program, you must declare a different file pointer. The file pointers that your input and output statements use determine which file they operate on. If you have to open many files, you can declare an array of file pointers.

Here is a way you can open the two payroll files:

```
#include <stdio.h>
FILE *file_in;                                      /* Input file */
FILE *file_out;                                     /* Output file */

main()
{
    file_in = fopen("payroll.dat", "r");   /* Existing file */
    file_out = fopen("payroll.BAK", "w");        /* New file */
```

When you finish with these files, be sure to close them with these two `fclose()` function calls:

```
fclose(file_in);
fclose(file_out);
```

Writing to a File

Any input or output function that requires a device performs input and output with files. You have seen most of these already. The most common file I/O functions are

`getc()` and `putc()`

`fprintf()`

`fgets()` and `fputs()`

There are a few more, but the most common I/O function left that you have not seen is the `fscanf()` function. `fscanf()` is to `scanf()` as `fprintf()` is to `printf()`. The only difference between `fscanf()` and `scanf()` is its first parameter. The first parameter to `fscanf()` must be a file pointer (or any C device, such as `stdin` and `stdaux`).

The following function reads three integers from a file pointed to by `file_ptr`:

```
fscanf(file_ptr, "%d %d %d", &num1, &num2, &num3);
```

As with `scanf()`, you do not have to specify the `&` before array variable names. The following `fscanf()` reads a string from the disk file:

```
fscanf(file_ptr, "%s", name);
```

The fscanf() is not as potentially dangerous as the scanf() function. scanf() gets input from the user. The user does not always enter data in the format that scanf() expects. When you get data from a disk file, however, you can be more certain about the format because you probably wrote the program that created the file in the first place. Errors still can creep into a data file, and you might be wrong about the file's format when using fscanf(), but generally, fscanf() is more secure than scanf().

There is always more than one way to write data to a disk file. Most of the time, more than one function will work. For instance, if you write many names to a file, both fputs() and fprintf() will work. You also can write the names using putc(). You should use whichever function you are most comfortable with for the data being written. If you want a newline character (\n) at the end of each line in your file, the fprintf() and fputs() probably are easier than putc(), but all three will do the job.

> **TIP:** Each line in a file is called a *record*. By putting a newline character at the end of file records, you make the input of those records easier.

Examples

1. The following program creates a file called NAMES.DAT. The program writes five names to a disk file using fputs().

   Identify the program and include the I/O header file. Open a new data file called NAMES.DAT. Write five names to the file, then close the file and return to the operating system.

```
/* Filename: C30WR1.C
   Writes five names to a disk file */
#include <stdio.h>

FILE *fp;

main()
{
```

```
fp = fopen("NAMES.DAT", "w");      /* Creates a new file */

fputs("Michael Langston\n", fp);
fputs("Sally Redding\n", fp);
fputs("Jane Kirk\n", fp);
fputs("Stacy Grady\n", fp);
fputs("Paula Hiquet\n", fp);

fclose(fp);                         /* Release the file */
return;
}
```

To keep this first example simple, no error checking was done on the fopen(). The next few examples check for the error.

NAMES.TXT is a text data file. If you like, you can read this file into your word processor (use your word processor's command for reading ASCII files) or use an operating system command to display this file on-screen (such as the MS-DOS TYPE command or the UNIX cat command). If you were to display NAMES.TXT, you would see

```
Michael Langston
Sally Redding
Jane Kirk
Stacy Grady
Paula Hiquet
```

2. The following file writes the numbers from 1 to 100 to a file called NUMS.1.

```
/* Filename: C30WR2.C
   Writes 1 to 100 to a disk file */
#include <stdio.h>

FILE *fp;

main()
{
    int ctr;
    fp = fopen("NUMS.1", "wt");      /* Creates a new file */
```

```
        if (fp == NULL)
          { printf("Error opening file.\n"); }
        else
          { for (ctr=1; ctr<101; ctr++)
            { fprintf(fp, "%d ", ctr); }    /* Writes the data */
          }
        fclose(fp);
        return;
}
```

The numbers are not written one per line, but with a space between each of them. The format of the `fprintf()` control string determines the format of the output data. When writing data to disk files, keep in mind that you will have to read the data later. You will have to use "mirror-image" input functions to read data you output to files.

Notice that this program opens the file using the `"wt"` access mode. This is equivalent to the `"w"` access mode because C opens all files as text files unless you specify a binary override access.

Writing to a Printer

The `fopen()` and other output functions were not designed to just write to files. They were designed to write to any device, including files, the screen, and the printer. If you need to write data to a printer, you can treat the printer as if it were a file. The following program opens a FILE pointer using the MS-DOS name for a printer located at LPT1 (the MS-DOS name for the first parallel printer port):

```
/* Filename: C30PRNT.C
   Prints to the printer device */
#include <stdio.h>
FILE *prnt;  /* Points to the printer */

main()
{
   prnt = fopen("LPT1", "w");
```

```
fprintf(prnt, "Printer line 1\n");   /* 1st line printed */
fprintf(prnt, "Printer line 2\n");   /* 2nd line printed */
fprintf(prnt, "Printer line 3\n");   /* 3rd line printed */

fclose(prnt);
return;
}
```

Make sure that your printer is turned on and that it has paper before you run this program. When you run the program, you see this printed on the printer:

```
Printer line 1
Printer line 2
Printer line 3
```

Adding to a File

You can easily add data to an existing file or create new files by opening the file in append access mode. Data files on the disk rarely are static; they grow almost daily due to (with luck!) increased business. Being able to add to data already on the disk is very useful indeed.

Files you open for append access (using `"a"`, `"at"`, `"ab"`, `"a+b"`, and `"ab+"`) do not have to exist. If the file exists, C appends data to the end of the file when you write the data. If the file does not exist, C creates the file (as is done when you open a file for write access).

Example

The following program adds three more names to the NAMES.DAT file created in an earlier example.

```
/* Filename: C30AP1.C
   Adds three names to a disk file */
#include <stdio.h>

FILE *fp;
```

```
main()
{
    fp = fopen("NAMES.DAT", "a");              /* Adds to file */

    fputs("Johnny Smith\n", fp);
    fputs("Laura Hull\n", fp);
    fputs("Mark Brown\n", fp);

    fclose(fp);                                /* Release the file */
    return;
}
```

If the file did not exist, C would create it and store the three names to the file. Here is what the file now looks like:

```
Michael Langston
Sally Redding
Jane Kirk
Stacy Grady
Paula Hiquet
Johnny Smith
Laura Hull
Mark Brown
```

Basically, you have to change only the fopen() function's access mode to turn a file creation program into a file appending program.

Reading from a File

As soon as the data is in a file, you must be able to read that data. You must open the file in a read access mode. There are several ways to read data. You can read character data a character at a time or a string at a time. The choice depends on the format of the data. If you stored numbers using fprintf(), you might want to use a mirror-image fscanf() to read the data.

Files you open for read access (using "r", "rt", and "rb") must exist already, or C gives you an error. You cannot read a file that does not exist. fopen() returns NULL if the file does not exist when you open it for read access.

> **TIP:** You can read a word at a time from a file using `fscanf()` with the `%s` control code.

Another event happens when reading files. Eventually, you read all the data. Subsequent reading produces errors because there is no more data to read. C provides a solution to the end-of-file occurrence. If you attempt to read from a file that you have completely read the data from, C returns the value EOF, defined in stdio.h. To find the end-of-file condition, be sure to check for EOF when performing input from files.

> **NOTE:** Because some compilers return –1 when the end-of-file condition is reached, ANSI C requires that you declare input variables as integers. If the end-of-file is not reached, you can treat the integer as if it were a character, as always.

Examples

1. This program asks the user for a filename and prints the contents of the file to the screen. If the file does not exist, the program displays an error message.

```
/* Filename: C30RE1.C
   Reads and displays a file */
#include <stdio.h>

FILE *fp;

main()
{
    char filename[12];              /* Holds user's filename */
    int in_char;                       /* Input character */

    printf("What is the name of the file you want to see? ");
    gets(filename);
```

```
if ((fp=fopen(filename, "r"))==NULL)
  { printf("\n\n*** That file does not exist ***\n");
    exit();                              /* Exits program */
  }

  in_char = getc(fp);            /* Reads first character */
  while (in_char != EOF)
    { putchar(in_char);
      in_char = getc(fp);
    }
  fclose(fp);
  return;
}
```

Notice that the program reads the input character in two places. It is possible, although rare, that a file with no data could exist. In such a file, the first character read would result in the end-of-file condition. Therefore, this program reads the first character and prints it as long as it is not EOF.

Although the program is written to help illustrate file input, most C programmers combine the file input with the test for EOF. This might seem like too much to do at once, but it is so common in C programs that you should become familiar with the algorithm. Here is a rewritten version of the previous program's I/O routine that is more common:

```
while ((in_char = getc(fp)) != EOF)        /* Reads first */
  { putchar(in_char); }                    /* character   */
```

Figure 30.1 shows what happens when the NAMES.DAT file is requested. Because newline characters are in the file at the end of each name, the names appear on the screen one per line. If you attempt to read a file that does not exist, the program displays the following message:

```
*** That file does not exist ***
```

```
What is the name of the file you want to see? names.dat
Michael Langston
Sally Redding
Jane Kirk
Stacy Grady
Paula Hiquet
Johnny Smith
Laura Hull
Mark Brown
```

Figure 30.1. Reading and displaying a disk file.

2. This program reads one file and copies it to another. You might want to use such a program to back up important data in case the original file gets damaged.

The program must open two files—the first for reading and the second for writing. The file pointer determines which of the two files is being accessed.

```c
/* Filename: C30RE2.C
   Makes a copy of a file */
#include <stdio.h>

FILE *in_fp;
FILE *out_fp;

main()
{
    char in_filename[12];       /* Holds original filename */
    char out_filename[12];       /* Holds backup filename */

    int in_char;                        /* Input character */
```

```
printf("What is the name of the file you want to back up? ");
gets(in_filename);

printf("What is the name of the file ");
printf("you want to copy %s to? ", in_filename);
gets(out_filename);

if ((in_fp=fopen(in_filename, "r"))==NULL)
  { printf("\n\n*** %s does not exist ***\n",
          in_filename);
    exit();                              /* Exits program */
  }
if ((out_fp=fopen(out_filename, "w"))==NULL)
  { printf("\n\n*** Error opening %s ***\n",
          out_filename);
    exit();                              /* Exits program */
  }

printf("\nCopying...\n");              /* Waiting message */
while ((in_char = getc(in_fp)) != EOF)    /* Gets input
                                            character */
  { putc(in_char, out_fp); }    /* Writes the character
                                   to the backup file */

printf("\nThe files are copied.\n");

fclose(in_fp);
fclose(out_fp);
return;
}
```

Review Questions

Answers to review questions are in Appendix B.

1. What are the three ways to access sequential files?

2. What advantages do disk files have over holding data in memory?

3. How do sequential files differ from random access files?

4. What happens when you open a file for read access and the file does not exist?

5. What happens when you open a file for write access and the file already exists?

6. What happens when you open a file for append access and the file does not exist?

7. How does C inform you that you have reached the end-of-file condition?

8. Why must you use an integer variable for performing character input?

Review Exercises

1. Write a program that creates a file that contains the following data:

   Your name
   Your address
   Your phone number
   Your age

2. Write a second program that reads and prints the data file you created in Exercise 1.

3. Write a program that takes the data you created in Exercise 1 and writes it to the screen, one word per line. (Hint: Use the fscanf() function and the %s control code.)

4. Write a program for PCs that backs up two important files: AUTOEXEC.BAT and CONFIG.SYS. Call the backup files AUTOEXEC.SAV and CONFIG.SAV.

5. Write a program that reads a file and creates a new file with the same data, but reverse the case on the second file. Everywhere uppercase letters appear in the first file, write lowercase letters to the new file, and everywhere lowercase letters appear in the first file, write uppercase letters to the new file.

Summary

You can now perform one of the most important requirements of data processing: writing and reading to and from disk files. Before this chapter, you could only store data in variables. The short life of variables (they last only as long as your program is running) makes long-term storage of data impossible. You can now save large amounts of data in disk files to process them later.

Reading and writing sequential files involves learning more concepts than actual commands or functions. The `fopen()` and `fclose()` are the most important functions you learned in this chapter. You are familiar with most of the I/O functions needed to get data to and from disk files.

The next chapter concludes this book's discussion of disk files. You will learn how to create and use random access files. By programming with random file access, you can read selected data from a file, as well as change data without having to rewrite the entire file.

Random Access Files

This chapter introduces the concept of random file access. Random file access enables you to read or write any data in your disk file without having to read or write every piece of data before it. You can quickly search for, add, retrieve, change, and delete information in a random access file. Although you need a few new functions to access files randomly, you will find that the extra effort pays off in flexibility, power, and speed of disk access.

This chapter introduces the following concepts:

◆ Random access files

◆ File records

◆ The fseek() function

◆ Special-purpose file I/O functions

This chapter concludes *C By Example*. With C's sequential and random access files, you can do everything you would ever want to do with disk data.

Random File Records

Random files exemplify the power of data processing with C. Sequential file processing is slow unless you read the entire file into arrays and process them in memory. As explained in the last chapter, however, you have much more disk space than RAM, and most disk files do not even fit in your RAM at one time. Therefore, you need a way to quickly read individual pieces of data from a file in any order needed and process them one at a time.

Generally, you read and write file *records*. A record to a file is analogous to a C structure. A record is a collection of one or more data values (called *fields*) that you read and write to disk. Generally, you store data in structures and write the structures to disk, where they are called records. When you read a record from disk, you generally read that record into a structure variable and process it with your program.

Unlike most programming languages, not all disk data has to be stored in record format. Typically, you write a stream of characters to a disk file and access that data either sequentially or randomly by reading it into variables and structures.

The process of randomly accessing data in a file is simple. Consider the data files of a large credit card organization. When you make a purchase, the store calls the credit card company to get an authorization. Millions of names are in the credit card company's files. There is no quick way the credit card company could read every record sequentially from the disk that comes before yours. Sequential files do not lend themselves to quick access. In many situations, looking up individual records in a data file with sequential access is not feasible.

The credit card companies must use a random file access so that their computers can go directly to your record, just as you go directly to a song on a compact disc or a record album. The functions you use are different from the sequential functions, but the power that results from learning the added functions is worth the effort.

Reading and writing files randomly is similar to thinking of the file as a big array. With arrays, you know that you can add, print, or remove values in any order. You do not have to start the first array element, sequentially looking at the next one, until you get the

A record is to a file like a structure is to variables.

You do not have to rewrite the entire file to change random access file data.

element you need. You can view your random access file in the same way, accessing the data in any order.

Most random file records are fixed-length records. That is, each record (usually a row in the file) takes the same amount of disk space. Most sequential files you read and wrote in the previous chapter were variable-length records. When you are reading or writing sequentially, there is no need for fixed-length records because you input each value one character, word, string, or number at a time, looking for the data you want. With fixed-length records, your computer can better calculate exactly where the search record is located on the disk.

Although you waste some disk space with fixed-length records (because of the spaces that pad some of the fields), the advantages of random file access compensate for the "wasted" disk space.

> **TIP:** With random access files, you can read or write records in any order. Therefore, even if you want to perform sequential reading or writing of the file, you can use random access processing and "randomly" read or write the file in sequential record number order.

Opening Random Access Files

Just as with sequential files, you must open random access files before reading or writing to them. You can use any of the read access modes mentioned in the last chapter (such as "r", "rt", and "rb") if you are going to only read a file randomly. To modify data in a file, however, you must open the file in one of the update modes, which Table 31.1 reviews.

You can randomly read a file, even if the file was opened without an update +. Therefore, there is really no physical difference between sequential files and random files in C. However, the methods you use to access and update them differ.

Table 31.1. Random access update modes.

Mode	Description
"r+"	Opens a file for update (reading and writing)
"w+"	Opens a file for update (creates it, then allows reading and writing)
"a+"	Opens a file for update (reads the entire file, or writes to the end of it)
"r+t"	Opens a text file for update (reading and writing; same as "r+")
"w+t"	Opens a text file for update (creates it, then allows reading and writing; same as "w+")
"a+t"	Opens a text file for update (reads the entire file or writes to the end of it; same as "a+")
"r+b"	Opens a binary file for update (reading and writing)
"w+b"	Opens a binary file for update (creates it, then allows reading and writing)
"a+b"	Opens a binary file for update (reads the entire file or writes to the end of it)

Examples

Prepare
file for
writing

1. Suppose that you want to write a program to create a file of friends' names. The following fopen() function call will suffice, assuming that fp is declared as a file pointer:

```
if ((fp = fopen("NAMES.DAT", "w"))==NULL)
    { printf("\n*** Cannot open file ***\n"); }
```

No update fopen() access mode is needed if you are only creating the file. However, what if you wanted to create the file, write names to it, and give the user a chance to change any of the names before closing the file? You would have to open the file like this:

```
if ((fp = fopen("NAMES.DAT", "w+"))==NULL)
    { printf("\n*** Cannot open file ***\n"); }
```

This lets you create the file, then change data that you wrote to the file.

2. As with sequential files, the only difference between using a binary `fopen()` access mode and a text `fopen()` access mode is that the file you create with the binary `fopen()` will be more compact and will save disk space. You could not, however, read that file from other programs as an ASCII text file. The previous `fopen()` function can be rewritten to create and allow updating of a binary file. All other file-related commands and functions work for binary files just as they do for text files.

```
if ((fp = fopen("NAMES.DAT", "w+t"))==NULL)
   { printf("\n*** Cannot open file ***\n"); }
```

3. Suppose that you want to read a binary inventory file, and want to change some of the data to reflect new pricing. The following `fopen()` function call suffices for such a file that you want to read and update:

```
if ((fp = fopen("INVENT.JUN", "r+b"))==NULL)
   { printf("\n*** Cannot open file ***\n"); }
```

The fseek() Function

You can read forward or backward from any point in the file with `fseek()`.

C provides a function that enables you to read to a specific point in a random access data file. This is the `fseek()` function. The format of `fseek()` is

```
fseek(file_ptr, long_num, origin);
```

The `file_ptr` is the pointer to the file that you want to access, initialized with an `fopen()` statement. The `long_num` is the number of bytes in the file you want to skip. C does not read this many bytes, but literally skips the data by the number of bytes specified in `long_num`. Skipping the bytes on the disk is much faster than reading them. If `long_num` is negative, C skips backward in the file (this allows for rereading of data several times). Because data files can be large, you must declare `long_num` as a long integer to hold a large number of bytes.

The origin is a value that tells C where to begin the skipping of bytes specified by long_num. The origin can be any of the three values shown in Table 31.2.

Table 31.2. Possible origin values.

Description	Equivalent	origins
Beginning of file	SEEK_SET	0
Current file position	SEEK_CUR	1
End of file	SEEK_END	2

The words SEEK_SET, SEEK_CUR, and SEEK_END are defined in stdio.h as the constants 0, 1, and 2, respectively. That is why it does not matter which (the defined constants or the numeric constants) you use as the origin.

> **NOTE:** Actually, the file pointer plays a much more important role than just "pointing to the file" on the disk. The file pointer continually points to the exact location of the *next byte to read or write*. In other words, as you read data, from either a sequential or a random access file, the file pointer increments with each byte read. By using fseek(), you can move the file pointer forward or backward in the file.

Examples

1. No matter how far into a file you have read, the following fseek() function positions the file pointer back at the beginning of a file:

```
fseek(fp, 0L, SEEK_SET); /* Positions the file pointer
                                    at the beginning */
```

The constant 0L passes a long integer 0 to the fseek() function. Without the L, C would pass a regular integer that would not match the fseek() prototype, which is located in stdio.h. Chapter 4, "Variables and Constants," explains the use of data type suffixes on numeric constants, but the suffixes have not been used since then until now.

This `fseek()` function literally reads "move the file pointer 0 bytes from the beginning of the file."

2. The following example reads a file named MYFILE.TXT twice, once to send the file to the screen and once to send the file to the printer. Three file pointers are used, one for each device (the file, the screen, and the printer). The device names for the screen and the printer are MS-DOS-compatible. If you run this program on a minicomputer or a mainframe, substitute your operating system's code for your local screen and printer in the `fopen()` function calls for these devices.

```
/* Filename: C31TWIC.C
   Writes a file to the screen, rereads it,
   and sends it to the printer */
#include <stdio.h>
FILE *in_file;                       /* Input file pointer */
FILE *scrn;                           /* Screen pointer */
FILE *prnt;                           /* Printer pointer */

main()
{
   int in_char;
   if ((in_file = fopen("MYFILE.TXT", "r"))==NULL)
     { printf("\n*** Error opening MYFILE.TXT ***\n");
       exit();  }

   scrn = fopen("CON", "w");          /* Open screen device */
   while ((in_char=getc(in_file))!=EOF)
     { putc(in_char,scrn); }          /* Output characters
                                          to the screen */

   fclose(scrn);                      /* Close screen because
                                        it is no longer needed */

   fseek(in_file, 0L, SEEK_SET);      /* Reposition
                                          file pointer */
```

```
prnt = fopen("LPT1", "w");        /* Open printer device */
while ((in_char=getc(in_file))!=EOF)
    { putc(in_char,prnt); }         /* Output characters
                                       to the printer */

fclose(prnt);              /* Always close all open files */
fclose(in_file);

return;
}
```

You also can close then reopen a file to position the file pointer back at the beginning, but using fseek() is a more efficient method.

Of course, you could have used regular I/O functions such as printf() to write to the screen, instead of having to open the screen as a separate device.

3. The following fseek() function positions the file pointer at the 30th byte in the file. (The next byte read is the 31st byte.)

```
fseek(file_ptr, 30L, SEEK_SET); /* Positions file pointer
                                   at the 30th byte */
```

This fseek() function literally reads "move the file pointer 30 bytes from the beginning of the file."

If you write structures to a file, you can quickly seek any structure in the file by using the sizeof() function. Suppose that you want the 123rd occurrence of the structure tagged with inventory. You would search using the following fseek() function:

```
fseek(file_ptr, (123L * sizeof(struct inventory)), SEEK_SET);
```

4. The following program writes the letters of the alphabet to a file called ALPH.TXT. The fseek() function is then used to read and display the 9th and 17th letters (I and Q).

Identify the program and include the I/O header file. This program will read some letters from a file. We need to store the alphabet in a file, so open the ALPH.TXT file for output. Loop through the letters of the alphabet, from A to Z, writing each to the file.

Position the file pointer so that it points to the 9th character in the file (the letter I). Read the character, then print it. Position the file pointer so that it points to the 17th character in the file (the letter Q). Read the character, then print it. Close the file and return to DOS.

```
/* Filename: C31ALPH.C
   Stores the alphabet in a file,
   then reads two letters from it */
#include <stdio.h>
FILE *fp;
main()
{
    int ch;                              /* Holds A through Z */

    /* Opens in update mode so that you can read
       the file after writing to it */
    if ((fp=fopen("alph.txt", "w+"))==NULL)      /* Create
                                              alphabet file */
      { printf("\n*** Error opening file ***\n");
        exit(); }

    for (ch=65; ch<=90; ch++)
      { putc(ch, fp); }                  /* Writes letters */

    fseek(fp, 8L, SEEK_SET);            /* Skips 8 letters,
                                              points to I */
    ch=getc(fp);
    printf("The first character is %c\n",ch);
    fseek(fp, 16L, SEEK_SET);           /* Skips 16 letters,
                                              points to Q */
    ch=getc(fp);
    printf("The second character is %c\n",ch );

    fclose(fp);
    return;
}
```

5. To point to the end of a data file, you can use the `fseek()` function to position the file pointer at the last byte. Subsequent `fseek()`s should then use a negative `long_num` value to skip backward in the file. The following `fseek()` function makes the file pointer point to the end of the file:

```
fseek(file_ptr, 0L, SEEK_END);   /* Positions file pointer
                                         at the end */
```

This `fseek()` function literally reads "move the file pointer 0 bytes from the end of the file." The file pointer now points to the end-of-file marker, but you can then `fseek()` backward to get to other data in the file.

6. The following program reads the ALPH.TXT file (created in Exercise 4) backward, printing each character as it skips back in the file.

```
/* Filename: C31BACK.C
   Reads and prints a file backward */
#include <stdio.h>
FILE *fp;
main()
{
   int ctr;   /* Steps through the 26 letters in the file */
   int in_char;

   if ((fp = fopen("ALPH.TXT", "r"))==NULL)
     { printf("\n*** Error opening file ***\n");
       exit(); }

   fseek(fp, 1L, SEEK_END);     /* Points to the last byte
                                        in the file */
   for (ctr=0;ctr<26;ctr++)
     {
     in_char = getc(fp);
     fseek(fp, -2L, SEEK_CUR);
     putchar(in_char); }

   fclose(fp);
   return;
}
```

This program also uses the SEEK_CUR origin value. The last `fseek()` in the program seeks two bytes backward from the *current position,* not from the beginning or the end as the previous examples do. The `for` loop toward the end of the program performs a "skip 2 bytes back, read 1 byte forward" method to skip through the file backward.

7. The following program performs the same actions as Example 4 (C31ALPH.C), with one addition. When the letters *I* and *Q* are found, an `fputc()` writes the letter *x* over the *I* and *Q*. The `fseek()` must be used to back up one byte in the file to overwrite the letter just read.

```c
/* Filename: C31CHANG.C
   Stores the alphabet in a file, reads two letters from
   it, and changes those letters to x's */
#include <stdio.h>
FILE *fp;
main()
{
   int ch;                            /* Holds A through Z */

   /* Opens in update mode so that you can read
      the file after writing to it */
   if ((fp=fopen("alph.txt", "w+"))==NULL)     /* Creates
                                                  alphabet file */
     { printf("\n*** Error opening file ***\n");
       exit(); }

   for (ch=65; ch<=90; ch++)
     { putc(ch, fp); }                   /* Writes letters */

   fseek(fp, 8L, SEEK_SET);           /* Skips 8 letters,
                                          points to I */
   ch=getc(fp);

   /* Changes the I to an x */
   fseek(fp, -1L, SEEK_CUR);
   fputc('x', fp);

   printf("The first character is %c\n",ch);
   fseek(fp, 16L, SEEK_SET);          /* Skips 16 letters,
                                          points to Q */
   ch=getc(fp);
   printf("The second character is %c\n",ch );
```

```
/* Changes the Q to an x */
fseek(fp, -1L, SEEK_CUR);
fputc('x', fp);

fclose(fp);
return;
}
```

The file named ALPH.TXT now looks like this:

ABCDEFGHxJKLMNOPxRSTUVWXYZ

This program forms the basis of a more complete data file management program. After you master the `fseek()` functions and become more familiar with disk data files, you will begin to write programs that store more advanced data structures and access them.

The mailing list application in Appendix F is a good example of what you can do with random file access. The user is given a chance to change names and addresses that are already in the file. You can use the program to change selected data without having to rewrite the entire disk file. Simply use random access to seek data and write to it.

Other Helpful I/O Functions

Several more disk I/O functions are available that you might find useful. They are mentioned here for completeness. As you write more powerful programs in C, you will find a use for many of these functions when performing disk I/O. Each of these functions is prototyped in the stdio.h header file.

◆ `feof(fp)` can be used to test for an end-of-file condition when reading binary files. Unlike text files, C might mistake the binary data for the end-of-file marker. The `feof()` function ensures that the end-of-file condition is properly tested.

◆ `fread(array, size, count, fp)` reads the amount of data specified by the integer *count*, each data size being *size* in bytes (use the `sizeof()` function), into the array or pointer specified by *array*. fread() is called a *buffered I/O* function. fread() enables you to read much data with a single function call.

♦ fwrite(*array, size, count, fp*) writes *count array* elements, each being size *size,* to the file specified by *fp*. fwrite() uses a buffered I/O function. fwrite() enables you to write much data in a single function call.

♦ remove(*fp*) erases the file pointed to by *fp*. remove() returns 0 if the file was erased successfully and –1 if an error occurred.

♦ rewind(*fp*) positions the file pointer at the beginning of the file.

Many of these (and other built-in I/O functions that you will learn in your C programming career) are helpful functions that you can duplicate using what you already know. For instance, the rewind() function simply positions the file pointer at the beginning of a file. rewind() is the third method you have seen that does this. These three methods all position the file pointer at the beginning of the file:

```
fclose(fp);
fopen(fp, "r");               /* Reopening a file always
                                 reinitializes the pointer */
```

and

```
fseek(fp, 0L, SEEK_SET);
```

and

```
rewind(fp);
```

The buffered I/O file functions enable you to read and write entire arrays (including arrays of structures) to the disk in a single function call.

Examples

1. The following program requests a filename from the user and uses the remove() function to erase the file from the disk:

Erase the file

```
/* Filename: C31ERAS.C
   Erases the file specified by the user */
#include <stdio.h>
FILE *fp;
main()
{
   char filename[12];

   puts("What is the filename you want me to erase? ");
   gets(filename);

   if (remove(filename) == -1)
      { printf("\n*** I could not remove the file ***\n"); }
   else
      { printf("\nThe file %s is now removed\n", filename); }
   return;
}
```

2. The following program reads a binary file, a character at a time, until `feof()` returns a true condition. (The regular end-of-file defined constant works only for text files.)

```
/* Filename: C31READ.C
   Reads and displays a binary file */
#include <stdio.h>

FILE *fp;

main()
{
   char filename[12];              /* Holds user's filename */
   int in_char;                    /* Input character */

   printf("What is the name of the file you want to see? ");
   gets(filename);

   if ((fp=fopen(filename, "rb"))==NULL)
     { printf("\n\n*** That file does not exist ***\n");
       exit();                     /* Exits program */
     }
```

```
    while (!feof(fp))
       { in_char = getc(fp);
         putchar(in_char); }

    fclose(fp);
    return;
}
```

3. The following function would be part of a larger program that gets inventory data, in an array of structures, from the user. This function is passed the array name and the number of elements (structure variables) in the array. The `fwrite()` function then writes the complete array of structures to the disk file pointed to by `fp`.

```
void write_str(struct inventory items[], int inv_cnt)
{
   fwrite(items, sizeof(struct inventory), inv_cnt, fp);
   return;
}
```

If the inventory array had 1,000 elements, this one-line function would still write the entire array to the disk file. You could use the `fread()` function to read the entire array of structures from the disk in a single function call.

Review Questions

Answers to review questions are in Appendix B.

1. What is the difference between records and structures?

2. True or false: You have to create a random access file before reading from it randomly.

3. What happens to the file pointer as you read from a file?

4. What are the two buffered file I/O functions?

5. What are two methods for positioning the file pointer at the beginning of a file?

6. What are the three starting positions (the `origins`) in the `fseek()` function?

7. What is wrong with this program?

```c
#include <stdio.h>
FILE *fp;
main()
{
  int in_char;
  fopen(fp, "rb");
  if((in_char=getc(fp))!=EOF)
    { putchar(in_char); }      /* Writes to the screen */
  fclose(fp);
  return;
}
```

Review Exercises

1. Write a program that asks the user for a list of five names, then writes the names to a file. Rewind the file and display its contents on the screen by using the `fseek()` and `getc()` functions.

2. Rewrite the program in Exercise 1 so that it displays every other character in the file of names.

3. Write a program that reads characters from a file. If the input character is a lowercase letter, change it to uppercase. If the input character is uppercase, change it to lowercase. Do not change other characters in the file.

4. Write a program that displays the number of nonalphabetic characters in a file.

5. Write a grade-keeping program for a teacher. Let the teacher enter as many as 10 students' grades. Each student has three grades for the semester. Store the students' names and their three grades in an array of structures and store the data on the disk. Make the program menu-driven. Let the teacher

have the option of adding more students, viewing the file's data, or printing the grades to the printer with a calculated class average.

Summary

C supports random access files with several functions. These functions include error-checking, file pointer positioning, and the opening and closing of files. You now have the tools you need to save your C program data to disk for storage and retrieval.

The mailing-list application in Appendix F offers a complete example of random access file manipulation. The program enables the user to enter names and addresses, store them to disk, edit them, change them, and print them from the disk file. The mailing-list program combines almost every topic from this book into a complete application that "puts it all together."

Memory Addressing, Binary, and Hexadecimal Review

You do not have to understand the concepts in this appendix to become well-versed in C. You can master C, however, only if you spend some time learning about the "behind-the-scenes" roles played by binary numbers. The material presented here is not difficult, but many programmers do not take the time to study it; hence, there are a handful of C masters who learn this material and understand how C works "under the hood," and there are those who will never be as expert in the language as they could be.

You should take the time to learn about addressing, binary numbers, and hexadecimal numbers. These fundamental principles are presented here for you to learn, and although a working knowledge of C is possible without knowing them, they will greatly enhance your C skills (and your skills in every other programming language).

After reading this appendix, you will better understand why different C data types hold different ranges of numbers. You also will see the importance of being able to represent hexadecimal numbers in C, and you will better understand C array and pointer addressing.

Computer Memory

Each memory location inside your computer holds a single character called a *byte*. A byte is any character, whether it is a letter of the alphabet, a numeric digit, or a special character such as a period, question mark, or even a space (a blank character). If your computer contains 640K of memory, it can hold a total of approximately 640,000 bytes of memory. This means that as soon as you fill your computer's memory with 640K, there is no room for an additional character unless you overwrite something else.

Before describing the physical layout of your computer's memory, it might be best to take a detour and explain exactly what 640K means.

Memory and Disk Measurements

K means approximately 1000 and exactly 1024.

By appending the K (from the metric word *kilo*) to memory measurements, the manufacturers of computers do not have to attach as many zeros to the end of numbers for disk and memory storage. The K stands for approximately 1000 bytes. As you will see, almost everything inside your computer is based on a power of 2. Therefore, the K of computer memory measurements actually equals the power of 2 closest to 1000, which is 2 to the 10th power, or 1024. Because 1024 is very close to 1000, computerists often think of K as meaning 1000, even though they know it only approximately equals 1000.

Think for a moment about what 640K exactly equals. Practically speaking, 640K is about 640,000 bytes. To be exact, however, 640K equals 640 times 1024, or 655,360. This explains why the PC DOS command CHKDSK returns 655,360 as your total memory (assuming that you have 640K of RAM) rather than 640,000.

M means approximately 1,000,000 and exactly 1,048,576.

Because extended memory and many disk drives can hold such a large amount of data, typically several million characters, there is an additional memory measurement shortcut called *M*, which stands for *meg*, or *megabytes*. The M is a shortcut for approximately one million bytes. Therefore, 20M is approximately 20,000,000 characters, or bytes, of storage. As with K, the M literally stands for 1,048,576 because that is the closest power of 2 (2 to the 20th power) to one million.

How many bytes of storage is 60 megabytes? It is approximately 60 million characters, or 62,914,560 characters to be exact.

Memory Addresses

Each memory location in your computer, just as with each house in your town, has a unique *address*. A memory address is simply a sequential number, starting at 0, which labels each memory location. Figure A.1 shows how your computer memory addresses are numbered if you have 640K of RAM.

Figure A.1. Memory addresses for a 640K computer.

By using unique addresses, your computer can keep track of memory. When the computer stores a result of a calculation in memory, it finds an empty address, or one matching the data area where the result is to go, and stores the result at that address.

Your C programs and data share computer memory with DOS. DOS must always reside in memory while you operate your computer. Otherwise, your programs would have no way to access disks, printers, the screen, or the keyboard. Figure A.2 shows computer memory being shared by DOS and a C program. The exact amount of memory taken by DOS and a C program is determined by the version of DOS you use, how many DOS extras (such as device drivers and buffers) your computer uses, and the size and needs of your C programs and data.

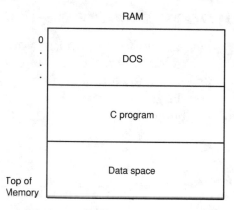

Figure A.2. DOS, your C program, and your program's data share the same memory.

Bits and Bytes

You now know that a single address of memory might contain any character, called a byte. You know that your computer holds many bytes of information, but it does not store those characters in the same way that humans think of characters. For example, if you type a letter *W* on your keyboard while working in your C editor, you see the *W* on the screen, and you also know that the *W* is stored in a memory location at some unique address. Actually, your computer does not store the letter *W*; it stores electrical impulses that stand for the letter *W*.

Electricity, which is what runs through the components of your computer, making it understand and execute your programs, can exist in only two states—on or off. As with a lightbulb, electricity is either flowing (it is on) or it is not flowing (it is off). Even though you can dim some lights, the electricity is still either on or off.

Today's modern digital computers employ this on-or-off concept. Your computer is nothing more than millions of on and off switches. You might have heard about integrated circuits, transistors, and even vacuum tubes that computers have contained over the years. These electrical components are nothing more than switches that rapidly turn electrical impulses on and off.

The binary digits 1 and 0 (called bits) represent on and off states of electricity.

This two-state on and off mode of electricity is called a *binary* state of electricity. Computer people use a 1 to represent an on state (a switch in the computer that is on) and a 0 to represent an off state (a switch that is off). These numbers, 1 and 0, are called *binary digits*. The term binary digits is usually shortened to *bits*. A bit is either a 1 or a 0 representing an on or an off state of electricity. Different combinations of bits represent different characters.

Several years ago, someone listed every single character that might be represented on a computer, including all uppercase letters, all lowercase letters, the digits 0 through 9, the many other characters (such as %, *, {, and +), and some special control characters. When you add the total number of characters that a PC can represent, you get 256 of them. The first 128 of these characters are found on all PCs and are listed in the ASCII (pronounced *ask-ee*) table in Appendix C. The remaining 128 characters can only be found on IBM-compatible computers and are not shown in Appendix C.

The order of the ASCII table's 256 characters is basically arbitrary, just as the telegraph's Morse code table is arbitrary. With Morse code, a different set of long and short beeps represent different letters of the alphabet. In the ASCII table, a different combination of bits (1s and 0s strung together) represent each of the 256 ASCII characters. The ASCII table is a standard table used by almost every PC in the world. ASCII stands for American Standard Code for Information Interchange. (Some minicomputers and mainframes use a similar table called the EBCDIC table.)

It turns out that if you take every different combination of eight 0s strung together, to eight 1s strung together (that is, from 00000000, 00000001, 00000010, and so on until you get to 11111110, and finally,

11111111), you will have a total of 256 of them. (256 is 2 to the 8th power.) Each memory location in your computer holds eight bits each. These bits can be any combination of eight 1s and 0s. This brings us to the following fundamental rule of computers.

> **NOTE:** Because it takes a combination of eight 1s and 0s to represent a character, and because each byte of computer memory can hold exactly one character, eight bits equal one byte.

To bring this into better perspective, consider that the bit pattern needed for the uppercase letter *A* is 01000001. No other character in the ASCII table "looks" like this to the computer because each of the 256 characters is assigned a unique bit pattern.

Suppose that you press the *A* key on your keyboard. Your keyboard does *not* send a letter *A* to the computer; rather, it looks in its ASCII table for the on and off states of electricity that represent the letter *A*. As Figure A.3 shows, when you press the *A* key, the keyboard actually sends 01000001 (as on and off impulses) to the computer. Your computer simply stores this bit pattern for *A* in a memory location. Even though you can think of the memory location as holding an *A*, it really holds the byte 01000001.

Figure A.3. Your computer keeps track of characters by their bit patterns.

If you were to print that *A*, your computer would not send an *A* to the printer; it would send the 01000001 bit pattern for an *A* to the printer. The printer receives that bit pattern, looks up the correct letter in the ASCII table, and prints an *A*.

From the time you press the *A* until the time you see it on the printer, it is *not* a letter *A*! It is the ASCII pattern of bits that the computer uses to represent an *A*. Because a computer is electrical, and because electricity is easily turned on and off, this is a nice way for the computer to manipulate and move characters, and it can do so very quickly. Actually, if it were up to the computer, you would enter everything by its bit pattern, and look at all results in their bit patterns. This would not be good, so devices such as the keyboard, screen, and printer know that they have to work part of the time with letters as we know them. That is why the ASCII table is such an integral part of a computer.

There are times when your computer treats two bytes as a single value. Even though memory locations are typically eight bits wide, many CPUs access memory two bytes at a time. If this is the case, the two bytes are called a *word* of memory. On other computers (commonly mainframes), the word size might be four bytes (32 bits) or even eight bytes (64 bits).

Summarizing Bits and Bytes

A bit is a 1 or a 0 representing an on or an off state of electricity.

Eight bits represents a byte.

A byte, or eight bits, represents one character.

Each memory location of your computer is eight bits (a single byte) wide. Therefore, each memory location can hold one character of data. Appendix C provides the first 128 characters of the ASCII table.

If the CPU accesses memory two bytes at a time, those two bytes are called a word of memory.

The Order of Bits

To further understand memory, you should understand how programmers refer to individual bits. Figure A.4 shows a byte and a two-byte word. Notice that the bit on the far right is called bit 0.

From bit 0, keep counting by ones as you move left. For a byte, the bits are numbered 0 to 7, from right to left. For a double-byte (a 16-bit word), the bits are numbered from 0 to 15, from right to left.

Figure A.4. The order of bits in a byte and a two-byte word.

Bit 0 is called the *least-significant bit*, or sometimes the *low-order bit*. Bit 7 (or bit 15 for a two-byte word) is called the *most-significant bit*, or sometimes the *high-order bit*.

Binary Numbers

Because a computer works best with 1s and 0s, its internal numbering method is limited to a *base-2* (binary) numbering system. People work in a *base-10* numbering system in the real world. The base-10 numbering system is sometimes called the decimal numbering system. There are always as many different digits as the base in a numbering system. For example, in the base-10 system, there are ten digits, 0 through 9. As soon as you count to 9 and run out of digits, you have to combine some that you already used. The number 10 is a representation of ten values, but it combines the digits 1 and 0.

The same is true of base 2. There are only two digits, 0 and 1. As soon as you run out of digits, after the second one, you have to reuse digits. The first seven binary numbers are 0, 1, 10, 11, 100, 101, and 110.

It is okay if you do not understand how these numbers were derived; you will see how in a moment. For the time being, you should realize that no more than two digits, 0 and 1, can be used to represent any base-2 number, just as no more than ten digits, 0 through 9, can be used to represent any base-10 number in the regular "real-world" numbering system.

You should know that a base-10 number, such as 2981, does not really mean anything by itself. You must assume what base it is. You get very used to working with base-10 numbers because that is what the world uses. However, the number 2981 actually represents a quantity based on powers of 10. For example, Figure A.5 shows what the number 2981 actually represents. Notice that each digit in the number represents a certain number of a power of 10.

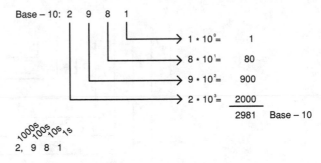

Figure A.5. The base-10 breakdown of the number 2981.

This same concept applies when you work in a base-2 numbering system. Your computer does this, because the power of 2 is just as common to your computer as the power of 10 is to you. The only difference is that the digits in a base-2 number represent powers of 2 and not powers of 10. Figure A.6 shows you what the binary numbers 10101 and 10011110 are in base-10. This is how you convert any binary number to its base-10 equivalent.

A binary number can contain only the digits 1 and 0.

A base-2 number contains only 1s and 0s. To convert any base-2 number to base-10, add each power of 2 everywhere a 1 appears in the number. The base-2 number 101 represents the base-10 number 5. (There are two 1s in the number, one in the 2 to the 0 power, which equals 1, and one in the 2 to the second power, which equals 4.) Table A.1 shows the first 18 base-10 numbers and their matching base-2 numbers.

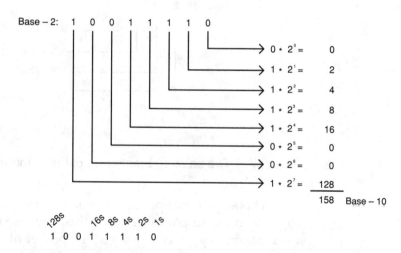

Figure A.6. The base-2 breakdown of the numbers 10101 and 10011110.

You do not have to memorize this table; you should be able to figure the base-10 numbers from their matching binary numbers by adding the powers of two for each 1 (on) bit. Many programmers do memorize the first several binary numbers, however, because it comes in handy in advanced programming techniques.

What is the largest binary number a byte can hold? The answer is all 1s, or 11111111. If you add the first eight powers of 2, you get 255.

Table A.1. The first 17 base-10 and base-2 (binary) numbers.

Base-10	Base-2
0	0
1	1
2	10
3	11
4	100
5	101
6	110
7	111
8	1000
9	1001
10	1010
11	1011
12	1100
13	1101
14	1110
15	1111
16	10000
17	10001

A byte holds either a number or an ASCII character, depending on how it is accessed. For example, if you were to convert the base-2 number 01000001 to a base-10 number, you would get 65. However, this also happens to be the ASCII bit pattern for the uppercase letter *A*. If you check the ASCII table, you will see that the *A* is ASCII code 65. Because the ASCII table is so closely linked with the bit patterns, the computer knows whether to work with a number 65 or a letter *A*—by the context of how the patterns are used.

A binary number is not limited to a byte, as an ASCII character is. Sixteen or 32 bits at a time can represent a binary number (and usually do). There are more powers of 2 to add when converting that number to a base-10 number, but the process is the same. By now you should be able to figure out that 1010101010101010 is 43,690 in base-10 decimal numbering system (although it might take a little time to calculate).

To convert from decimal to binary takes a little more effort. Luckily, you rarely need to convert in that direction. Converting from base-10 to base-2 is not covered in this appendix.

Binary Arithmetic

At their lowest level, computers can only add and convert binary numbers to their negative equivalents. Computers cannot truly subtract, multiply, or divide, although they simulate these operations through judicious use of the addition and negative-conversion techniques.

If a computer were to add the numbers 7 and 6, it could do so (at the binary level). The result is 13. If, however, the computer were instructed to subtract 7 from 13, it could not do so. It can, however, take the negative value of 7 and add that to 13. Because –7 plus 13 equals 6, the result is a simulated subtraction.

To multiply, computers perform repeated addition. To multiply 6 by 7, the computer adds seven 6s together and gets 42 as the answer. To divide 42 by 7, a computer keeps subtracting 7 from 42 repeatedly until it gets to a 0 answer (or less than 0 if there is a remainder), then counts the number of times it took to reach 0.

Because all math is done at the binary level, the following additions are possible in binary arithmetic:

$$0 + 0 = 0$$

$$0 + 1 = 1$$

$$1 + 0 = 1$$

$$1 + 1 = 10$$

Because these are binary numbers, the last result is not the number 10, but the binary number 2. (Just as the binary 10 means "no ones, and carry an additional power of 2," the decimal number 10 means "no ones, and carry a power of 10.") No binary digit represents a 2, so you have to combine the 1 and the 0 to form the new number.

Because binary addition is the foundation of all other math, you should learn how to add binary numbers. You will then understand how computers do the rest of their arithmetic.

Using the binary addition rules shown previously, look at the following binary calculations:

```
 01000001  (65 decimal)
+00101100  (44 decimal)
 01101101  (109 decimal)
```

The first number, 01000001, is 65 decimal. This also happens to be the bit pattern for the ASCII A, but if you add with it, the computer knows to interpret it as the number 65 rather than the character A.

The following binary addition requires a carry into bit 4 and bit 6:

```
 00101011  (43 decimal)
+00100111  (39 decimal)
 01010010  (82 decimal)
```

Typically, you have to ignore bits that carry past bit 7, or bit 15 for double-byte arithmetic. For example, both of the following binary additions produce incorrect positive results:

```
 10000000  (128 decimal)        1000000000000000  (65536 decimal)
+10000000  (128 decimal)       +1000000000000000  (65536 decimal)
 00000000  (0 decimal)          0000000000000000  (0 decimal!)
```

There is no 9th or 17th bit for the carry, so both of these seem to produce incorrect results. Because the byte and 16-bit word cannot hold the answers, the magnitude of both these additions is not possible. The computer must be programmed, at the bit level, to perform *multiword arithmetic,* which is beyond the scope of this book.

Binary Negative Numbers

Negative binary numbers are stored in their 2's complement format.

Because subtracting requires understanding binary negative numbers, you need to learn how computers represent them. The computer uses *2's complement* to represent negative numbers in binary form. To convert a binary number to its 2's complement (to its negative) you must

1. Reverse the bits (the 1s to 0s and the 0s to 1s).

2. Add 1.

This might seem a little strange at first, but it works very well for binary numbers. To represent a binary –65, you need to take the binary 65 and convert it to its 2's complement, such as

```
01000001   (65 decimal)
10111110   (Reverse the bits)
      +1   (Add 1)
10111111   (-65 binary)
```

By converting the 65 to its 2's complement, you produce –65 in binary. You might wonder what makes 10111111 mean –65, but by the 2's complement definition it means –65.

If you were told that 10111111 is a negative number, how would you know which binary number it is? You perform the 2's complement on it. Whatever number you produce is the positive of that negative number. For example:

```
10111111   (-65 decimal)
01000000   (Reverse the bits)
      +1   (Add 1)
01000001   (65 decimal)
```

Something might seem wrong at this point. You just saw that 10111111 is the binary –65, but isn't 10111111 *also* 191 decimal (adding the powers of 2 marked by the 1s in the number, as explained earlier)? It depends whether the number is a *signed* or an *unsigned* number. If a number is signed, the computer looks at the most-significant bit (the bit on the far left), called the *sign bit*. If the most-significant bit is a 1, the number is negative. If it is 0, the number is positive.

Most numbers are 16 bits long. That is, two-byte words are used to store most integers. This is not always the case for all computers, but it is true for most PCs.

In the C programming language, you can designate numbers as either signed integers or unsigned integers (they are signed by default if you do not specify otherwise). If you designate a variable as a signed integer, the computer interprets the high-order bit as a sign bit. If the high-order bit is on (1), the number is negative. If the high-order bit is off (0), the number is positive. If, however, you designate a variable as an unsigned integer, the computer uses the high-order bit as just another power of 2. That is why the range of unsigned integer variables goes higher (generally from 0 to 65535, but it depends on the computer) than for signed integer variables (generally from –32768 to +32767).

After so much description, a little review is in order. Assume that the following 16-bit binary numbers are unsigned:

0011010110100101

1001100110101010

1000000000000000

These numbers are unsigned, so the bit 15 is not the sign bit, but just another power of 2. You should practice converting these large 16-bit numbers to decimal. The decimal equivalents are

13733

39338

32768

If, on the other hand, these numbers are signed numbers, the high-order bit (bit 15) indicates the sign. If the sign bit is 0, the numbers are positive and you convert them to decimal in the usual manner. If the sign bit is 1, you must convert the numbers to their 2's complement to find what they equal. Their decimal equivalents are

+13733

–26198

–32768

To compute the last two binary numbers to their decimal equivalents, take their 2's complement and convert it to decimal. Put a minus sign in front of the result and you find what the original number represents.

> **TIP:** To make sure that you convert a number to its 2's complement correctly, you can add the 2's complement to its original positive value. If the answer is 0 (ignoring the extra carry to the left), you know that the 2's complement number is correct. This is like saying that decimal opposites, such as –72 + 72, add up to zero.

Hexadecimal Numbers

All those 1s and 0s get confusing. If it were up to your computer, however, you would enter *everything* as 1s and 0s! This is unacceptable to people because we do not like to keep track of all those 1s and 0s. Therefore, a *hexadecimal* numbering system (sometimes called *hex*) was devised. The hexadecimal numbering system is based on base-16 numbers. As with other bases, there are 16 unique digits in the base-16 numbering system. Here are the first 19 hexadecimal numbers:

0 1 2 3 4 5 6 7 8 9 A B C D E F 10 11 12

Hexadecimal numbers use 16 unique digits, 0 through F.

Because there are only 10 unique digits (0 through 9), the letters A through F represent the remaining six digits. (Anything could have been used, but the designers of the hexadecimal numbering system decided to use the first six letters of the alphabet.)

To understand base-16 numbers, you should know how to convert them to base-10 so that they represent numbers people are familiar with. Perform the conversion to base-10 from base-16 the same way you did with base-2, but instead of using powers of 2, represent each hexadecimal digit with powers of 16. Figure A.7 shows how to convert the number 3C5 to decimal.

Figure A.7. Converting hexadecimal 3C5 to its decimal equivalent.

> **TIP:** There are calculators available that convert numbers between base-16, base-10, and base-2, and also perform 2's complement arithmetic.

You should be able to convert 2B to its decimal 43 equivalent, and E1 to decimal 225 in the same manner. Table A.2 shows the first 20 decimal, binary, and hexadecimal numbers.

Table A.2. The first 20 base-10, base-2 (binary), and base-16 (hexadecimal) numbers.

Base-10	Base-2	Base-16
1	1	1
2	10	2
3	11	3
4	100	4
5	101	5
6	110	6
7	111	7
8	1000	8
9	1001	9
10	1010	A

continues

Table A.2. continued

Base-10	Base-2	Base-16
11	1011	B
12	1100	C
13	1101	D
14	1110	E
15	1111	F
16	10000	10
17	10001	11
18	10010	12
19	10011	13
20	10100	14

Why Learn Hexadecimal?

Because of its close association to the binary numbers your computer uses, hexadecimal notation is extremely efficient for describing memory locations and values. It is much easier for you (and more importantly at this level, for your computer) to convert from base-16 to base-2 than from base-10 to base-2. Therefore, you sometimes want to represent data at the bit level, but using hexadecimal notation is easier (and requires less typing) than using binary numbers.

To convert from hexadecimal to binary, convert each hex digit to its four-bit binary number. You can use Table A.2 as a guide for this. For example, the following hexadecimal number

5B75

can be converted to binary by taking each digit and converting it to four binary numbers. If you need leading zeroes to "pad" the four digits, use them. The number becomes

0101 1011 0111 0101

It turns out that the binary number 0101101101110101 is exactly equal to the hexadecimal number 5B75. This is much easier than converting them both to decimal first.

To convert from binary to hexadecimal, reverse this process. If you were given the following binary number

110100001110111111010

you could convert it to hexadecimal by grouping the bits into groups of four, starting with the bit on the far right. Because there is not an even number of groups of four, pad the one on the far left with zeroes. You then have the following:

0011 0100 0011 1101 1111 1010

Now you only have to convert each group of four binary digits into their hexadecimal number equivalent. You can use Table A.2 to help. You then get the following base-16 number:

343DFA

The C programming language also supports the base-8 *octal* representation of numbers. Because octal numbers are rarely used with today's computers, they are not covered in this appendix.

How Binary and Addressing Relates to C

The material presented here may seem foreign to many programmers. The binary and 2's complement arithmetic reside deep in your computer, shielded from most programmers (except assembly language programmers). Understanding this level of your computer, however, explains everything else you learn.

Many C programmers learn C before delving into binary and hexadecimal representation. For them, much about the C language seems strange, but it could be explained very easily if they understood the basic concepts.

For example, a signed integer holds a different range of numbers than an unsigned integer. You now know that this is due to the sign bit being used in two different ways, depending on whether the number is designated as signed or unsigned.

The ASCII table also should make more sense to you after this discussion. The ASCII table is an integral part of your computer. Characters are not actually stored in memory and variables; rather, their ASCII bit patterns are. That is why C can move easily between characters and integers. The following two C statements are allowed, whereas they probably would not be in another programming language:

```
char c = 65;    /* Puts the ASCII letter A in c */
int ci = 'A';  /* Puts the number 65 in ci */
```

The hexadecimal notation taught to many C programmers also makes much more sense if they truly understand base-16 numbers. For example, if you see the following line in a C program

```
char a = '\x041';
```

you could convert the hex 41 to decimal (65 decimal) if you want to know what is being assigned. Also, C systems programmers find that they can better interface with assembly language programs when they understand the concepts presented in this appendix.

If you gain only a cursory knowledge of this material at this point, you will be very much ahead of the game when you program in C.

Answers to Review Questions

Chapter 1 Answers

1. BCPL or Algol

2. 1970s

3. False. C's compact size makes it an excellent programming language for smaller computers.

4. The hard disk

5. A modem

6. b. Input. By moving the mouse, you give cursor-direction commands to the computer.

7. Num Lock

8. UNIX

9. When you turn off the computer, the contents of RAM are destroyed.

10. True

11. 524,288 (512 times 1,024)

12. *Mo*dulate *dem*odulate

Chapter 2 Answers

1. A set of detailed instructions that tells the computer what to do

2. Buy one or write it yourself.

3. False

4. The program produces the output.

5. A program editor

6. The .c extension

7. You must first plan the program by deciding which steps you will take to produce the final program.

8. To get the errors out of your program

9. So that your programs work with various compilers and computer equipment

10. False. You must compile a program before linking it. Most compilers link the program automatically.

Chapter 3 Answers

1. /* and */

2. A holding place for data that can be changed

3. A value that cannot be changed

4. False. ANSI C does not support nested comments.

5. The +, -, *, and / operators

6. The = assignment operator

7. False. There are floating-point, double floating-point, short integers, long integers, and many more variable data types.

8. `printf()`

9. `city` must be a variable name because it is not enclosed in quotation marks.

10. All C commands must be in lowercase.

Chapter 4 Answers

1. `my_name` and `sales_89`

2. Characters: `'X'` and `'0'`

   Strings: `"2.0"` and `"X"`

   Integer: `0` and `-708`

   Floating-point: `-12.0` and `65.4`

3. Seven variables are declared: three integers, three characters, and one floating-point variable.

4. A null zero, also called a binary zero or an ASCII zero

5. True

6. 1

7. As a series of ASCII values, representing the characters and blanks in the string, ending in an ASCII 0

8. A single ASCII 0

Chapter 5 Answers

1. `char my_name[] "This is C";`

2. 9 characters

3. 10

4. Binary zero

5. Two character arrays are declared, each with 25 elements.

6. False. The keyword char must precede the variable name.

7. True. The binary zero terminates the string.

8. False. The characters do not represent a string because there is no terminating zero.

Chapter 6 Answers

1. False. You can define only constants with the #define preprocessor directive.

2. #include

3. #define

4. True

5. The preprocessor changes your source code before the compiler sees the source code.

6. Use angled brackets when the include files reside in the compiler's include subdirectory. Use quotation marks when the include file resides in the same subdirectory as the source program.

7. Defined constants are easier because you have to change only the line with #define and not several other lines in the program.

8. stdio.h

9. False. You cannot define constants enclosed in quotation marks (as "MESSAGE" is in the printf() function).

10. Amount is 4

Chapter 7 Answers

1. `printf()` sends output to the screen, and `scanf()` gets input from the keyboard.

2. The prompt tells the user what is expected.

3. Four values are entered: two integers, a floating-point, and a string.

4. True

5. Arrays

6. The `scanf()` function gets its values from the keyboard. The assignment statement gets its value from data in the program.

7. `The backslash, "\" character is special`

8. The following value prints, with one leading space: 123.456

9. False

10. 1234560   .000001234   −1234000   −.000001234

Chapter 8 Answers

1. a. 5

   b. 6

   c. 5

2. a. 5

   b. 7

3. a. `a = (3+3) / (4+4);`

   b. `x = (a-b)*( (a-c) * (a-c));`

   c. `d = ( (8=x*x)/(x-9) ) - ((4*2-1) / (x*x*x));`

4.

```
#include <stdio.h>
#define PI 3.14159
main()
{
    printf("%f", (PI*(4*4)));
    return;
}
        5.
r = 100%4;
printf("%d", r);
```

Chapter 9 Answers

1. The `==` operator

2. a. True

   b. True

   c. True

   d. True

3. True

4. The `if` statement determines what code executes when the relational test is true. The `if-else` statement determines what happens for both the True and the False relational test.

5. Yes

6. a. False

   b False

   c. False

Chapter 10 Answers

1. The &&, ¦¦, and ¦ operators

2. a. False

   b. False

   c. True

   d. True

3. a. True

   b. 11

   c. True

4. g is 25 and f got changed to 35

5. a. True

   b. True

   c. False

   d. True

6. Yes

Chapter 11 Answers

1. The if-else statement

2. The conditional operator is the only C operator with three arguments.

3.
```
if (a == b)
    { ans = c + 2; }
else
    { ans = c + 3; }
```

4. True

5. The increment and decrement operators compile into single assembly instructions.

6. A comma operator (,) that forces a left-to-right execution of the statements on either side

7. The output cannot be determined reliably. Do not pass an increment operator as an argument.

8. `The size of name is 20`

Chapter 12 Answers

1. Bitwise logical operators: !, &, ^, and ¦
   Compound bitwise logical operators: &=, ^=, and ¦=
   Bitwise shift operators: << and >>

2. a. 1

   b. 1

   c. 0

   d. 0

3. True

4. The 2's complement converts a number to its negative. The 1's complement simply reverses the bit pattern.

Chapter 13 Answers

1. The `while` loop tests for a true condition at the top of the loop. The `do-while` tests at the bottom.

2. A counter variable increments by one. A total variable increments by the addition to the total you are performing.

3. The ++ operator

4. If the body of the loop is a single statement, the braces are not required. However, braces are always recommended.

5. There are no braces. The second `printf()` will always execute, regardless of the result of the `while` loop's relational test.

6. stdlib.h

7. One time

8. By returning a value inside the `exit()` function's parentheses

9. `This is the outer loop`

   `This is the outer loop`

   `This is the outer loop`

   `This is the outer loop`

Chapter 14 Answers

1. A sequence of one or more instructions executed repeatedly

2. False

3. A loop within a loop

4. Because the expressions might be initialized elsewhere, such as before the loop or in the body of the loop

5. The inner loop

6. `10`

   `7`

   `4`

   `1`

7. True

8. The body of the `for` loop stops repeating.

9. False, due to the semicolon after the first `for` loop

10. There is no output. The value of `start` is already less than end when the loop begins; therefore, the `for` loop's test is immediately False.

Chapter 15 Answers

1. To force a program to pause

2. Because some computers are faster than others

3. If the `continue` and `break` statements were unconditional, there would be little use for them.

4. Because of the unconditional `continue` statement, there is no output.

5. `*****`

6. A single variable rarely can hold a large enough value for the timer's count.

Chapter 16 Answers

1. The program does not execute sequentially, as it would without `goto`.

2. The `switch` statement

3. A `break` statement

4. False

5.
```
switch (num)
{ case (1) : { printf("Alpha");
              break; }
  case (2) : { printf("Beta");
              break; }
  case (3) : { printf("Gamma");
              break; }
  default :  { printf("Other");
              break; }
}
```

6.
```
do
  { printf("What is your first name? ");
    scanf(" %s", name);
  } while ((name[0] < 'A') |\ (name[0] > 'Z'));
```

Chapter 17 Answers

1. True

2. `main()`

3. Several smaller functions are better because each function can perform a single task

4. Function names always end with a pair of parentheses.

5. By putting separating comments between functions

6. The function `sq_25()` cannot be nested in `calc_it()`.

7. A function definition (a prototype)

8. True

Chapter 18 Answers

1. True

2. Local variables are passed as arguments.

3. False

4. The variable data types

5. Static

6. You should never pass global variables—they do not need to be passed.

7. 2 arguments

Chapter 19 Answers

1. Arrays

2. Nonarray variables are always passed by value, unless you override the default with & before each variable name.

3. False

4. No

5. Yes

6. The data types of variables x, y, and z are not declared in the receiving parameter list.

7. c

Chapter 20 Answers

1. By putting the return type to the right of the function name

2. 1

3. To prototype built-in functions

4. Integer

5. False

6. Prototypes ensure that the correct number of parameters is being passed.

7. Global variables are already known across functions.

8. The return type is float. Three parameters are passed: a character, an integer, and a floating-point variable.

Chapter 21 Answers

1. For portability between different computers

2. False. The standard output can be redirected to any device through the operating system.

3. `getchar()` assumes `stdin` for the input device.

4. `getch()` does not wait for the Enter keypress.

5. `fprintf()`

6. `>` and `<`

7. `getche()`

8. False. The input from `getchar()` goes to a buffer as you type it.

9. Enter

10. True

Chapter 22 Answers

1. The character-testing functions do not change the character passed to them.

2. `gets()` and `fgets()`

3. `floor()` rounds down and `ceil()` rounds up.

4. False. The inner function returns 1.

5. `PeterParker`

6. `8 9`

7. True

8. `Prog` with a null zero at the end

9. True

Chapter 23 Answers

1. False

2. The array subscripts differentiate array elements.

3. C does not initialize, or "zero out," arrays for you.

4. `0`

5. Yes. All arrays are passed by address because an array name is nothing more than an address to that array.

6. C initializes all global variables (and every other static variable in your program) to zero or null zero.

Chapter 24 Answers

1. False

2. From the low numbers "floating" to the top of the array like bubbles

3. Ascending order

4. The name of an array is an address to the starting element of that array.

5. a. `Eagles`

   b. `Rams`

   c. `les`

   d. invalid

   e. `E`

   f. invalid

   g. `g`

Chapter 25 Answers

1. `int scores[5][6];`

2. `char initials[4][10][20]`

3. The first subscript represents rows and the last represents columns.

4. 30 elements

5. a. 2

   b. 1

   c. 91

   d. 8

6. Nested `for` loops step through multidimensional tables very easily.

7. a. 78
   b. 100
   c. 90

Chapter 26 Answers

1. a. Integer pointer
   b. Character pointer
   c. Floating-point pointer
2. "Address of "
3. The * operator
4. `pt_sal = &salary;`
5. False
6. Yes
7. a. 2313.54
   b. 2313.54
   c. invalid
   d. invalid
8. b

Chapter 27 Answers

1. Array names are pointer constants, not pointer variables.
2. 8
3. a, c, d, e. Parentheses are needed around `iptr+1` and `iptr+4` to make b and f valid.
4. You have to move only pointers, not entire strings.
5. a and d

Chapter 28 Answers

1. Structures hold groups of more than one value, each of which can be a different data type.

2. Members

3. At declaration time and at run time

4. Structures pass by copy.

5. False. Memory is reserved only when structure variables are declared.

6. Globally

7. Locally

8. 4

Chapter 29 Answers

1. True

2. Arrays are easier to manage.

3. a. `inventory[32].price = 12.33;`

   b. `inventory[11].part_no[0] = 'X';`

   c. `inventory[96] = inventory[62];`

4. a. `item` is not a structure variable.

   b. `inventory` is an array and must have a subscript.

   c. `inventory` is an array and must have a subscript.

Chapter 30 Answers

1. Write, append, and read

2. Disks hold more data than memory.

3. You can access sequential files only in the same order that they were originally written.

4. An error condition occurs

5. The old file is overwritten.

6. The file is created.

7. C returns the EOF constant, defined in stdio.h, when an end-of-file condition is met.

8. The EOF return value might be a negative number.

Chapter 31 Answers

1. Records are stored in files and structures are stored in memory.

2. False

3. The file pointer continually updates to point to the next byte to read.

4. `fwrite()` and `fread()`

5. `rewind()` and `fseek(fp, 0, SEEK_SET);`

6. SEEK_SET (or 0), SEEK_CUR (or 1), and SEEK_END (or 2)

7. You must use the `feof()` function to check for the end-of-file condition in binary files.

ASCII Table

Dec X_{10}	Hex X_{16}	Binary X_2	ASCII Character
000	00	0000 0000	null
001	01	0000 0001	☺
002	02	0000 0010	●
003	03	0000 0011	♥
004	04	0000 0100	♦
005	05	0000 0101	♣
006	06	0000 0110	♠
007	07	0000 0111	●
008	08	0000 1000	■
009	09	0000 1001	○
010	0A	0000 1010	■
011	0B	0000 1011	♂
012	0C	0000 1100	♀
013	0D	0000 1101	♪
014	0E	0000 1110	♪♪
015	0F	0000 1111	☼
016	10	0001 0000	►
017	11	0001 0001	◄
018	12	0001 0010	↕

Dec X_{10}	Hex X_{16}	Binary X_2	ASCII Character
019	13	0001 0011	‼
020	14	0001 0100	¶
021	15	0001 0101	§
022	16	0001 0110	–
023	17	0001 0111	↕
024	18	0001 1000	↑
025	19	0001 1001	↓
026	1A	0001 1010	→
027	1B	0001 1011	←
028	1C	0001 1100	FS
029	1D	0001 1101	GS
030	1E	0001 1110	RS
031	1F	0001 1111	US
032	20	0010 0000	SP
033	21	0010 0001	!
034	22	0010 0010	"
035	23	0010 0011	#
036	24	0010 0100	$
037	25	0010 0101	%
038	26	0010 0110	&
039	27	0010 0111	'
040	28	0010 1000	(
041	29	0010 1001	)
042	2A	0010 1010	*
043	2B	0010 1011	+
044	2C	0010 1100	'
045	2D	0010 1101	-
046	2E	0010 1110	.
047	2F	0010 1111	/
048	30	0011 0000	0
049	31	0011 0001	1
050	32	0011 0010	2

Dec X_{10}	Hex X_{16}	Binary X_2	ASCII Character
051	33	0011 0011	3
052	34	0011 0100	4
053	35	0011 0101	5
054	36	0011 0110	6
055	37	0011 0111	7
056	38	0011 1000	8
057	39	0011 1001	9
058	3A	0011 1010	:
059	3B	0011 1011	;
060	3C	0011 1100	<
061	3D	0011 1101	=
062	3E	0011 1110	>
063	3F	0011 1111	?
064	40	0100 0000	@
065	41	0100 0001	A
066	42	0100 0010	B
067	43	0100 0011	C
068	44	0100 0100	D
069	45	0100 0101	E
070	46	0100 0110	F
071	47	0100 0111	G
072	48	0100 1000	H
073	49	0100 1001	I
074	4A	0100 1010	J
075	4B	0100 1011	K
076	4C	0100 1100	L
077	4D	0100 1101	M
078	4E	0100 1110	N
079	4F	0100 1111	O
080	50	0101 0000	P
081	51	0101 0001	Q
082	52	0101 0010	R

Dec X_{10}	Hex X_{16}	Binary X_2	ASCII Character
083	53	0101 0011	S
084	54	0101 0100	T
085	55	0101 0101	U
086	56	0101 0110	V
087	57	0101 0111	W
088	58	0101 1000	X
089	59	0101 1001	Y
090	5A	0101 1010	Z
091	5B	0101 1011	[
092	5C	0101 1100	\
093	5D	0101 1101	]
094	5E	0101 1110	^
095	5F	0101 1111	–
096	60	0110 0000	`
097	61	0110 0001	a
098	62	0110 0010	b
099	63	0110 0011	c
100	64	0110 0100	d
101	65	0110 0101	e
102	66	0110 0110	f
103	67	0110 0111	g
104	68	0110 1000	h
105	69	0110 1001	i
106	6A	0110 1010	j
107	6B	0110 1011	k
108	6C	0110 1100	l
109	6D	0110 1101	m
110	6E	0110 1110	n
111	6F	0110 1111	o
112	70	0111 0000	p
113	71	0111 0001	q

DecHex X_{10}	Binary X_{16}	ASCII X_2	Character
114	72	0111 0010	r
115	73	0111 0011	s
116	74	0111 0100	t
117	75	0111 0101	u
118	76	0111 0110	v
119	77	0111 0111	w
120	78	0111 1000	x
121	79	0111 1001	y
122	7A	0111 1010	z
123	7B	0111 1011	{
124	7C	0111 1100	¦
125	7D	0111 1101	}
126	7E	0111 1110	~
127	7F	0111 1111	DEL

C Precedence Table

Precedence

Level	Symbol	Description	Associativity
1	++	Prefix increment	Left to right
	--	Prefix decrement	
	()	Function call and subexpression	
	[ ]	Array subscript	
	->	Structure pointer	
	.	Structure member	
2	!	Logical negation	Right to left
	~	1's complement	
	-	Unary negation	
	+	Unary plus	

Precedence continued

Level	Symbol	Description	Associativity
2 (cont.)	(type)	Type cast	
	*	Pointer dereference	
	&	Address of	
	sizeof	Size of	
3	*	Multiplication	Left to right
	/	Division	
	%	Modulus (integer remainder)	
4	+	Addition	Left to right
	-	Subtraction	
5	<<	Bitwise left shift	Left to right
	>>	Bitwise right shift	
6	<	Less than	Left to right
	<=	Less than or equal to	
	>	Greater than	
	>=	Greater than or equal to	
7	==	Equal test	Left to right
	!=	Not equal test	
8	&	Bitwise AND	Left to right
9	^	Bitwise exclusive OR	Left to right
10	¦	Bitwise inclusive OR	Left to right
11	&&	Logical AND	Left to right

Level	Symbol	Description	Associativity
12	¦¦	Logical inclusive OR	Left to right
13	?:	Conditional test	Right to left
14	=	Assignment	Right to left
	+=	Compound add	
	-+	Compound subtract	
	*=	Compound multiply	
	/=	Compound divide	
	%=	Compound modulus	
	<<=	Compound bitwise left shift	
	>>=	Compound bitwise right shift	
	&=	Compound bitwise AND	
	^=	Compound bitwise exclusive OR	
	¦=	Compound bitwise inclusive OR	
15	,	Sequence point	Left to right
	++	Postfix increment	
	--	Postfix decrement	

Keyword and Function Reference

These are the 32 ANSI C standard keywords:

auto	double	int	struct
break	else	long	switch
case	enum	register	typedef
char	extern	return	union
const	float	short	unsigned
continue	for	signed	void
default	goto	sizeof	volatile
do	if	static	while

The following are the built-in function prototypes, listed by their header files. The prototypes describe the parameter data types that each function requires.

`<stdio.h>`

```
int fclose(FILE *stream);
int feof(FILE *stream);
int ferror(FILE *stream);
int fflush(FILE *stream);
int fgetc(FILE *stream);
char *fgets(char *, int, FILE *stream);
FILE *fopen(const char *filename, const char *mode);
int fprintf(FILE *stream, const char *format, ...);
int fputc(int, FILE *stream);
int fputs(const char *, FILE *stream);
size_t fread(void *, size_t, size_t, FILE *stream);
int fscanf(FILE *stream, const char *format, ...);
int fseek(FILE *stream, long offset, int origin);
size_t fwrite(const void *, size_t, size_t, FILE *stream);
int getc(FILE *stream);
int getchar(void);
char *gets(char *);
void perror(const char *);
int putc(int, FILE *stream);
int putchar(int);
int puts(const char *);
int remove(const char *filename);
void rewind(FILE *stream);
int scanf(const char *format, ...);
```

`<ctype.h>`

```
int isalnum(unsigned char);
int asalpha(unsigned char);
int iscntrl(unsigned char);
int isdigit(unsigned char);
int isgraph(unsigned char);
int islower(unsigned char);
int isprint(unsigned char);
int ispunct(unsigned char);
int isspace(unsigned char);
int isupper(unsigned char);
int isxdigit(unsigned char);
```

```
int tolower(int);
int toupper(int);
```

<string.h>

```
char *strcat(char *, char *);
int strcmp(char *, char *);
int strcpy(char *, char *);
size_t strlen(char *);Ce
```

<math.h>

```
double ceil(double);
double cos(double);
double exp(double);
double fabs(double);
double floor(double);
double fmod(double, double);
double log(double);
double log10(double);
double pow(double, double);
double sin(double);
double sqrt(double);
double tan(double);
```

<stdlib.h>

```
double atof(const char *);
int atoi(const char *);
long atol(const char *);
void exit(int);
int rand(void);
void srand(unsigned int);
```

The Mailing List Application

This appendix shows a complete program that contains most of the commands and functions you learned throughout the book. This program manages a mailing list for your personal or business needs.

When you run the program, you are presented with a menu of choices that guide you through the program's operation. Comments throughout the program offer improvements you might want to make. As your knowledge and practice of C improves, you might want to expand this mailing list application into your entire contact database.

Here is the listing of the complete program:

```
/* Filename: MAILING.C
   * Mailing List Application *
   ----------------------

   This program enables the user to enter, edit, maintain, and
   print a mailing list of names and addresses.

   All commands and concepts included in this program are
   explained throughout the text of C By Example.              */
```

```
/* These are items you might want to add or change:
    1. Find your compiler's clear screen function to improve on
       the screen-clearing function.
    2. Add an entry for the 'code' member to track different
       types of names and addresses (that is, business codes,
       personal codes, and so on).
    3. Search for a partial name (that is, typing "Sm" finds
       "Smith" and "Smitty" and "Smythe" in the file).
    4. When searching for name matches, ignore case (that is,
       typing "smith" finds "Smith" in the file).
    5. Print mailing labels on your printer.
    6. Allow for sorting a listing of names and addresses by
       name or ZIP code.
*/

/* Header files used by the program */
#include <stdio.h>
#include <ctype.h>

/* Global structure of a name and address */
struct mail_struct
    { char name[25];            /* Name stored here should
                                    be last, first order */
      char address[25];
      char city[12];
      char state[3];            /* Save room for null zero */
      char zipcode[6];
      char code[7];     /* For additional expansion. You
                           might want to use this member for
                           customer codes, vendor codes, or
                           holiday card codes */
    };
/* Global file pointer */
FILE *fp;

/* Defined constants */
/* MAX is the total number of names allowed in memory for
   reading mailing list */
#define MAX 250
#define BELL '\x07'
```

```
#define FILENAME "ADDRESS.DAT"

/* Prototype all of this program's functions */
void main(void);
void disp_menu(void);
void clear_sc(void);
void enter_na(void);
void change_na(void);
void print_na(void);
void err_msg(char err_msg[]);
void delay(void);
void add_to_file(struct mail_struct item);
void pause_sc(void);
void pr_data(struct mail_struct item);
void get_new_item(struct mail_struct *item);
void getzip(char zipcode[]);

/*************************************************************/
void main(void)
{
   struct mail_struct list[MAX];
   char ans;
   do
     { disp_menu();        /* Display the menu for the user */
       scanf(" %d", &ans);
       switch (ans)
       {  case (1) : { enter_na();
                 break; }
       case (2) : { change_na();
                 break; }
       case (3) : { print_na();
                 break; }
       case (4) : { break; }
       default  : { err_msg("*** You need to enter");
                    printf(" 1 through 4 ***");
                 break; }
       }
     } while (ans!=4);
   return;
}


/*************************************************************/
```

```
void disp_menu()  /* Display the main menu of the program */
{
   clear_sc();                        /* Clear the screen */
   printf("\t\t*** Mailing List Manager ***\n");
   printf("\t\t    ------------------\n\n\n\n");
   printf("Do you want to:\n\n\n");
   printf("\t1. Add names and addresses to the list\n\n\n");
   printf("\t2. Change names and addresses in the list\n\n\n");
   printf("\t3. Print names and addresses in the list\n\n\n");
   printf("\t4. Exit this program\n\n\n");
   printf("What is your choice? ");
   return;
}


/**************************************************************/
void clear_sc()              /* Clear the screen by sending
                                        25 blank lines to it */
{
   int ctr;               /* Counter for the 25 blank lines */
   for(ctr=0;ctr<25;ctr++)
      { printf("\n"); }
   return;
}


/**************************************************************/
void enter_na(void)
{
   struct mail_struct item;
   char ans;
   do
   { fflush(stdin);                    /* Clear input buffer
                                    before getting strings */
     printf("\n\n\n\n\nWhat is the name? ");
     gets(item.name);
     printf("What is the address? ");
     gets(item.address);
     printf("What is the city? ");
     gets(item.city);
     printf("What is the state? (2-letter abbreviation only) ");
     gets(item.state);

     getzip(item.zipcode);           /* Ensure that ZIP code
                                         is all digits */
```

```
        strcpy(item.code, " ");  /* Null out the code member */
        add_to_file(item);              /* Write new information
                                                    to disk file */
     printf("\n\nDo you want to enter another name");
     printf(" and address? (Y/N) ");
     ans=getchar();
     getchar();                 /* Discard carriage return */
   } while (toupper(ans)=='Y');

   return;
}


/**************************************************************/
void change_na(void)
{
   /* This search function can be improved by using the   */
   /* code member to assign a unique code to each person   */
   /* in the list. Names are difficult to search for       */
   /* because there are so many variations (such as        */
   /* Mc and Mac, and St. and Saint.                       */

   struct mail_struct item;
   int ans, s;               /* Holds size of structure */
   int change_yes = 0;          /* Will be True if user
                                    finds a name to change */
   char test_name[25];

   printf("\nWhat is the name of the person you want");
   printf(" to change? ");
   fflush(stdin);   /* Clear out anything in input buffer */
   gets(test_name);
   fflush(stdin);

   s = sizeof(struct mail_struct);      /* To ensure that
                                    fread() reads properly */
   if((fp=fopen(FILENAME, "r+"))==NULL)
      { err_msg("*** Read error—ensure file exists ***");
      return; }
   do
      { if(fread(&item, sizeof(struct mail_struct), 1, fp)!=s)
      { if(feof(fp))               /* If EOF, quit reading */
         { break; }
```

```
        }
        if (strcmp(item.name, test_name)==0)
        {  pr_data(item);           /* Print name and address */
           printf("\nIs this the name and address to");
           printf(" change? (Y/N) ");
           ans=getchar();
           getchar();              /* Discard carriage return */
           if (toupper(ans)=='N')
             { continue; }              /* Get another name */
           get_new_item(&item);      /* Let user type new
                                              information */
           fseek(fp, (long)-s, SEEK_CUR);   /* Back up one
                                                structure */
           fwrite(&item, s, 1, fp);           /* Rewrite
                                              information */
           change_yes = 1;               /* Changed flag */
           break;                        /* Finished */
        }
     } while (!feof(fp));
   fclose(fp);
   if (!change_yes)
     { err_msg("*** End of file—couldn't find name ***"); }
   return;
}

/*************************************************************/
void print_na(void)
{
   struct mail_struct item;
   int s, linectr=0;

   s = sizeof(struct mail_struct);       /* To ensure that
                                      fread() reads properly */
   if((fp=fopen(FILENAME, "r"))==NULL)
     { err_msg("*** Read error—ensure file exists ***");
     return; }
   do
     { if(fread(&item, sizeof(struct mail_struct), 1, fp)!=s)
       { if(feof(fp))                /* If EOF, quit reading */
         { break; }
     }
       if (linectr>20)                    /* Screen is full */
```

```
      { pause_sc();
        linectr=0; }
       pr_data(item);          /* Print the name and address */
       linectr+=4;
     } while (!feof(fp));
   fclose(fp);
   printf("\n- End of list -");
   pause_sc();              /* Give the user a chance to see
                               the names remaining on-screen */

   return;
}


/**************************************************************/
void err_msg(char err_msg[])
{
   printf("\n\n%s\n", err_msg);
   printf("%c", BELL);
   delay();
   return;
}


/**************************************************************/
void delay()
{
   /* This function loops for about three seconds on a fast  */
   /* computer. You might have to change the value for delay */
   /* if the loop is too fast or too slow on your computer.  */

   int time1, time2;
   int delay=20000;
   for(time1=0;time1<500;time1++)
     { for(time2=0;time2<delay;time2++); }   /* Do nothing
                                        for three seconds */
   return;
}


/**************************************************************/
void add_to_file(struct mail_struct item)
{
   if((fp = fopen(FILENAME, "a"))==NULL)  /* Open file in
                                             append mode */
     { err_msg("*** Disk error—please check disk drive ***");
      return; }
```

```
          fwrite(&item, sizeof(item), 1, fp);   /* Add structure
                                                       to the file */
       fclose(fp);
       return;
    }

    /**************************************************************/
    void pause_sc()
    {
       char ans;
       fflush(stdin);              /* Remove any extra characters
                                              from the input buffer */
       printf("\nPress the Enter key to continue...");
       ans=getchar();
       fflush(stdin);              /* Remove any extra characters
                                              from the input buffer */
       return;
    }

    /**************************************************************/
    void pr_data(struct mail_struct item)
    {
       /* Prints the name and address sent to it */
       printf("\nName    : %-25s\n", item.name);
       printf("Address: %-25s\n", item.address);
       printf("City    : %-12s\tState: %-2s  Zipcode: %-5s\n",
              item.city, item.state, item.zipcode);
       return;
    }

    /**************************************************************/
    void get_new_item(struct mail_struct *item)
    {
       struct mail_struct temp_item;         /* Holds temporary
                                                   changed input */
       printf("\nEnter new name and address information");
       printf(" below\n(Press the ");
       printf("Enter key without typing data to retain old");
       printf(" information)\n\n");
       printf("What is the new name? ");
       if (strlen(gets(temp_item.name))>0)   /* Save new data
                                                  only if the user */
```

```
       { strcpy((*item).name, temp_item.name); } /* presses
                                        the Enter key */
     printf("What is the address? ");
     if (strlen(gets(temp_item.address))>0)
       { strcpy((*item).address, temp_item.address); }
     printf("What is the city? ");
     if (strlen(gets(temp_item.city))>0)
       { strcpy((*item).city, temp_item.city); }
     printf("What is the state? (2-letter abbreviation only) ");
     if (strlen(gets(temp_item.state))>0)
       { strcpy((*item).state, temp_item.state); }
     printf("What is the ZIP code? ");
     if (strlen(gets(temp_item.zipcode))>0)
       { strcpy((*item).zipcode, temp_item.zipcode); }
     (*item).code[0] = 0;    /* Null out the code member (unused
                                 here) */

     return;      /* Return structure with changed member(s) */
   }

   void getzip(char zipcode[])        /* Ensure that ZIP code
                                         is all digits */
   {
      int ctr, bad_zip;

      do
        { bad_zip = 0;
          printf("What is the ZIP code? ");
          gets(zipcode);
          for(ctr=0;ctr<5;ctr++)
        { if (isdigit(zipcode[ctr]))
            { continue; }
          else
            { err_msg("*** The ZIP code must be digits only ***");
            bad_zip = 1;
            break; }
        }
        } while (bad_zip);
      return;
   }
```

Glossary

address Each memory (RAM) location (each byte) has a unique address. The first address in memory is 0, the second RAM location's address is 1, and so on until the last RAM location (which comes thousands of bytes later).

argument The value sent *to* a function or procedure. This can be a constant or a variable. The argument is enclosed in parentheses.

array A list of variables, sometimes called a table of variables.

ASCII Acronym for **A**merican **S**tandard **C**ode for Information Interchange.

ASCII file A file containing characters that can be used by any program on most computers. Sometimes it is called a text file or an ASCII text file.

AUTOEXEC.BAT An optional batch file in a PC that executes a series of commands whenever you start or reset the computer.

backup file A duplicate copy of a file that preserves your work in case you damage the original file. Files on a hard disk are commonly backed up on floppy disks.

binary A numbering system based on only two digits. The only valid digits in a binary system are 0 and 1. See also *bit*.

binary zero Another name for *null zero*.

bit Binary digit, the smallest unit of storage on a computer. Each bit can have a value of 0 or 1, indicating the absence or presence of an electrical signal. See also *binary*.

bitwise operators C operators that manipulate the binary representation of values.

block One or more statements treated as if they are a single statement. A block is always enclosed within braces.

boot To start a computer with the operating system software in place. You must boot your computer before using it.

bubble sort An easy-to-code sorting routine that sorts arrays of values.

bug An error in a program that prevents the program from running correctly. This term originated when a moth short-circuited a connection in a printer, preventing the computer from working.

byte A basic unit of data storage and manipulation. A byte is equivalent to eight bits and can contain a value ranging from 0 through 255.

cathode ray tube (CRT) The television-like screen of a computer, also called the *monitor*. It is one place to which you can send the output of the computer.

code A set of instructions written in a programming language. See *source code*.

compile To translate a program written in a programming language, such as C or Pascal, into machine code that your computer understands.

central processing unit (CPU) The controlling circuit responsible for operations within the computer. These operations generally include system timing, logical processing, and logical operations. The CPU controls every operation of the computer system. On PCs, the central processing unit is called a *microprocessor* and is stored on a single integrated circuit chip.

concatenation   The process of attaching one string to the end of another or combining two or more strings into a longer string.

conditional loop   A series of C instructions that occurs a fixed number of times.

constant   Data that remain the same during a program run.

CPU   See *central processing unit.*

CRT   See *cathode ray tube.*

data   Information stored in the computer as numbers, letters, and special symbols such as punctuation marks. *Data* refers also to the characters you input to your program so that the program can produce meaningful *information.*

data processing   This is what computers really do: They take data and manipulate it into meaningful output. The meaningful output is called *information.*

debug   The process of locating an error (bug) in a program and removing it.

default   A predefined action or command that the computer chooses unless you specify otherwise.

dereference   The process of finding a value pointed to by a pointer variable.

digital computer   A term that comes from the fact that your computer operates on binary (*on* and *off*) digital impulses of electricity.

directory   A list of the files that are stored on a disk. Directories within existing directories are called *subdirectories.*

disk   A round, flat, magnetic storage medium. Floppy disks are made of flexible material and enclosed in 5 1/4-inch or 3 1/2-inch protective cases. Hard disks consist of a stack of rigid disks housed in a single unit. A floppy disk is sometimes called *external memory.* Hard disk storage and floppy disk storage are nonvolatile. When you turn off your computer, the disk's contents do not go away.

disk drive   A device that reads and writes data to a floppy disk or hard disk.

diskette   Another name for a removable floppy disk.

display   A screen or monitor.

display adapter   Located in the system unit, the display adapter determines the amount of resolution and the possible number of colors on the screen.

DOS   Disk operating system.

dot-matrix printer   One of the two most common PC printers (the laser printer is the other). A dot-matrix printer is inexpensive and fast; it uses a series of small dots to represent printed text and graphics.

element   An individual variable in an array.

execute   To run a program.

expanded memory   See *extended memory*.

extended memory   The amount of RAM that is beyond the basic 640K in most PCs. You cannot access this extra RAM without special programs.

external modem   A modem that sits in a box outside your computer. See also *internal modem*.

file   A collection of data stored as a single unit on a floppy disk or hard disk. Files always have a file name that identifies them.

file extension   Used by PCs to denote file types, the file extension consists of a period followed by up to three characters. The file extension follows the file name.

file name   A unique name that identifies a file. File names can be up to eight characters long, and may have a period followed by an extension (which is normally three characters long).

fixed disk   See *hard disk*.

fixed-length records   A record in which each field takes the same amount of disk space, even if that field's data value does not fill the field.

floppy disk   See *disk*.

format To create a "map" on a disk that tells the operating system how the disk is structured. This is how the operating system keeps track of where files are stored.

function A self-contained coding segment designed to do a specific task. All C programs must have at least one function called `main()`. Some functions are built-in routines that manipulate numbers, strings, and output.

function keys The keys labeled F1 through F12 (some keyboards go only to F10).

global variable A variable that can be seen from (and used by) every statement in the program.

hard copy The printout of a program (or its output). Also a safe back-up copy for a program in case the disk is erased.

hard disk Sometimes called a *fixed disk*. The hard disk holds much more data and is many times faster than a floppy disk. See *disk*.

hardware The physical parts of the computer. Hardware has been defined as "anything you can kick," and consists of the things you can see, such as the system unit, the monitor, and the printer.

hexadecimal A numbering system based on 16 elements. Digits are numbered 0 through F as follows: 0, 1, 2, 3, 4, 5, 6, 7, 8, 9, A, B, C, D, E, F.

hierarchy of operators See *order of operators*.

indeterminate loop A loop in which you do not know in advance how many cycles of the loop will be made (unlike with the `for` loop).

infinite loop The never-ending repetition of a block of C statements.

information The meaningful product of a program. Data go *into* a program to produce *meaningful* output (information).

input To enter data into a computer through a device such as the keyboard. *Input* can also refer to the data itself.

input-process-output This model is the foundation of everything that happens in your computer. Data are input, then processed by your program in the computer, and finally information is output.

integer variables   Variables that can hold integers.

internal modem   A modem that resides inside the system unit. See also external modem.

I/O   Acronym for Input/Output.

kilobyte (K)   A unit of measurement that is equal to 1,024 bytes.

laser printer   A type of printer that in general is faster than a dot-matrix printer. Laser printer output is much sharper than that of a dot-matrix printer, because a laser beam actually burns toner ink into the paper. Laser printers are more expensive than dot-matrix printers.

least significant bit   The rightmost bit of a byte. For example, a binary 00000111 would have a 1 as its least significant bit.

line printer   Another name for your printer.

local variable   A variable that can be seen from (and used by) only the block in which it is defined.

loop   The repeated circular execution of one or more statements.

machine language   The series of binary digits that a microprocessor executes to perform individual tasks. People seldom (if ever) program in machine language. Instead, they program in assembly language, and an assembler translates their instructions into machine language.

main module   The first function of a modular program called `main()` that controls the execution of the other functions.

maintainability   The computer industry's word for the ability to change and update programs that were written in a simple style.

math operator   A symbol used for addition, subtraction, multiplication, division, or other calculations.

megabyte (M)   In computer terminology, approximately a million bytes. 1,048,576 bytes.

member   A piece of a structure variable that holds a specific type of data.

memory   A storage area inside the computer, which is used to store data temporarily. The computer's memory is erased when you turn off the power.

menu   A list of commands or instructions displayed on the screen. These lists organize commands and make a program easier to use.

menu-driven   Describes a program that provides menus for choosing commands.

microchip   A small wafer of silicon that holds computer components and occupies less space than a postage stamp.

microcomputer   A small version of a computer that can fit on a desktop, sometimes called a PC. The microchip is the heart of the microcomputer.

microprocessor   The chip that does the calculations for a PC. Sometimes it is called the central processing unit (CPU).

modem   A piece of hardware that modulates and demodulates signals so that your computer can communicate with other computers over telephone lines. See also *external modems, internal modems.*

modular programming   The process of writing your programs in several modules rather than as one long program. By breaking a program into several smaller program-line routines, you can isolate problems better, write correct programs faster, and produce programs that are much easier to maintain.

modulate   Before your computer can transmit data over a telephone line, the information to be sent must be converted (modulated) into analog signals. See also *demodulate.*

modulus   The integer remainder of division.

monitor   A television-like screen that lets the computer display information. The monitor is known as an output device.

mouse   A hand-held device that you move across the desktop to move an indicator, called a mouse pointer, across the screen. The mouse is used instead of the keyboard to select and move items (such as text or graphics), execute commands, and perform other tasks.

MS-DOS An operating system for IBM and compatible computers.

multidimensional arrays Arrays with more than one dimension. As two-dimensional arrays, they are sometimes called tables or matrices, which have rows and columns.

nested loop A loop within a loop.

null zero The string-terminating character. All C string constants and strings stored in character arrays end in null zero. The ASCII value for the null zero is 0.

null string An empty string, the first character of which is the null zero and the length of which is zero.

numeric functions Built-in routines that work with numbers.

object code A "halfway step" between source code and executable machine language. Object code consists mostly of machine language; however, it is not directly executable by the computer. Object code must first be linked in order to resolve external references and address references.

operator An operator works on data and might perform math calculations or change data to other data types. Examples include the +, -, and `sizeof()`.

order of operators Sometimes called the *hierarchy of operators* or the *precedence of operators*, the order of operators determines exactly how C computes formulas.

output device Where the results of a program are output, such as the screen, the printer, or a disk file.

parallel arrays Two arrays working side-by-side. Each element in each array corresponds to one in the other array.

parallel port A connector used to plug a device, such as a printer, into the computer. Transferring data through a parallel port is much faster than transferring data through a serial port.

parameter A list of variables enclosed in parentheses that follow the name of a function or procedure. Parameters indicate the number and type of arguments that will be sent to the function or procedure.

passing by address   Also called *passing by reference*. When an argument (a local variable) is passed by address, the variable's address in memory is sent to, and is assigned to, the receiving function's parameter list. (If more than one variable is passed by address, each of their addresses is sent to and assigned to the receiving function's parameters.) A change made to the parameter within the function will also change the value of the argument variable.

passing by copy   Another name for *passing by value*.

passing by reference   Another name for *passing by address*.

passing by value   By default, all C variable arguments are passed *by value*. When the value contained in a variable is passed to the parameter list of a receiving function, changes made to the parameter within the routine will *not* change the value of the argument variable. Also called *passing by copy*.

path   The route the computer travels from the root directory to any subdirectories when locating a file. The path also refers to the subdirectories that MS-DOS examines when you type a command that requires it to find and access a file.

peripheral   A device attached to the computer, such as a modem, a disk drive, a mouse, or a printer.

personal computer   A microcomputer, sometimes called a PC.

pointer   A variable that holds the address of another variable.

precedence of operators   See *order of operators*.

preprocessor directive   A command, preceded by a #, that you place in your source code that directs the compiler to modify the source code in some fashion. The two most common preprocessor directives are #define and #include.

printer   A device that prints data from the computer to paper.

program   A group of instructions that tell the computer what to do.

programming language   A set of rules for writing instructions for the computer. Popular programming languages include BASIC, C, Visual Basic, QBasic, C++, and Pascal.

RAM   Random-access memory.

random-access file   Records in a file that can be accessed in any order you want.

random-access memory   What your computer uses to temporarily store data and programs. RAM is measured in kilobytes and megabytes. Generally, the more RAM a computer has, the more powerful programs it can run.

read-only memory (ROM)   A permanent type of computer memory. It contains the BIOS (Basic Input/Output System), which is a special chip used to provide instructions to the computer when you turn on the computer.

real numbers   Numbers that have decimal points and a fractional part to the right of the decimal.

record   An individual row in a file.

relational operators   Operators that compare data; they tell how two variables or constants relate to each other. Relational operators tell you whether two variables are equal or not equal, or which one is less than or more than the other.

ROM   Read-only memory.

scientific notation   A shortcut method of representing numbers of extreme values.

sectors   A pattern of pie-shaped wedges on a disk. Formatting creates a pattern of tracks and sectors where your data and programs will be stored.

sequential-access file   A file that has to be accessed one record at a time beginning with the first record.

serial port   A connector used to plug in serial devices, such as a modem or a mouse.

single-dimensional arrays   Arrays that have only one subscript. Single-dimensional arrays represent a list of values.

software   The data and programs that interact with your hardware. The C language is an example of software.

sorting   A method of putting data in a specific order (such as alphabetical or numerical order), even if that order is not the same order in which the elements were entered.

source code   The C language instructions, written by humans, that the C compiler translates into object code.

spaghetti code   A term used when there are too many occurrences of `goto` in a program. If a program branches all over the place, it is difficult to follow, and the logic resembles a "bowl of spaghetti."

stream   Literally, a stream of characters, one following another, flowing between devices in your computer.

string constant   One or more groups of characters that end in a null zero.

string literal   Another name for a *string constant.*

structure   A unit of related information containing one or more members, such as an employee number, employee name, employee address, employee pay rate, and so on.

subscript   A number inside brackets that differentiates one element of an array from another.

syntax error   The most common error a programmer makes—usually a misspelled word.

system unit   The large box component of the computer. The system unit houses the PC's microchip (the CPU).

tracks   A pattern of paths on a disk. Formatting creates a pattern of tracks and sectors where your data and programs will go.

truncation   The fractional part of a number (the part of the number to the right of the decimal point) is taken off the number. No rounding is done.

two's complement   A method your computer uses to take the negative of a number. This method plus addition allows the computer to simulate subtraction.

unary operator   The addition or subtraction operator used before a single variable or constant.

UNIX   A multiuser operating system used by minicomputers.

user-friendliness   A program is user-friendly if it makes the user comfortable and simulates what the user is already familiar with.

variable   Data that can change as the program runs.

variable-length record   A record that takes up no wasted space on the disk. As soon as a field's data value is saved to the file, the next field's data value is stored immediately after it. There is usually a special separating character between the fields so that your programs know where the fields begin and end.

variable scope   Sometimes called the *visibility of variables*, variable scope describes how variables are "seen" by your program. See also *global variables* and *local variables*.

volatile   Temporary. For example, when you turn the computer off, all the RAM (volatile memory) is erased.

word   In PC usage, a word is two consecutive bytes (16 bits) of data. On a minicomputer or mainframe, a word can be larger.

Index

Symbols

-- decrement operator, 221
#define directive, 112-119
#include directive, 106-110
% modulus operator, 161-162
% modulus or remainder operator, 158
%c (character) conversion character, 129-130
%d (integer) conversion character, 130-133
%e (exponential) conversion character, 135-137
%f (floating-point) conversion character, 130-133
%g (exponential) conversion character, 135-136
%o (octal) conversion character, 134-135
%s (string) conversion character, 128-129
%s control code, 502, 551
%x (hex) conversion character, 134-135
& (address of) pointer operator, 532
" " quotation marks, double, 79, 109
! NOT operator, 204, 442
!= not equal to operator, 182
pound sign, 106
&& AND operator, 204
& ampersand, 147, 392
& bitwise AND logical operator, 234
, comma operator, 228-230
" quotation mark, 83
* asterisk, 159
* (dereferencing) pointer operator, 532
* multiplication operator, 158
+ addition operator, 158
- hyphen, 338

- subtraction operator, 158
. dot operator, 580
/ division operator, 158-162
; semicolon, 52
< > angled brackets, 109
< input redirection symbol, 421
< less than operator, 182
<= less than or equal to operator, 182
= equal sign, 240
= equal sign, assignment operator, 59
== equal to operator, 182
> greater than operator, 182
> output redirection symbol, 421
>= greater than or equal to operator, 182
[ ] braces, 338, 470
\ backslash, 85
^ bitwise exclusive OR logical operator, 234
_ underscore character, 337
¦ bitwise inclusive OR logical operator, 234
¦¦ OR operator, 204
~ bitwise one's complement logical operator, 234
++ increment operator, 221
\n (newline) character, 146, 419, 431
\r conversion characters, 299
2's complement, 666, 725

A

absolute value, 451
access
  append, 627
  files, disk, 615-616
  modes
    files, 615, 618-619
    read, 628
    random, 615
    sequential, 615
accessing
  elements, arrays, 93
  files
    random access, 615
    sequential, 613-615
  keyboard values, 392
  memory, 615
adapters, display, 718
addresses, 715
  memory, 385, 655-656
  passing arrays by, 387-394
  passing by, 723
  passing variables, 384-394, 536
  pointers, 532
  variables, 385-386
addressing, 653
aggregate variable type, 69
Algol, 14
alphabetic conditions, function tests, 440
alphabetic testing functions, 441-442
American National Standards Institute, see ANSI
ampersand (&), 147, 392
analog signals, 27
angled brackets < >, 109
ANSI (American National Standards Institute), 12
ANSI C-compatible, 12
append access mode, 627
appending to files, 627-628
application-specific keys, 26
arguments, 715
  character, passing to functions, 440
  passing, 364
    to internal code, 392
  separating, 228

arithmetic
 binary, 664-665
 multiword, 665
arithmetic, pointer, *see* pointer
  arithmetic
array of arrays, 515
arrays, 715
 as members, 603-610
 assigning to another, 477
 character, 91, 389
  reserving, 470
  sorting, 498
  strings, 551
  see also character arrays
 character pointers, defining,
  562
 declaring, 91, 466
 defining, 465
  multiple values, 559
 double floating-point, 465
 elements, 718
  accessing, 93
  calculating with, 547
  character, 469
  initializing, 469-472, 476-480
  manipulating, 464
  overwriting, 94
  printing with, 547
  reserving, 95
  storage, 466
  strings, pointing to, 563
 filling, 388
 floating-point
  defining, 560
  with pointer, 558
 initializing, 469-480
 integer, 465
 mapping to memory, 515-516
 multidimensional, 509-512, 722
  defining, 517-520
  reserving, 512-514

 row order storage, 516
 names, as pointers, 546-547
 notation, mixing, 597
 of structures, 577
 parallel, 722
 passing
  by address, 387
  to erase, 389
  to functions, 386, 475
 pointers, 541-542
  notation, 549
  reference, 549
 printing, 94
 protecting, 468
 ragged-edge, 562
 referencing, 498-505, 546
 reserving, 92
 searching, 484-491
 single-dimensional, 724
 sizes, 467
  defined constants, 476
 sorting, 484, 491-498
  ascending sort, 496
  bubble sort, 492
  descending sort, 484, 496
  quicksort, 492
  shell sort, 492
 storage, 466
 storing, 546
 strings, 562-566
  declaring, 469
  printing, 551
 structures, 593
  declaring, 594-602
  disk drive, 599
 subscripts, 93-94, 464, 597
  matching, 519
 values, assigning new, 548
 variables, 464
arrow keys, 25
ascending sort, 496

ASCII (American Standard Code for Information Interchange)
characters, 84
table, 672
ascii( ) function, 410
assigning
arrays to another, 477
character data to character variables, 75
strings to character pointers, 551
values
character arrays, 95
initial, 370
members, 589
pointers, 535-536
strings, 99
variables, 73-74
assignment operators, 59
assignment statements, 73, 145
compound, 171-173
multiple, 168-171
pointers, initializing, 538
start expressions, 276
tables, initializing, 524
associating, 170
asterisk (*), 159
atof( ) function, 450
atoi( ) function, 449
atol( ) function, 450
auto keyword, 369-370
automatic
carriage returns, 125
conversion, data types, 174
automatic variables, 369

B

backslash (\), 85
backup files, 715
BCPL, 14
BEEP directive, 316
Bell Labs, 13

binary
arithmetic, 664-665
calculations, 665
data files, 619
digits, 657, 716
files, 639, 648
format, 619
level string storage, 82
mode, 619-620
numbers, 653, 660-663, 716
converting from decimals, 664
converting to 2's complement, 666
converting to hexadecimal, 671
negative, 666-668
operators, 158
operations, 158
state of electricity, 19, 657
zeros, 82, 716
bit mask, 239
bit patterns
characters, 82
internal
character, 234
integer, 234
bits, 656-659, 716
binary digits, 657
high-order, 660
least significant, 660, 720
low-order, 660
most-significant, 660
order, 659-660
sign, 666
propagation, 242
bitwise
compound operators, 240-241
inclusive OR operator, 235
logical operators, 234-240
operators, 233, 716
combining, 240

shift operators, 242-244
truth tables, 234
blank expressions, 286
blanks, printing, 299
block statements, 716
blocks
inside blocks, 338
programs, 51-52
body of statement, 186
boilerplates, 109
booting, 716
braces, 52
arrays, initializing, 470
closing, 61
function names, 338
loops, 250, 251
nested, 519
branching programs
(spaghetti code), 322
break statement, 260-264,
300-305
conditional, 303
unconditional, 301
breaks, conditional, 262
bubble sort, 492, 716
buffered I/O functions, 647
buffered input functions, 429
buffers
multiuser computers, 429
size, 429
typeahead, 429
bugs, 45, 716
see also debugging, 45
built-in editors, 38
built-in functions, 61
prototypes, 702 703
string, 255
bytes, 19, 654, 716
megabytes, 22
reserved for arrays, 467
skipping, 639-640

two as single value, 659
see also bits

C

calculations
binary, 665
data types, mixing,
174-177
parentheses, 164-169
structure members, 585
sum of the digits, 403
with array elements, 547
calling functions, return values,
398
calls, function, see function calls
carriage return character (\r), 299
carriage returns
adding, 427
automatic, 125
case expressions, 312
case statements
arrangements for speed, 313
order, 320
cathode ray tube (CRT), 716
ceil( ) function, 451
central processing unit, see CPU
character
constants, 83-86
data, reading, 628
elements, arrays, 469
functions, I/O, 424-436
internal bit patterns, 234
variables, incrementing, 286
character arguments, passing to
functions, 440
character arrays, 91, 95-101, 389
characters, printing, 504
filenames, storing, 621
reserving, 92, 470
sorting, 498

strings
  printing, 126, 500, 504
  storing, 96, 551
  values, 97
values, assigning, 95
character constants
  storing, integer variables, 86
character functions, 440-445
character pointers, 551-556
  arrays, defining, 562
  incrementing, 560
  string constants, changing, 554
  strings, assigning, 551
character stream I/O, 418-419
character testing functions, 440
character variables, 72, 75
characters
  \r (carriage return), 299
  arrays, 92-95
  ASCII, storing, 84
  bit patterns, 82
  conversion, 127-131
    %c (character), 129-130
    %d (integer), 130-133
    %e (exponential), 135-137
    %f (floating-point), 130-133
    %g (exponential), 135-136
    %o (octal), 134-135
    %s (string), 128-129
    %x (hex), 134-135
    \r, 299
    modifiers, 137-142
  conversion functions, 443-445
  echoing, 434
  escape, 85
  escape sequence, 85-86
  internal size requirements, 547
  mathematic operations, 86
  newline (\n), 419
    discarding, 431
    scanf( ) control strings, 146
  null, 81

special, test functions, 442-443
string-terminating, 447
suffix, numeric constants, 73
underscore (_), 337
writing to printer, 425
closing files, disk, 617-623
COBOL, 13
code, 716
  blocks, inside blocks, 338
  expressions, 222
  internal, passing arguments, 392
  non-executing, 307
  object, 722
  source, 725
  spaghetti, 322, 725
  unreachable, 307
  see also source code
codes, control (%s), 502, 551
combining operators, bitwise, 240
comma (,) operator, 228-230
commas (,), values, 75
comments, 43, 53-56
  functions, 346
  nested, 54
comparing internal data, 234
comparison, statements, 183
compiled languages, 35
compilers, 34, 40-41
compiling, 35, 716
complement, 2's, 666, 725
complete structures, assigning to one another, 596
compound
  assignment statements, 171-173
  operators, 171-172
  relational operators, 203
  relational tests, 203
computers
  digital, 27, 717
  multiuser, buffers, 429

personal, *see* PCs
see also microcomputers
CON (console), 420
concatenation, 717
conditional
  break statement, 303
  breaks, 262
  control of statements, 181
  loop, 717
  operator, 218-221
  test, 205
conditional_expression,
  218-219
conditions, 185-186
  end-of-file, testing, 646
  EOF (end-of-file), 629
console, (CON), 420
constants, 57-58, 76, 717
  character, 83-86
    appending null zeros, 83
    storing in integer variables,
    86
  defined, 476
  hexadecimal, 77-78
  integer, 76-78
  numeric, suffix characters, 73
  octal, 77
  pointers, 548-550
  string, 78, 95, 725
    endings, 81-82
    lengths, 82-83
    numeric digits, 79
    printing, 79, 124, 128
  unsigned, 73
construct statements, 250
constructs, 311
continue statement, 305-309
control strings, printing, 131
control code, %s, 502, 551
control strings, matching with
    values, 142-144
control_string, 124

controlling
  execution, 315
  statements conditionally, 181
conversion
  data types, 174
  to lowercase, 240
  to uppercase, 239
conversion characters, 127
  %c (character), 129-130
  %d (integer), 130-133
  %e (exponential), 135-137
  %f (floating-point), 130-133
  %g (exponential), 135-136
  %o (octal), 134-135
  %s (string), 128-129
  %x (hex), 134-135
  \r, 299
  modifiers, 137-142
conversion functions, character,
  443-445
convert( ) function, 405
converting
  numbers
    binary to 2's complement,
    666
    binary to hexadecimal, 671
    decimal to binary, 664
    hexadecimal to binary,
    670-671
  strings to numbers,
    449-450
copying variables, structures, 586
cos( ) function, 454
count expression, 283
countdown, 275
counters, 264-268
CPU (central processing unit), 18,
  716
creating
  files, 624-625
  programs, data-driven, 181
CRT, *see* monitor, 22

ctype.h header file, 702-703
cursor, 22, 125
cycling
    for loops, 298
    while loops, 298

D

data, 717
    files, binary, 619
    internal, comparing, 234
    overwriting, 620
    processing, 28, 717
    validation, 191
data types, 14, 65-66, 69-73
    calculations, mixing, 174-177
    changing temporarily, 175
    conversion, 174
    defining, 575
    floating-point, double, 73
    mixing, 76
    pointers, 539
    truncating, 174
    see also type casting
data-driven programs, 181
debugging, 45, 717
DEC (Digital Equipment
        Corporation), 13
decimal numbers, converting to
        binary, 664
decimal points, 70
decision statement, 185
declaring
    arrays, 91, 466
        of structures, 594-602
        of strings, 469
    pointers, 533-535
    variables, 57, 67-69, 369
decrement operators, 221-226,
    229
decrementing
    pointers, 556
    variables, 221-226

loop, 284
    postfix operator, 223
    prefix operator, 222
defaults, 717
#define directive, 112-119
defined constants, 476
defining
    arrays, 465
        character pointers, 562
        floating-point, 560
        multidimensional, 517-520
        multiple values, 559
    data types, 575
    functions, 342
    newline (\n) character, 428
    operators, logical, 203-205
    pointers
        file, 618
        floating-point, 560
    relational operators, 182-185
    structures, 575-578
        globally, 583
    variables, 355
        structure, with structure
            tags, 583
definitions
    member, consolidating, 578
    structure
        consolidating, 588
        nesting, 588
delimiters, strings
    zeros, 81
demodulation, 27
dereferencing, 717
    elements, pointers, 564
descending sort, 484, 496
designing programs, 36-37
determinate loops, 275
devices
    flushing, 448
    I/O, 419-424
    output, 124, 722

peripherals, 723
redirecting, 421
standard input, 419
standard output, 419
digital computer, 27, 717
digital signals, demodulation, 27
digital testing functions, 441-442
digits, test functions, 441
directives, 105
  `#define`, 112-119
  `#include`, 106-110
  `BEEP`, 316
  preprocessor, 41, 723
directories, 617, 717
disappearing variables, 355
disk files, 598-599
  access, 615-616
  closing, 617-623
  displaying, 631
  formats, 599
  merging into program, 106
  opening, 617-623
  reading, 631
disks, 20-22, 717
  data, changing, 614
  drives, 599, 717
  fixed, 21, 718
  floppy, 21, 718
  formatting, 719
  hard, 21-22, 719
  memory, 614
  sectors, 724
  structures, saving to, 599
  tracks, 22, 725
  see also floppy disks
display adapter, 23, 718
displaying
  disk files, 631
  messages, error, 298
`do-while` loop, 256-259, 279
DOS, 718
  see also MS-DOS

dot operator (.), 580, 589, 596, 605
dot-matrix printer, 23, 718
double floating-point,
  see floating-point
double subscripts, 605

E

echoing characters, 434
`EDIT`, 39
editing, link editing, 41
editors, 34, 40
  built-in, 38
  `EDIT`, 39
  `EDLIN`, 39
  `ISPF`, 39
  `vi`, 39
`EDLIN`, 39
electricity
  binary state, 19, 657
elements
  arrays, 718
    accessing, 93
    character, 469
    initializing, 469-480
    manipulating, 464
    storage, 466
    strings, pointing to, 563
  overwriting, 94
  pointers, dereferencing, 564
  reserving, 95
`else` statement, 195-199
`else-if` construct, 311
`end-of-file`, 629
  condition, testing, 646
  marker, pointing to, 644
  pointing to, 643
endless loops, 323
environments
  integrated, 38
  variables, 260

equal sign (=), 240
  assignment operator, 59
erasing
  arrays by passing to functions,
    389
  files, 647
error checking, 625
error handling, 44-45
error level, 260
error messages
  displaying, 298
  overwriting, 299
errors
  bugs, 716
  debugging, 717
  file opening, 620
  syntax, 44, 725
Escape key, 25
escape character, 85
escape sequences, 85-86
executable
  files, 40
  statements, 52
executing, 718
execution
  controlling, 315
  falling through, 312-318
exit( ) function, 260-264
exp( ) function, 455
expanded memory, 19, 718
  accessing, 615
exponents, 71
expressions
  blank, 286
  case, 312
  code, 222
  conditional_expression,
    218-219
  count, 283
  multiple, in one line, 229
  null, 286

start, 276
test, loop statements, 250-251
see also subexpressions
extended memory, 19, 655, 718
  accessing, 615
extensions, files, 718
external
  functions, 109
  memory, 20
  modems, 26, 718

F

fabs( ) function, 451
factorials, 292
falling through, 312-318
fclose( ) function, 617, 621
feof( ) function, 646
fflush( ) function, 448
fgets( ) function, 447
fields, records, 636
file formats, system-specific, 619
file pointer
  defining, 618, 621
  moving, 640
  positioning, 647
  repositioning to beginning, 642
filenames, 718
  lowercase, 618
  specifying upon file opening,
    622
  storing character arrays, 621
files, 718
  access mode, 615, 618-619
  appending to, 627-628
  backup, 715
  binary, 639
    reading, 648
  closed, 620
  creating, 624-625
  data, binary, 619
  directories, 617, 717

disk, 598-599
    access, 615-616
    closing, 617-623
    displaying, 631
    formats, 599
    merging into program, 106
    opening, 617-623
    reading, 631
erasing, 647
executable, 40
extensions, 718
functions, I/O, 623
header
    ctype.h, 702-703
    math.h, 703
    prototypes, 409
    stdio.h, 617, 702
    stdlib.h, 260, 703
    strcpy( ) function, 409
    string.h, 703
    see also header files
include, 109-110
modes, binary, 619
opening
    errors, 620
    for writing, 620
    multiple, 622
    specifying filenames, 622
pointers, 618
pointing to end, 643
protecting, 620
random access, 635
    accessing, 615
    opening, 637-639
    records, 636-637
reading, 628-632
    binary format, 619
    character by characer, 628
    end-of-file, 629
    randomly, 636
records, 624

sequential, 615-617
sequential access, 613, 724
text, 619
writing structures to, 642
writing to, 623-626
    multiple, 622
    randomly, 636
FILES= statement, 617
fixed disks, 21, 718
fixed-length records, 637, 718
floating-point
    arrays
        defining, 560
        double, 465
        with pointer, 558
    data types, double, 73
    internal size requirements, 547
    numbers, 70
        printing, 135
    pointer, defining, 560
    variables, 59
floor( ) function, 452
floppy disks, 21, 718
    drives, 22
    formatting
flushing devices, 448
fmod( ) function, 452
fopen( ) function, 617, 639
for loops, 275-287, 520, 523-527
    character variables,
        incrementing, 286
    cycling, 298
    empty, 298
    nested, 288-293, 524
    terminating, 302
for statement, 275-276, 300-305
format strings, 60
formats
    binary, reading files, 619
    conditional operator, 218
    disks, 21, 719

files
 disk, 599
 system-specific, 619
 programs, 49-50
formatted output, printing,
 423-424
FORTRAN, 13
fprintf( ) function, 423
fputs( ) function, 447
fread( ) function, 646
free-form languages, 49
fscanf( ) function, 623-624
fseek( ) function, 639-646
function calls, 15
 nested, 402
 operators, 229
 replacing with values, 400
 return values, 339
 tracing, 341
function invocations, 341
function keys, 26, 719
function-calling statements, 342
functions, 719
 ascii( ), 410
 atof( ), 450
 atoi( ), 449
 atol( ), 450
 blocks inside blocks, 338
 built-in, 61
  prototypes, 702-703
 ceil( ), 451
 character, 440-445
 comments, 346
 conversion character, 443-445
 convert( ), 405
 cos( ), 454
 defining, 342
 exit( ), 260-264
 exp( ), 455
 external, 109
 fabs( ), 451
 fclose( ), 617, 621

feof( ), 646
fflush( ), 448
fgets( ), 447
floor( ), 452
fmod( ), 452
fopen( ), 617, 639
fprintf( ), 423
fputs( ), 447
fread( ), 646
fscanf( ), 623-624
fseek( ), 639-646
fwrite( ), 647
getc( ), 424-428
getch( ), 434-436
getchar( ), 428-433
gets( ), 447
I/O, 646, 648-649
 buffered, 647
 character, 424-436
 files, 623
 macros, 425
 string, 446-449
input
 buffered, 429
 mirror-image, 626
isalnum( ), 441
iscntrl( ), 443
isdigit( ), 441
isgraph( ), 443
islam( ), 440
isomer( ), 440
isprint( ), 443
ispunct( ), 443
isspace( ), 443
isxdigit( ), 441
length, 337
log( ), 455
log10( ), 455
logarithmic, 454-455
main( ), 51, 57, 334
mathematical, 451-454
mirror-image, 430

names, 337-338
next_fun( ), 340
nonbuffered, 434
numeric, 451-457, 722
passing, 364-365
    arrays to, 386, 475
    character arguments, 440
pow( ), 452
printf( ), 79, 124, 340
prototyping, 397, 405-412
putc( ), 424-428
putch( ), 434-436
putchar( ), 428-433
puts( ), 447
rand( ), 455
receiving, 364-365
receiving parameters, 364
remove( ), 647
rewind( ), 647
scanf( ), 123, 144-151, 253, 392
separating, 346
sin( ), 454
sipped( ), 440
sizeof( ), 467, 642
sort, saving, 498
sqrt( ), 452
srand( ), 455-456
strcpy( ), 99, 409
string, 445-450
    built in, 255
    strcat( ), 446
    strcmp( ), 446
    strlen( ), 446
strlen( ), 255
tan( ), 454
testing
    alphabetic, 441-442
    alphabetic arguments, 441
    alphabetic conditions, 440
    character, 440

digital, 441-442
    digits, 441
    numeric arguments, 441
    special characters, 442-443
third_fun( ), 340
tolower( ), 443
toupper( ), 443
trigonometric, 454
values, return, 398-405
writing, 333
see also subfunctions
fwrite( ) function, 647

G

getc( ) function, 424-428
getch( ) function, 434-436
getchar( ) function, 428-433
gets( ) function, 447
global variables, 67, 354-358, 363, 719
goto statement, 321-327
graphics monitors, 23

H

hard copy, 719
hard disks, 21-22, 719
hardware, 17-27, 719
hardware independent routines, 15
header files, 109-110
    ctype.h, 702-703
    math.h, 703
    prototypes, 409
    stdio.h, 109-110, 617, 702
    stdlib.h, 703
    strcpy( ) function, 409
    string.h, 703
hexadecimal
    constants, 77-78
    notation, 670

numbers, 84, 653, 668-669, 719
  converting to binary,
    670-671
  printing, 134
  storing, 78
hierarchy of operators, 719
high-order bit, 660
hyphen (-), 338

▌

I/O (input/output), 417
  character stream, 418-419
  devices, 419-424
  functions, 646-649
    buffered, 647
    character, 424-436
    files, 623
    macros, 425
    string, 446-449
  redirecting, 420
if
  construct, 311
  loop, 259
  statement, 185-194
if-else logic, 218
if-else statements, 220
#include directive, 106-110
include files, 109-110
increasing variables, see
    incrementing variables
increment operators, 221-226
  ++, 221
  counters, 265
  function calls, 229
incrementing
  pointers, 556-558
    character, 560
  variables, 221-226
    character variables, 286
    postfix operator, 223
    prefix operator, 222

indeterminate loops, 719
infinite loops, 250, 254, 719
initial values, assigning, 370
initializing
  arrays, 473-479
    braces [ ], 470
    elements, 469-472
    multdimensional, 519
  elements, arrays, 476-480
  members, structures, 579
  pointers, assignment state-
    ments, 538
  structures
    data, 579-587
    dot operator (.), 580
  variables, 279
input
  devices, standard, 419
    flushing, 448
  functions
    buffered, 429
    mirror-image, 626
  statements, 15
  terminating, 447
  user, storing in strings, 553
  variables, declaring as integers,
    629
  see also I/O devices
input redirection symbol (<), 421
input/output, see I/O
integer arrays, 465
integer constants, 76-78
integer pointers, 535
integer variables, 59, 720
  character constants, storing, 86
integers, 69
  declaring input variables as,
    629
  internal bit patterns, 234
  internal size requirements, 547
  signed, 667, 671
  unsigned, 667

integrated environment, 38
internal
  bit patterns, 234
  data, comparing, 234
  modems, 27, 720
interpreted languages, 35
invalid loops, 254
isalnum( ) function, 441
iscntrl( ) function, 443
isdigit( ) function, 441
isgraph( ) function, 443
islam( ) function, 440
isomer( ) function, 440
ISPF editor, 39
isprint( ) function, 443
ispunct( ) function, 443
isspace( ) function, 443
isxdigit( ) function, 441
iteration
  loops, forcing another, 305
  timing loops, 298

J–K

Job Control Language (JCL), 420
K (kilo) memory measurement,
    19, 654
keyboard, 23-26
  numeric keypad, 25
  values, accessing, 392
keys
  application-specific, 26
  arrows, 25
  escape, 25
  function, 26, 719
  numeric, 25
keywords, 701
  auto, 369-370
  void, 406
kilobyte, 720

L

labels
  lines, 322
  output, 80, 126
  statement, 321-322
  structures, see structure tag
languages
  Algol, 14
  BCPL, 14
  COBOL, 13
  compiled, 35
  FORTRAN, 13
  free-form, 49
  interpreted, 35
  machine, 720
  Pascal, 13
  programming, 723
  translating, 716
  UNIX, 13
  weakly-typed, 14
laser printers, 23, 720
least-significant bit, 660, 720
line printer, 720
lines
  labels, 322
  skipping during printing, 85
link editing, 41
linking, 41
lists
  strings, sorting, 564
  variables, arrays, 715
literals, string, see string
    constants
local variables, 354-355, 720
  automatic, 369
  disappearing, 355
  names, overlapping, 361
log( ) function, 455
log10( ) function, 455
logarithmic functions,
    454-455

logic
  if-else, 218
  relational, 183-184
logical operators, 203-211
  ! (NOT), 204
  & (bitwise AND), 234
  && (AND), 204
  ^ (bitwise exclusive OR), 234
  ¦ (bitwise inclusive OR), 234
  ¦¦ (OR), 204
  ~ (bitwise one's complement), 234
  defining, 203-205
  order of precedence, 211-213
  test expression, 250
  truth tables, 204-205
looping statement, 250
loops, 251-256, 720
  braces, 250-251
  conditional, 717
  determinate, 275
  do-while, 256-259, 279
  endless, 323
  for, 275-288, 520, 523-527
    cycling, 298
    empty, 298
    incrementing character
      variables, 286
    nested, 288-293, 524
    terminating, 302
  if, 259
  indeterminate, 719
  infinite, 250, 254, 719
  iteration, forcing another, 305
  non-executing, 253
  terminating, 300
  timing, 297-300
  variables, decrementing, 284
  while, 249, 259
    cycling, 298
    invalid, 254

low-order bit, 660
lowercase, 51
  converting to, 240
  filenames, 618

M

M (meg) memory measurement, 655
machine language, 720
macros, 425
main module, 720
main( ) function, 51, 57
mapping arrays to memory, 515-516
markers, end-of-file, 644
math hierarchy, *see* order of precedence
math operators, 720
math.h header file, 703
mathematical
  functions, 451-454
  operators, 60
    % (modulus or remainder), 158
    % (modulus), 161-162
    * (multiplication), 158
    + (addition), 158
    - (subtraction), 158
    / (division), 158, 161-162
    binary operations, 158
    results, 158
  summation symbol, 292
matrices, 509
maximum routines, 220
measurements, memory
  K, 654
  M (meg), 655
megabytes, 22, 655, 720
members, 720
  arrays as, 603-610
  definitions, 576-578

structure, 572
    calculating with, 585
    initializing, 579
    redefining, 583
    values, assigning, 589
memory, 18, 721
    addresses, 385, 655-656, 715
    arrays, 546
        mapping, 515-516
    buffer, 429
    bytes, 19, 654
    disk, 614
    expanded, 19, 615, 718
    extended, 19, 615, 655, 718
    external, 20
    K, 19
    measurement
        K, (kilobyte), 654, 720
        M (megabyte), 655, 720
    RAM (random-access
        memory), *see* RAM
    read-only (ROM), 724
    running out of, 595
    structure tags, 573
    variables, storing, 386
    volatile, 20
    word, 659
menus, 721
merging files into program, 106
messages
    error, *see* error messages
    printing, 348-350
microchips, 16, 721
microcomputers, 13-17, 721
microprocessor, 716, 721
minimum routine, 220
mirror-image functions, 430, 626
modems, 721
    external, 26, 718
    internal, 27, 720

modes
    access, 618-619
        files, 615
        read, 628
    binary, 619-620
    update, random access, 638
modifiers, conversion characters,
    137-142
modular programming, 334, 721
modulate, 721
modulated information, 27
modules, main, 720
modulus, 721
monitors, 22, 716-721
    graphics, 23
    monochrome, 23
    resolution, 23
most-significant bit, 660
mouse, 26, 721
moving file pointers, 640
MS-DOS, 28, 30, 722
    redirecting output, 422
multidimensional arrays,
    509-511, 722
    defining, 517-520
    initializing, 519
    reserving, 512-514
    storing, row order, 516
    subscripts, matching with
        arrays, 519
multiple-choice statement, *see*
    switch statement
multiplication, 664
multiword arithmetic, 665

N

names
    arrays, as pointers,
        546-547
    files, 718

functions, 337
  braces ([ ]), 338
  parentheses, 338
pointers, 533
structure tags, 573
variables, 360
  pointer, 533
  structures, 580
naming variables, 64-65
negative numbers
  binary, 666-668
  unary, 160
nested
  braces, 519
  comments, 54
  for loops, 288-293, 524
  function calls, 402
  loops, 722
  structures, 588-590
newline (\n) character, 419
  defining as constant, 428
  discarding, 431
  scanf( ) control strings, 146
next_fun( ) function, 340
nonarrays, passing by address,
  390-394
not operator (!), 442
notation
  array, mixing, 597
  hexadecimal, 670
  pointers, 546
    as arrays, 549
    mixing, 597
  scientific, 724
nth root, 452-453
null
  character, 81
  expressions, 286
  string, 722
  zeros, 722
    string-terminating, 82
NULL value, 620

numbers
  binary, 653, 660-664, 716
    converting to 2's
      complement, 666
    digits, 657
    negative, 666-668
  converting
    binary to hexadecimal, 671
    decimal to binary, 664
    from strings, 449-450
    hexadecimal to binary,
      670-671
  decimal points, 70
  exponents, 71
  factorials, 292
  floating-point, 70, 135
  hexadecimal, 78, 84, 134, 653,
    668-672, 719
  negative, unary, 160
  nth root, 452-453
  octal, 134, 671
  printing, 131
    floating-point, 135
    hexadecimal, 134
    octal, 134
    width, 137-138
  random, 455-457
  real, 70, 724
  rounding, 452
  scientific notation, 135-136
  signed, 666
  truncating, 725
  unsigned, 666
numeric
  bases, constants, 77
  constants, suffix characters, 73
  digits, string constants, 79
  functions, 451-457, 722
  keypad, 25
  values, in character variables,
    72
  variables, signed, 72

O

object code, 722
octal
    constants, 77
    numbers, 134, 671
opening files
    disk, 617-623
    errors, 620
    for writing, 620
    multiple, 622
    random access, 637-639
    specifying filenames, 622
operator precedence, 15
operators, 15, 722
    binary, 158
    bitwise, 233, 716
        combining, 240
        compound, 240-241
        logical, 234-240
        shift, 242-244
    bitwise inclusive OR, 235
    comma (,), 228-230
    compound, 171-172
    conditional, 218-221
    decrement, 221-226
        function calls, 229
    dot., 589-596, 605
    hierarchy, 719
    increment, 222-226
        ++, 221
        counters, 265
        function calls, 229
    logical, 203-211
        ! (NOT), 204
        & (bitwise AND), 234
        && (AND), 204
        ^ (bitwise exclusive OR), 234
        ¦ (bitwise inclusive OR), 234
        ¦¦ (OR), 204
        ~ (bitwise one's comple-
            ment), 234

defining, 203-205
        order of precedence, 211-213
        test expression, 250
        truth tables, 204-205
    mathematical, 60, 158, 720
        % (modulus or remainder),
            158, 161-162
        * (multiplication), 158
        + (addition), 158
        - (subtraction), 158
        / (division), 158, 161-162
        results, 158
    order, 722-723
    order of precedence, 162-169
    overloaded, 532
    pointer
        & (address of), 532
        * (dereferencing), 532
    postfix, incrementing/
        decrementing, 223
    precedence, 723
    prefix, incrementing/
        decrementing, 222
    relational, 181, 724
        != (not equal to), 182
        < (less than), 182
        <= (less than or equal to), 182
        == (equal to), 182
        > (greater than), 182
        >= (greater than or equal to),
            182
        compound, 203
        defining, 182-185
        primary, 185
        test expression, 250
    sizeof, 226-228
    ternary, 218
    truth tables, 235
    unary, 159-160, 725

order
  bits, 659-660
  case statements, 320
  include files, 110
  of operators, 722-723
order or precedence, 162-169
  logical operators, 211-213
  primary operators, 163
origin values, 640
outlines, 337
output
  devices, 124, 722
    standard, 419
    see also I/O devices
  formatted, printing, 423-424
  labeling, 80, 126
  redirecting, MS-DOS, 422
  redirection symbol (>), 421
  screen, 22, 124
  statement, 15
overloaded operators, 532
overwriting
  data, 620
  elements, arrays, 94
  error messages, 299

P

parallel ports, 722
parameters, 722
  mismatched, 143
  passing, 374, 375
  receiving, 364
  scanf( ), 394
parentheses, 61
  calculations, 164-169
  function names, 338
  order of precedence, 164-169
Pascal, 13
passing
  addresses, variables, 536
  arguments, 364
    to internal code, 392

arrays, 389
  by address, 387
  to erase, 389
  to functions, 386, 475
by address, 723
by reference, 723
by values, 723
nonarrays, by address, 390-394
parameters, 374-375
variables, 363-369
  by address, 384-394
  by copy (value), 379
  by value, 379-384
  renaming, 382-383
  structure, 583
passing function, 364-365
passwords, 266-267
paths, 723
patterns, bit, 82
PCs, 16
peripherals, 723
point of definition, variables, 356
pointer
  arithmetic, 556-562
  operators
    & (address of), 532
    * (dereferencing), 532
  variables, see pointers
pointers, 483, 531, 723
  addresses, 532
  array, 541-547
  changing, 548
  character, 551-556
    see also character pointers
  constants, 548-550
  data types, 539
  declaring, 533-535
  decrementing, 556
  elements, dereferencing, 564
  file
    defining, 618
    globally defining, 621

moving, 640
  positioning, 647
  repositioning to beginning, 642
floating-point, defining, 560
incrementing, 556-558
initializing, assignment statements, 538
integer, 535
names, 533
notation, 546
  as arrays, 549
  mixing, 597
reference, as arrays, 549
reserving, 541
to files, 618
values, assigning, 535-536
variable, changing, 548
pointing
  end of file, 643
  end-of-file marker, 644
ports
  parallel, 722
  serial, 724
postfix operator, incrementing/ decrementing, 223
pound sign (#), 106
pow( ) function, 452
precedence of operators, 722
prefix operator, incrementing/ decrementing, 222
prefixing variables, 372
preprocessor directives, *see* directives
preprocessors, 41, 105
printers, 23, 723
  characters, writing to, 425
  dot-matrix, 23, 718
  laser, 23, 720
  line, 720
  writing to, 626-627
printf( ) function, 79, 124, 340

printing
  arrays, 94
  blanks, 299
  characters, character arrays, 504
  constants, string, 79, 128
  hard copy, 719
  lines, skipping, 85
  messages, 348, 350
  numbers, 131
    floating-point, 135
    hexadecimal, 134
    octal, 134
    width, 137-138
  output, formatted, 423-424
  strings, 124-127, 502
    arrays, 551
    character arrays, 126, 504
    control, 131
    in character arrays, 500
    pointed to, 551
    width, 139
  with array elements, 547
procedures, repeating, 251
processors/preprocessors, 41
  see also preprocessors
program editor, 38-40
programming
  languages, 723
  modular, 334, 721
  structured, 334
programs, 34, 723
  blocks, 51-52
  branching, spaghetti code, 322
  compiling, 35
  data-driven, 181
  designing, 36-37
  executing, 718
  files, merging, 106
  format, 49-50
  linking, 41
  listings, 36

lowercase letters, 51
outlines, 337
skeletons, 335-337
spaghetti code, 322
string-length, 254
termination, *see* termination
uppercase letters, 51
white space, 50-51
propagation of sign bits, 242
protecting arrays, 468
prototypes
 files, header, 409
 functions, 397, 405-412, 702-703
putc( ) function, 424-428
putch( ) function, 434-436
putchar( ) function, 428-433
puts( ) function, 447

Q

quicksort, 492
quotation marks, 58, 83, 79, 109

R

ragged-edge arrays, 562
RAM, 18-20, 724
rand( ) function, 455
random access
 files, 615, 635, 724
 opening, 637-639
 memory, *see* RAM
 records, 636-637
random-number processing,
 455-457
ranges, variables, 70-72
read access mode, 628
read-only memory, *see* ROM
reading
 character data, 628
 disk files, 631
 files, 628-632
  binary, 648

character by character, 628
end-of-file, 629
randomly, 636
string by string, 628
word by word, 629
real numbers, 70, 724
receiving function, 364-365
recognition, variables, 359
records, 724
 fields, 636
 files, 624, 636-637
 fixed-length, 637, 718
 variable-length, 726
redirecting
 devices, 421
 output, MS-DOS, 422
reference pointers as arrays, 549
references, passing by, 723
referencing, arrays, 498-505, 546
relational
 logic, 183, 184
 operators, 181, 724
  != (not equal to), 182
  < (less than), 182
  <= (less than or equal to), 182
  == (equal to), 182
  > (greater than), 182
  >= (greater than or equal to),
   182
  compound, 203
  defining, 182-185
  primary, 185
  test expression, 250
 tests, 203, 206
remove( ) function, 647
renaming variables, passed,
 382-383
repeating statements, 249
reserving
 arrays, character, 470
 character arrays, 92
 elements, 95

multidimensional arrays, 512-514
  pointers, 541
  storage, 542
  variables, 365
resolution, 23
return command, 61
return statement, 339
return values, 399-405
  calling functions, 398
  fopen( ), 622
  types, 400
returning variables, 400
rewind( ) function, 647
ROM, 724
rounding numbers, 452
routines, 334
  hardware independent, 15
  maximum, 220
  minimum, 220
  screen-clearing, 480
  see also subroutines

S

saving
  sort functions, 498
  structures to disk, 599
scanf( ) control string, 146
scanf( ) function, 123, 144-151, 253, 392-394
scientific notation, 135-136, 724
scope, variable, 726
screen-clearing routine, 480
screens, 718
  output, 22, 124
  scrolling, 22, 480
searching arrays for values, 484-491
sectors, 724
seed value, 456
semicolon (;), 52
separating arguments, 228

sequence point, 228
sequential files, 613-617, 724
serial ports, 724
shell sort, 492
sign bits, 242, 666
signals
  analog, 27
  digital
signed
  integers, 667, 671
  numbers, 666
  variables, 72
sin( ) function, 454
single-dimensional arrays, 724
sipped( ) function, 440
sizeof operator, 226-228
sizeof( ) function, 467, 642
skeleton programs, 335-337
skipping bytes, 639-640
software, 27-30
sort functions, 498
sorting, 725
  arrays, 484, 491
    ascending sort, 496
    bubble sort, 492
    character, 498
    descending sort, 496
    quicksort, 492
    shell sort, 492
  bubble, 716
  descending sort, 484
  lists, strings, 564
source code, 38-40, 725
  changing, 106
spaghetti code, 322, 725
specifying
  filenames upon file opening, 622
  structure variables, 576
sqrt( ) function, 452
square root, 452
srand( ) function, 455-456

standard input device, 419, 448
standard output device, 419
start expressions, assignment
statements, 276
statements
assignment, 73, 145, 276
compound, 171-173
initializing pointers, 538
initializing tables, 524
multiple, 168-171
block, 716
body, 186
break, 260-264, 300-305
case, order, 320
comparison, 183
construct, 250
continue, 305-309
controlling, conditionally, 181
decision, 185
else, 195-199
executable, 52
FILES=, 617
for, 275-276, 300-305
function-calling, 342
goto, 321-327
if, 185-194
if-else, 220
input, 15
labels, 321-322
looping, 250
multiple-choice, see switch
statement
output, 15
repeating, 249
return, 339
struct, 575
switch, 311-321, 342
while, 250-251
static variables, 369-374
stdin, 419
stdio.h header file, 109-110, 617,
702
stdlib.h header file, 703

stdout, 419
storage, reserving, 542
storing
arrays, 466, 546
characters, 84
filenames, 621
multidimensional arrays, row
order, 516
numbers, hexadecimal, 78
strings
binary level, 82
character arrays, 96, 551
in variables, 92
user input strings, 553
variables, 386
strcat( ) function, 446
strcmp( ) function, 446
strcpy( ) function, 99, 409
stream, 725
string
constants, 95, 725
changing character pointers,
554
endings, 81-82
lengths, 82-83
numeric digits, 79
printing, 79, 124, 128
functions, 445-450
I/O, 446-449
strcat( ), 446
strcmp( ), 446
strlen( ), 446
literals, 725
values, character arrays, 97
string-length program, 254
string-terminating characters,
447
string-terminating null zero, 82
string.h header file, 703
strings, 95-101
arrays, 562-566
declaring, 469
printing, 551

assigning character pointers, 551
character arrays, printing, 504
control
    matching with values, 142-144
    printing, 131
control_string, 124
converting to numbers, 449-450
delimiters, zeros, 81
format, 60
functions, built-in, 255
lists, sorting, 564
null, 722
pointing to, array elements, 563
printing, 94, 124-127, 502, 551
    character arrays, 126
    in character arrays, 500
    pointed to, 551
    width, 139
storing
    binary level, 82
    character arrays, 96, 551
    in variables, 92
user input, storing, 553
values, assigning, 99
strlen( ) function, 255, 446
struct statement, 575
structure tags
  memory, 573
  names, 573
  variables, defining, 583
structure variables, specifying, 576
structured programming, 334
structures, 571-575, 725
  arrays, 577
  arrays of, 593-602
  complete, assigning to one another, 596
  data, initializing, 579-587
  defining, 575-578, 583

definitions, consolidating, 588
disk drive, 599
functions, filling with, 583
initializing, dot operator (.), 580
members, 572, 720
  arrays as, 603-610
  calculating with, 585
  definitions, 576
  initializing, 579
  redefining, 583
names, variables, 580
nested, 588-590
saving, to disk, 599
variables
  copying, 586
  filling with values, 583
  passing, 583
writing to file, 642
subdirectories, 717
subexpressions, 312
subfunctions, 398
subroutines, 398
subscripts, 93, 464, 725
  arrays, 94, 597
    manipulating, 464
    referencing, 546
  double, 605
  matching with multidimensional arrays, 519
suffix characters, 73
sum of the digits calculation, 403
swapping
  values, 540
  variables, 540
switch statements, 311-321, 342
syntax errors, 44, 725
system unit, 17, 725
system-specific file formats, 619

T

tables, 509, 520, 523-527
  ASCII, 672
  initializing, assignment
    statements, 524
  justified, 563
  operator precedence, 15
  truth, 235
    bitwise, 234
    logical operators, 204-205
  two-dimensional, 523, 562
tan( ) function, 454
terminating, 260
  input, 447
  loops, 300-302
ternary operators, 218
test expressions
  loop statements, 250-251
  operators
    logical, 250
    relational, 250
test functions, special characters,
  442-443
tests
  conditional, 205
    end-of-file, 646
  functions
    alphabetic arguments, 441
    alphabetic conditions, 440
    digits, 441
    numeric arguments, 441
  relational, 203, 206
text
  boilerplates, 109
  files, 619
third_fun( ) function, 340
timing loops, 297-300
tolower( ) function, 443
totals, 268-272
toupper( ) function, 443
tracks, 22, 725

transistors, 19
trigonometric functions, 454
truncation, 174, 725
truth tables, 235
  bitwise, 234
  logical operators, 204-205
two-dimensional tables, 523, 562
type casting, 175
typeahead buffers, 429
types, return values, 400

U

unary operators, 159-160, 725
unconditional break statements,
  301
underscore (_) character, 337
UNIX, 13
unreachable code, 307
unsigned
  constants, 73
  integers, 667
  numbers, 666
  variables, 78
  see also signed variables *and*
    variables
update modes, random access,
  638
uppercase letters, 51, 239

V

values
  absolute, 451
  arrays
    assigning new, 548
    searching for, 485-491
  assigning
    character arrays, 95
    pointers, 535-536
  commas, 75
  control strings, matching,
    142-144

data validation, 191
initial, assigning, 370
keyboard, accessing, 392
members, assigning, 589
multiple, defining arrays, 559
NULL, 620
numeric, in character variables,
    72
origin, 640
passing by, 723
passing variables, 379-384
replacing function calls, 400
return, 398-405
    calling functions, 398
    fopen( ), 622
    types, 400
seed, 456
string
    assigning, 99
    character arrays, 97
structure variables, filling with
    values, 583
swapping, 540
variables, assigning, 73-74
variable scope, 726
variable-length records, 726
variables, 57, 64-76, 726
    addresses, 385-386
        passing, 536
    aggregate type, 69
    array, 464
    automatic, *see* automatic
        variables
    character, 72
        assigning data, 75
        numeric values, 72
    data types, 14, 65-66
    declaring, 57, 67-69
    decrementing, 221-224
        postfix operator, 223
        prefix operator, 222
    defining, 355

environment, 260
floating-point, 59
global, 67, 719
global, *see* global variables
incrementing, 221-224
    character variables, 286
    postfix operator, 223
    prefix operator, 222
initializing, 279
input, declaring as integers,
    629
integer, 59, 86, 720
lists, 715
local, *see* local variables
long, 71-72
loop, decrementing, 284
naming, 64, 65, 360, 580
numeric, signed, 72
over-typing, 71
parameters, 722
passing, 363-369
    by address, 384-394
    by value, 379-384
    renaming, 382-383
point of definition, 356
pointer, *see* pointers, 531
prefixing, 372
ranges, 70-72
recognition, 359
reserving, 365
returning, 400
static, *see* static variables
storing, 92, 386
structures
    copying, 586
    defining with structure tags,
        583
    filling with values, 583
    passing, 583
    specifying, 576
swapping, 492, 540
unsigned, 78

values, assigning, 73-74
    visibility, 726
vi editor, 39
visibility of variables, 358, 726
void keyword, 406
volatile memory, 20, 726

W

weakly-typed languages, 14
while loops, 249, 259
    cycling, 298
    invalid, 254
while statement, 250-251
white space, 50-51
word of memory, 659
writing
    structures to file, 642
    to files, 623-626, 636
    to printers, 626-627
writing functions, 333

Z

zeros
    binary, 82, 716
    null, 722
        appending to constants, 83
        string-terminating, 82
    string delimiter, 81

Computer Books from Que Mean PC Performance!

Spreadsheets

1-2-3 Beyond the Basics	$24.95
1-2-3 for DOS Release 2.3 Quick Reference	$ 9.95
1-2-3 for DOS Release 2.3 QuickStart	$19.95
1-2-3 for DOS Release 3.1+ Quick Reference	$ 9.95
1-2-3 for DOS Release 3.1+ QuickStart	$19.95
1-2-3 for Windows Quick Reference	$ 9.95
1-2-3 for Windows QuickStart	$19.95
1-2-3 Personal Money Manager	$29.95
1-2-3 Power Macros	$39.95
1-2-3 Release 2.2 QueCards	$19.95
Easy 1-2-3	$19.95
Easy Excel	$19.95
Easy Quattro Pro	$19.95
Excel 3 for Windows QuickStart	$19.95
Excel for Windows Quick Reference	$ 9.95
Look Your Best with 1-2-3	$24.95
Quattro Pro 3 QuickStart	$19.95
Quattro Pro Quick Reference	$ 9.95
Using 1-2-3 for DOS Release 2.3, Special Edition	$29.95
Using 1-2-3 for Windows	$29.95
Using 1-2-3 for DOS Release 3.1+, Special Edition	$29.95
Using Excel 4 for Windows, Special Edition	$29.95
Using Quattro Pro 4, Special Edition	$27.95
Using Quattro Pro for Windows	$24.95
Using SuperCalc5, 2nd Edition	$29.95

Databases

dBASE III Plus Handbook, 2nd Edition	$24.95
dBASE IV 1.1 Quick Reference	$ 9.95
dBASE IV 1.1 QuickStart	$19.95
Introduction to Databases	$19.95
Paradox 3.5 Quick Reference	$ 9.95
Paradox Quick Reference, 2nd Edition	$ 9.95
Using AlphaFOUR	$24.95
Using Clipper, 3rd Edition	$29.95
Using DataEase	$24.95
Using dBASE IV	$29.95
Using FoxPro 2	$29.95
Using ORACLE	$29.95
Using Paradox 3.5, Special Edition	$29.95
Using Paradox for Windows	$26.95
Using Paradox, Special Edition	$29.95
Using PC-File	$24.95
Using R:BASE	$29.95

Business Applications

CheckFree Quick Reference	$ 9.95
Easy Quicken	$19.95
Microsoft Works Quick Reference	$ 9.95
Norton Utilities 6 Quick Reference	$ 9.95
PC Tools 7 Quick Reference	$ 9.95
Q&A 4 Database Techniques	$29.95
Q&A 4 Quick Reference	$ 9.95
Q&A 4 QuickStart	$19.95
Q&A 4 Que Cards	$19.95
Que's Computer User's Dictionary, 2nd Edition	$10.95
Que's Using Enable	$29.95
Quicken 5 Quick Reference	$ 9.95
SmartWare Tips, Tricks, and Traps, 2nd Edition	$26.95
Using DacEasy, 2nd Edition	$24.95
Using Microsoft Money	$19.95
Using Microsoft Works: IBM Version	$22.95
Using Microsoft Works for Windows, Special Edition	$24.95
Using MoneyCounts	$19.95
Using Pacioli 2000	$19.95
Using Norton Utilities 6	$24.95
Using PC Tools Deluxe 7	$24.95
Using PFS: First Choice	$22.95
Using PFS: WindowWorks	$24.95
Using Q&A 4	$27.95
Using Quicken 5	$19.95
Using Quicken for Windows	$19.95
Using Smart	$29.95
Using TimeLine	$24.95
Using TurboTax: 1992 Edition	$19.95

CAD

AutoCAD Quick Reference, 2nd Edition	$ 8.95
Using AutoCAD, 3rd Edition	$29.95

Word Processing

Easy WordPerfect	$19.95
Easy WordPerfect for Windows	$19.95
Look Your Best with WordPerfect 5.1	$24.95
Look Your Best with WordPerfect for Windows	$24.95
Microsoft Word Quick Reference	$ 9.95
Using Ami Pro	$24.95
Using LetterPerfect	$22.95
Using Microsoft Word 5.5: IBM Version, 2nd Edition	$24.95
Using MultiMate	$24.95
Using PC-Write	$22.95
Using Professional Write	$22.95
Using Professional Write Plus for Windows	$24.95
Using Word for Windows 2, Special Edition	$27.95
Using WordPerfect 5	$27.95
Using WordPerfect 5.1, Special Edition	$27.95
Using WordPerfect for Windows, Special Edition	$29.95
Using WordStar 7	$19.95
Using WordStar, 3rd Edition	$27.95
WordPerfect 5.1 Power Macros	$39.95
WordPerfect 5.1 QueCards	$19.95
WordPerfect 5.1 Quick Reference	$ 9.95
WordPerfect 5.1 QuickStart	$19.95
WordPerfect 5.1 Tips, Tricks, and Traps	$24.95
WordPerfect for Windows Power Pack	$39.95
WordPerfect for Windows Quick Reference	$ 9.95
WordPerfect for Windows Quick Start	$19.95
WordPerfect Power Pack	$39.95
WordPerfect Quick Reference	$ 9.95

Hardware/Systems

Batch File and Macros Quick Reference	$ 9.95
Computerizing Your Small Business	$19.95
DR DOS 6 Quick Reference	$ 9.95
Easy DOS	$19.95
Easy Windows	$19.95
Fastback Quick Reference	$ 8.95
Hard Disk Quick Reference	$ 8.95
Hard Disk Quick Reference, 1992 Edition	$ 9.95
Introduction to Hard Disk Management	$24.95
Introduction to Networking	$24.95
Introduction to PC Communications	$24.95
Introduction to Personal Computers, 2nd Edition	$19.95
Introduction to UNIX	$24.95
Laplink Quick Reference	$ 9.95
MS-DOS 5 Que Cards	$19.95
MS-DOS 5 Quick Reference	$ 9.95
MS-DOS 5 QuickStart	$19.95
MS-DOS Quick Reference	$ 8.95
MS-DOS QuickStart, 2nd Edition	$19.95
Networking Personal Computers, 3rd Edition	$24.95
Que's Computer Buyer's Guide, 1992 Edition	$14.95
Que's Guide to CompuServe	$12.95
Que's Guide to DataRecovery	$29.95
Que's Guide to XTree	$12.95
Que's MS-DOS User's Guide, Special Edition	$29.95
Que's PS/1 Book	$22.95
TurboCharging MS-DOS	$24.95
Upgrading and Repairing PCs	$29.95
Upgrading and Repairing PCs, 2nd Edition	$29.95
Upgrading to MS-DOS 5	$14.95
Using GeoWorks Pro	$24.95
Using Microsoft Windows 3, 2nd Edition	$24.95
Using MS-DOS 5	$24.95
Using Novell NetWare, 2nd Edition	$29.95
Using OS/2 2.0	$24.95
Using PC DOS, 3rd Edition	$27.95
Using Prodigy	$19.95
Using UNIX	$29.95
Using Windows 3.1	$26.95
Using Your Hard Disk	$29.95
Windows 3 Quick Reference	$ 8.95
Windows 3 QuickStart	$19.95
Windows 3.1 Quick Reference	$ 9.95
Windows 3.1 QuickStart	$19.95

Desktop Publishing/Graphics

CorelDRAW! Quick Reference	$ 8.95
Harvard Graphics 3 Quick Reference	$ 9.95
Harvard Graphics Quick Reference	$ 9.95
Que's Using Ventura Publisher	$29.95
Using DrawPerfect	$24.95
Using Freelance Plus	$24.95
Using Harvard Graphics 3	$29.95
Using Harvard Graphics for Windows	$24.95
Using Harvard Graphics, 2nd Edition	$24.95
Using Microsoft Publisher	$22.95
Using PageMaker 4 for Windows	$29.95
Using PFS: First Publisher, 2nd Edition	$24.95
Using PowerPoint	$24.95
Using Publish It!	$24.95

Macintosh/Apple II

Easy Macintosh	$19.95
HyperCard 2 QuickStart	$19.95
PageMaker 4 for the Mac Quick Reference	$ 9.95
The Big Mac Book, 2nd Edition	$29.95
The Little Mac Book	$12.95
QuarkXPress 3.1 Quick Reference	$ 9.95
Que's Big Mac Book, 3rd Edition	$29.95
Que's Little Mac Book, 2nd Edition	$12.95
Que's Mac Classic Book	$24.95
Que's Macintosh Multimedia Handbook	$24.95
System 7 Quick Reference	$ 9.95
Using 1-2-3 for the Mac	$24.95
Using AppleWorks, 3rd Edition	$24.95
Using Excel 3 for the Macintosh	$24.95
Using FileMaker Pro	$24.95
Using MacDraw Pro	$24.95
Using MacroMind Director	$29.95
Using MacWrite Pro	$24.95
Using Microsoft Word 5 for the Mac	$27.95
Using Microsoft Works: Macintosh Version, 2nd Edition	$24.95
Using Microsoft Works for the Mac	$24.95
Using PageMaker 4 for the Macintosh	$24.95
Using Quicken 3 for the Mac	$19.95
Using the Macintosh with System 7	$24.95
Using Word for the Mac, Special Edition	$24.95
Using WordPerfect 2 for the Mac	$24.95
Word for the Mac Quick Reference	$ 9.95

Programming/Technical

Borland C++ 3 By Example	$21.95
Borland C++ Programmer's Reference	$29.95
C By Example	$21.95
C Programmer's Toolkit, 2nd Edition	$39.95
Clipper Programmer's Reference	$29.95
DOS Programmer's Reference, 3rd Edition	$29.95
FoxPro Programmer's Reference	$29.95
Network Programming in C	$49.95
Paradox Programmer's Reference	$29.95
Programming in Windows 3.1	$39.95
QBasic By Example	$21.95
Turbo Pascal 6 By Example	$21.95
Turbo Pascal 6 Programmer's Reference	$29.95
UNIX Programmer's Reference	$29.95
UNIX Shell Commands Quick Reference	$ 8.95
Using Assembly Language, 2nd Edition	$29.95
Using Assembly Language, 3rd Edition	$29.95
Using BASIC	$24.95
Using Borland C++	$29.95
Using Borland C++ 3, 2nd Edition	$29.95
Using C	$29.95
Using Microsoft C	$29.95
Using QBasic	$24.95
Using QuickBASIC 4	$24.95
Using QuickC for Windows	$29.95
Using Turbo Pascal 6, 2nd Edition	$29.95
Using Turbo Pascal for Windows	$29.95
Using Visual Basic	$29.95
Visual Basic by Example	$21.95
Visual Basic Programmer's Reference	$29.95
Windows 3.1 Programmer's Reference	$39.95

For More Information,
Call Toll Free!
1-800-428-5331

All prices and titles subject to change without notice.
Non-U.S. prices may be higher. Printed in the U.S.A.

Find It Fast with Que's Quick References!

Que's Quick References are the compact, easy-to-use guides to essential application information. Written for all users, Quick References include vital command information under easy-to-find alphabetical listings. Quick References are a must for anyone who needs command information fast!

 To Order, Call: (800) 428-5331
OR (317) 573-2500

Professional Training
Is Available Using This Text!

"C by Example" comes alive with professional training offered by Innovative Computer Services. Expert "C" programmers/trainers build on the text's presentation of "C" and add real live tips and techniques for efficient, portable "C" programming. The five day course covers the entire text and will allow you to ask questions about your first "C" application. Because the course was designed for programmers, time is not wasted on programming theory, or the simple, almost universal use of operators. Rather, programming theory and simple operator usage will be covered as a matter of fact, allowing more time to be spent on the peculiarities of "C" and efficient "C" implementation. Special attention will be paid to writing portable, ANSI "C" programs so that your applications will be platform independent.

The course material is applicable to DOS, UNIX/ZENIX or VMS platforms. All classes are hands-on and are limited in size to assure individual attention. Innovative Computer Services will provide each attendee the use of a 386sx computer with a choice of the Microsoft or Borland compilers and editors. The attendee may provide his or her own compiler and editor if desired.

On-Site Training

Innovative Computer Services will send a trainer to your company for groups of five or more students.

For More Information

For more information on class schedules and locations, group discounts, on-site training, or consulting services, contact:

Innovative Computer Services Training Center

(800) 877-9809

(This offer is made by Innovative Computer Services, not by Que Corporation.)

Order Your Program Disk Today!

You can save yourself hours of tedious, error-prone typing by ordering the companion disk to *C By Example*. This disk contains the source code for all complete programs and all sample code in the book, as well as the complete mailing list application from Appendix F. Also included are the answers to many of the review exercises in the book.

You will get code that shows you how to use all the beginning and advanced features of C. Samples include code for keyboard and screen control, file I/O, control construct statements, structures, and pointers. Every complete program in this book is included on one disk, giving you more than 200 programs to help you learn C. Each 3 $1/2$-inch disk is $10.00.

Just make a copy of this page, fill in the blanks, and mail it with your check or money order to:

C Diskette
Greg Perry
P.O. Box 35752
Tulsa, OK 74153-0752

Please **print** the following information:

Number of 3 $1/2$-inch disks: _____ @ $10.00 = _____

Name:_____

Street Address: _____

City: _____ State: _____

ZIP: _____

On foreign orders, please use a separate page to give your exact mailing address in the format required by your post office, and add $5 (US currency only) to cover the additional postage.

Make checks and money orders payable to:
Greg Perry

(This offer is made by the author,
not by Que Corporation.)

Free Catalog!

Mail us this registration form today, and we'll send you a free catalog featuring Que's complete line of best-selling books.

Name of Book _____

Name _____

Title _____

Phone (   ) _____

Company _____

Address _____

City _____

State _____ ZIP _____

Please check the appropriate answers:

1. Where did you buy your Que book?
   - ☐ Bookstore (name: _____)
   - ☐ Computer store (name: _____)
   - ☐ Catalog (name: _____)
   - ☐ Direct from Que
   - ☐ Other: _____

2. How many computer books do you buy a year?
   - ☐ 1 or less
   - ☐ 2-5
   - ☐ 6-10
   - ☐ More than 10

3. How many Que books do you own?
   - ☐ 1
   - ☐ 2-5
   - ☐ 6-10
   - ☐ More than 10

4. How long have you been using this software?
   - ☐ Less than 6 months
   - ☐ 6 months to 1 year
   - ☐ 1-3 years
   - ☐ More than 3 years

5. What influenced your purchase of this Que book?
   - ☐ Personal recommendation
   - ☐ Advertisement
   - ☐ In-store display
   - ☐ Price
   - ☐ Que catalog
   - ☐ Que mailing
   - ☐ Que's reputation
   - ☐ Other: _____

6. How would you rate the overall content of the book?
   - ☐ Very good
   - ☐ Good
   - ☐ Satisfactory
   - ☐ Poor

7. What do you like *best* about this Que book?
   _____
   _____

8. What do you like *least* about this Que book?
   _____
   _____

9. Did you buy this book with your personal funds?
   - ☐ Yes   ☐ No

10. Please feel free to list any other comments you may have about this Que book.
    _____
    _____
    _____

que

Order Your Que Books Today!

Name _____

Title _____

Company _____

City _____

State _____ ZIP _____

Phone No. (   ) _____

Method of Payment:

Check ☐   (Please enclose in envelope.)

Charge My: VISA ☐   MasterCard ☐

American Express ☐

Charge # _____

Expiration Date _____

Order No.	Title	Qty.	Price	Total

You can **FAX** your order to **1-317-573-2583**. Or call **1-800-428-5331, ext. ORDR** to order direct.
Please add $2.50 per title for shipping and handling.

Subtotal	_____
Shipping & Handling	_____
Total	_____

BUSINESS REPLY MAIL

First Class Permit No. 9918   Indianapolis, IN

Postage will be paid by addressee

11711 N. College
Carmel, IN 46032

BUSINESS REPLY MAIL

First Class Permit No. 9918   Indianapolis, IN

Postage will be paid by addressee

11711 N. College
Carmel, IN 46032